BEGINNING STRUCTURED COBOL
2nd Edition

BEGINNING STRUCTURED COBOL
KEITH CARVER 2nd Edition

Sacramento City College

Brooks/Cole Publishing Company

Monterey, California

Brooks/Cole Publishing Company
A Division of Wadsworth, Inc.

Printed in the United States of America

10 9 8 7 6 5 4 3 2 1

Library of Congress Cataloging in Publication Data
Carver, D. K.
    Beginning structured COBOL.

    Includes index.
    1. COBOL (Computer program language)
2. Structured programming.   I. Title.
QA76.73.C25C36   1984   001.64'24   84-11340
ISBN 0-534-03795-X

Sponsoring Editor: *Neil Oatley*
Editorial Assistant: *Lorraine McCloud*
Production Editor: *Ellen Brownstein*
Manuscript Editor: *Dex Ott*
Permissions Editor: *Carline Haga*
Interior and Cover Design: *Stan Rice*
Art Coordinator: *Rebecca Ann Tait/Michèle Judge*
Interior Illustration: *Art by AYXA*
Photo Editor: *Judy Blamer*
Typesetting: *Graphic Typesetting Service, Los Angeles*
Printing and Binding: *The Maple-Vail Book Manufacturing Group*

Acknowledgment

The following extract is reproduced from *American National Standard Programming Language
COBOL, X3.23-1974*, published by the American National Standards Institute, Inc.
    Any organization interested in reproducing the COBOL standard and specifications in whole
or in part, using ideas from this document as the basis for an instruction manual or for any other
purpose, is free to do so. However, all such organizations are requested to reproduce the
following acknowledgment paragraphs in their entirety as part of the preface to any such
publication (any organization) using a short passage from this document, such as in a book
review, is requested to mention "COBOL" in acknowledgment of the source, but need not quote
the acknowledgment:

    COBOL is an industry language and is not the property of any company or group of companies,
    or of any organization or group of organizations.
        No warranty, expressed or implied, is made by any contributor or by CODASYL
    Programming Language Committee as to the accuracy and functioning of the programming
    system and language. Moreover, no responsibility is assumed by any contributor, or by the
    committee, in connection therewith.

The authors and copyright holders of the copyrighted material used herein

    FLOW-MATIC (trademark of Sperry Rand Corporation), Programming for the Univac® I and II,
    Data Automation Systems copyrighted 1958, 1959, by Sperry Rand Corporation; IBM
    Commercial Translator Form No. F28-8013, copyrighted 1959 by IBM; FACT, DSI 27A5260-2760;
    copyrighted 1960 by Minneapolis-Honeywell

have specifically authorized the use of this material in whole or in part, in the COBOL
specifications. Such authorization extends to the reproduction and use of COBOL specifications in
programming manuals of similar publications.

Photo credits

P. 12, IBM Corporation; pp. 12-13, 53, 105, 178, 235, 317, 331, 361, 450, Frank Keillor.

Preface

This edition of *Beginning Structured* COBOL follows the same basic premise that was at the heart of the first edition: to present COBOL in a clear, easy to understand and yet enjoyable manner. As the title indicates, emphasis has been placed on program structure and every program has been written using the structured techniques so widely accepted today. To help the student understand these techniques, problem analysis is developed early in the book through the use of top-down design charts, program flowcharts, Warnier/Orr diagrams, and pseudocode. Thus, the teacher and the student may choose from among several planning techniques to find the one best suited to class conditions and local preference. Many of the examples are analyzed using more than one method; these side-by-side comparisons should be extremely helpful to the beginning programmer.

As with the first edition, many problems are presented, analyzed, and coded so that the beginning student can see the sequence of steps that must be followed in order to arrive at a successful conclusion. You will see that the programs have been kept short and relate directly to the material covered within the chapter. This is in keeping with the author's feeling that short, concise examples are far more useful to the student than long, multipage problems.

The text is designed to avoid one of the more common difficulties of COBOL texts—that of not getting students into programming quickly. In the first chapter a sample program is presented that can be entered by the students and used as a project to familiarize themselves with the peculiarities of their computer systems. Through the next few chapters this program is used as a teaching/learning vehicle to present the basics of the language. For those schools that operate in more of an interactive environment, an on-line, screen-oriented sample program is presented in Chapter 2. Since both batch and on-line versions of COBOL are used in schools today, the text covers both approaches. In contrast, many of today's COBOL texts omit any significant reference to on-line systems.

Your students should be encouraged to make use of the special sections at the end of each chapter. The Common Errors section includes examples of errors beginning programmers tend to make. The errors are discussed in detail: how and why they have been made and how they can be avoided. The Programming Tips section follows with advice about a variety of problems that can arise in programming and how they can be solved. The Self-Study: Questions and Answers section, retained in response to a great many favorable comments by instructors, contains typical student questions (and answers) the author has encountered over many years of COBOL instruction. Finally, the Chapter Terms section lists the important terms encountered in the chapter.

Those of you who used the first edition will note that this edition contains much more material. You will find enough material within the text to allow you to pick and choose according to your needs and still have enough left to challenge your fastest student.

Summary of Added Items

Extended material on the IF statement

Character manipulation statements EXAMINE and INSPECT

Extended coverage of on-line, screen-oriented operations involving DISPLAY and ACCEPT

On-line data manipulation

Two chapters on table handling

Sorting with INPUT/OUTPUT PROCEDURE

A separate chapter on working with sequential files

A separate chapter on indexed files: creating indexed files, sequential retrieval, random retrieval, updating indexed files

Writing reports with the Report Writer feature

Appendix Section on COBOL programming and documentation standards

Of course, these new sections and chapters are in addition to all the standard subjects you would expect in a beginning COBOL text. Of all the added items, manuscript reviewers have been most enthusiastic about the extended coverage of tables. Traditionally, tables have been a bit of a stumbling block for the beginner. There is every indication that these two chapters should lighten the burden considerably for both you and the student.

Another major addition to the text is a short but very useful section, located in Appendix F, on COBOL programming and documentation standards. It addresses over-all program design considerations and sub-module design, examples of documentation within the program, and typical COBOL coding or format conventions.

This section was not meant to be the end-all, authoritative source on the topic but should serve as a starting point. I am sure you have your own standards and I urge you to add to, delete from, and modify this material to suit your own needs.

My thanks go to the following people who provided constructive criticism and advice on technical matters during the production of the text: Angela Blas, State University of New York at Farmingdale; David P. Hale, University of Wisconsin at Milwaukee; Jerry Hattaway, Troy State University, Troy, Alabama; Jack Kendall, Grove City College, Grove City, Pennsylvania; Clarence Krantz, Mansfield University, Mansfield, Pennsylvania; Marilyn Meyers, California State University at Fresno; Joseph F. Morales, Atlanta University; James Walters, Pikes Peak Community College, Colorado Springs, Colorado; and Knox Wasley, California State University at Los Angeles.

I'd like to express my appreciation to the entire production team at Brooks/Cole, especially Mike Needham, whose support and encouragement were a constant throughout this project.

Finally, a special word of thanks to my wife, June, for typing through several revisions in order to bring the text to fulfullment.

Keith Carver

Note to the Student

COBOL—*Common Business Oriented Language*—is the predominant computer language used in the world today. It was developed in the late 1950s when there was urgent need for an easy–to–understand programming language that could be used on any machine and that would meet the needs of a wide range of users. The CODASYL committee (Conference on Data Systems Languages) was formed for this purpose and the result was the COBOL language.

Since its original formation, COBOL has undergone two major changes under the direction of the American National Standards Institute (ANSI) in 1968 and 1974. At the present time, the third major revision of COBOL—COBOL 80—is in the final stages of acceptance but the majority of users, particularly the smaller shops, are likely to continue to use the older versions for some years. However, you should realize that other versions exist. Developed for specific machines or specific applications, some of these versions have extended the language while others have pared it down and become subsets of the original. Many of today's microcomputers use a subset of COBOL 74 that omits the less frequently used statements.

This condition leads us to the next major point. Let us suppose you do a superb job of learning ANSI 74 COBOL, or whatever version is available on your machine. In theory, you are now ready to enter the outside world to seek fame and fortune as a COBOL programmer. Is it likely that company X will use the same version of COBOL you learned in school? Obviously, the answer is "No"—you will have to modify your learning to fit the new workplace. This is only a minor problem but a second, even more important, truth must be met and dealt with. In most COBOL classes, the student enjoys an almost unthinkable luxury: you are allowed, encouraged, and even required to write your own, totally new programs! The outside world, however, is likely to differ dramatically from the classroom since 50–80% of the programming effort is usually devoted to maintaining (that is, modifying or changing) old programs. Your mind will probably be reeling under the impact of this last statement as you realize you may be dealing with a multitude of programming styles, coding conventions, and language versions, and, most vexing of all, perhaps a total lack of program documentation. In fact, some of my former students have programmed professionally for over 3 years before getting the opportunity to write a new program. Therefore, the emphasis in the text is on the development of a solid understanding of how COBOL works and on the use of a clear, easy-to-follow code that gets the job done with a reasonable degree of efficiency.

The last few words in the preceding paragraph may cause a few wrinkled brows. Why speak of "reasonable efficiency"? Why not talk in terms of totally efficient programs? There is an old (perhaps 20 years old!) programming proverb that says: Beware of efficiency. As with all things, you must define your terms and efficiency can be defined in at least two ways: programmer efficiency and machine efficiency. Computers are fast; we humans are not. And in the long run it may be more "efficient" to produce a program that may not be internally efficient but that can be written quickly and in an easy-to-understand format.

The intention of the last sentence is not to have you forget machine efficiency entirely, but it is important for you to weigh the two kinds of efficiency. From a practical standpoint, however, there is a middle position that can be taken. First, write the program as you normally would. Then look at it to find those parts that will be executed most frequently. If you do decide to spend some time optimizing your program for machine efficiency, these are the places to which to devote your time. In other words, don't spend your time trying to optimize the whole program. It usually is not worth the effort.

Along with the changes in the COBOL language, we have seen a decided change in programming style in recent years. Until the mid 1960s, a "good" program was any program that worked. Because of this outlook, we tolerated programs that were a Gordian knot of code lines tangled in obscure and convoluted logic. Hopefully, today's programmer will be able to eliminate his or her personality from the program itself and to produce clear, maintainable code ("ego-less programming").

One of the major advantages of COBOL is its "self-documenting" feature, which means that a person with rudimentary knowledge of programming should be able to read through the program and get a general sense of what is happening. This is true to the extent that you use meaningful names within the program and to the extent that you insert explanatory notes and "open spaces" to highlight the entries. If you do not, you will have negated the "self-documenting" feature of the language. This text does not presume that you know how to program. If you do know another language, so much the better, since there can be great transfer of knowledge from one to another. If not, the text will lead you through the steps.

Finally, a bit of advice based on years of teaching beginning COBOL classes. At the start of the semester or quarter, the class will be composed of two kinds of students: those who read the text (any COBOL text) carefully and notice the exact format of COBOL entries, and those who do not. The class also will be composed of those who recognize that an extra hour spent in the planning stage of programming (problem analysis; program design) saves countless hours of looking for hidden errors later, versus those eager to jump into programming. As you would suspect, at the end of the semester, only those in the first group are left in the class. In general, resist the urge to code. Plan first, code later! With these golden words of advice tucked safely away, you are now ready to confront COBOL and to learn its mysteries.

Contents

Chapter 1
Computers and Problem Solving

LEARNING OBJECTIVES

1. To understand how our everyday problem-solving methods are identical to those used on problems for computer solution.

2. To become familiar with some of the more popular design tools such as top-down design, pseudocode, flowcharting, and Warnier/Orr diagrams.

3. To be able to read through a sample COBOL program in order to get a general feeling for the structure of the language.

For many of you, this will be your first exposure to a programming language. If this is true, you will really be wrestling with two tasks rather than one: learning how to solve a problem on the computer and learning the details of the COBOL language. Fortunately, neither of these tasks is as formidable as it sounds. The first part—the problem-solving process—follows the same general pattern you have used for years. The second part—learning how COBOL works—is relatively easy since COBOL is a very straightforward, logical language.

The problem-solving process

Since you have been solving problems all your life, you already know that the problem-solving process involves several identifiable steps. From a practical standpoint, most problems you encounter in everyday living tend to fall into certain well-known categories and, upon recognizing the category, you initiate a semi-automatic series of actions to accomplish the desired result. Typically, problems for solution on the computer follow a fairly predictable pattern in that most of them fall into three general categories.

1. Report programs that, for the most part, are simple listings of inventory on hand, customer accounts, and so on. The basic pattern is a repetition of: Read a data record; write a line; and so on; until the listing is complete.
2. Edit programs whose main purpose is to detect errors on incoming data records. Our basic pattern now changes slightly and becomes: Read a record; test for validity; if valid, perform action A; if invalid, perform action B; read another record; and so on.
3. File manipulation programs that add records to or delete records from or change records within single or multiple data files.

Indeed, these types of problems are so common that virtually every programming teacher requires his or her students to complete specific programs in these areas.

In detailing the problem-solving steps for computer programs, we will have to make some minor changes to account for the nature of man/machine interaction. Generally, the solution to all problems on all machines involves the following steps:

1. Analyze the problem.
2. Design a solution.
3. Write the COBOL program.
4. Compile and run the program.
5. Debug, if necessary.
6. Complete the documentation.

Analyzing the problem

Analyzing the problem means that you have to study the problem until you understand its nature completely. The key word is "completely." Large or complex problems may have to be broken into smaller and smaller subtasks until the demands of each task are recognized. Most beginning programmers are not willing to devote the time to this most crucial step. They are often too eager to get to the "fun" part of the process—coding or writing the actual COBOL statements. Of course, the computer's power lies in its ability to perform repetitive tasks, particularly those in which the relationships of all the elements in the problem are clearly understood. A crucial part of the analysis phase is to isolate and identify these tasks so that they can be worked on. As you will see throughout the text, the steps of input, processing, and output are the three basic building blocks of any computer program.

Let's set up a simple problem (that falls into the report program category) and follow it through the various steps. We will suppose that, at your school, the Campus Students' Association has access to a computer and to a *data file* that contains the name, street address, and city of each student currently enrolled. A friend of yours works in the office and comes to you asking that you prepare a computer listing or printout of this information.

On the surface, this is a very simple request since the program will have to follow the traditional read-a-data-record and write-a-line pattern over and over until the data file has been exhausted. However, as simple as this program is, you need to determine some other facts before proceeding to the design phase. First, you need to know the exact format of the incoming data records.

Undoubtedly, you are aware that data files can take several forms—magnetic disk, magnetic tape, or punched cards, to name a few. Throughout the text we will focus our attention on magnetic storage media rather than cards, but for this first example we will use cards. Whatever the storage media, a record layout diagram or description will help the programmer to visualize what the data look like. Note that in our example the data *fields* have been appropriately spaced across the card record. Since our friend wants nothing more than a simple listing of the records, our program becomes a straightforward read-a-record, write-a-record process. Later you will see that, in most programs, the programmer must manipulate the individual fields within the record. See Figure 1-1.

Record layout	
Student name	Columns 1–20
Street address	Columns 31–50
City	Columns 61–80

The next step is to describe the output format for the report. Most reports will require several different types of output lines such as heading lines, main report lines, and ending lines. Normal procedure is to lay out these formats on a Printer Spacing Chart (Figure 1-2), but in our case, neither a heading nor an ending line is required. Since our friend only needs an exact listing of the input records, the output format will be identical to the input format.

FIGURE 1-1

Sample input record

```
STUDENT NAME            ADDRESS                    CITY
0000000000000000000000000000000000000000000000000000000000000000000000000000000000
1 2 3 4 5 6 7 8 9 10 11 12 13 14 15 16 17 18 19 20 21 22 23 24 25 26 27 28 29 30 31 32 33 34 35 36 37 38 39 40 41 42 43 44 45 46 47 48 49 50 51 52 53 54 55 56 57 58 59 60 61 62 63 64 65 66 67 68 69 70 71 72 73 74 75 76 77 78 79 80
11111111111111111111111111111111111111111,1111111111111111111111111111111111111111
2222222222222222222222222222222222222222222222222222222222222222222222222222222222
3333333333333333333333333333333333333333333333333333333333333333333333333333333333
4444444444444444444444444444444444444444444444444444444444444444444444444444444444
5555555555555555555555555555555555555555555555555555555555555555555555555555555555
j6666666666666666666666666666666666666666666666666666666666666666666666666666666666
77777777777777777777777777777777777777777777777777777777777777777777777777i7777777
8888888888888888888888888888888888888888888888888888888888888888888888888888888888
9999999999999999999999999999999999999999999999999999999999999999999999999999999999
1 2 3 4 5 6 7 8 9 10 11 12 13 14 15 16 17 18 19 20 21 22 23 24 25 26 27 28 29 30 31 32 33 34 35 36 37 38 39 40 41 42 43 44 45 46 47 48 49 50 51 52 53 54 55 56 57 58 59 60 61 62 63 64 65 66 67 68 69 70 71 72 73 74 75 76 77 78 79 80
```

Designing a solution—Top-down design

Theoretically, by the time you get to this second step, you have analyzed or defined all the components of the problem and understand their relationships. You are now ready to design a solution. From a historical standpoint, program design and coding have been considered art forms that reflected programmers' individual styles. Each person had his or her own way of doing things, an approach that worked reasonably well during the early years of data processing. As computers became more complex and powerful, and as programming costs continued to soar during the late 1960s and early 1970s, business and industry could no longer afford the luxury of such methods. Because the design and coding had been done almost randomly, old programs were extremely difficult to maintain. They became "maintenance nightmares." It was imperative that a disciplined, structured approach to program design and coding be found. This overall sense of discipline was provided by two interrelated ideas: top-down design and structured programming.

Professor E. W. Dijkstra laid the foundation for the new disciplined technique in 1966 in the article "Structured Programming." His ideas were incorporated in the so-called "New York Times Project," in which an IBM team programmed an on-line retrieval system for the newspaper. Over 80,000 lines of coding were produced in just under 2 years—productivity nearly five times as great as the industry standards—and the coding was nearly free of errors. In contrast, unstructured programming had produced around 2000 lines of coding per year (using a high-level language such as COBOL or FORTRAN) with perhaps one error per 100 lines of code. Using structured methods, it is estimated that individual output has gone up by at least 25%.

Although we often see productivity figures such as those quoted above, sheer volume of coded lines is not the main benefit of this new approach. Of greater importance is that properly designed and coded programs are more likely to be correct, are easier to follow and maintain, and are easier to debug if an error is found.

FIGURE 1-2

Printer spacing chart

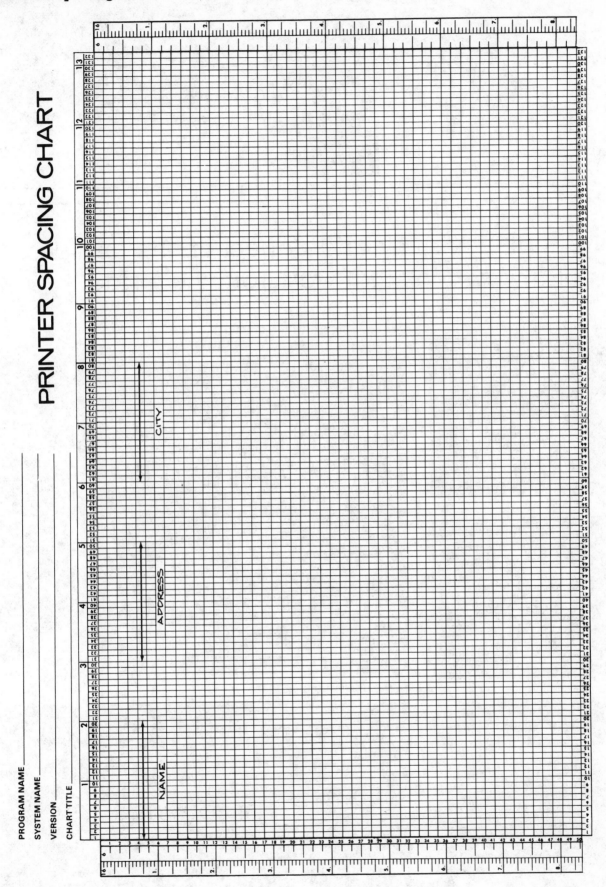

Systems that look shiny and perfect on the outside ... may not always look that way from the inside!

If the wrong button is pushed ...

Or the wiring is incorrect ...

Or the data are misfiled ...

Or the documentation is missing ...

Or the printer jams ...

If you look at the advertisements, or read the magazine articles, or even study the books, it may occasionally seem that, in the never-never-land of big computer systems, nothing can go wrong, that everything just hums along. Well, when it hums, it's people that call the tune. In a big COBOL shop, making things hum can take a lot of talent and cooperation, especially if . . . (fill in the blank).

Or there is a bug in the system somewhere ...

Or everything has to be done at once .

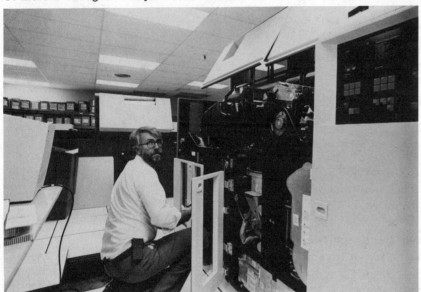

Or the machine can't handle the load ...

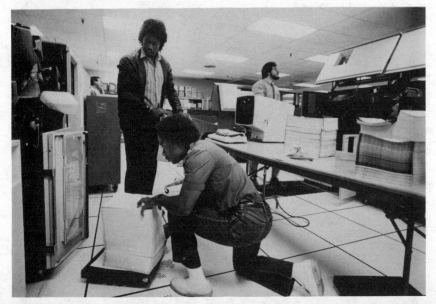

Using the top-down approach to program design, the programmer logically analyzes the problem by starting at the top with the most general function and carefully working down to the lowest-level function. As each function is identified, the process is carried on down to the lesser functions that are part of the major ones. Notice that this is a method of isolating the processing steps—that is, of determining *what* is to be done. The result is a hierarchical chart that breaks the overall job into a set of related tasks. This chart becomes a visual method of checking the *design* logic. Other sections of this book describe how the programmer uses other design tools, such as program flowcharts and pseudocodes, to lay out the *program* logic *after* the top-down analysis has been completed.

Now let's apply the top-down technique to a payroll operation, which is a typical business task run on the computer. We will assume that the employees are paid under one of three different methods: salary, hourly, and commission. Further, payroll data are available in an input file, and output will be in the form of paychecks and a payroll report that will be stored on a disk file that our program creates.

Our top-down chart will start with a single block at the top that will be our *control module*.

The next step in our analysis of the problem is to determine the specific tasks, or functions, that will have to take place. Three functions immediately come to mind.

First, you have to prepare for the main job of payroll processing. This is shown in a box marked *Initialization*, which would include all the "getting ready," or housekeeping, activities that must be performed prior to starting the next task. The second function gets to the heart of the matter—the main processing activities. Third, ending activities, which are equally distinct from both the beginning and main processing functions, should be isolated in a separate box. At this point the top-down chart has two layers in its hierarchy. Note that each module is lettered and numbered so that its position in the chart can be determined easily.

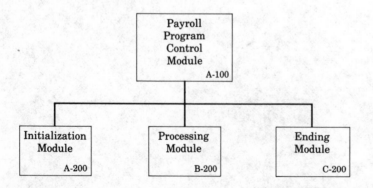

The next step is to analyze the previous layer of blocks to see if any of them needs to be broken into smaller functions. After you have had a little experience with programming, you will recognize the possibility of two Initialization activities: getting data files ready and printing headings on our payroll report.

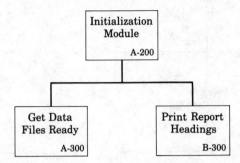

The processing module can be broken into the three basic parts we have identified before: Data Input, Processing, and Data Output.

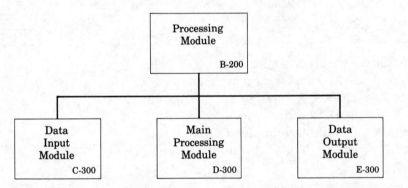

The Ending module is almost the reverse of the Initialization module because we will need to print ending lines to the reports (totals, and so on) in addition to closing the data files (Figure 1-3).

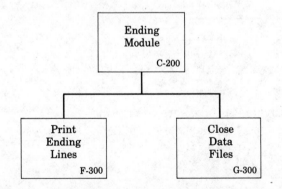

At this point we can again pause to examine our design logic for its correctness. As a matter of fact, one of the major advantages of top-down design is that the correctness of the design logic can be verified as the chart is being developed. If we assume that our design is correct so far, then we must again analyze the previous level of blocks, or modules, to see if any of them needs to be broken down. How detailed should the design chart

---

FIGURE 1-3

Partial top-down chart

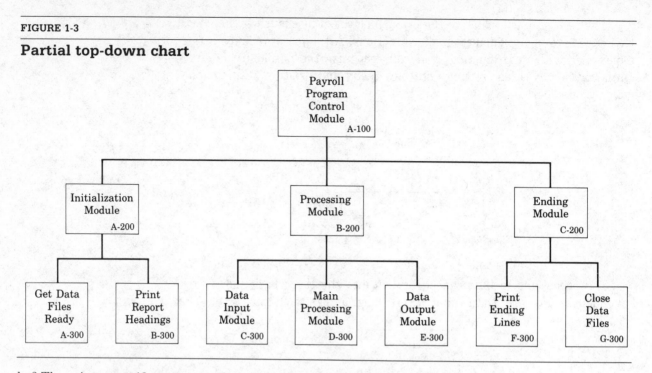

be? There is no specific answer to the question, but a general answer would be that the design must be detailed enough so that no one can misunderstand what is taking place. In the top-down chart generated so far, it appears that the Main Processing Module and the Data Output Module need to be described further. The first of these will be broken into lesser modules to take care of employees who are compensated under the three different payment methods.

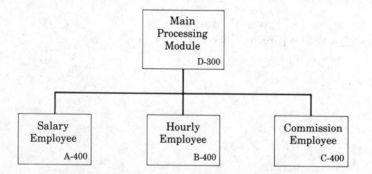

Next, the Data Output Module is subdivided to take care of printing the paychecks and the output of the payroll report to a disk storage file.

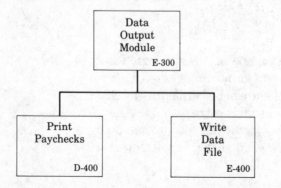

After that, only the Hourly Employee block will have to be further subdivided to account for regular pay and overtime pay calculations. The completed top-down chart is shown in Figure 1-4.

The use of top-down and structured programming logic is at the root of modern programming concepts. The top-down approach is illustrated by the use of groups of program statements (or modules) to accomplish specific tasks at specific levels within the program. The most obvious of these is a *control module*, or paragraph, that is at the top of the design structure and that directly or indirectly controls the actions of all other modules in the program.

If we apply our top-down approach to our record listing program we should come up with the chart shown in Figure 1-5. Our top-down or hierarchical chart shows four boxes: a Control Module and three secondary modules. These three are likely to be present in any program, since almost

---

FIGURE 1-4

Completed top-down chart

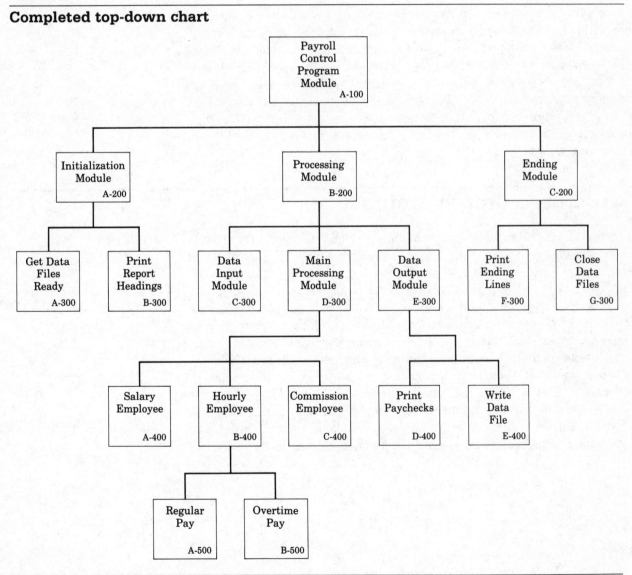

FIGURE 1-5

Top-down design of record lister program

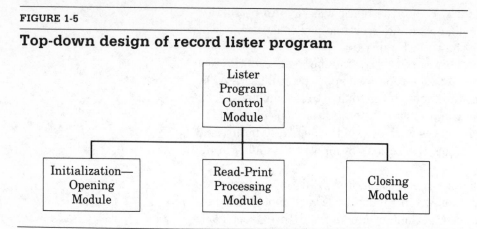

every program requires beginning housekeeping activities (Initialization), a repetitive processing loop (Read-Print), and an ending operation (Closing module).

At this point we should step back and assess what has been accomplished. Notice that we have broken the problem into a series of "bite-sized" chunks. More to the point, we have identified *what* tasks must be accomplished in order to complete the program. Perhaps even more important is to see what we have *not* done. Nowhere in any of the previous discussion was anything said about *how* we were going to get these tasks done. That is the function of the next step: program logic design. Today, virtually all programs are written in a manner that incorporates the idea of a disciplined, structured approach.

Structured programming

The basic idea of structured programming is to produce a program that is easy to read, easy to maintain, and easy to correct or debug. By now you should have grasped the very important point that programming is not simply a matter of stringing together a series of instructions, or COBOL statements. Programming involves the application of logic (which is defined as the use of valid reasoning and correct inference), which means arranging the right statements in the proper order to achieve an exact planned result.

The disciplined approach to programming introduces the idea that good programs can be developed using a limited number of logical programming structures. This idea is based on the mathematically developed structure theorem developed by C. Bohm and G. Jacopini in 1966, which states that a proper program can be coded using only three logical structures or patterns: linear sequence, selection structure, and the controlled loop structure.

Linear sequence structure

The linear sequence structure is nothing more than the sequential execution of two or more program statements. The form for this construct is the straight connection of processing steps shown in the diagram in the margin.

Although we have not yet discussed any specific COBOL statements, the following series of statements is very much self-explanatory. We are simply moving a series of fields from an input area to an output area and then writing a line of output on the printer. The statements will be executed sequentially—that is, one after another:

```
MOVE NAME-IN TO NAME-OUT.
MOVE ID-NBR-IN TO ID-NBR-OUT.
MOVE ADDRESS-IN TO ADDRESS-OUT.
MOVE BODY-LINE TO PRINT-LINE.
WRITE PRINT-LINE AFTER ADVANCING 2 LINES.
```

The series above would appear as shown in Figure 1-6.

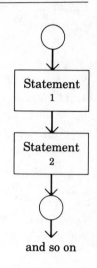

FIGURE 1-6

Linear sequence structure

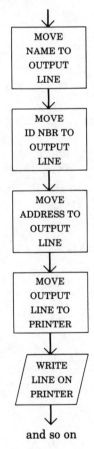

Selection structure (IFTHENELSE)

Every programming language has some statement that permits the programmer to perform logical (true–false) testing. The statement usually is very simple in its operation (as it is in COBOL), and is normally known as an IF statement. The actual statement will be discussed later, but a typical use of such a statement would be to test whether an employee has worked overtime. If the employee has worked in excess of 40 hours, we would want to follow one set of statements, whereas a different set of statements would be followed if no overtime were involved.

Although IF statements may be combined in complicated ways, their use in structured programming is severely limited. They are to be used in such a manner that there is only one entry point and one exit point from the module, as shown in the following diagram.

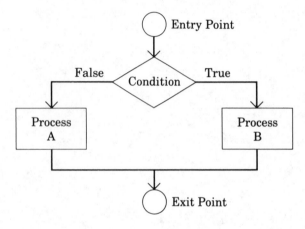

The following program segment again is self-explanatory and follows the selection structure format (which is also known as the IFTHENELSE structure). Note that both the true and the false conditions of the IF test end at the same statement (ADD PAY TO TOTAL-PAY) (Figure 1-7).

```
IF HOURS-WORKED IS GREATER THAN 40
    COMPUTE PAY = (((HRS - 40) * 1.5 * RATE) + (RATE * 40))
ELSE
    COMPUTE PAY = RATE * HOURS.
ADD PAY TO TOTAL-PAY.
```

Selection structure (IFTHENELSE)

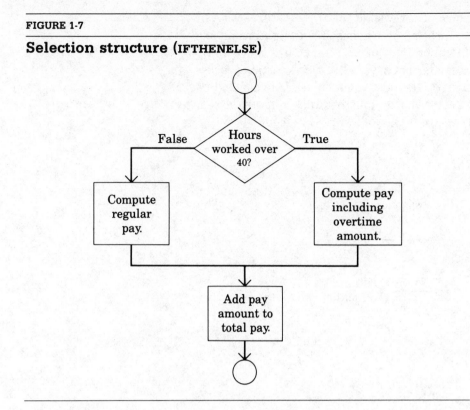

Controlled loop structure (DOWHILE)

In the controlled loop structure (also called the DOWHILE, or *iteration*, structure) a processing block is combined with a test of some type. The DOWHILE construct says "Do Process A as long as the test condition is false. When the test condition is true, exit from the loop."

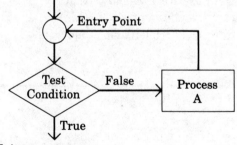

Note that with this structure, it is possible that Process A may *never* be executed at all. In either case, the structure has only one entry and one exit point from the module. In COBOL the DOWHILE structure is set up by means of a PERFORM UNTIL statement that says "PERFORM a certain process UNTIL a specific test has been met." Its most common use is in controlling a processing loop until there are no more input records to be processed. The classic example of this structure is the following statement:

```
PERFORM 020-READER
      UNTIL EOF-INDICATOR = 1.
```

This statement executes (PERFORMS) a block of code (020-READER) until a test condition (EOF − INDICATOR = 1) has been satisfied.

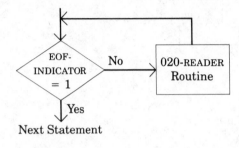

Now you know the three basic programming structures with which any problem can be programmed. There are some variations to the selection structure and the controlled loop structure, but they are not important now and will be discussed later.

Before leaving this section you should understand that these three structures can be put together like building blocks to solve whatever problem you have. It is up to you to use your logical problem-solving ability to decide on the correct structures for your program. Figure 1-8a shows that a linear sequence structure and a selection structure can be combined within a larger selection structure. Figure 1-8b illustrates a controlled loop structure within a selection structure.

A sample COBOL program

At this point, some of you may be getting eager to see what a COBOL program looks like. Every COBOL program consists of four major parts called DIVISIONS. The first of these, the IDENTIFICATION DIVISION, is very short and serves to identify, or name, the program. The second part is known as the ENVIRONMENT DIVISION, and its most obvious function is to describe the physical environment in which your program will operate. The term "physical environment" refers to the various pieces of hardware that will be used, such as card readers, printers, tape drives, or disk drives.

Next, in the DATA DIVISION the programmer describes to the system the exact nature of the data records and fields that will be used in the program. Finally, the PROCEDURE DIVISION is the part in which you actually

FIGURE 1-8

Combined structures

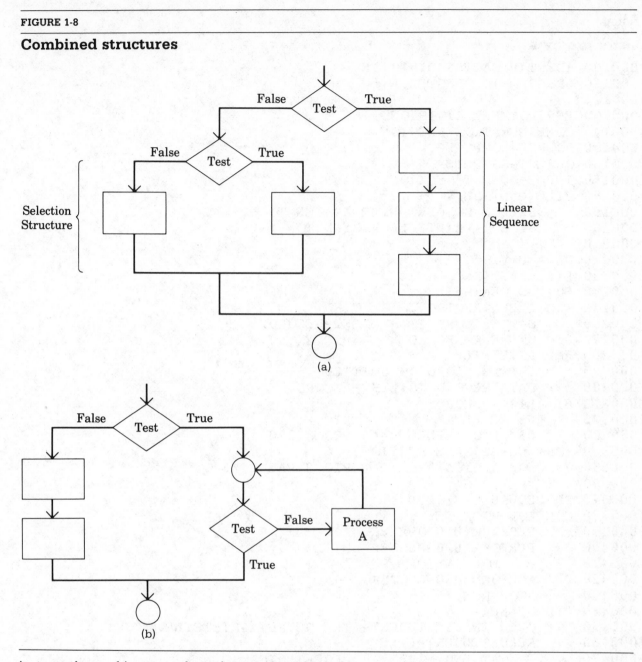

instruct the machine to perform the specific task of adding, moving, printing, and so on.

Our program (Figure 1-9) will read a record of data into memory and print a line of output and will continue doing so until all the records in the file are processed. (*Note:* Many of you may be working with on-line, video-oriented systems that do not use cards. Instead, the data file would be stored on magnetic disk. There would be only a few changes between this program and yours, but the general action of the processing would be identical.)

As mentioned earlier, the IDENTIFICATION DIVISION is very short, and, in this case, the programmer has decided to name the program LISTER.

FIGURE 1-9

Lister program

```
000100 IDENTIFICATION DIVISION.
000110 PROGRAM-ID. LISTER.
000120*
000130 ENVIRONMENT DIVISION.
000140 CONFIGURATION SECTION.
000150 SOURCE-COMPUTER. - - -.
000160 OBJECT-COMPUTER. - - -.
000170 INPUT-OUTPUT SECTION.
000180 FILE-CONTROL.
000190     SELECT STUDENT-FILE ASSIGN TO - - -.
000200     SELECT PRINTFILE ASSIGN TO - - -.
000210*
000220 DATA DIVISION.
000230 FILE SECTION.
000240 FD  STUDENT-FILE
000250     LABEL RECORD IS OMITTED
000260     DATA RECORD IS STUDENT-RECORD.
000270 01  STUDENT-RECORD      PIC X(80).
000280 FD  PRINTFILE
000290     LABEL RECORD IS OMITTED
000300     DATA RECORD IS LIST-RECORD.
000310 01  LIST-RECORD.
000320     03  FILLER          PIC X.
000330     03  LIST-LINE       PIC X(120).
000340 WORKING-STORAGE SECTION.
000350 77  EOF-INDICATOR       PIC 9 VALUE ZERO.
000360*
000370 PROCEDURE DIVISION.
000380 CONTROL-ROUTINE.
000390     PERFORM 010-OPENER.
000400     PERFORM 020-READER UNTIL
000410        EOF-INDICATOR = 1.
000420     PERFORM 030-CLOSER.
000430     STOP RUN.
000440 010-OPENER.
000450     OPEN INPUT STUDENT-FILE OUTPUT PRINTFILE.
000460     READ STUDENT-FILE
000470        AT END MOVE 1 TO EOF-INDICATOR.
000480 020-READER.
000490     MOVE STUDENT-RECORD TO LIST-LINE.
000500     WRITE LIST-RECORD AFTER ADVANCING 2 LINES.
000510     READ STUDENT-FILE
000520        AT END MOVE 1 TO EOF-INDICATOR.
000530 030-CLOSER.
000540     MOVE 'END OF PROGRAM' TO LIST-LINE.
000550     WRITE LIST-RECORD AFTER ADVANCING 3 LINES.
000560     CLOSE STUDENT-FILE PRINTFILE.
```

Next, in the CONFIGURATION SECTION of the ENVIRONMENT DIVISION, the programmer identifies the computer on which the program will be run (shown here by a broken line).

```
IDENTIFICATION DIVISION.
PROGRAM-ID.  LISTER.
*
ENVIRONMENT DIVISION.
CONFIGURATION SECTION.
SOURCE-COMPUTER.  ----------·
OBJECT-COMPUTER.  ----------·
```

The INPUT-OUTPUT SECTION is the place where the system is first informed of the names of the data files the programmer will use (STUDENT-FILE and PRINTFILE) and the specific hardware devices through which they will pay (again shown by a broken line).

```
INPUT-OUTPUT SECTION.
FILE-CONTROL.
     SELECT STUDENT-FILE ASSIGN TO ------·
     SELECT PRINTFILE   ASSIGN TO ------·
```

The DATA DIVISION is appropriately named, since it is here that the programmer describes to the system the nature of the incoming and outgoing data elements. Note that each of the files named in the INPUT-OUTPUT SECTION of the ENVIRONMENT DIVISION is further described in the FILE SECTION of the DATA DIVISION. The incoming card record (80 columns) and the outgoing print line (120 characters) are clearly shown.

```
DATA DIVISION.
FILE SECTION.
FD  STUDENT-FILE
    LABEL RECORD IS OMITTED
    DATA RECORD IS STUDENT-RECORD.
01  STUDENT-RECORD          PIC X(80).
FD  PRINTFILE
    LABEL RECORD IS OMITTED
    DATA RECORD IS LIST-RECORD.
01  LIST-RECORD.
    03  FILLER              PIC X.
    03  LIST-LINE           PIC X(120).
```

You already know that the computer is particularly well suited to performing repetitive tasks. In this example—a report type of program—there must be some mechanism by which the computer can stop the Read-Process-Print activity. This will be accomplished by means of a field of data (EOF-INDICATOR) that is set up in the WORKING-STORAGE SECTION with a beginning value of zero. Later, when the system tries to READ and there are no more cards, a 1 will be moved to the EOF-INDICATOR field. This action becomes a signal that tells the system to stop processing the Read-Print module and to go on to the Closing, or ending, module.

```
WORKING-STORAGE SECTION.
77 EOF-INDICATOR              PIC 9 VALUE ZERO.
```

The last part, the PROCEDURE DIVISION, is the easiest of all to understand, since it is here that the COBOL statements are most similar to the English language.

```
000370 PROCEDURE DIVISION.
000380 CONTROL-ROUTINE.
000390     PERFORM 010-OPENER.
000400     PERFORM 020-READER.
000410         UNTIL EOF-INDICATOR = 1.
000420     PERFORM 030-CLOSER.
000430     STOP RUN.
000440 010-OPENER.
000450     OPEN INPUT STUDENT-FILE OUTPUT PRINTFILE.
000460     READ STUDENT-FILE
000470         AT END MOVE 1 TO EOF-INDICATOR.
000480 020-READER.
000490     MOVE STUDENT-RECORD TO LIST-LINE.
000500     WRITE LIST-RECORD AFTER ADVANCING 2 LINES.
000510     READ STUDENT-FILE
000520         AT END MOVE 1 TO EOF-INDICATOR.
000530 030-CLOSER.
000540     MOVE 'END OF PROGRAM' TO LIST-LINE.
000550     WRITE LIST-RECORD AFTER ADVANCING 3 LINES.
000560     CLOSE STUDENT-FILE PRINTFILE.
```

As with most COBOL programs, the PROCEDURE DIVISION is broken into smaller parts called paragraphs (modules) at the discretion of the programmer. Typically, they are numbered and/or named (CONTROL-ROUTINE, 010-OPENER, and so on). The most important thing to notice is that the entire program is controlled from the first paragraph, or control module. The general steps in the program are as follows:

1. All modules are controlled from CONTROL-ROUTINE, including program termination, by means of the STOP RUN statement.

2. The first PERFORM statement causes the system to go out and execute the statements in the 010-OPENER paragraph and then automatically return to the next statement after the PERFORM. The first statement (OPEN) simply gets the data files ready for processing. Those of you with a sharp eye will note that the program contains two READ statements. The reason for the two READS will be discussed in detail later, but for now you can think of the first READ as a "priming" read that is necessary to get the Read-Print processing started.

3. The PERFORM UNTIL statement causes the 020-READER paragraph to be executed until a specific condition is met—until EOF-INDICATOR is equal to 1. This process of repeating a section of code over and over is known as a *program loop*. Note that this is a *controlled* loop using the DOWHILE structure discussed earlier. Specifically, this segment moves the record to the print area, prints a line, and then reads another record.

4. The third PERFORM causes the system to move a message (END OF PROGRAM) to the print area, print the message, and close the data files.

5. The automatic return to the CONTROL-ROUTINE stops the program (STOP RUN).

In theory, the self-documenting nature of the program should have made it easy to read. The names of the data files, data fields, and paragraphs were chosen by the programmer with readability in mind. Also, to a great extent, the readability of the program was enhanced by indenting certain entries and by putting in blank lines between the DIVISION entries.

Now we encounter a slight problem in that you have already seen the sample lister program that was supposed to be the *result of* the design process; in other words, the program should be written after the program design is complete. In this case it was shown first because many people get a better perspective of the design process after having seen a typical program. However, keep in mind the old rule—*plan first; code later.*

Program design tools

In designing the *program logic* that will accomplish the tasks shown in the boxes of the top-down chart, the programmer often turns to a specific tool or method that will make the job easier. For some, a visual design tool such as *flowcharting* or *Warnier/Orr diagrams* is used because they convey the relationships between the parts of the program in a quick, easy-to-understand manner. For others, *pseudocode*—an abbreviated written narrative of the program steps—works equally well.

Unfortunately, there is no one design method or tool that has been accepted by the majority of data-processing practitioners. Individual programmers and individual shops each have design methods they swear by; yet any method is appropriate if it does what it is supposed to do. Generally, any design tool is supposed to aid in the design process by showing the relationships of the parts of the solution and by serving as a form of documentation for the program.

Pseudocode

Pseudocode is a short narrative form of English used to describe the flow of control within the program and the function of the various modules. No iron-clad rules exist as to how the pseudocode must be written. However, frequently we find that the actual COBOL statements (such as PERFORM, READ, WRITE, MOVE, and so on) will be written in capital letters while all other terms are in lower case (Figure 1-10).

Notice that we adhered to the original top-down design format by having all program actions controlled from one, main module (CONTROL-ROUTINE). The steps in this routine, in turn, controlled the action of several other modules or *paragraphs* within the program. If, at some later date, someone wanted to see exactly what the program was doing, he or she would start by looking at the CONTROL-ROUTINE. This would tell the reader the order in which other paragraphs are being performed and the conditions of their performance. For example, the initialization (010-OPENER) and closing (030-CLOSER) modules need only be performed once but the main processing paragraph (020-READER) must be performed repeatedly until the data file is exhausted.

FIGURE 1-10

Pseudocode specifications: LISTER program

```
CONTROL-ROUTINE
     PERFORM opening module
     PERFORM write-read module
          UNTIL there are no more records
     PERFORM end module
     STOP RUN
010-OPENER
     OPEN the files
     READ a record
020-READER
     MOVE data record to print area
     WRITE a line on the printer
     READ a record
030-CLOSER
     MOVE end message to print area
     WRITE end message
     CLOSE the files
```

Program flowcharting

As indicated before, most programmers realize the need for some kind of design tool that will help them determine the best way to solve the problem. For some, pseudocode works well; but for those who are more visually oriented, program flowcharts seem to have more impact.

As with pseudocode, a flowchart depicts the program logic and is developed *before* attempting to write the program instructions. It would seem foolish to spend a lot of time writing the detailed instructions for an entire program only to discover that your method of approach was wrong. Thus, a few minutes devoted to any design tool is usually time well spent.

From a practical standpoint, some problems to be solved on the computer are so simple that a flowchart is not necessary. In these cases the programmer can remember the sequence of steps without reference to diagrams. For more difficult problems, however, the programmer usually devises a rough flowchart as a guide through the complex part of the program. When actually writing the program statements, the programmer may find that the flowchart was faulty or lacked certain details. This is nothing to worry about since the critical point is that some thought had been given to the proper sequence of events. The final flowchart can then be corrected to reflect the actual logic of the program.

A number of special symbols have been adopted for use in flowcharting, but in an effort to keep it simple, only a few will be used in this text.

The oval is used to indicate the start or end of a program.

(Start)   or   (End)

The parallelogram indicates any type of input or output of data.

The rectangle depicts any type of calculation or general processing of data.

The diamond-shaped symbol is used whenever a decision is made or a test is performed.

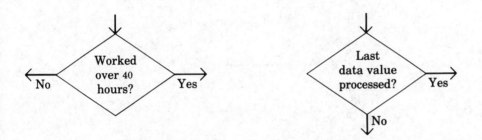

Note that arrows are used to document the flow of events.

One difficulty beginning programmers seem to encounter with flow-charts revolves around the question of how much detail to put into the chart. The answer is that it should show all the major steps of your plan but should not be so detailed that it becomes a duplicate of the program you intend to write. Figure 1-11 shows a flowchart of the LISTER program. Note that each PERFORMed paragraph is shown in the flowchart of the CONTROL-ROUTINE and that, in turn, each of these paragraphs is *individually* flowcharted. This process is indicated by the vertical lines within the rectangular processing symbol.

An important point to remember is that a flowchart depicts the sequence of statements used in the PROCEDURE DIVISION. The other divisions, although of equal importance with the PROCEDURE DIVISION, exist to identify data and other elements of COBOL to the computer system. Since they are not concerned with the flow of logic, or the sequence of the programming steps, they do not appear as entries in the flowchart.

FIGURE 1-11

Flowchart of LISTER program

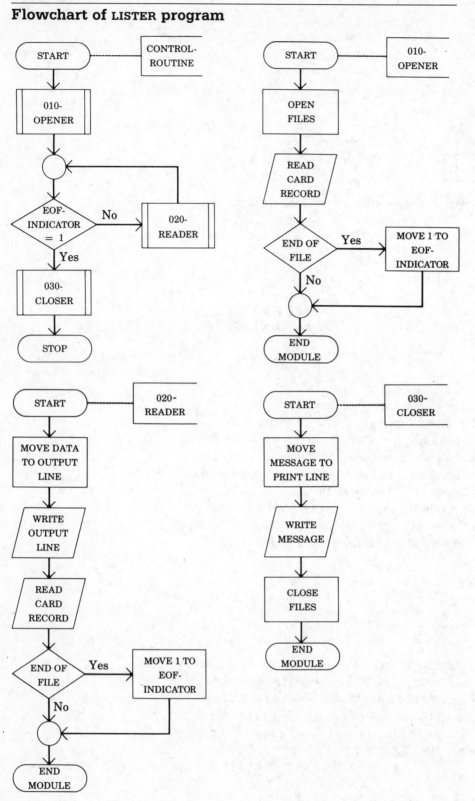

Warnier/Orr diagrams

The increased use of top-down design and structured programming concepts fueled the need for tools that would provide more and better information about logical program design. Today, many programming shops use Warnier/Orr diagrams because they can show logic at the system, program, or module level.

The diagrams are named after Jean-Dominique Warnier, who developed the system of logical design of programs. Ken Orr modified the work of Warnier to make it compatible with structured systems design and programming. These diagrams are hierarchical; but, unlike hierarchical charts or top-down charts, Warnier/Orr diagrams proceed from left to right rather than top to bottom. Braces show a process, and repetition of a process is indicated by a number, letter, or symbol within parentheses. Figure 1-12 compares traditional flowcharting with a Warnier/Orr diagram for the top levels of the LISTER program. Note that the 010-OPENER, or initialization process, is performed only once, as is the 020-CLOSER routine. The 020-READER paragraph is performed until the EOF-INDICATOR field is equal to 1.

One of the advantages of Warnier/Orr diagrams is that they show the relationship of each module within the total program. As the reader progresses from left to right, the hierarchical nature of the modules is apparent and the relationship of one module to another is clearly shown. In addition,

FIGURE 1-12

Warnier/Orr contrasted with a flowchart

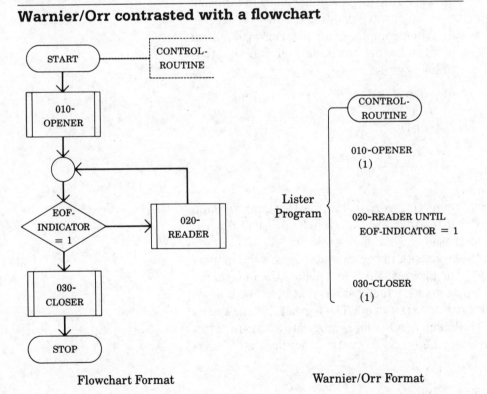

Flowchart Format   Warnier/Orr Format

Warnier/Orr diagrams allow the programmer to show the three logical forms of structured programming that were presented in this chapter: sequence, selection (IFTHENELSE), and the controlled loop, or repetition structure (DOWHILE).

The sequential execution of program statements is shown by listing the operations from top to bottom within the process (as indicated by the braces). Earlier in the chapter you saw an example of the *selection structure* in which one of two processes (regular pay or overtime pay) was executed depending upon a test. The two processes were mutually exclusive; that is, only one or the other could be executed. In Warnier/Orr format, this relationship is shown by a plus symbol within a circle: ⊕. Both the positive and negative sides of the test are shown with the negative indicated by a solid line drawn over the process.

$$\begin{array}{cll} \text{HOURS-WORKED} & & \left\{ \begin{array}{l} \text{Compute} \\ \text{pay including} \\ \text{overtime} \end{array} \right. \\ \text{over 40} & \text{— — —} & \\ (0,1) & & \\ \oplus & & \end{array}$$

$$\begin{array}{cll} \overline{\text{HOURS-WORKED}} & & \left\{ \begin{array}{l} \text{Compute} \\ \text{regular pay} \end{array} \right. \\ \text{over 40} & \text{— — —} & \\ (0,1) & & \end{array}$$

The numbers within parentheses indicate that the process is executed either zero or one time depending upon the test. Just as with any diagramming method, different shops interpret the diagramming rules in different ways. For example, some firms use an upward pointing arrow to represent the negative condition of a test. When complete, our diagram will appear as follows. In either case the word IF is not shown, since it is understood to be there whenever the ⊕ symbol is present.

$$\begin{array}{c} \text{HOURS-WORKED} \\ \text{over 40} \\ (0,1) \\ \oplus \\ \overline{} \\ \uparrow \end{array}$$

Figure 1-13 illustrates flowcharting versus Warnier/Orr diagramming of the selection structure. Other testing variations will be presented when the COBOL IF statement is discussed.

We can now get back to the LISTER program and diagram the actions of the 010-OPENER paragraph. The process starts by opening the files (once) and then goes into the READ statement, which has a conditional event associated with it (AT END MOVE 1 TO EOF-INDICATOR). The logic of the statement is that if the end of file (EOF) is detected, a 1 value is moved to EOF-INDICATOR and program control returns to the CONTROL-ROUTINE without any intervening action.

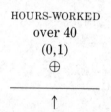

FIGURE 1-13

Selection structure: Warnier/Orr format

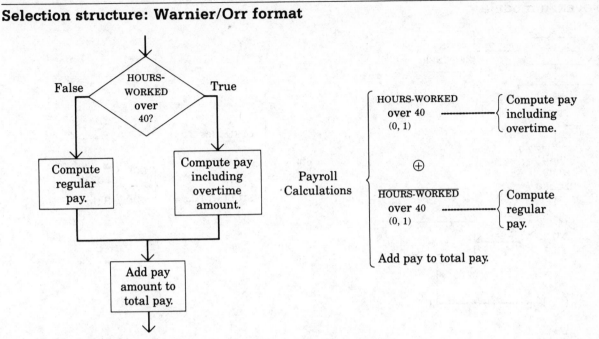

Note that the ⊕ symbol indicated two alternatives that are *mutually exclusive*; that is, only one or the other will be executed. Figure 1-14 contrasts the 010-OPENER module using flowcharting and a Warnier/Orr diagram.

Other shops require the paragraph, or module, name to appear in front of the braces.

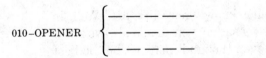

The complete Warnier/Orr diagram for our LISTER program is shown in Figure 1-15. The program was so short that it contained only four paragraphs, but the Warnier/Orr diagram shows the hierarchy of the program structure. The CONTROL-ROUTINE paragraph was shown to the left of the others because it was at a higher level than the other three. The diagram also shows that the other paragraphs are at the *same* level yet subsidiary to the CONTROL-ROUTINE. If the 020-READER paragraph had contained a statement such as PERFORM 100-CALC-ROUTINE, it would have been shown within and to the right of the 020-READER diagram.

FIGURE 1-14

010-OPENER module

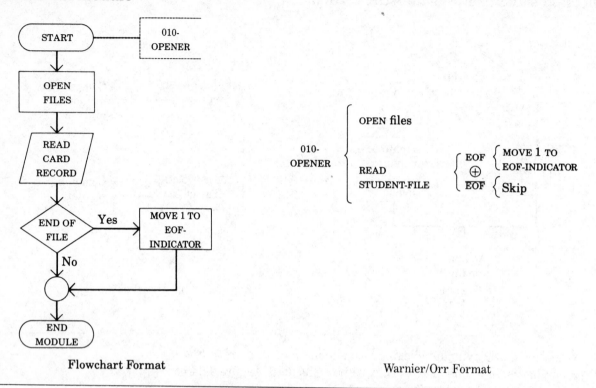

Flowchart Format   Warnier/Orr Format

As just shown, Warnier/Orr diagrams can be used to represent a problem solution, but they also can be used to show the interrelationship of the problem solution and data elements, or to show the structure of data alone. These additional uses are outside the scope of the text, but obviously add to the versatility of the Warnier/Orr method.

PROGRAMMING TIPS

How do you solve a problem if you do not know where to start? Well, in theory you should never experience this sensation; you should always know where to start in your program design even though it may not be the best place.

The advice here is simple: Start someplace, anyplace—but start! Get something down on paper! It may be wrong and you may erase it, scratch it out, move it, and so on; but write something. One possibility is to design the Initialization and Ending modules in great detail. For unknown reasons, just the act of designing, flowcharting, or coding *something—anything—* seems to get the vital "juices" flowing. You can study a problem forever and perhaps never know enough about it; but the design phase must begin sometime. As you try your design, questions you forgot to ask will emerge and the solution will become more and more apparent. The key point, however, is that you must make a start, even if it is wrong.

Another way of getting around this starting difficulty is shown by a

FIGURE 1-15

Warnier/Orr diagram of LISTER program

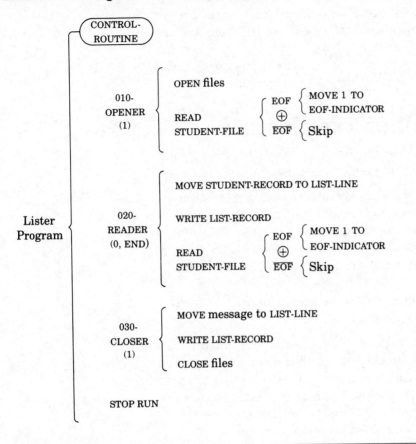

statement a great many beginning programmers make (it seems to be prevalent in all languages). Their cry is "I don't know how to do this part!" The best answer to this is "Don't worry about what you don't know!" Instead, write down, design, or code what you *do* know, and things will start happening. Build upon similar instances in previous problems. These instances may not have been exactly the same, but surely they will suggest different approaches.

Some other bits of advice are equally pertinent here.

Plan first. Code later.   Actually, this statement should be the first two rules of programming. Resist the urge to program! Much like the old saying that one picture is worth a thousand words, a few minutes of planning are certainly worth hours of coding, logic errors, and debugging. The particular planning method you use (flowcharts, pseudocode, Warnier/Orr diagrams, and so on) is not as important as the fact that you *have* planned. Understand the problem *completely* before coding!

Program in a "top-down" manner.   This statement means that you must think in terms of levels of programming modules in the PROCEDURE DIVISION. The main advantage of this approach is that it allows the programmer to think in terms of the action of the program rather than getting bogged down in the semantics of COBOL.

Keep it simple.   Take the normal, straightforward approach to the problem. Don't try to get "cute" and use obscure statements or fancy techniques. Remember that somewhere between 50% and 80% of the total cost of a program comes *after* the program has been completed and run successfully. Think and program in terms of the effort required to make changes to the program later.

SELF-STUDY: QUESTIONS AND ANSWERS

1. The problem-solving process sounds like something I have been doing all along. Why should it be any different when working on the computer?

   Answer: You are exactly right. The only difference now is that you are likely to be working in an area totally new to you, and the problems you encountered before will now have to be analyzed in a little more detail and with greater precision. Remember to continue breaking the problem into smaller and smaller parts until you are comfortable with them.

2. Why do I need a formal plan in order to solve a problem on the computer? So far everything seems very simple.

   Answer: The beginning illustrations and problems used in most textbooks are, of necessity, very simple and you should not have any great difficulty with the concepts. However, seemingly simple programs have a way of getting complex very quickly. The best solution is to use some planning method for all programs. The time to learn this process is now, while it is easy, rather than later when it may be too late.

3. I think that I am going to have trouble using a top-down hierarchical chart. How do I know that I am doing it correctly?

   Answer: The first part of the answer is to remind you to reread the text section since it tells you exactly how to proceed. Another way of answering your question is to quote an old programming proverb that says that the three most important things about programming are experience, experience, and experience. More to the point, it is not a question of whether your attempt is "right" or "wrong." The crucial point is whether it covers the needs of the situation. If it does not, you will discover your error in a later stage when you try to complete the program logic. With experience, this will happen less and less frequently.

4. What do you mean by "program maintenance"?

   Answer: In a classroom situation, such as that set up in this text, you are always writing new, short programs. In the "outside world," in a job situation, this is not the case. First, you are likely to write much, much longer programs—perhaps thousands of statements long. Second, it is very likely you will write few new programs. Instead, you will be making changes in existing programs. Recent estimates show that maintenance programming accounts for somewhere between 50% and 80% of the programs written.

You can readily see why as various changes in state and federal laws require changes in payroll calculations, welfare payments, unemployment compensations, tax deductions, and so on.

5. What good is a flowchart? Isn't a written plan such as pseudocode just as good?

Answer: The most important thing to be concerned about is that the design tool does the job. Actually, written plans and flowcharts are very closely related. The value of flowcharts is that they can act as a visual extension to the steps of a written plan. Because a flowchart is a visual device, it is much easier for some people to understand the relationships between the various parts of a program.

6. What do you mean by "debugging" a program?

Answer: Most programs contain errors, or "bugs"—even the so-called simple programs. The process of getting these errors out of your program is known as debugging and involves a logical thought process to determine where the error, or errors, might be.

CHAPTER TERMS

controlled loop structure (DOWHILE)
control module
DATA DIVISION
data file
design logic
edit programs
ending lines
ENVIRONMENT DIVISION
fields of data
file manipulation programs
flowcharting
heading lines
hierarchical chart (top-down chart)
IDENTIFICATION DIVISION
initialization
linear sequence structure

loop (program loop)
magnetic disk
modules (program modules)
paragraph
PROCEDURE DIVISION
program flowcharts
program logic
pseudocode
punched cards
record layout
record of data
report programs
selection structure (IFTHENELSE)
structured programming
top-down chart
Warnier/Orr diagrams

EXERCISES

1. What are the three general categories or types of computer programs?

2. One of the greatest strengths of computers lies in their ability to perform _____?

3. Why is it that most old programs are so difficult to maintain?

4. What are two good reasons for writing your programs in a structured manner?

5. The *How to* part of a problem starts at what point in the development of a program?

6. Of what three logical structures are all programs comprised?

7. Using top-down design techniques and either pseudocode or flowcharts, diagram the functional tasks required to determine your current checkbook balance. You may assume that your previous balance was correct and that all the checks were correctly recorded by the bank. Be sure to account for all checks written, deposits made, and special charges imposed by the bank. If the result of your calculations does not balance with the bank statement, you are to print the message ERROR IN CHECKSTUB CALCULATIONS and stop. If you do balance, you are to print the message IT BALANCES and stop.

8. Grade-point averages are always important to students, so here is your chance to develop a solution to determine your GPA on the computer. Assume your school gives letter grades of A, B, C, D, and F, where an A has a numerical value of 4.0, a B is 3.0, a C is 2.0, a D is 1.0, and an F is zero. Design the solution and draw the flowchart to calculate your grade-point average based on the number of courses taken. For example, if you had taken five courses, you would read-in five grades and ultimately divide by five to get the grade-point average.

9. Revise Exercise 8 to take into account the units granted in each course. Your GPA will now be calculated by dividing the numerical grade value achieved by the number of units. Design the solution and draw the flowchart as before. Note that an F grade generates no grade value, but it does count toward the number of units taken.

10. A school of engineering has far more applicants than it can handle. You are to design a computer program (using either pseudocode or flowchart) that will print a list of those who will be admitted. A file of data consists of records containing the student name and high school grade-point average. A grade of 3.5 or better is required in order to be admitted. You may assume that the data file will always contain at least one card record.

11. Revise the above exercise as follows: each student data record will contain three fields of data (student name, grade-point average, and a residency code). If the residency code is not equal to an "X," the student will not be considered for admittance. If it is an "X," the student may be considered.

12. Revise Exercise 10 as follows: print a list of those who will be admitted; however, print a second list of those whose grade-point average is between 3.0 and 3.49. (The people on the second list may be admitted if there are not enough people on the first list.)

13. Name the four COBOL divisions in order and explain briefly what each does.

14. Refer to the sample COBOL program (Figure 1-9) to answer the following questions.
    a. What was the name assigned to the incoming data file?
    b. What was the name of the data record within the outgoing printer data file?
    c. What were the names of the PROCEDURE DIVISION paragraphs?
    d. What was the purpose of the PERFORM 020-READER UNTIL statement in the CONTROL-ROUTINE?
    e. What does the OPEN statement do?
    f. In general terms, how does the program get out of the READ-PRINT loop?

15. What is the purpose of the EOF-INDICATOR field in the sample program?

16. What causes the LISTER program to end?

17. If your instructor allows you to do so, enter the LISTER program as indicated in the text and run it so that you can see the output. (*Note:* Your instructor

will have to supply additional specific information about your system before you can do so.)

18. Try some of these other possibilities with the LISTER program.
    a. Leave out the first priming read entirely. Run your program *with* data and see what happens. However, before running the program, write down exactly what you think will happen.
    b. Do the same as above, but leave out the data cards entirely. Again, write down exactly what you think will happen.

Chapter 2
Getting Started in COBOL

CHAPTER OUTLINE

LEARNING OBJECTIVES

1. To establish the basic rules for coding a COBOL program.

2. To understand the nature of the compiling process.

3. To see how literals and figurative constants are formed and used.

4. To learn the entries that comprise the IDENTIFICATION and ENVIRONMENT DIVISIONS.

5. To understand the relationship between characters, fields, records, and files.

6. To see how a screen-oriented program works and be able to contrast it with a card-oriented example.

After completing the design phase, the next step is to use the designs you have formulated (flowcharts, pseudocode, Warnier/Orr diagrams) to help you write the actual COBOL code or statements. In order to write the code, however, you must first understand the format of a COBOL program.

Coding the program

A special coding sheet is used for writing COBOL program statements. Each space on the coding sheet (Figure 2-1) corresponds to a column on an 80-column punched card or to a comparable screen position for on-line, video-oriented systems. Some COBOL entries must begin at specific columns on the sheet; but within these limitations the programmer may use a free-form approach to coding. When writing COBOL programs, the best approach is to have an example in front of you, such as shown in this text, or perhaps an old COBOL program. This technique will help eliminate simple format errors.

Columns 1 through 6 (of the sheet and the card) are used for sequence numbering of your program statements, such as 000001, 000002, and so on. If your program is short, the work of numbering your statements is probably not worth the effort. For a long program, however, the sequence numbers allow you to reassemble a dropped deck quickly. Fortunately, most on-line systems have an automatic line-numbering feature that automatically fills in these positions, thus saving you a lot of effort.

Column 7 has two uses. An asterisk keyed here will cause the system to treat the entire line as a comment. In the text you will see many examples of how the use of this feature can help make your program more readable by providing white space between parts of the program.

The second use for column 7 is for the continuation of what is known as a *non-numeric literal*. You saw an example of this in the LISTER program when we moved 'END OF PROGRAM' to LIST-LINE. By definition, anything enclosed within quotation marks (even numeric values) is considered to be a non-numeric literal. If a literal is so long that it goes onto more than one line, special provision (Figure 2-1) must be made for this on the coding sheet.

The actual statements in your COBOL program are written, or keyed, in columns 8 through 72. Look closely at the book examples, since they illustrate just which entries must begin in area A (columns 8 through 11) and which must be within area B (columns 12 through 72). Although you can enter a COBOL statement up to and including column 72, this often results in an awkward division of COBOL words. A better method is to break the statement between words and continue onto the next line.

Figure 2-2 repeats the LISTER program from the previous chapter with appropriate comments on the entries.

Finally, columns 73 through 80 may be used to key an identification code for the program. For practice or non-production programs, these columns would ordinarily be left blank.

FIGURE 2-1

Coding sheet

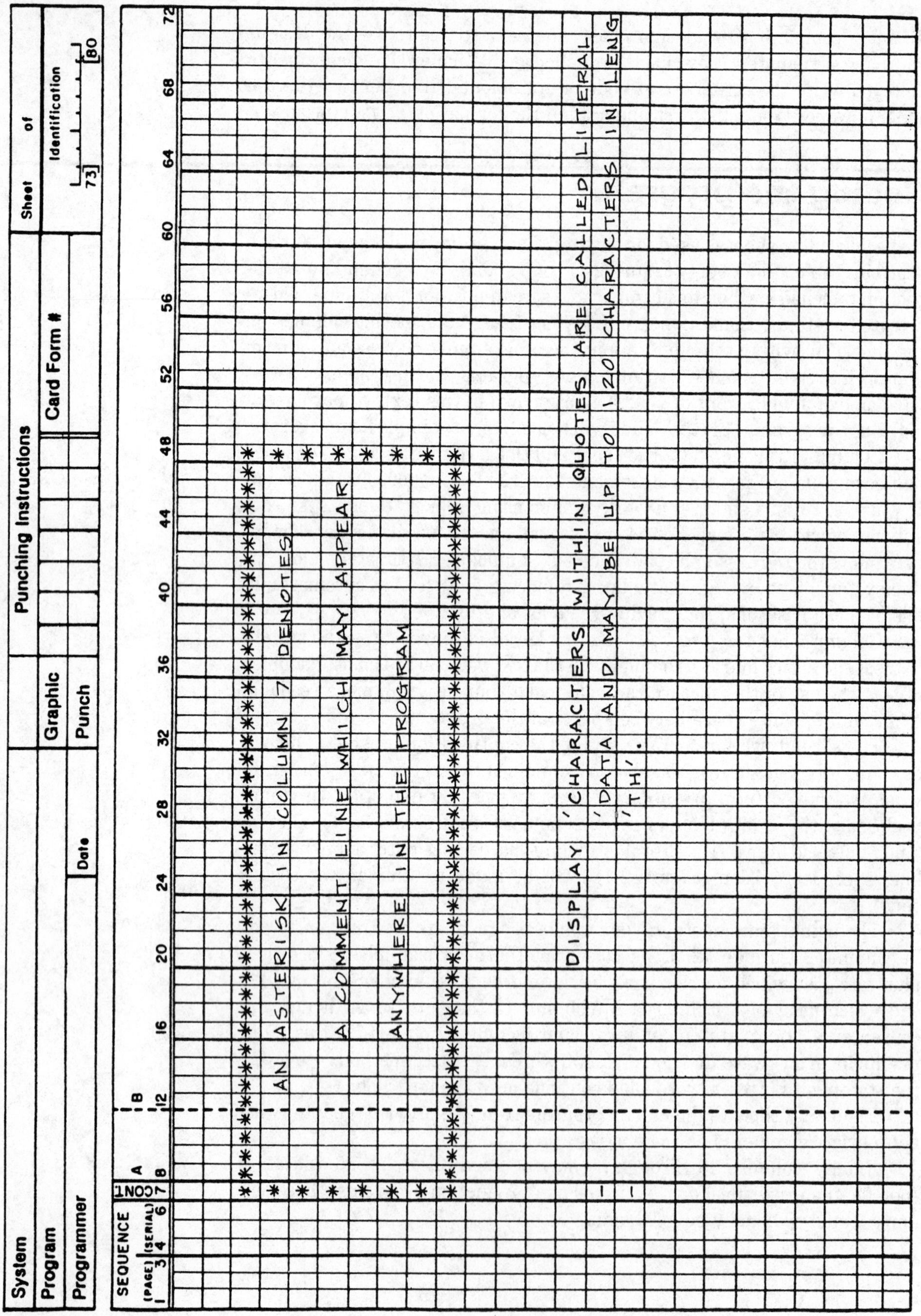

COBOL PROGRAM SHEET

System

Program

Programmer

Punching Instructions

Graphic

Punch

Date

Card Form #

Sheet   of

Identification

73]   [80

SEQUENCE (PAGE) (SERIAL) CONT A B

```
*******************************
AN ASTERISK IN COLUMN 7 DENOTES
A COMMENT LINE WHICH MAY APPEAR
ANYWHERE IN THE PROGRAM
*******************************
DISPLAY 'CHARACTERS WITHIN QUOTES ARE CALLED LITERAL
       'DATA AND MAY BE UP TO 120 CHARACTERS IN LENG
       'TH'.
```

FIGURE 2-2

LISTER program

```
                    COLUMN 7
                    COLUMN 8

000100  IDENTIFICATION DIVISION.
000110  PROGRAM-ID. LISTER.
000120* ←——————————————— ASTERISK USED TO CREATE BLANK LINE
000130  ENVIRONMENT DIVISION.
000140  CONFIGURATION SECTION.
000150  SOURCE-COMPUTER. - - -.
000160  OBJECT-COMPUTER. - - -.
000170  INPUT-OUTPUT SECTION.
000180  FILE-CONTROL.
000190      SELECT STUDENT-FILE ASSIGN TO - - -.
000200      SELECT PRINTFILE ASSIGN TO - - -.
000210* ————————————————————————— COLUMN 12
000220  DATA DIVISION.
000230  FILE SECTION.
000240  FD  STUDENT-FILE
000250      LABEL RECORD IS OMITTED
000260      DATA RECORD IS STUDENT-RECORD.
000270  01  STUDENT-RECORD        PIC X(80).
000280  FD  PRINTFILE
000290      LABEL RECORD IS OMITTED
000300      DATA RECORD IS LIST-RECORD.
000310  01  LIST-RECORD.
000320      03  FILLER           PIC X.
000330      03  LIST-LINE        PIC X(120).
000340  WORKING-STORAGE SECTION.
000350  77  EOF-INDICATOR        PIC 9 VALUE ZERO.
000360* ——————————————— LINED-UP FOR READABILITY
000370  PROCEDURE DIVISION.
000380  CONTROL-ROUTINE.
000390      PERFORM 010-OPENER.
000400      PERFORM 020-READER UNTIL
000410          EOF-INDICATOR = ①  ←——— NUMERIC LITERAL
000420      PERFORM 030-CLOSER.
000430      STOP RUN.
000440  010-OPENER.
000450      OPEN INPUT STUDENT-FILE OUTPUT PRINTFILE.
000460      READ STUDENT-FILE
000470          AT END MOVE ① TO EOF-INDICATOR.
000480  020-READER.                    NUMERIC LITERAL
000490      MOVE STUDENT-RECORD TO LIST-LINE.
000500      WRITE LIST-RECORD AFTER ADVANCING 2 LINES.
000510      READ STUDENT-FILE
000520          AT END MOVE 1 TO EOF-INDICATOR.
000530  030-CLOSER.                NON-NUMERIC LITERAL
000540      MOVE "END OF PROGRAM" TO LIST-LINE.
000550      WRITE LIST-RECORD AFTER ADVANCING 3 LINES.
000560      CLOSE STUDENT-FILE PRINTFILE.

        SEQUENCE NUMBERING DONE BY ON-LINE SYSTEM
```

Compiling and running a COBOL program

Step 4 in the problem-solving process involves the act of compiling (or translating) your COBOL program into machine language before execution can take place. The translator, which is only one small part of the total system software or *operating system*, is usually stored on magnetic disk and brought into memory as required. The over-all software control program, called Supervisor or Executive, is in memory all the time and has the task of determining which of the other software programs are needed at any given moment. In turn, Supervisor is controlled by the operator working at the system console device. Figure 2-3 shows the relationship of the hardware and software elements of the system at this point.

FIGURE 2-3

Computer system: Hardware and software relationship

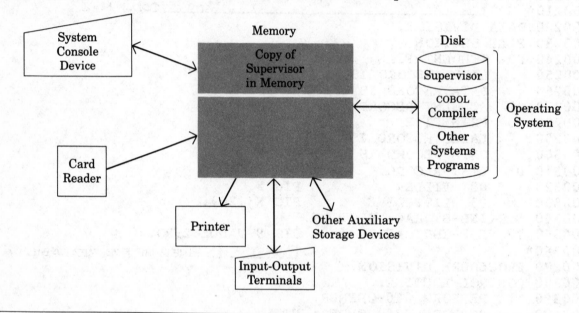

The steps that take place during the translation of a COBOL program are simple, but important for you to understand. The writer feels very strongly that the more you understand how the system operates, the fewer errors you will make and the more efficiently you will program. Figure 2-4 illustrates the major steps of the compiling process in batch-oriented systems. On-line systems go through the same general process, but the steps are often not as easy to see.

1. The COBOL program is punched into cards and placed in the card reader. The operator starts the process by executing the supervisor program, which reads your COBOL program into memory (Step 1). (*Note:* This is the traditional way COBOL programs have been entered into the computer system. For many of you, the COBOL program may be entered via an on-line video terminal.)

2. Supervisor recognizes that it is a COBOL program and that the services of the COBOL translator are needed (Step 2). A copy of the COBOL translator is brought into memory.

3. The translator program changes your COBOL program into a machine language program. The memory area originally occupied by the COBOL compiler is no longer needed and reverts back to a general usage area (Step 3).

4. Your program (now in machine language form) is executed. Depending upon the nature of the problem you are solving, data may be brought in from cards, tape, or disk. Output may be to the printer or to any of the other output and/or auxiliary storage devices (Step 4).

In theory, every computer program works perfectly the first time. Real life, however, is very different from theory, and your program may not produce what you want. Even the use of an elaborate pseudocode or flowchart does not guarantee that your program is *logically* correct. Indeed, you may get some proper-looking answers that are entirely incorrect. The

FIGURE 2-4

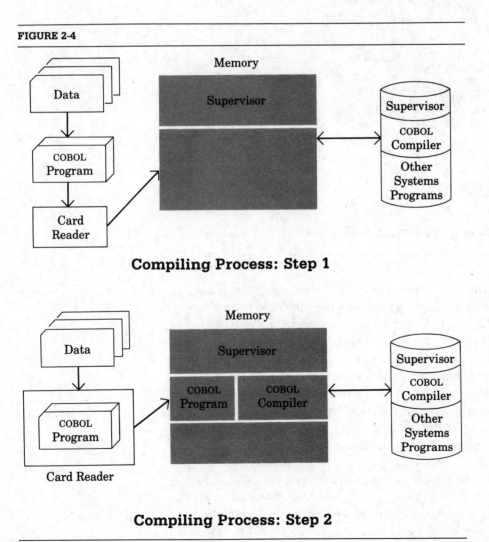

Compiling Process: Step 1

Compiling Process: Step 2

(Continued)

FIGURE 2-4

continued

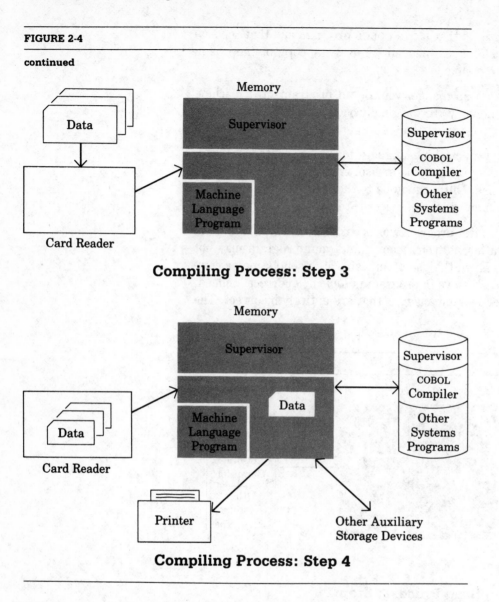

Compiling Process: Step 3

Compiling Process: Step 4

computer is incapable of correcting your errors in design logic since it only does what it is instructed to do. In programmer's terminology, you have a "bug" in your program. It is up to you to remove the error, or "debug," by reasoning to the point, or points, where the errors were made.

The three general error possibilities are that you have left out a needed instruction, that you have included an unnecessary instruction, or that you have all the proper instructions but in the wrong order. Later chapters show many examples of errors that are commonly made. Don't be afraid of errors, since making them is a beautiful learning device. However, you can avoid the majority of errors and derive the same learning values by analyzing the problem thoroughly and designing a correct solution.

When an error occurs, you must go back to these two steps. You may not have analyzed the problem completely, or if your analysis was correct, you may have forgotten a step during the design of the computer solution. Each chapter, however, contains information on how one solves problems on the computer because, ultimately, this is what programming is all about.

Beginning with Chapter 3, you will encounter a section called Common Errors. Having taught COBOL to a great many beginning students, I have seen a familiar pattern of errors emerge. Hopefully, you will pay close attention to this section and thus be able to avoid many of the difficulties that others have experienced.

At this point, we are talking about compile-time errors—that is, errors that prevent the correct compilation of your program. Most errors of this kind are simple and relatively easy to correct. Run-time errors are a different matter entirely and will be discussed throughout the text.

Compile-time errors are indicated by reference to a program line number along with the error message itself. Some of the messages may be a little cryptic, but, in time, you will be able to understand what the system is telling you. In addition, some versions of COBOL indicate the severity of the error with abbreviations such as W (Warning), C (Conditional), and E (Execution). Warning level errors (if available on your system) are of programmer's interest but have no effect on the compilation or execution of the program. C, or Conditional, level errors may affect the execution of the program, but are not severe enough to stop compilation of the program. E, for Execution level, errors are serious enough to prevent execution, and compiling continues only in an effort to identify further errors. (Different systems may use different letters, such as S for Severe, F for fatal, or D for Disaster. (I like that last designation!)

The fundamentals

COBOL, a business-oriented language, was designed to handle a wide range of problems encountered in business activities. And, although the language does have extensive data manipulation capabilities, it is not truly applicable to scientific programming tasks. Another feature, one that was demonstrated in the sample program, is that it was designed to resemble English and thus be relatively easy to read. However, a word to the wise at this point: because the language is similar to English, the rules of punctuation are extremely important. The sooner you adjust to these rules, the sooner you will eliminate many simple and annoying errors.

Punctuation

The rules of punctuation generally are the same as those you would follow in typing, such as always having a space after a period or spacing between two successive words. Another rule is that a space cannot appear directly after a left parenthesis symbol [(] or before a right parenthesis [)]. Commas may be inserted in COBOL statements to improve readability, but are *not* required elements of punctuation.

The critical point for you to understand about punctuation is that there is one major difference between English and COBOL punctuation: in English, a misplaced element of punctuation or a misspelled word may be noticed, but the message still gets through to the reader. In COBOL, a single error of this type may be serious enough to cause your whole program to be aborted. The period is used to end a COBOL entry and must be followed by at least one space. It is just as important to learn where the period goes as it is to know where it does *not* go. The easiest way to learn this is to look at the sample entries very closely.

Words and names

The programmer assigns names to data fields according to specific rules. Names are limited to a maximum of 30 characters made up of digits, alphabetic characters, and the hyphen. A word cannot start or end with a hyphen, and the programmer must take special care to avoid the use of reserved words. Certain words called reserved words (Appendix A) have preassigned meanings and can be used as shown in the text examples. Many of these words are obvious (ADD, SUBTRACT, MOVE, READ, WRITE, and so on), but many others are not. Normally, they do not cause much trouble because you will quickly learn to avoid their improper usage. In addition, the software normally signals improper usage during the compiling process.

For example, suppose we wish to move a field of data, called SS-NUMBER, to another area, called SS-NUMBER-PRINTER. (Both these names, by the way, are typical of names that a programmer chooses for the fields of data.) The COBOL statement to accomplish our move operation is:

```
MOVE SS-NUMBER TO SS-NUMBER-PRINTER.
```

The words MOVE and TO are reserved words that are required in the MOVE operation, along with a period that terminates the statement. The self-documenting nature of this English-like statement tells you that the social security number is going to be moved from one location in memory to another. The use of the PRINTER with the second data field indicates that the value contained in this field will be output on a printing device. Also note that since blanks are not permitted in COBOL names, the hyphen is used to separate the parts of the word to make them more readable.

```
ADD TAX-AMOUNT-1, TAX-AMOUNT-2 TO TOTAL.
```

The second example illustrates the use of the reserved words ADD and TO and the use of the comma (which is not required). In this illustration the numeric values stored in the first two fields will be added to the value already in the field called TOTAL. Also note that the programmer chose names that were meaningful in relation to the problem being solved. It would be correct, but very foolish, for the programmer to use names such as those shown below.

```
ADD APPLES, NUTS-AND-BOLTS TO ICE-CREAM.
```

Many data processing shops today, as part of their effort to apply some discipline to the programming effort, have lists of commonly used names or terms and how they shall appear in programs. Thus, terms such as month, day, year, social security number, accounts receivable, accounts payable, and so on, will have specific formats that are to be used by every COBOL programmer.

Literals

Literals are actual values used in the program. Numeric literals may be up to 18 digits in length and may contain a sign and a decimal point.

```
ADD 1 TO COUNTER.
```

The numeric literal 1 will be added to the contents of the field called COUNTER.

```
DIVIDE AREA-AMOUNT BY 3.1415 GIVING RESULT-1.
```

The value stored at AREA-AMOUNT will be divided by the literal 3.1415 (the value of pi) and the answer stored in a field called RESULT-1.

Non-numeric literals may be used in a similar way. They may be up to 120 characters long and must be enclosed within quotation marks. (On most machines the single apostrophe is the quotation mark.)

```
MOVE 'COBOL IS NOT SO HARD' TO OUTPUT-AREA.
```

All characters, including blanks, count toward the maximum literal length of 120 characters.

```
DISPLAY 'MARCH 17, 1985' UPON CONSOLE.
```

Numeric characters enclosed within quotation marks are valid parts of non-numeric literals. This statement causes the message to be printed on the console typewriter.

Figurative constants

A figurative constant is a special type of literal to which a reserved name has been given. The two most commonly used figurative constants are ZERO (ZEROS, ZEROES) and SPACE (SPACES).

```
MOVE ZEROS TO COUNTER.
```

The correct number of zeros is moved to the field called COUNTER. (The computer system always knows the exact size and the nature of data fields because the fields have been defined earlier in your program.) The action of this statement is that the value previously in the COUNTER field is destroyed when zeros are moved in.

```
MOVE SPACES TO PRINTER-LINE.
```

Spaces are moved to the field called PRINTER-LINE.

The identification division

Those readers who took a good look at the LISTER program shown in the previous chapter undoubtedly noticed that a clear and simple relationship exists between the various DIVISIONS in COBOL. Actually, the first three divisions—IDENTIFICATION, ENVIRONMENT, and the DATA DIVISION—are there to prepare the computer system for the actual processing statements (such as ADD, READ, or WRITE) that will be used in the PROCEDURE DIVISION. Only one entry—PROGRAM-ID—is required within the IDENTIFICATION DIVISION. In the PROGRAM-ID entry the programmer tells the system the name by which the program is identified. On most systems the name may be up to 30 characters long, but only the first eight will be considered by most systems. Also, the name cannot begin with a hyphen or contain blanks, but it may contain numeric values.

```
IDENTIFICATION DIVISION.
PROGRAM-ID.  LISTER.
```

In the example, LISTER is the program name assigned by the programmer. Also note that the period is a required element of punctuation necessary in COBOL. The following format is also permissible, but note that the program name—LISTER—is in the B margin area.

```
IDENTIFICATION DIVISION.
PROGRAM-ID.
    LISTER.
```

Other entries are permitted in the IDENTIFICATION DIVISION but are optional to be used at the programmer's discretion. Many shops require that these entries be included as part of the over-all program documentation.

```
AUTHOR.   comment entry
INSTALLATION.   comment entry
DATE-WRITTEN.   comment entry
DATE-COMPILED.   (On many versions of COBOL, the system will insert
                 the appropriate date.)
SECURITY.   comment entry
REMARKS.   comment entry
```

Example:
```
IDENTIFICATION DIVISION.
PROGRAM-ID.  LISTER.
AUTHOR.   BENJAMIN BUGLESS.
INSTALLATION.  ABC SCHOOL DISTRICT.
DATE-WRITTEN.  MAY 14, 1984.
DATE-COMPILED.
SECURITY.   NONE, THIS PROGRAM MAY BE COPIED.
REMARKS.   PROGRAM MAY BE MODIFIED AS REQUIRED.
```

The environment division

The entries in the ENVIRONMENT DIVISION are also simple and very logical. The division consists of two sections: the CONFIGURATION SECTION and INPUT-OUTPUT SECTION. Our sample program was as follows:

```
ENVIRONMENT DIVISION.
CONFIGURATION SECTION.
SOURCE-COMPUTER. -----.
OBJECT-COMPUTER. -----.
```

The SOURCE-COMPUTER entry specifies the exact machine on which the *source program* will be compiled, and the OBJECT-COMPUTER entry indicates the machine on which the *object program* will be run or executed. Normally, the two entries are identical, but it is possible to compile on one machine for execution on another. The dashed lines were used in the sample program to indicate that the specific entry will vary from machine to machine but generally include the brand followed by the model number.

Example:
```
SOURCE-COMPUTER.   IBM-370-145.
OBJECT-COMPUTER.   IBM-370-145.
```

or

```
SOURCE-COMPUTER.   PRIME-650.
OBJECT-COMPUTER.   PRIME-650.
```

The INPUT-OUTPUT SECTION entries are easy, but they do require a little more explanation.

```
INPUT-OUTPUT SECTION.
FILE-CONTROL.
     SELECT STUDENT-FILE ASSIGN TO ------.
     SELECT PRINTFILE ASSIGN TO ------.
```

The SELECT entry does two things.

1. It assigns a name (called an *internal file name*) to a file of data that will be used in the program. In the above example, STUDENT-FILE and PRINT-FILE are programmer-chosen internal file names. (The topic of files will be discussed in more detail in the next section.) The maximum size of the file name is 30 characters; it cannot contain any special characters or blanks; and, on most systems, must begin with a letter.

2. The ASSIGN portion of the entry informs the system of the physical piece of hardware through which the file will be passing. In our example, we again used dashed lines since this entry is entirely machine-dependent.

A typical IBM SELECT entry for card input and printer output is:

```
SELECT STUDENT-FILE
     ASSIGN TO SYS007-UR-2540R-S.
SELECT PRINTFILE
     ASSIGN TO SYS009-UR-1403-S.
```

where:

SYS007 is the *system number* assigned to a specific I/O device (a card reader).

UR identifies it as a Unit Record piece of equipment. UR is used for card readers and printers as opposed to magnetic tape or disk devices, which have a different designation.

2540 is a specific model IBM card reader.

R indicates a Reading device (as opposed to P for a Punching device).

S indicates that the device will handle a Sequential file.

The SELECT PRINTFILE entry follows the same pattern, but, as you would expect, with a different SYS number and device number. On many computer systems the SELECT entries are simplified by using preassigned names for the commonly used devices such as the card reader, card punch, and printer. Then, your entry might look as follows:

```
SELECT STUDENT-FILE
     ASSIGN TO SYSTEM-INPUT
```

or

```
     ASSIGN TO SYSRDR
```

or

```
SELECT PRINTFILE
     ASSIGN TO SYSTEM-OUTPUT
```

or

```
     ASSIGN TO SYSLST
```

Up to this point our sample program looks as shown in Figure 2-5.

FIGURE 2-5

Partial LISTER program
```
000100 IDENTIFICATION DIVISION.
000110 PROGRAM-ID. LISTER.
000120*
000130 ENVIRONMENT DIVISION.
000140 CONFIGURATION SECTION.
000150 SOURCE-COMPUTER. ----.
000160 OBJECT-COMPUTER. ----.
000170 INPUT-OUTPUT SECTION.
000180 FILE-CONTROL.
000190     SELECT STUDENT-FILE ASSIGN TO ----.
000200     SELECT PRINTFILE ASSIGN TO ----.
```

Files and the structure of data

This is a good time to become acquainted with the nature of the data handled by COBOL. The smallest units of data with which COBOL can work are *characters*. Any of the digits, the alphabetic symbols (A, B, C, and so on), or the permissible special symbols, such as the decimal point or the comma, are considered characters (Figure 2-6). Characters are normally grouped together to form *fields of data*, such as social security number field, rate of pay field, amount owed field, and so on. Fields are usually numeric (such as those indicated above) or alphabetic (customer name field), but COBOL also can work with alphanumeric fields that mix the two types of data (for example, customer address field).

Early computers relied heavily on the punched card as the storage medium for a single record of data. The customary practice has been to

---

FIGURE 2-6

Permissible COBOL characters

Digits 0 through 9
Letters A through Z
Special characters:

    Blank or space
+   Plus sign
−   Minus sign or hyphen
*   Check protection symbol, asterisk
/   Slash
=   Equal sign
>   Inequality sign (greater than)
<   Inequality sign (less than)
$ Dollar sign
,   Comma
.   Period or decimal point
'   Quotation mark (also called an apostrophe; it is a 5-8 card punch.)
(Left parenthesis
)   Right parenthesis

Of the previous set, the following characters are used for words:

0 through 9
A through Z
- Hyphen

The following characters are used for punctuation:

' Quotation mark
(Left parenthesis
) Right parenthesis
, Comma
. Period

The following characters are used in arithmetic expressions:

+   Addition
−   Subtraction
*   Multiplication
/   Division
**   Exponentiation

The following characters are used in relation tests:

>   Greater than
<   Less than
=   Equal to

punch all the pertinent information on one transaction into one card *record* (hence the term *unit record* applied to cards). Today, the trend is away from card files and toward various forms of magnetic data storage such as *magnetic tape*, *hard disk*, and the *floppy* disks that are used on most microcomputer systems.

There are several reasons for this change.

1. The card format limits the user to a maximum 80-character record, while magnetic storage media can handle individual records of almost any size.
2. Card reading is much slower than reading magnetic data files.
3. Card punching is far slower and more prone to error than non-card methods.

However, the major point to understand is this: since a record is defined in terms of the individual fields of which it is comprised, the programmer then knows that *every* record in the file will have exactly the same format. Thus, in Figure 2-7, *every* record, whether it be tape, disk, or cards, will contain the student name in positions 1–20, address in positions 21–50, and so forth.

In a business situation, a firm is likely to have thousands of files of data on hand (Figure 2-8). Therefore, it becomes imperative that the correct file be located and mounted on the specific input/output device when called for. All languages have some provision for checking to be sure that the correct file is being used, and in COBOL it revolves around the relationship between the *external* and the *internal file name*.

When a file is created on magnetic media (tape or disk), the programmer assigns to it an *external file name*. However, different shops have different rules for the construction of file names; for example, the May 1984 accounts receivable file for the West Coast Division created by the accounting programming department might be called WC-0584-ACP-AR. Most likely, this file would become input data to a variety of programs. Again, note that this is the external file name, and, in the case of magnetic tape, the system software writes this information in a *label area* at the beginning of the tape. Names of this type, however, may be awkward to use *within* a particular COBOL program. COBOL requires that the programmer identify the external file name but allows the programmer to assign a different *internal file name*—that is, the name of the file used *within* the program—in the SELECT entry. Thus, in our LISTER program, STUDENT-FILE and PRINTFILE are internal file names created by the programmer for use in that program only. It is possible for the internal and external file names to be the same, but this is usually not done.

The subject of data files can get rather complex, but, in a beginning COBOL class, the coursework is centered around *sequential* files. By definition, a sequential file is one in which the only access for a specific record is by reading or accessing all prior records. Card and tape files are, by their very nature, classified as sequential. Disk files, however, can take several forms including sequential, and *indexed*. These topics will be discussed in Chapters 11 and 12.

FIGURE 2-7

Relationship of fields and records

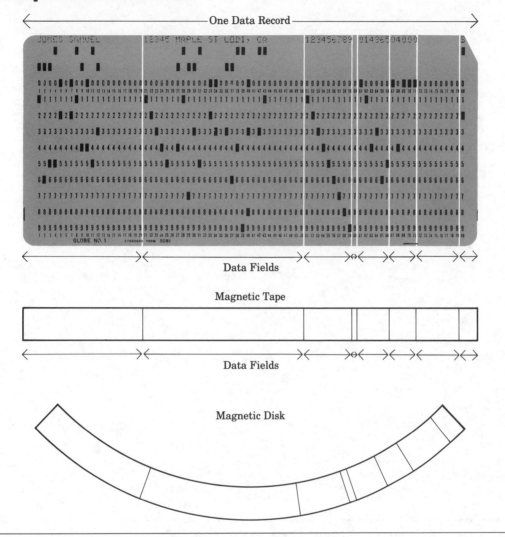

FIGURE 2-8

Data files

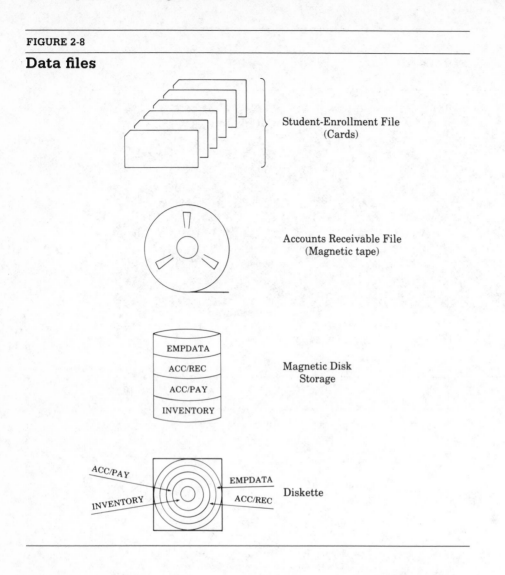

Student-Enrollment File
(Cards)

Accounts Receivable File
(Magnetic tape)

Magnetic Disk
Storage

Diskette

An on-line, screen-oriented program

This second example program varies considerably from the previous one in that it is an interactive, screen-oriented program built around two statements: ACCEPT and DISPLAY. As with the previous example, it contains the required four DIVISIONs, but note that it does *not* use any files. Instead, the program ACCEPTs data values keyed into specific memory areas in response to a prompt message DISPLAYed on the screen. Also note that this is a one-time program because there is no provision for looping back (PERFORM UNTIL), which was used in the previous example. Figure 2-9 illustrates the general action of the program, while Figure 2-10 shows the actual program listing.

On-line videoscreen activities are rapidly replacing other methods of input.

FIGURE 2-9

Schematic: An on-line program

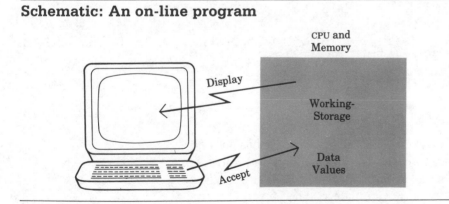

FIGURE 2-10

Screen-oriented, on-line program

```
000100 IDENTIFICATION DIVISION.
000110 PROGRAM-ID. SAMPLE1.
000120*
000130 ENVIRONMENT DIVISION.
000140 CONFIGURATION SECTION.
000150 SOURCE-COMPUTER. - - -.
000160 OBJECT-COMPUTER. - - -.
000170*
000180 DATA DIVISION.
000190 WORKING-STORAGE SECTION.
000200 01  OUTPUT-LINE.
000210     03  FILLER        PIC X(05).
000220     03  FULL-NAME     PIC A(20).
000230     03  FILLER        PIC X(05).
000240     03  HOME-ADDRESS  PIC X(20).
000250     03  FILLER        PIC X(05).
000260     03  SS-NBR        PIC 9(09).
000270     03  FILLER        PIC X(16).
000280*
000290 PROCEDURE DIVISION.
000300 CONTROL-ROUTINE.
000310     MOVE SPACES TO OUTPUT-LINE.
000320     PERFORM 010-ENTER-DATA.
000330     STOP RUN.
000340 010-ENTER-DATA.
000350     DISPLAY 'ENTER YOUR FULL NAME. IF YOU MAKE AN ERROR'.
000360     DISPLAY 'DEPRESS THE BACKSPACE KEY AND CONTINUE'.
000370     DISPLAY 'IF YOUR NAME DOES NOT FILL THE WHOLE FIELD'.
000380     DISPLAY 'DEPRESS THE "ENTER" KEY AFTER THE LAST CHARACTER'.
000390     ACCEPT FULL-NAME.
000400     DISPLAY 'ENTER YOUR HOME ADDRESS'.
000410     ACCEPT HOME-ADDRESS.
000420     DISPLAY 'ENTER YOUR SOCIAL SECURITY NUMBER'.
000430     ACCEPT SS-NBR.
000440     DISPLAY 'WELCOME TO COBOL PROGRAMMING!', LINE 13, ERASE.
000450     DISPLAY OUTPUT-LINE, LINE 15.
```

PROGRAMMING TIPS

The problem-solving techniques we need to consider here are not as directly related to the program as they are to your programming habits. First, it is very important for you to understand as much as possible about compiling a COBOL program. The more thoroughly you understand the process, the greater will be your feeling for the language, which will result in fewer logic and coding errors.

Second, get to know the machine on which your COBOL programs are going to be run. Try to get a copy of that manufacturer's COBOL manual. If possible, look at the machine. Study the card reader or magnetic tape drive or disk drive so that you can visualize these devices when writing your programs. Later, the physical association with these pieces of hardware will not be so important, but identifying these devices seems to help beginning students.

Third, you can save yourself a lot of trouble by developing neat, precise work habits *now*. Print your COBOL statements with clear, bold marks and be extremely careful with punctuation and spelling, since the compiler is very intolerant of even the smallest error. Learn the rules of the game *now*.

Finally, this chapter and the previous one indicated that every COBOL program contains four DIVISIONs, and that in almost every case you will have an Initialization, a Processing, and an Ending module. Since there is such a great likelihood that specific sections of one COBOL program are going to be very similar (or identical) to the same section in another COBOL program, it would be wise for you to code in a manner such that these sections can be used from one program to another. The suggestion, therefore, is for you to develop programming patterns and habits that will increase the use and portability of programming modules.

> *Collect documentation material right away.*   Don't wait until the program is running—documentation may be hard to find then.
>
> *Every program can be improved.*   A corollary to this rule is that every program can be made one statement shorter. The question is: Is it worth the time to do so?
>
> *Programming productivity is not just output per hour; it is a function of usefulness.*   Three lines of code per hour that work are far better than 30 lines that do not work.

SELF-STUDY: QUESTIONS AND ANSWERS

1. If I do make a lot of compile-time errors, they should be easy to correct, shouldn't they?

   Answer: Yes, these errors are simple to correct but the problem is finding them in your program. The computer system will print an error message for each mistake, but the messages themselves are not always very clear. The best plan is to learn the rules and the format of COBOL right away and not make these types of errors.

2. The text discusses fields, records, and files that seem to be simple enough. What I want to know is whether this arrangement is always true or is it true just for COBOL?

   Answer: The relationship of fields, records, and files is true for any language, not just COBOL. For that reason it is good that you understand it now so you won't have to relearn it later when working with another language.

3. As I understand it, the programmer gives names to fields of data. Is that correct?

Answer: Generally, in all languages the programmer is able to assign names to fields of data. The rules for naming are very liberal in COBOL, which makes it easy to give meaningful names to the fields, rather than nonsense syllables. This point will become extremely important later when you have to refer back to a part of your program that was written earlier. It is very easy to forget what some of these field names stand for.

4. I looked at the reserved word list and there is no way I can learn all of those names.

Answer: Don't worry, you really won't have to learn all the reserved words. Most of them are required words you will be learning very quickly as you program in COBOL. Many of the rest are such that plain "horse sense" would tell you they might be on the list. A good idea is to read the list over from time to time just to become familiar with some of the words. Even so, you may still end up using a reserved word in an incorrect way. This should happen very infrequently and the problem is usually very easy to correct.

5. When moving figurative constants such as SPACES or ZEROS, how does the system "know" how many to move to the field?

Answer: The complete answer to your question will come later when the DATA DIVISION is discussed in detail. Right now, the main point to understand is that in just about any programming language the system somehow has to be informed of the size and type of every field. This is the major function of the DATA DIVISION.

6. Explain again the difference between the SOURCE-COMPUTER and OBJECT-COMPUTER entries. I don't see the need for both entries.

Answer: If you recall, the COBOL program you write is called a source program. It is translated by the COBOL compiler, and the output from the compiler software is known as an object program. It is this object program that actually gets run, or executed, on the computer. Perhaps well over 99% of the time you will compile your program on the same computer (SOURCE-COMPUTER) on which it is executed (OBJECT-COMPUTER). In these cases the two entries in the CONFIGURATION will be the same. On rare occasions when the compiling and executing computer are not the same, COBOL provides for this possibility.

CHAPTER TERMS

batch processing system
characters
compiling (compiler)
disk (magnetic disk)
diskettes
external file name
fields

figurative constants
floppy disk (diskettes)
hard disk
indexed file
internal file name
label area (magnetic tape)
literals

magnetic tape
object program
on-line systems
operating system
reserved words
sequential file
soft disk (diskette; floppy disk)

source program
supervisor program
system number (sys number)
tape (magnetic tape)
translator program (compiler)
unit record

EXERCISES

1. In your program, any material contained within quotes is called a _____ .

2. In which column does Area A begin?
   In which column does Area B begin?
   To what column does Area B extend?

3. The COBOL compiler is part of more software that goes by the name _____ .

4. Errors which prevent correct compilation of a program are called _____ errors.

5. Errors which are detected upon execution of a program are called _____ errors.

6. What is the maximum size of a programmer-supplied name that COBOL allows?

7. Using Appendix A, note which of the names shown below are reserved words.
   DATA
   NAME
   DATE
   IFTHENORELSE
   IFTHENELSE
   LOW-VALUE
   TERMINAL
   SENTENCES

8. In the statement
        MOVE SPACES TO DATA-FIELD-A.
   SPACES is a _____ constant.

9. What is wrong with this program segment?
        IDENTIFICATION DIVISION.
        PROGRAM-ID.   WRONG-PROG

10. What 2 sections are part of the ENVIRONMENT DIVISION?

11. What is the smallest accessible unit of data in COBOL?

12. What unit of data is grouped together to make up a field of data?

13. How important are commas in COBOL statements?

14. Why are blanks not permitted in COBOL names?

15. Determine whether the following statements are correct or incorrect COBOL statements. If the statement is incorrect, change it so it is correct.
    a. MOVE NUMBER TO COUNTER.
    b. MOVE AMOUNT TO TOTAL.
    c. MOVE SUZIE TO TOWN.
    d. ADD, GROSS, TO, TOTAL.
    e. ADD REG-PAY.
    f. ADD REG-PAY TO OVERFLOW.

g. ADD 123-ANSWER TO ANS-OUT.
h. MORE INV-ITEM TO INV-ITEM-PR.
i. MOVE SS NUMBER TO PRINT-FIELD-1.

16. Determine whether the following are correct or incorrect COBOL statements. If the statement is incorrect, change it so it is correct.
    a. ADD 7 TO AMOUNT.
    b. ADD - 6.4 TO TOTAL.
    c. MOVE 'THE ANSWER IS' TO OUTPUT-AREA.
    d. ADD 'AN ANSWER' TO TOTAL-1.
    e. DISPLAY 'ERROR #2' UPON CONSOLE
    f. MOVE 17 SPACES TO OUTPUT-AREA-E.
    g. ADD 16 TO 'GRAND-TOTAL'.
    h. MOVE ZEROS TO COUNTER.
    i. MOVE COUNTER TO ZEROS.

17. What is the maximum size of a numeric literal? of a non-numeric literal?

18. Define a figurative constant and give two examples of how they are used.

19. Identify or name each of the following.
    a. 456
    b. '456'
    c. 'END OF REPORT'
    d. 3,165
    e. '$3644.14'
    f. -21.85
    g. ZERO
    h. 0
    i. 'ZERO'
    j. 'MARCH 17, 1984'

20. What is the only required entry in the IDENTIFICATION DIVISION, other than the division entry itself?

21. Under what conditions would the entries for SOURCE-COMPUTER and OBJECT-COMPUTER be different?

22. What is the purpose of the SELECT entry in the FILE-CONTROL section?

23. Describe the difference between an internal and an external file name. Why would they be different?

24. Explain in your own words the relationship between fields, records, and files.

25. Could a file ever contain just one record? Could a record consist of a single field? What is the minimum size of a field? What is the maximum size of a field?

26. What is the label area on magnetic tape?

27. Name two other types of files other than sequential files.

28. Refer to Figure 2-10 to answer these questions.
    a. What is the purpose of the entries in lines 350 through 380?
    b. Explain what takes place when line 390 is executed by the computer sytem.
    c. What is displayed by line 450 in the program?

29. Why is there no FILE-CONTROL entry in the chapter SAMPLE 1 program (Figure 2-10)?

30. Why is there no FILE SECTION entry in the chapter SAMPLE 1 program?

Chapter 3
Setting Up the Program

CHAPTER OUTLINE

The file section
    Describing an input record—level numbers
    Describing a printer record
The working-storage section
Basic procedure division statements
    The OPEN and CLOSE statements
    The READ statement
    The MOVE statement
    The WRITE statement
    The PERFORM and PERFORM UNTIL statements
    The STOP statement
Common errors
Programming tips
Self-study: Questions and answers
Chapter terms
Exercises

LEARNING OBJECTIVES

1. To learn the function of the FILE SECTION and how the programmer goes about describing both input and output files.

2. To see how independent fields and entire records are set up in the WORKING-STORAGE SECTION.

3. To become acquainted with seven of the most commonly used statements in COBOL: OPEN, CLOSE, READ, MOVE, WRITE, PERFORM, and STOP.

4. To see how two structured programming formats are used: linear sequence structure and the controlled loop or DOWHILE STRUCTURE.

After the IDENTIFICATION and ENVIRONMENT DIVISION, the next part of a COBOL program is the DATA DIVISION that often is quite long but not difficult to understand. As explained earlier, the purpose of the division is to tell the system the specific details about the data that will be handled, or processed, in the PROCEDURE DIVISION. A word of caution is due here. Few programmers would ever describe the DATA DIVISION as "fun"—the PROCEDURE DIVISION maybe, but not the DATA DIVISION. However, it is an extremely important part of the over-all program, and extra effort devoted here will pay off later when writing the PROCEDURE DIVISION.

The file section

Recall that in the ENVIRONMENT DIVISION you named the files of data you intended to use, such as STUDENT-FILE and PRINTFILE. At this point the system is expecting the programmer to provide a more detailed description of the file. This description begins with the FILE SECTION entry and continues with FD, which stands for "file description," and the name of the file that will be described.

```
000220 DATA DIVISION.
000230 FILE SECTION.
000240 FD   STUDENT-FILE
000250      LABEL RECORD IS OMITTED
000260      DATA RECORD IS STUDENT-RECORD.
000270 01  STUDENT-RECORD      PIC X(80).
000280 FD   PRINTFILE
000290      LABEL RECORD IS OMITTED
000300      DATA RECORD IS LIST-RECORD.
000310 01  LIST-RECORD.
000320      03  FILLER          PIC X.
000330      03  LIST-LINE       PIC X(120).
```

Immediately after the FD entry you will have a series of entries that further describe the file, the record, and the individual fields that are part of the record. All this, of course, goes back to the basic idea of a *file*, which is comprised of *records* made up of a series of *fields*. To be even more exact, the system *must* find an FD—file description entry—for *every* file named in a SELECT. Not only must there be a corresponding entry, but the SELECT file name *must* exactly match the FD name, as Figure 3-1 indicates. Later in this chapter you will see what happens when this rule is violated. What is important now, however, is that you understand that a SELECT and FD entry are *always* tied together by the file name. The relationship is nothing more than that dictated by common sense: The SELECT entry only names the file; the FD entries will break the file down into its component parts.

As you can see from Figure 3-1, the file description contains several entries, some of which are dependent upon the particular computer you use. Some of the entries are required, and some are optional but are used to provide good program documentation.

FIGURE 3-1

Relationship of FILE-CONTROL and FILE SECTION

```
000180  FILE-CONTROL.
000190       SELECT STUDENT-FILE ASSIGN TO - - -.
000200       SELECT PRINTFILE ASSIGN TO - - -.
000210*
000220  DATA DIVISION.
000230  FILE SECTION.
000240  FD  STUDENT-FILE
000250       LABEL RECORD IS OMITTED
000260       DATA RECORD IS STUDENT-RECORD.
000270  01   STUDENT-RECORD        PIC X(80).
000280  FD  PRINTFILE
000290       LABEL RECORD IS OMITTED
000300       DATA RECORD IS LIST-RECORD.
000310  01   LIST-RECORD.
000320       03  FILLER            PIC X.
000330       03  LIST-LINE         PIC X(120).
```

The first entry after the FD indicates that LABEL RECORD IS OMITTED. This is a required entry and tells the system whether there is or is not a label associated with the file. Magnetic tape and disk storage devices do have labels (a series of magnetic spots, or bits, that indicate the name given to that particular file) that usually follow a standard format. (If we are using tape or disk, we would use the entry LABEL RECORD IS STANDARD.) However, card files and printer files do *not* have labels, and so our entry is correct in stating that LABEL RECORD IS OMITTED.

The next entry is one in which the programmer assigns a name to the series of incoming data records. Earlier, in the SELECT statement, you named the entire file of data. Now you are naming the *entire record* (an 80-column card) of data. You must follow the rules of naming and, in this case, the programmer has chosen the name STUDENT-RECORD. Note that the programmer could have chosen any name (except a reserved word) for the record, but could *not* have used STUDENT-FILE. STUDENT-FILE is the *file* name, STUDENT-RECORD is the *record* name. Also, note that the period is at the end of the *last* entry in the file description. Periods *do not* go at the end of each line in the FD entry.

Describing an input record—level numbers

As previously indicated, you just finished assigning a name to a record. Immediately after this, the system must find an 01 entry beginning at column 8. The 01 is required and is the programmer's way of telling the system that he or she is now ready to show how the record is broken into a series of fields. In our sample program the entry was extremely simple since the entire record (80 columns) was treated as a single field. In most cases, however, a record is comprised of many fields. Suppose our incoming data record was called STORE-DATA and looked as follows:

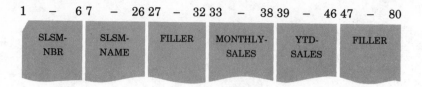

1 – 6	7 – 26	27 – 32	33 – 38	39 – 46	47 – 80
SLSM-NBR	SLSM-NAME	FILLER	MONTHLY-SALES	YTD-SALES	FILLER

We must start the record description with 01 since this number is reserved for a record as a whole. After this, the programmer has the chance to break the record into component fields. Following the diagram shown earlier, our complete record description entry is shown below.

```
01    STORE-DATA.
      03    SLSM-NBR          PIC 9(6).
      03    SLSM-NAME         PIC A(20).
      03    FILLER            PIC X(6).
      03    MONTHLY-SALES     PIC 9(4)V99.
      03    YTD-SALES         PIC 9(6)V99.
      03    FILLER            PIC X(34).
```

The 03 entries associated with each field named indicate that these fields are part of and subordinate to the whole record STORE-DATA. As a matter of fact, any number from 02 through 49 could have been used to show the next level of breakdown within a record. Some shops use an odd numbering system of 01, 03, 05, and so on, while others use increments of five: 01, 05, 10, 15, and so on.

The field names conform to the rules of naming and make some sort of sense so that a person reading the program could guess the contents of the field. Some shops require that all field names describe the source of the data. Thus, we might have appended IN or something similar onto all the names shown above. Doing this serves two purposes: (1) it provides necessary documentation, and (2) it almost certainly rules out the possibility of using a reserved word for the name of a data field. This, and other *programming conventions*, are designed to reduce the chance of error.

```
01    STORE-DATA-CARD.
      03    SLSM-NBR-CARD-IN  ------
      03    SLSM-NAME-CARD-IN ------
            etc.
```

The PIC clause entries (the full word PICTURE is also permissible) are usually lined up as an aid to detecting misspellings and other common key entry errors. The 9 entry indicates to the system that the field is numeric and is six digits long. Any of the entries in this area may be written with or without parentheses. For example, PIC 9(6) and PIC 999999 are equally correct. The second field is alphabetic, as designated by the letter A, and is 20 characters long.

The next entry describes a six-column blank field, or a field that may be present in the record but is not going to be used by the programmer. The reserved word FILLER is used for this purpose although, in theory, the programmer could make up names for unused fields. The x indicates that the field could contain any type of character—numeric, alphabetic, or mixed alphanumeric.

The monthly sales field is obviously numeric and contains dollars and cents information. Decimal points are seldom keyed into the record (it slows the data entry process), but the system *must* be informed of the location of the assumed or unpunched decimal point. This is done by means of the v character inserted in the PIC entry. (PIC 9(4)V99 says that the numeric field is a total of six positions wide and has two places to the right of the assumed, or implied, decimal point.) The next field follows the same pattern except that it is eight digits long. The last entry simply accounts for the unused portion of the record out to the 80th position.

Another programming convention that has become popular is that of always using two-digit PIC entries, even if the field is less than ten characters long. As you can see in the example below, this enables the programmer to line up the entries so that errors will be easier to detect.

```
01   STORE-DATA.
     03   SLSM-NBR          PIC 9(06).
     03   SLSM-NAME         PIC A(20).
     03   FILLER            PIC X(06).
     03   MONTHLY-SALES     PIC 9(04)V99.
     03   YTD-SALES         PIC 9(06)V99.
     03   FILLER            PIC X(34).
```

A second example will illustrate another aspect of the breakdown of fields within a record. In this case, let's assume our record is 32 characters long and is called DATE-RECORD and that the first six columns contain the date in the following form: month (two digits), day (two digits), and year (two digits). We could correctly describe the record as shown below.

```
01   DATE-RECORD.
     03   DATE-INFO         PIC 9(06).
     03   FILLER            PIC X(26).
```

In this case the DATE-INFO field is six digits long and can be handled *only* as a six-digit field. Thus, the following PROCEDURE DIVISION statement moves the entire six digits:

```
MOVE DATE-INFO TO DATE-AREA.
```

With this arrangement there is no problem in handling the entire field, but it is not possible for the programmer to get to any of the sub-fields that make up DATE-INFO.

If the programmer had any idea that it might be necessary to process the sub-parts of the DATE-INFO field, he or she should have broken the field down further. One method is shown below.

```
01  DATE-RECORD.
    03  DATE-INFO.
        05  MONTH        PIC 99.
        05  DAY          PIC 99.
        05  YEAR         PIC 99.
    03  FILLER           PIC X(26).
```

Now the programmer has the best of all possibilities. The PROCEDURE DIVISION statement

MOVE DAY TO DAY-DATA.

moves only those two digits, while the statement

MOVE DATE-INFO TO DATE-AREA.

moves all six digits of the DATE-INFO field. The system "understands" that DATE-INFO is comprised of lesser fields because of the numbering system. The 05 entries indicate a breakdown of the 03 entry. Also, note that the breakdown stops when the 03 is encountered again. The range of numbers permitted—02 through 49—allows for an extremely fine breakdown if it is required. A sensible policy is to use level numbers spaced sufficiently apart to allow for future entries to be inserted (program maintenance).

DATE-INFO is known as a *group item* because it is further broken down. A PIC entry *cannot* be used on a group item. MONTH, DAY, and YEAR are called *elementary items* because they are not broken down any further. A PIC entry *must* be used with every elementary item.

Describing a printer record

After this bit of diversion into the description of records within a field, we should again look at the file entries in our sample program. As you would expect, we have a similar series of entries for our PRINTFILE. Label records are omitted and the data record is called LIST-RECORD. Subordinate to LIST-RECORD is a very simple breakdown consisting of two entries. The first entry is typical on most printers in that a single position must be set aside for use by the system for controlling the spacing of the printer (single, double, triple spacing, and so on) (Figure 3-2). This topic will be discussed more fully in a later chapter. The second entry describes the width of a fairly standard print line of 120 characters. Perhaps the single most important point to understand right now is that *all* printing will take place from the record area designated as LIST-RECORD. This point will be discussed and illustrated when we deal with the second part of the DATA DIVISION—the WORKING-STORAGE SECTION.

At this point we have completed the entries within the FILE SECTION. The rule is that for every file SELECTed, you must have a complete FD—file description. By the way, we did not have to describe the files in the order in which they appeared in the FILE-CONTROL area. The compiler is only concerned that all files be described. However, common sense would indicate that they be done in order so that a file doesn't get lost in the process.

Note that you have been setting aside two areas in memory: one for the incoming card record, and one for the data record going to the printer.

FIGURE 3-2

Carriage control position

```
000100 IDENTIFICATION DIVISION.
000110 PROGRAM-ID. LISTER.
000120*
000130 ENVIRONMENT DIVISION.
000140 CONFIGURATION SECTION.
000150 SOURCE-COMPUTER. - - -.
000160 OBJECT-COMPUTER. - - -.
000170 INPUT-OUTPUT SECTION.
000180 FILE-CONTROL.
000190     SELECT STUDENT-FILE ASSIGN TO - - -.
000200     SELECT PRINTFILE ASSIGN TO - - -.
000210*
000220 DATA DIVISION.
000230 FILE SECTION.
000240 FD   STUDENT-FILE
000250     LABEL RECORD IS OMITTED
000260     DATA RECORD IS STUDENT-RECORD.
000270 01  STUDENT-RECORD      PIC X(80).
000280 FD   PRINTFILE
000290     LABEL RECORD IS OMITTED
000300     DATA RECORD IS LIST-RECORD.
000310 01  LIST-RECORD.
000320     03  FILLER          PIC X.◄————— CARRIAGE CONTROL POSITION
000330     03  LIST-LINE       PIC X(120).
```

All this is typical of DATA DIVISION activities: setting up data areas within memory for manipulation by COBOL statements within the PROCEDURE DIVISION. This relationship will be illustrated in greater detail later in the chapter.

The WORKING-STORAGE SECTION

A second—and optional—part of the DATA DIVISION, called the WORKING-STORAGE SECTION, is usually present in most COBOL programs. Our sample program was so short that we had only one entry in WORKING-STORAGE.

```
77  EOF-INDICATOR           PIC 9 VALUE ZERO.
```

WORKING-STORAGE is exactly what the term indicates. As opposed to the FILE SECTION where you set aside room for *incoming* and *outgoing* *records*, the WORKING-STORAGE SECTION is the place where you set aside either independent data fields (not part of a record) or entire records according to the needs of the problem you are solving. In our sample program we needed a field that would act as a triggering device to detect the end of our card file. The VALUE entry was used to fill the one position EOF-INDICATOR field with a specific value—zero in this case. If VALUE is *not* specified, the programmer should assume that the area will be filled with *garbage*.

For example, one of the most common uses of WORKING-STORAGE is to set aside total areas—that is, fields in which you wish to total certain values. The following example shows how we would create two total areas (TOTAL-1 and TOTAL-2) in addition to the EOF-INDICATOR field.

```
WORKING-STORAGE SECTION.
77   EOF-INDICATOR        PIC 9 VALUE ZERO.
77   TOTAL-1              PIC 9(5).
77   TOTAL-2              PIC 9(4)V99.
```

Although the entry above is correct, it is likely to lead to serious difficulties later. In fact, this "error" is perhaps the most common one made by beginning COBOL students. For some reason, they assume that a field without the VALUE entry will automatically contain whatever should be there. Reflecting on the matter, it would seem absurd to attempt to add into an area without first knowing that it contained zeros. The easiest way to do this is by means of the VALUE clause. VALUE may also be used to create values other than zero as shown below. Note that the PIC entry must correspond *exactly* to the size of the value created.

```
WORKING-STORAGE SECTION.
77   EOF-INDICATOR        PIC 9 VALUE ZERO.
77   TOTAL-1              PIC 9(5) VALUE ZERO.
77   TOTAL-2              PIC 9(4)V99 VALUE ZERO.
77   PI-AMOUNT            PIC 9V9999 VALUE 3.1415.
77   HOLD-AREA            PIC 9(3).
```

The last entry illustrates another important point: that, for some fields, using a VALUE entry would be a waste of time. For example, it would make no sense to initialize HOLD-AREA to a particular value if the programmer intended to MOVE data into that area, since the act of moving from one area to another destroys the contents of the receiving field. Note that the use of the VALUE entry to create specific values is permitted *only* in the WORKING-STORAGE SECTION, *not* in the FILE SECTION.

Many installations, particularly those using IBM equipment, know that level 77 entries make inefficient use of storage. Because of this, there is a general trend to discourage or eliminate their use. An 01 entry can be used to group these fields under a common heading as shown below.

```
WORKING-STORAGE SECTION.
01   MISC-FIELDS.
     03   TOTAL-1         PIC 9(5) VALUE ZEROS.
     03   TOTAL-2         PIC 9(4)V99 VALUE ZEROS.
     03   PI              PIC 9V9999 VALUE 3.1415.
```

As shown in the sample program, it is entirely permissible to use *both* level 77's and 01's in the WORKING-STORAGE SECTION. Versions of COBOL prior to 1974 required that if both level 77's and 01's were used in WORKING-STORAGE, all level 77's must precede the 01 entries. ANS 74 COBOL, however, permitted the 77's to be intermixed with 01's. In the interest of program portability, you should adhere to the earlier rule despite the change. However, most programs written today do not use level 77's.

The VALUE clause may be used to create whatever values you wish—not just numerics. For example, you can create alphabetic and alphanumeric values by means of the A and X PICTURE characters.

```
WORKING-STORAGE SECTION.
01  MISC-FIELDS.
    03   TOTAL-1            PIC 999V99 VALUE ZEROS.
    03   PROJECT-LEADER     PIC X(11) VALUE 'SUSAN JONES'.
    03   ROUNDING-AMT       PIC V999 VALUE .005.
```

As indicated earlier, you must be particularly careful that the PIC and the created value match exactly. Note the following in which the first field contains a numeric zero while the second is defined as X and contains an *alphanumeric* seven.

```
01  WORK-AREAS.
    03   EOF-SWITCH         PIC 9 VALUE 0.
    03   SEVEN              PIC X VALUE '7'.
```

The next example is *incorrect* because the PIC and VALUE do not match.

```
    03   DOZEN             PIC XX VALUE 12.
```

By now you must realize that, since COBOL is a business-oriented language, output from your programs normally will involve printed material such as reports to management, pay checks, inventory listings, and the like. Almost always these reports are going to have at least three general kinds of output lines: *heading lines* at the top of the report, a *main body line* for the center of the report, and *ending lines* for totals, and so forth. We can modify our sample program to show how this would look.

Card Listing

End of Report

The easy way to handle all of these different output lines is to set up each one in WORKING-STORAGE. Printer output, of course, *has* to come from the record area established for the print file. Here, all we do is set up a record large enough for printer output with the following entries:

```
FD  PRINTFILE
    LABEL RECORD IS OMITTED
    DATA RECORD IS PRINT-LINE.
01  PRINT-LINE             PIC X(121).
```

The next step is to set up the individual lines in WORKING-STORAGE for *exactly* the same length—121 characters. Then when you are ready to print, you MOVE the particular heading, body, or ending line to the PRINT-LINE, and then WRITE PRINT-LINE.

In setting up the heading line, we will have to account for all the *printing* positions across the page (121 in this case). To center it on the page, we will have to create 54 spaces (120 minus 12 divided by 2) on both sides of the message. This is best seen when using a Printer Spacing Chart (Figure 3-3). The actual entry is shown below and would be followed by additional entries for the main body line and the ending line.

```
WORKING-STORAGE SECTION.
01  MISC-FIELDS.
    03  -----.
    03  -----.
01  HEAD-LINE.
    03  FILLER          PIC X.
    03  FILLER      ·   PIC X(54) VALUE SPACES.
    03  FILLER          PIC X(12).
        VALUE 'CARD LISTING'.
    03  FILLER          PIC X(54) VALUE SPACES.
01  MAIN-BODY-LINE.
    .
    .

    .
01  ENDING-LINE.

    .
```

Now, when you are ready to print, you MOVE the particular heading, body, or ending line to the PRINT-LINE and WRITE it. This method makes for a very clean, simple way of handling multiple types of output lines. Figure 3-4 shows, in skeletal form, how this would look in your program. Figure 3-5 illustrates that all the lines are of the same length and are moved to the PRINT-LINE when required. Again, notice that, in this example, the only place from which you can print is PRINT-LINE. In the original LISTER program the only place from which printing could occur was LIST-RECORD.

Basic PROCEDURE DIVISION statements

The PROCEDURE DIVISION usually is the most interesting part of a COBOL program because it is here that the programmer finally gets the chance to direct the computer to perform specific operations such as adding, subtracting, and so on. However, the ease or difficulty of programming in the PROCEDURE DIVISION is, to a great extent, dependent upon how well you have laid out the files, records, and fields you will be using.

By now you should be thoroughly familiar with the individual statements in the first three divisions of our sample program, but let's see the whole COBOL program, including the PROCEDURE DIVISION (Figure 3-6).

COBOL was designed to closely resemble the English language, and, as a result, many of the terms are taken from English grammar. The individual instructions are called *statements* and a series of logically related statements are grouped under *paragraph headers*. In the sample program, CONTROL-ROUTINE, 010-OPENER, 020-READER, and 030-CLOSER are paragraph

FIGURE 3-3

Report format

PROGRAM NAME

SYSTEM NAME

VERSION

CHART TITLE

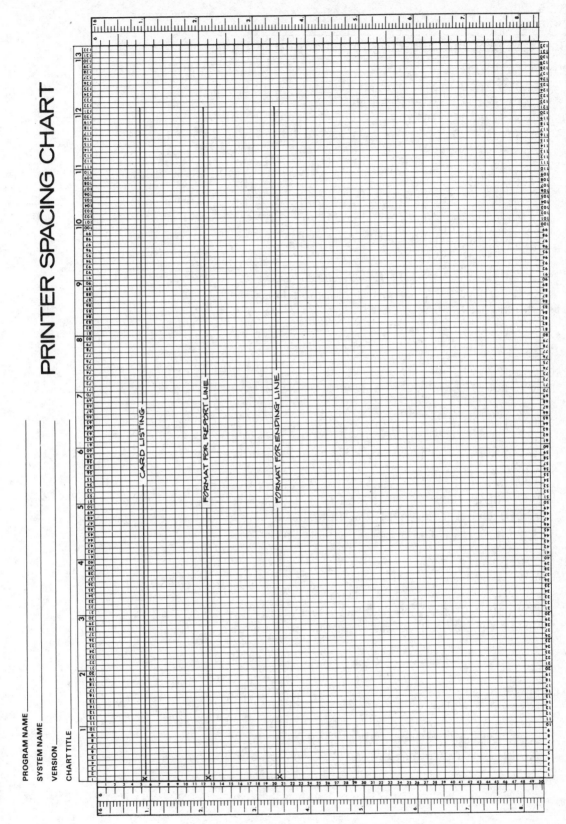

PRINTER SPACING CHART

FIGURE 3-4

Skeletal program showing types of output lines

```
FD   PRINTFILE
     LABEL RECORD IS OMITTED
     DATA RECORD IS PRINT-LINE.
WORKING-STORAGE SECTION.
01   MISC-FIELDS.
     03---
     03---
01   HEAD-LINE.
     .
     .                    } 121 characters as described earlier
     .
01   MAIN-BODY-LINE.
     .
     .                    } 121 characters including numeric,
     .                      alphabetic fields, spaces, blanks, etc.
01   ENDING-LINE.
     .
     .                    } 121 characters
     .
PROCEDURE DIVISION.
CONTROL-ROUTINE.
     .
     .
     .

INITIALIZATION-MODULE
     ------
     ------
     MOVE HEAD-LINE TO PRINT-LINE.
     WRITE PRINT-LINE AFTER ADVANCING 2 LINES.
     ------
     ------
READ-WRITE-MODULE.
     ------
     ------                                         } Main
     MOVE MAIN-BODY-LINE TO PRINT-LINE.               Program
     WRITE PRINT-LINE AFTER ADVANCING 2 LINES.         Loop
     .
     .
     .

ENDING-MODULE.
     ------
     ------
     MOVE ENDING-LINE TO PRINT-LINE.
     WRITE PRINT-LINE AFTER ADVANCING 3 LINES.
     .
     .
     .
```

FIGURE 3-5

Schematic: Output lines in storage

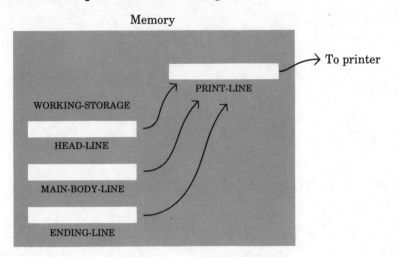

headers. They follow the rules of naming that have been discussed before, and are created by the programmer as needed.

The first paragraph header is our control module, which was discussed in the top-down section presented earlier in the text. Complete control of the program occurs from this paragraph.

The second header (010-OPENER) is there because the programmer wanted to show, set aside, or document the fact that he or she was doing some opening, or "housekeeping," or initialization activities prior to getting into the main part of the program.

The third header (020-READER) not only separates one part of the program from another, but also provides a point for the programmer to branch to later on. A quick look at all the statements within the PROCEDURE DIVISION shows that this paragraph is the heart of the program. It is here that we move the contents of the record to the output line, print it, and read another record. Since this is a task we wish to repeat over and over, we use the UNTIL version of the PERFORM statement to control the looping process, which executes that paragraph over and over until there are no more data records.

The last header (020-CLOSER) establishes the ending paragraph, which will be executed when the READ statement recognizes that the last valid data record has been processed.

By now you are probably wondering why the headers are numbered. They don't have to be numbered at all, but it is good programming practice to do so since you can waste a great amount of time trying to find a particular paragraph header in a long program. If they are numbered in some logical way, the task is much easier. Remember, however, that the number is part of the paragraph name.

FIGURE 3-6

Sample LISTER program

```
000100  IDENTIFICATION DIVISION.
000110  PROGRAM-ID. LISTER.
000120*
000130  ENVIRONMENT DIVISION.
000140  CONFIGURATION SECTION.
000150  SOURCE-COMPUTER. - - -.
000160  OBJECT-COMPUTER. - - -.
000170  INPUT-OUTPUT SECTION.
000180  FILE-CONTROL.
000190      SELECT STUDENT-FILE ASSIGN TO - - -.
000200      SELECT PRINTFILE ASSIGN TO - - -.
000210*
000220  DATA DIVISION.
000230  FILE SECTION.
000240  FD  STUDENT-FILE
000250      LABEL RECORD IS OMITTED
000260      DATA RECORD IS STUDENT-RECORD.
000270  01  STUDENT-RECORD       PIC X(80).
000280  FD  PRINTFILE
000290      LABEL RECORD IS OMITTED
000300      DATA RECORD IS LIST-RECORD.
000310  01  LIST-RECORD.
000320      03  FILLER           PIC X.
000330      03  LIST-LINE        PIC X(120).
000340  WORKING-STORAGE SECTION.
000350  77  EOF-INDICATOR        PIC 9 VALUE ZERO.
000360*
000370  PROCEDURE DIVISION.
000380  CONTROL-ROUTINE.
000390      PERFORM 010-OPENER.
000400      PERFORM 020-READER UNTIL
000410          EOF-INDICATOR = 1.
000420      PERFORM 030-CLOSER.
000430      STOP RUN.
000440  010-OPENER.
000450      OPEN INPUT STUDENT-FILE OUTPUT PRINTFILE.
000460      READ STUDENT-FILE
000470          AT END MOVE 1 TO EOF-INDICATOR.
000480  020-READER.
000490      MOVE STUDENT-RECORD TO LIST-LINE.
000500      WRITE LIST-RECORD AFTER ADVANCING 2 LINES.
000510      READ STUDENT-FILE
000520          AT END MOVE 1 TO EOF-INDICATOR.
000530  030-CLOSER.
000540      MOVE 'END OF PROGRAM' TO LIST-LINE.
000550      WRITE LIST-RECORD AFTER ADVANCING 3 LINES.
000560      CLOSE STUDENT-FILE PRINTFILE.
```

The time has come to get down to the specifics of the individual COBOL statements in our sample program. You will find that most of these statements are easy to learn and remember.

In general, COBOL statements can be grouped into a few broad categories: input/output, data movement, arithmetic, sequence control, and miscellaneous. Our sample program used seven statements basic to almost every program. In describing and explaining these statements, we will follow the rules concerning format.

1. Uppercase words, such as OPEN, READ, WRITE, and so on, are reserved words. If underlined, they are required when the entry is used.
2. Lowercase words, such as *file name*, are words, or terms, chosen by the programmer.
3. Brackets [   ] enclose entries that are optional.
4. Braces {   } are used to indicate a choice is to be made between two or more clauses.
5. Ellipses . . . indicate repetition of an entry.

For example, the first statement that will be discussed is OPEN, which has the following format:

$$\underline{\text{OPEN}} \quad \left[\begin{Bmatrix} \underline{\text{INPUT}} \\ \underline{\text{OUTPUT}} \end{Bmatrix} \text{ file-name-1} . . . \right] . . .$$

The format indicates that the word OPEN is required and that the programmer must make a choice between the words INPUT and OUTPUT followed by a programmer-supplied file name. The ellipses after file-name-1 indicate that once INPUT or OUTPUT is chosen, any number of file names can be used. The ellipses after the bracket indicate that the process of selecting INPUT or OUTPUT files can be repeated as many times as needed within the statement.

The OPEN and CLOSE statements

Both the OPEN and CLOSE statements are very simple as far as the programmer is concerned, but are very complex in their internal operations. The OPEN statement causes the system software to get the file ready for processing and has the following format:

$$\underline{\text{OPEN}} \quad \left[\begin{Bmatrix} \underline{\text{INPUT}} \\ \underline{\text{OUTPUT}} \end{Bmatrix} \text{ file-name-1} . . . \right] . . .$$

In our sample program the statement is written as:

```
OPEN INPUT STUDENT-FILE OUTPUT PRINTFILE.
```

Commas may be inserted in COBOL statements if you feel they are needed, but they have no effect on the statement.

Examples:

```
OPEN INPUT STUDENT-FILE, OUTPUT PRINTFILE.
```

Multiple OPEN statements are also permissible although it is more efficient to use a single OPEN statement.

```
OPEN INPUT STUDENT-FILE.
OPEN OUTPUT PRINTFILE.
```

The CLOSE statement performs the reverse function in that it closes files that have been previously OPENed. It differs from the OPEN statement in that you *must not* indicate whether the file is INPUT or OUTPUT; CLOSE followed by the file name(s) is sufficient.

```
CLOSE STUDENT-FILE PRINTFILE.
```

Also, as with OPEN statements, multiple CLOSE statements may be used within your program.

The READ statement

For sequential files such as cards, magnetic tape, and sequential disk, the READ statement brings the next available record into memory. (For non-sequential files the operation is a little different and will not be considered here.) To be more specific, the data record is brought into the memory area you set aside in the DATA DIVISION when you said DATA RECORD is STUDENT-RECORD. It is from this input area that you are able to manipulate the various fields by means of statements such as ADD, SUBTRACT, MOVE, and so forth. Figure 3-7 shows a schematic of the READ statement.

When a card is read in, the *whole* card enters memory, not just those fields you want to work with. In our sample program we had no need for breaking the record into fields, so the whole record was treated as a single field. On the other hand, if we had a card record such as that shown earlier in the chapter, the only difference would be that the record would be divided into a series of fields, as shown in Figure 3-8.

The READ statement, when used with sequential files, requires the words AT END followed by one or more COBOL statements. The basic format of the statement is shown below.

READ file-name AT END statement(s)

FIGURE 3-7

Schematic: READ operation

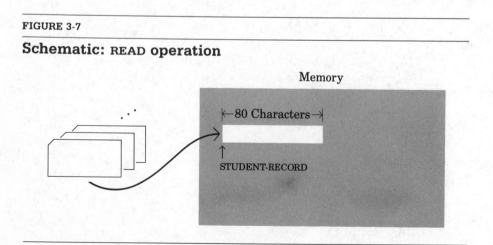

FIGURE 3-8

Read—in area showing fields within a record

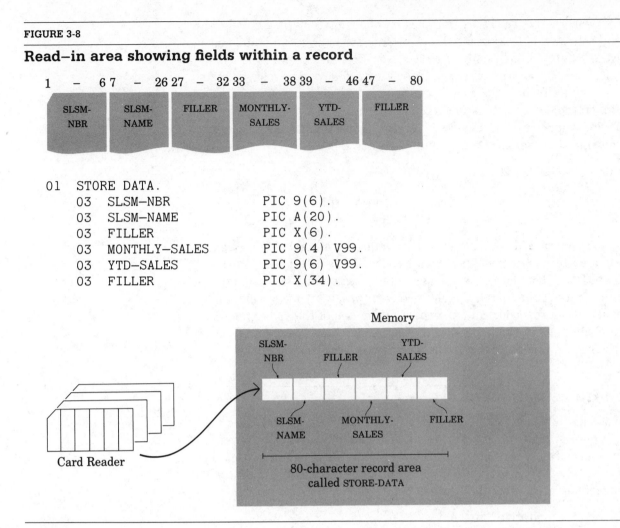

```
01   STORE DATA.
     03   SLSM—NBR            PIC 9(6).
     03   SLSM—NAME           PIC A(20).
     03   FILLER              PIC X(6).
     03   MONTHLY—SALES       PIC 9(4) V99.
     03   YTD—SALES           PIC 9(6) V99.
     03   FILLER              PIC X(34).
```

The AT END clause is necessary because the system must know what to do after the last data record has passed through the input device. With card files, the AT END condition is detected when a special combination of punches (often a / * in columns one and two) is read.

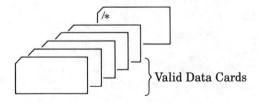

For tape and disk files, the end-of-file condition (EOF) is triggered when the system recognizes a unique bit pattern written after the last regular record. Note that the AT END situation is triggered when your program *executes* the READ statement *once too often*. In this case the system detects the EOF and activates the AT END portion of the statement. Actually, the COBOL software is looking for the EOF *every* time the READ statement is executed, but will find it only *after* the last record has been processed.

In the sample program the AT END entry is followed by a single statement—MOVE. Technically, the AT END may be followed by any number of COBOL statements—not just one, and not always MOVE. For example, the following sequence of statements is correct. (Note that the period appears at the end of the series of statements you want executed.)

```
READ STUDENT-FILE
    AT END
        MOVE 'END OF DATA' TO LIST-LINE
        WRITE LIST-RECORD AFTER ADVANCING 2 LINES.
```

The general rule is that AT END is required when reading sequential files. However, a few systems permit the use of a sequential READ without AT END. Even though this may be permitted it is not wise to do so, for two reasons. First, it limits the portability of your program, and second, the AT END serves a proper logical function—to take care of the end-of-file situation. Even if your system handles this automatically, the end-of-file activities should be readily visible to the user of your program.

The MOVE statement

The MOVE might very well be the most used statement in COBOL. As with most COBOL statements, it is simple but does a lot of work for the programmer. Generally, it makes a *copy* of a data field and moves this copy to another location. Wherever this copy arrives, it destroys the old value that was in the receiving area. Note that the sending field data remain the same.

$$\underline{\text{MOVE}} \quad \begin{Bmatrix} \text{figurative constant} \\ \text{identifier-1} \\ \text{literal} \end{Bmatrix} \quad \underline{\text{TO}} \quad \text{identifier-2 [identifier-3] ...}$$

The simplest form of the MOVE statement uses a figurative constant. The statement

```
MOVE SPACES TO AREA-A.
```

causes the correct number of spaces to be moved into the area called AREA-A. In the sample program we used another version of the statement

```
MOVE STUDENT-RECORD TO LIST-LINE.
```

In this case the contents of the card input area (80 characters) are moved into the area called LIST-LINE (120 characters), as shown below.

Memory

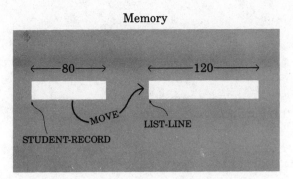

Both fields were defined as PIC X, and when one PIC X field is moved into another, the move goes from left to right and the *remaining characters on the right (if any) are cleared to spaces.*

Examples:

```
MOVE FIELD-A TO FIELD-B.
```

		Before	**After**
1.	FIELD-A PIC X(8)	15 R ST.	15 R ST.
	FIELD-B PIC X(8)	ABCDEFGH	15 R ST.

Both fields are the same size and the incoming data replace the old data in FIELD-B.

		Before	**After**
2.	FIELD-A PIC X(8)	15 R ST.	15 R ST.
	FIELD-B PIC X(10)	ABCDEFGHIJ	15 R ST.bb

The receiving field is larger and the extra positions on the right are automatically filled with blanks.

		Before	**After**
3.	FIELD-A PIC X(8)	15 R ST.	15 R ST.
	FIELD-B PIC X(6)	ABCDEF	15 R S

The receiving field is too small and the first six characters are moved in from left to right. The rightmost two characters are lost (truncated) and the compiler may produce an error message during compilation.

In the sample program we showed another way of moving non-numeric data to a field: by means of a literal. The statement

```
MOVE 'END OF PROGRAM' TO LIST-LINE
```

moves the actual characters END OF PROGRAM from left to right into the 120-character LIST-LINE area. The extra positions on the right are automatically filled with blanks.

When numeric fields are moved, the action is a little different since the system automatically aligns the data on the decimal point.

Examples:

```
MOVE NUMBER-A TO NUMBER-B.
```

		Before	**After**
1.	NUMBER-A PIC 999V99	123∧45	123∧45
	NUMBER-B PIC 999V99	777∧77	123∧45

Both fields are of the same size, and the numeric values are aligned on the assumed (V) decimal point.

		Before	**After**
2.	NUMBER-A PIC 999V99	123∧45	123∧45
	NUMBER-B PIC 9999V999	7777∧777	0123∧450

When a smaller numeric field is moved to a larger numeric field, zeros are automatically inserted where needed.

		Before	**After**
3.	NUMBER-A PIC 999V99	123∧45	123∧45
	NUMBER-B PIC 99V9	77∧7	23∧4

The receiving field is smaller on both sides of the decimal point and a digit is lost at both ends. On most systems the software will produce an error message during compilation. Other MOVE options will be discussed later in the text.

The WRITE statement

The purpose of the WRITE statement is to send a data record to an output device such as a printer, card punch, tape, or disk. The complete format is:

$$\text{WRITE record-name} \quad \begin{Bmatrix} \text{BEFORE} \\ \text{AFTER} \end{Bmatrix} \quad \text{ADVANCING} \quad \begin{Bmatrix} \text{identifier} \\ \text{integer} \\ \text{mnemonic name} \\ \text{PAGE} \end{Bmatrix} \quad \begin{matrix} \text{LINE} \\ \text{LINES} \end{matrix}$$

For the printer, the most common form is:

$$\underline{\text{WRITE}}\ \text{record-name}\ \left\{ \begin{array}{c} \underline{\text{BEFORE}} \\ \underline{\text{AFTER}} \end{array} \right\}\ \underline{\text{ADVANCING}}\ \text{integer}\ \underline{\text{LINES}}.$$

Note that the READ statement reads a *file name* while the WRITE statement writes a *record name*. In our sample program we moved the STUDENT-RECORD record to LIST-LINE and then wrote the *record* with the following statement:

```
WRITE LIST-RECORD AFTER ADVANCING 2 LINES.
```

The following are *incorrect* since they do not use the record name:

```
WRITE LIST-LINE AFTER ADVANCING 2 LINES.
```

or

```
WRITE PRINTFILE AFTER ADVANCING 2 LINES.
```

Earlier in the text we said that the programmer normally sets aside one character just before the beginning of the print line for system use. (Not all systems work this way, so check your machine to be sure.) The operation is quite simple and logical. The system looks at the number of lines you wish to advance (such as two lines in this case) and generates a single character inserted into the one position area located just before the print line. Then, when this line of 121 characters (1 + 120) is sent to the printer, the printer "knows" how many lines to advance.

Please note that if you fail to set aside room for this extra character, the system will take it anyway. Therefore, if your printout seems to be missing the first character, the chances are very good that you forgot about the one character printer requirement. ANS 74 COBOL permits the use of both LINE (singular) and LINES (plural), but older COBOL versions use only the plural form LINES. On these systems you must always use LINES even when spacing only a single line. The correct COBOL format then becomes

```
WRITE LIST-RECORD AFTER ADVANCING 1 LINES.
```

Check your system concerning this requirement.

The PERFORM and PERFORM UNTIL statements

The PERFORM statement has many variations, or options, that may be strung together to provide a very versatile statement. Two of the PERFORM formats are shown below.

Format 1 PERFORM paragraph-name.
Format 2 PERFORM paragraph-name UNTIL test condition.

Example: Format 1

```
PERFORM 010-OPENER-ROUTINE.
ADD 1 TO COUNTER-1.
```

Upon encountering the PERFORM statement, the system *branches* or *jumps* to the 010-OPENER-ROUTINE paragraph in your program and sequentially executes the statements found there. In the example shown above, the system will *automatically* return to the next statement after the PERFORM (in this case, the ADD statement).

The second form of the PERFORM statement (PERFORM UNTIL) allows us to use one of the three programming structures discussed earlier—the *controlled loop* or DOWHILE *structure*. The flowchart of the DOWHILE or controlled loop structure exactly fits the action of the PERFORM UNTIL statement.

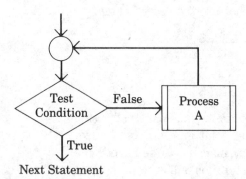

Example: Format 2

```
PERFORM 020-READER
    UNTIL EOF-INDICATOR = 1.
--------.
```

When the system reaches the PERFORM UNTIL statement, it will check the condition *first* (as shown by the flowchart). This is a critical point because the result of the test determines whether or not 020-READER will be executed. If the result of the test is false—that is, the EOF-INDICATOR field is *not* equal to 1—the module will be PERFORMED. If EOF-INDICATOR *is* equal to 1, the paragraph is *not* PERFORMed and the system will go to the next statement in sequence.

Now let's get back to a very critical idea we skimmed over in Chapter 1. At that time we presented the same sample program you just saw in Figure 3-6 and noted that the program contained two READ statements: one in the 010-OPENER paragraph and one at the end of the 020-READER paragraph. On the surface it appears foolish to have the first READ at all. Why not make things easier and simply omit the first READ and then move the *second* READ up to the top of the 020-READER paragraph, as shown below?

```
010-OPENER.
    OPEN -------.
020-READER.
    READ -------.
        AT END MOVE 1 TO EOF-INDICATOR.
    MOVE -------.
    WRITE -------.
```

This approach will work for a while, but then we run into a problem because of the way in which the PERFORM UNTIL statement works. Quite correctly the system will PERFORM the 020-READER paragraph until EOF-INDICATOR = 1. For example, on the first card the condition of the EOF-INDICATOR field will be tested before the system goes back to execute the 020-READER paragraph again. But what happens *after* the last record has been processed? The sequence of events is as follows:

1. The last valid data record is read.
2. The data are moved to the output area.
3. A line of data is written.
4. The system checks the EOF-INDICATOR field to see if it contains a value of 1. Since it does not, the 020-READER paragraph will be PERFORMed again.
5. The system now reads in the end-of-file configuration, which activates the AT END portion of the READ statement and moves a 1 to EOF-INDICATOR.
6. The problem is that the system cannot get back to the PERFORM UNTIL to do this testing until *it comes to the end of the* 020-READER *paragraph*. Thus, even though the value of the INDICATOR is changed to 1 right away, the MOVE and WRITE statements in the remainder of that paragraph will be executed and invalid data will be moved and printed.

The solution to the problem is to put the READ statement at the *end* of the paragraph so that the EOF-INDICATOR can be tested as soon as that statement is completed. In order to make this plan work, we must have an *extra* READ statement that is executed *before* going into the 020-READER paragraph loop. Note that this statement is placed in the 010-OPENER paragraph to act as a "priming" sort of device so that the 020-READER paragraph can use the sequence MOVE-WRITE-READ, rather than READ-MOVE-WRITE.

The STOP statement

The STOP statement terminates the execution of your program and normally transfers control to the system software.

```
STOP RUN.
```

COMMON ERRORS

Starting now, and in each following chapter, you will see some of the more common errors programmers make. When you do get compile-time error messages, do more than just correct the error—analyze what is happening within your program. Errors provide you with an excellent opportunity to see how COBOL works—don't miss this chance.

The first error that will be discussed illustrates exactly what I mean. In Figure 3-9 you can see that the programmer has not matched the SELECT file name (PRINTFILE) with the FD file name (PRINT-FILE). This is a fatal level error that will generate *multiple* error messages. Let's analyze what has taken place.

FIGURE 3-9

LISTER program with error

```
000100 IDENTIFICATION DIVISION.
000110 PROGRAM-ID. LISTER.
000120*
000130 ENVIRONMENT DIVISION.
000140 CONFIGURATION SECTION.
000150 SOURCE-COMPUTER. - - -.
000160 OBJECT-COMPUTER. - - -.
000170 INPUT-OUTPUT SECTION.
000180 FILE-CONTROL.
000190     SELECT STUDENT-FILE ASSIGN TO - - -.
000200     SELECT PRINTFILE ASSIGN TO - - -.
000210*
000220 DATA DIVISION.
000230 FILE SECTION.
000240 FD  STUDENT-FILE
000250     LABEL RECORD IS OMITTED
000260     DATA RECORD IS STUDENT-RECORD.
000270 01  STUDENT-RECORD       PIC X(80).
000280 FD  PRINT-FILE
000290     LABEL RECORD IS OMITTED
000300     DATA RECORD IS LIST-RECORD.
000310 01  LIST-RECORD.
000320     03  FILLER           PIC X.
000330     03  LIST-LINE        PIC X(120).
000340 WORKING-STORAGE SECTION.
000350 77  EOF-INDICATOR        PIC 9 VALUE ZERO.
000360*
000370 PROCEDURE DIVISION.
000380 CONTROL-ROUTINE.
000390     PERFORM 010-OPENER.
000400     PERFORM 020-READER UNTIL
000410         EOF-INDICATOR = 1.
000420     PERFORM 030-CLOSER.
000430     STOP RUN.
000440 010-OPENER.
000450     OPEN INPUT STUDENT-FILE OUTPUT PRINTFILE.
000460     READ STUDENT-FILE
000470         AT END MOVE 1 TO EOF-INDICATOR.
000480 020-READER.
000490     MOVE STUDENT-RECORD TO LIST-LINE.
000500     WRITE LIST-RECORD AFTER ADVANCING 2 LINES.
000510     READ STUDENT-FILE
000520         AT END MOVE 1 TO EOF-INDICATOR.
000530 030-CLOSER.
000540     MOVE 'END OF PROGRAM' TO LIST-LINE.
000550     WRITE LIST-RECORD AFTER ADVANCING 3 LINES.
000560     CLOSE STUDENT-FILE PRINTFILE.
```

FILE NAMES DO NOT MATCH

First, the system will generate an error message (FILE NAME NOT DEFINED. DESCRIPTION IGNORED) that refers to line 300, DATA RECORD IS LIST-RECORD. The reason is that, although the entry started on line 280, it ended on line 300. Then, note that the entire description of that file was *ignored* by the system. That, in turn, means that *any* references to the *file or any part of the file* throughout the remainder of the program will generate appropriate error messages. Thus, that one error will generate errors on the following statements:

Line 450 OPEN—a non-existent file cannot be opened

Line 490 MOVE—a record cannot be moved to LIST-LINE since LIST-LINE does not exist

Line 500 WRITE—a non-existent file cannot be written

Line 540 MOVE—a literal cannot be moved to an area (LIST-LINE) that does not exist

Line 550 WRITE—a non-existent file cannot be written

Line 560 CLOSE—an unopened (and non-existent) file cannot be closed.

The same thing could have happened on a far grander scale had the record contained a series of subordinate fields. In that case you would have gotten an error message every time one of these fields was used. The moral to the story: a single well-placed error can generate a great many nasty messages.

PROGRAMMING TIPS

For most beginners the IDENTIFICATION and ENVIRONMENT divisions cause no difficulty at all. Typically, the data files that will be used by your program have been described in a statement of the problem given to you by the instructor. Even if you think you understand the problem, a good technique at this point is to draw yourself a quick, simple diagram of the files that will be used. The diagram doesn't have to be a work of art—it is just for you to get a better visual picture of what is happening. As shown below, label the diagram with the file names to reinforce the idea even further.

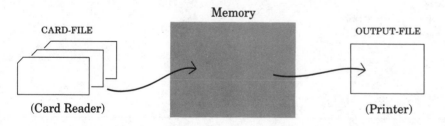

Memory

CARD-FILE   OUTPUT-FILE

(Card Reader)   (Printer)

Now, on to the DATA DIVISION, which is an entirely different matter. It starts out easily enough since you know that for each file appearing in a SELECT entry in the ENVIRONMENT DIVISION you must have an FD entry in the DATA DIVISION. The first entries are standard, but the big question is "How far should I break down the fields within the record?" Of course, there is no set answer to that question, other than "It depends."

The degree of breakdown of fields in the DATA DIVISION depends upon how you expect to use these fields in the PROCEDURE DIVISION. If you think you will have to work with subfields (such as MONTH, DAY, and YEAR) within a field, then break it down now. If you are not sure, then don't break it down. After all, you can always go back to the DATA DIVISION later and make the changes necessitated by your statements in the PROCEDURE DIVISION.

Some beginning COBOL programmers seem to have difficulty understanding the use of or need for the WORKING-STORAGE section. Although this section appears at the end of the DATA DIVISION, you should be thinking of it early in the design phase of the problem-solving process. WORKING-STORAGE is exactly what it says it is: a storage area for fields and records you will be working with in the program. Using it is much like packing a suitcase for a trip: You take those items you think you will need. In COBOL, as in packing a suitcase, the decision is yours. If you think you will need a working area during PROCEDURE DIVISION operations, then set up whatever is required.

The most common usages of WORKING-STORAGE were shown in the chapter examples: total areas, indicators, and various heading and ending lines. Constant values such as pi (3.1415), which might be used in mathematical applications, pay rate increases, and so forth, are commonly set up here. So, during the coding stage, set up those fields you know you are going to need. Later, when coding the PROCEDURE DIVISION entries, you may find that you need another WORKING-STORAGE field, but it should be no problem to add it as required. The general rule is that unless you intend to MOVE (GIVING) into a WORKING-STORAGE field, it should contain an initial value established by the VALUE entry.

Be sure to use meaningful names. One of the major advantages of COBOL is that you can use names up to 30 characters long to name data fields or paragraphs. Again and again we see beginning students use data names such as A1, A2, A3, and so on. It is true that this reduces the number of key-entry strokes required in a program, but the ultimate penalty is far too great: A program of this type becomes impossible for anyone else to follow. Thus, the programming has negated the self-documenting advantage of COBOL. Note the following examples of data names:

Horrible: C1, FIELD-1
Bad: C-NAME, A-FIELD
Fair: CUST-NAME, AMOUNT
Good: CUSTOMER-NAME, NET-PAY-AMOUNT

Thus the statement

```
MOVE C1 TO OUT-1
```

is almost meaningless. But the statement

```
MOVE CUSTOMER-NAME TO
    CUSTOMER-NAME-OUT
```

is better.

Line up the PICTURE (or PIC) entries to make it easier to detect key-stroking errors.

Poor:
```
03  NAME PIC X(20).
03  CUSTOMER-ID-NBR PIC 9(5).
03  FILLER PIC X(10).
03  DATE FIELD PIC 9(6).
```
Good:
```
03  NAME                    PIC X(20).
03  CUSTOMER-ID-NBR         PIC 9(5).
03  FILLER                  PIC X(10).
03  DATE-FIELD              PIC 9(6).
```

Make all PICs two digits for clarity.
```
03  NAME                    PIC X(20).
03  CUSTOMER-ID-NBR         PIC 9(05).
03  FILLER                  PIC X(10).
03  DATE-FIELD              PIC 9(06).
```

Identify the source or nature of data fields, records, and files.

We discussed this point earlier by saying that one frequently used technique is to identify WORKING-STORAGE fields with a WS prefix or suffix. The same holds true for input/output records and fields. For example, CUSTOMER-NAME-TAPE-IN or CUSTOMER-NAME-PR.

Using the words FILE and RECORD serves the same purpose of further identifying the nature of the data element with which you are dealing. For example, CARD-INPUT-FILE is better than INPUT-FILE, but ACC-REC-CARD-INPUT-FILE is even better.

SELF-STUDY: QUESTIONS AND ANSWERS

1. I understand that the purpose of a SELECT statement is to give a name to a file of data that will be going through a specific input/output device. However, it seems that every example I have ever seen shows names like STUDENT-FILE, PRINTFILE, TAPE-FILE, and so on. Do I have to use the FILE in the name?

   Answer: No, you don't have to use the word "FILE" at all in the file name. However, since it actually is a file, it is good practice to do so because it makes it easier for you and anyone who reads your program to understand that it is a *file* and nothing else.

2. Several times in the chapter you stressed the relationship between files, records, and fields. It seems simple enough, but is it really that important?

   Answer: It sure is! As the section on common errors showed, one simple mistake in this area gets compounded because of the file-record-field relationship. Unfortunately, this seems to be an area of some confusion, or at least an area in which students make many errors.

3. Do the FD entries in the FILE SECTION have to be in the same order as the SELECT statement?

   Answer: No, they don't, but every SELECT must have an FD entry. Still, it is good practice to do the FD entries in the same order as the SELECT entries so that they are easy to find and so that you don't forget any of them.

4. Could you explain a little more about an external file label? Why isn't there a label on card or print files?

Answer: Right now we cannot take the time to go into labels in detail, but perhaps a few comments will relieve your mind on the question. Card and printer files do not have labels, simply because there is no room or place for them. On disk and tape, however, an area is set aside for label data. When the programmer creates a file, he or she gives the file a name, such as "ACC-RECV", and this is written magnetically on the recording surface. Later, when a program tries to access a particular file, the label is checked by the system to be sure that the correct reel or disk was mounted on the I/O device. If the label does not match, the job is automatically canceled.

5. Since a field described as X can contain any type of character, why can't I just use PIC X for every field?

Answer: Technically you could do so, but don't—it is a bad habit to get into. The problem is that a field with a picture of X cannot be worked upon arithmetically. So the general rule is that, unless you have an extraordinary reason for not doing so, you make all numeric fields PIC 9. This would be true even for numeric fields (such as an ID number) that are not going to be processed arithmetically. By identifying them as PIC 9, there is no doubt to anyone else that the field is numeric.

6. Why are there two parts to the DATA DIVISION? It seems as though all the entries could go in the FILE SECTION so that WORKING-STORAGE wouldn't be needed.

Answer: The two parts of the DATA DIVISION serve two different functions, and there are slightly different rules concerning the entries in each part. The FILE SECTION identifies the files named in the SELECT entries made earlier. The WORKING-STORAGE SECTION, on the other hand, is the place where you create fields and records that are not directly part of the files you are using. In addition to the obvious difference between the two sections, there is also a difference in philosophy. In WORKING-STORAGE you not only create fields, but also have the capability of placing actual values into specific areas. In the FILE SECTION (with one exception) you cannot use the VALUE clause. All you can do is identify the nature, size, and sequence for the data fields. So, both sections are necessary.

7. Do I always have to use the VALUE entry with fields that I create in the WORKING-STORAGE SECTION?

Answer: No, you do not. There would be nothing gained by assigning a specific value to a field into which you are going to move some data. The move, of course, would destroy the old contents of the field anyway.

Also, you are not obligated to say VALUE ZEROS even for fields such as TOTAL-1 or TOTAL-2, as shown in the chapter example. Rather than use the VALUE entry at that point, you could use the MOVE ZEROS statement in the PROCEDURE DIVISION to accomplish the same result. However, this is not nearly as efficient as using VALUE. Perhaps even more important is that it is very easy to forget the MOVE ZEROS when actually writing the PROCEDURE DIVISION statements.

It should be mentioned that there are times when you will want to use both methods. As explained above, VALUE ZEROS sets the area to zero *before* any PROCEDURE DIVISION statements are executed. Then, after parts of the PROCEDURE DIVISION are executed, you may wish to reset the value of certain areas to zero prior to continuing on with more processing.

CHAPTER TERMS

alphanumeric fields
assumed decimal point
body-line (main body-line)
carriage control position
CLOSE statement
controlled loop structure (DOWHILE)
DOWHILE structure
elementary item
ending lines
EOF (end-of-file)
file description (FD)
group item
heading lines
independent data fields

initialization module
label (file label)
level numbers
MOVE statement
OPEN statement
paragraph headers
PERFORM (PERFORM UNTIL) statement
priming READ
printer spacing chart
programming conventions (practices)
READ statement
statements (COBOL statements)
STOP statement
WRITE statement

EXERCISES

1. What is the purpose of the DATA DIVISION?

2. FD stands for _____ .

3. What types of devices require the LABEL RECORD IS STANDARD entry?

4. What is wrong with this program segment?

```
FD  DATA-FILE
    LABEL RECORD IS OMITTED.
    DATA RECORD IS DATA-REC.
```

5. Once you have ended the FD portion of the file description what must the computer see next?

6. What is the alternate form of PIC 9999999?

7. What does the entry PIC A(20) tell the computer about a data field?

8. The common field name for unused portions of a record is _____ .

9. Alphanumeric data is designated by the character _____ .

10. An assumed decimal point is designated by the character _____ .

11. How does the computer know if one field is subordinate to another (for example, part of a larger field)?

12. An item which is further broken down is known as a _____ item.

13. An item which is not further broken down is known as an _____ item.

14. If you do not put a value on a field description, the field will be initialized with what value?

15. What is wrong with this statement?

```
77  DATA-FIELD        PIC 99V99 VALUE '98.65'.
```

16. What is wrong with this statement?

```
CLOSE INPUT FILE-C OUTPUT FILE-D.
```

17. What is the probable cause for this bad output?

```
EPORT FOR JUNE 19--
EADING LINE #1
ARRY SMITH  $   127.93
OM JONES    $    36.96
OHN DOE     $   168.97
IKE STACK   $1,699.87

OTAL        $2,033.73
```

18. Define or explain each of the following terms or phrases.
    a. group item
    b. elementary item
    c. 01 versus 77
    d. 02-49
    e. SOURCE-COMPUTER
    f. OBJECT-COMPUTER
    g. the function of the SELECT entry
    h. the function of the ASSIGN entry
    i. FILLER
    j. PICTURE, or PIC
    k. paragraph header
    l. LABEL RECORD IS STANDARD
    m. LABEL RECORD IS OMITTED

19. Indicate whether the following entries are correct or incorrect. If the entry is incorrect, change it so it is correct.
    a. IDENTIFICATION DIVISION
    b. PROGRAM-ID. NBR ONE.
    c. PROGRAM ID. LISTER.
    d. CONFIGURATION SECTION.
    e. ENVIRONMENT DIVISION
    f. FD OUTPUT-FILE
       LABEL RECORDS ARE OMITTED
       DATA RECORD IS OUTPUT-LINE.
    g. PROCEDURE-DIVISION.

20. Look at the following statements that apply to the sample LISTER program. If you see any mistake, make the appropriate correction.
    a. WRITE LIST-LINE AFTER ADVANCING 2 LINES.

b. READ CARD DATA
   AT END
      MOVE 'END OF REPORT' TO LIST-LINE
      WRITE LIST AFTER ADVANCING 1 LINE.
c. MOVE 'END OF REPORT' TO PRINT-LINE
   WRITE PRINT-LINE BEFORE ADVANCING 3 LINES.
d. MOVE SPACES TO LIST-LINE
e. MOVE '1' TO INDICATOR

21. In the next exercise you are to write the record description based on the following information: Record name is Inventory-data, fields are as follows:

Position or column	Field description
1–10	Part number
11–15	Blank
16–30	Part name
31–35	Bin number
36–40	Shelf number
41–79	Blank

22. Write the record description based on the following information: Record name is Employee-record, fields are as follows:

Position or column	Field description
1–20	Blank
21–29	Social security number
30–50	Name
51–70	Address
71–72	Numeric pay code

23. Modify Exercise 22 so that the social security number is broken down into its component parts. Each of these fields must be at the elementary level, but also create a social security number field so that the whole field can be moved by a single instruction.

24. Explain the difference between an assumed (or implied) decimal point and a real decimal point.

25. Draw the controlled loop structure (DOWHILE) so that Process A, Process B, and Process C will be executed as long as the test condition is false.

26. Write the PICTURE entry for the following numeric values.
    a. 3645
    b. 0039
    c. 156.93
    d. 0001.75
    e. 00.01
    f. .456
    g. .00059

27. Explain in detail the action of the PERFORM UNTIL statement. If necessary, use diagrams in your explanation.

28. Is it possible to PERFORM a single statement? If so, how?

29. Indicate the outcome of the following MOVE statements. The caret (^) indicates the position of the assumed decimal point.

		First field	Receiving field
a.	MOVE AMT-1 TO AMT-2.	4 5 6 7^	□ □ □.^
b.	MOVE AMT-3 TO AMT-4.	4 5^5 0	□ □.^□ □
c.	MOVE AMT-5 TO AMT-6.	1 2 3^0	□.^□ □ □
d.	MOVE AMT-7 TO AMT-8.	^1 2 3 4	□ □ □ □.^
e.	MOVE ZEROS TO TOTAL.		□ □ □ □ □ □
f.	MOVE SPACES TO TOTAL.		□ □ □ □ □ □

Indicate the outcome of the following MOVE statements.

		Sending field	Receiving field
a.	MOVE ALPHA-1 TO ALPHA-2.	A B C	□ □ □ □ □
b.	MOVE ALPHA-3 TO ALPHA-4.	A B C D E	□ □ □
c.	MOVE ALPHA-5 TO ALPHA-6.	A B b C D	□ □ □ □ □ □
d.	MOVE SPACES TO ALPHA-7.		□ □ □ □ □

30. Write the *complete* FD and record description based on the following information: file name is ACCOUNT-FILE; record name is ACCOUNT-REC. Fields are as follows and decimal points are *not* keyed in the card record.

Position or column	Field description
1–7	Account number
8–13	Location code (all numeric)
14–19	Retail price (dollar and cents figure)
20–30	Blank
31–35	Cost price (dollar and cents figure)
36–45	Item description
46–50	Salesperson code (mixed numeric and alphabetic)
51–55	Credit code (numeric)

31. Modify the sample program as follows: Change the file names, record names, and field names throughout the program. Use names of your own choice, but make sure they are appropriate to the problem.

32. Change the paragraph header names in the sample program and make whatever other changes in the program statements that this would require.

33. Address label exercise: You have an unknown number of data records containing information on subscribers to a magazine. The record format (assume tape or disk unless told otherwise by your instructor) is as follows:

Position or column	Field description
1–20	Customer name
21–40	Street address
41–60	City, state, ZIP code
61–66	Expiration date

Write a program that prints mailing labels in the following format:

Name

Street address

City, state ZIP expiration date

34. As a refinement to the previous exercise, you are to print two mailing labels for each subscriber. Use the following format:

Name	Name
Street address	Street address
City, state ZIP	City, state ZIP
Expiration date	Expiration date

Chapter 4
Handling Data (Part I)

LEARNING OBJECTIVES

1. To see how to use the INTO variation of the READ statement and the FROM option of the WRITE statement.

2. To understand the basic difference between the FILE SECTION and the WORKING-STORAGE SECTION.

3. To learn about the editing capabilities of COBOL and how these capabilities can be used to turn out professional looking business reports.

4. To see how COBOL handles arithmetic manipulations by means of either the four basic statements (ADD, SUBTRACT, MULTIPLY, and DIVIDE) or by means of the COMPUTE statement.

Chapter 3 introduced you to a set of basic COBOL statements that are needed in virtually every program: OPEN, CLOSE, READ, WRITE, MOVE, and PERFORM. In this chapter you will see more ways that data can be handled to produce the types of reports commonly required in business situations. Then, four arithmetic statements—ADD, SUBTRACT, MULTIPLY, and DIVIDE—will be shown along with the multiple-use COMPUTE statement.

More about data input and output

One of the nice features of COBOL is that the language is rich in its capability for handling data. Some of these features are well worth knowing about as they can save you a great deal of effort, particularly in complex programs.

READ INTO and WRITE FROM

So far you have seen only the basic form of the READ statement:

READ file-name
    AT END imperative statement

The action of the statement is straightforward and has already been diagramed: a record from the file is read into the *buffer* area that you established in the file description. Let's use the example that was shown earlier.

```
FD   DATA-FILE
     LABEL RECORD IS OMITTED
     DATA RECORD IS STORE-DATA.
01   STORE-DATA.
     03   SLSM-NBR        PIC 9(06).
     03   SLSM-NAME       PIC A(20).
     03   FILLER          PIC X(06).
     03   MONTHLY-SALES   PIC 9(04)V99.
     03   YTD-SALES       PIC 9(06)V99.
     03   FILLER          PIC X(34).
          .
          .
          .

     READ DATA-FILE
          AT END MOVE 1 TO INDICATOR.
```

As indicated earlier, the action of the READ statement brings the record into the designated input buffer area (STORE-DATA). The data in the named fields (SLSM-NBR, SLSM-NAME, etc.) may now be accessed/manipulated by the appropriate COBOL statements such as MOVE, ADD, SUBTRACT, and so on. However, for several reasons that will be noted below, some programmers and some shops prefer that all data manipulation take place in WORKING-STORAGE rather than in the FILE SECTION buffer area. This technique can be used fairly easily by following the same pattern that we did earlier when handling multiple types of print lines.

```
FD   DATA-FILE
     LABEL RECORD IS OMITTED
     DATA RECORD IS STORE-DATA.
01   STORE-DATA            PIC X(80).
WORKING-STORAGE SECTION.
01   STORE-DATA-WS.
     03   SLSM-NBR          PIC 9(06).
     03   SLSM-NAME         PIC A(20).
     03   FILLER            PIC X(06).
     03   MONTHLY-SALES     PIC 9(04)V99.
     03   YTD-SALES         PIC 9(06)V99.
     03   FILLER            PIC X(34).
             .
             .
             .
     READ DATA-FILE
          AT END -----.
     MOVE STORE-DATA TO STORE-DATA-WS.
```

The action of the READ and MOVE statements is that the incoming record
is in two places: STORE-DATA and STORE-DATA-WS. The same result could have
been achieved by using READ INTO (Figure 4-1).

```
READ DATA-FILE INTO STORE-DATA-WS
     AT END MOVE 1 TO INDICATOR.
```

Why would you want to do your processing in WORKING-STORAGE rather
than the input buffer area?

1. The process lends itself to a standardized programming method in
   which all input and output records (such as the printer record) are
   simply described in terms of their total size in the FILE SECTION.
   The detailed breakdown of the records is then done in the WORKING-
   STORAGE SECTION.

2. When the AT END condition is reached, the programmer no longer
   has access to the last valid record in the FILE SECTION buffer area.

FIGURE 4-1

Schematic: READ INTO

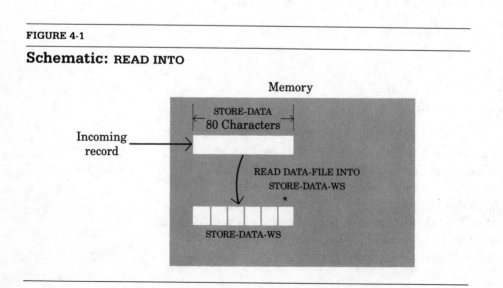

However, the last record can still be accessed in the WORKING-STOR-AGE area.

3. Depending upon the debugging aids available on your machine, it may be easier to debug from the WORKING-STORAGE SECTION rather than from the FILE SECTION.

The FROM option of the WRITE statement is the output counterpart of the READ INTO combination and can save you a few lines of code. The statement

```
WRITE PRINT-LINE FROM ENDING-LINE
     AFTER ADVANCING 2 LINES.
```

is exactly equivalent to the following statements:

```
MOVE ENDING-LINE TO PRINT-LINE.
WRITE PRINT-LINE
     AFTER ADVANCING 2 LINES.
```

And now we come to another point that should help illustrate the difference between the FILE SECTION and WORKING-STORAGE. In the previous chapter you saw that almost every report is likely to contain several different types of output lines, each of which was described in the WORKING-STORAGE SECTION. In truth, you really don't have any other method of describing these lines because of the way COBOL works. These lines must be described in WORKING-STORAGE because, with one exception, this is the *only place that the* VALUE *entry is permitted.* Typically you wish to create output lines in which some of the fields contain values such as SPACES (FILLER PIC X(10) VALUE SPACES) or specific terms (FILLER PIC X(7) VALUE 'ABC CO.'). The reason for this is entirely logical. The contents of the WORKING-STORAGE SECTION (individual fields and/or entire records) are created *during* the *compiling process.* However, file buffer areas as described in the FD are not created until the file is OPENed in the PROCEDURE DIVISION—in other words, during the execution of your program. Thus, according to what you have learned so far, there is no reason to have VALUE in the FILE SECTION. Later you will see that there is one exception to the rule—an exception that is permitted because of the unique way in which VALUE is used.

Printer control—SPECIAL-NAMES

Until now you have had only one way of controlling the action of the printer: by using BEFORE OR AFTER ADVANCING so many lines. The maximum number of lines you can advance with a single WRITE statement is 99, which certainly gives you a lot of room for choice. However, there is a way of providing even more control over the printer.

On IBM computers and many pre-1974 compilers, an additional entry in the ENVIRONMENT DIVISION called SPECIAL-NAMES allows you to assign a name to the first printing line on the top of a new page. The reserved word C01 (pronounced Cee zero one) identifies the top line and is used as shown below:

```
OBJECT-COMPUTER.
SPECIAL-NAMES.   C01 IS TOP-OF-PAGE.
        .
        .
        .

PROCEDURE DIVISION.
        .
        .
        .

     WRITE PRINT-LINE FROM HEADING-LINE
         AFTER ADVANCING TOP-OF-PAGE.
```

Of course, there is no "magic" in the name TOP-OF-PAGE, and any name that is not a reserved word can be used. This is an easy and efficient way to get your heading lines positioned at the top of a new page. With ANS 74 COBOL the process is even easier. Use of the reserved word PAGE causes the system to skip to the top of a new page; the SPECIAL-NAMES entry is not required. The statement

```
WRITE PRINT-LINE FROM HEADING-LINE
    AFTER ADVANCING PAGE.
```

achieves the same result as the previous example.

Actually, virtually all printers have a carriage control feature that can be triggered by appropriate COBOL entries. Twelve printer *channels* or controls can be accessed by the programmer. Channel 1 (C01) is always used to advance the paper to the first designated printing line on the page. Note that this printing line is not necessarily the first available line on the page. Most likely it will be the third, fourth, or fifth printing line. As you would suspect, the programmer or operator will set up the printer control prior to running the program.

In a corresponding way, Channel 12 (C12) is normally used to indicate the last desired printing line on the page since you don't want to print over the page perforations.

```
SPECIAL-NAMES.   C01 IS TOP-OF-PAGE.
                 C12 IS LAST-LINE.

PROCEDURE DIVISION.
        .
        .
        .

     WRITE PAGE-NUMBER-LINE
         AFTER ADVANCING LAST-LINE.
```

On IBM systems, the remaining channels, C02 through C11, can be used to designate intermediate stopping points on the page. Although virtually all modern computers have internal software to take care of end-of-page problems, many programmers prefer to set up a counter in WORKING-STOR-AGE and count the number of lines used down the page. Their count, of course, must include both printing lines and spacing lines. When their counter reaches the predetermined amount, they execute a WRITE _____ AFTER ADVANCING PAGE, reset the counter, and continue. The most commonly used line count on a standard 8½″ page is between 50 and 56 printing lines.

Output editing

Since COBOL is a business-oriented language, it has the capability of providing for very precisely arranged, printed output that can contain a wide range of special characters. The general term used to describe output that contains characters such as dollar signs, commas, debit and credit symbols, decimal points, and so on, is that of *editing*, or, more exactly, *output editing*. In an earlier example, data were read in and moved to the output line without any regard for editing. In actual practice, however, editing is the more common situation. In business situations we are likely to want to edit most numeric fields such as social security numbers, dates, job codes, and, of course, dollar amounts.

Fortunately, editing is very simple in COBOL. It is so simple that we don't even have an edit instruction; instead, editing takes place when an unedited field is *moved* to a receiving field that contains edit characters. The instruction that is normally used for this purpose is one you already know: MOVE. Later you will see that there are some other statements that, when executed, also result in a move operation. Suppose we have an incoming data field called

```
03   AMOUNT-IN          PIC 999V99.
```

that contains the value 31462. To edit this field into a "dollar and cents" format we would set up the following field in the output line.

```
03   EDITED-AMT         PIC $999.99.
```

The statement

```
MOVE AMOUNT-IN TO EDITED-AMT.
```

will cause editing to take place as shown below.

```
$314.62
```

The action is rather obvious as you will see from the following examples. However, there is one important point to remember when editing: The edit field must *exactly* match the *format* of the sending field. In the above example, the picture for EDITED-AMT contains two *edit characters* (a dollar sign and a decimal point) *plus* sufficient printing room (as indicated by the 9's) for the incoming five digits.

The following charts show some of the more common editing capabilities of COBOL.

Numeric data—decimal point

Source field picture	Contents	Edit field picture	Result
PIC 999V99	12345	PIC 999.99	123.45
PIC 999V99	05678	PIC 999.99	056.78

Numeric data—dollar sign and commas

PIC 999V99	12345	PIC $999.99	$123.45
PIC 9999V99	684021	PIC $9,999.99	$6,840.21
PIC 9999V99	039550	PIC $9,999.99	$0,395.50

In two of the above examples the left-most, or insignificant, zero digit was printed. This is technically correct, but usually unacceptable for reports. The z edit character allows you to suppress leading zeros as far as you want. Normal practice is to suppress up to the decimal point, but not beyond it. The small "b" (blank) in the following examples shows the suppression of leading zeros.

Source field picture	Contents	Edit field picture	Result
PIC 999V99	12345	PIC ZZZ.99	123.45
PIC 999V99	05678	PIC ZZZ.99	b56.78
PIC 9999V99	684021	PIC Z,ZZZ.99	6,840.21
PIC 9999V99	039550	PIC Z,ZZZ.99	bb395.50

Earlier you saw the use of the dollar sign ($) printed immediately to the left of the left-most digit. If the source field contains leading zeros, the output will not look very professional. A better way is to "float" the dollar sign so that it is always printed next to the first significant digit.

Source field picture	Contents	Edit field picture	Result
PIC 999V99	49763	$$$$.99	$497.63
PIC 999V99	09763	$$$$.99	b$97.63
PIC 999V99	00763	$$$$.99	bb$7.63
PIC 9999V99	157875	$$,$$$.99	$1,578.75
PIC 9999V99	057875	$$,$$$.99	b$578.75
PIC 9999V99	157875	$,$$$.99	----

An error condition will result when there is an insufficient number of dollar signs to accommodate all the digits in the output field.

The last example is incorrect because when floating a dollar sign, there must always be one dollar sign more than the number of digits to the left of the decimal point.

Although most numbers you will encounter are positive, negative numbers can arise in two ways. One, of course, is as the result of arithmetic calculations. The second source is from negative values that come in from the input file. In the case of card data, negative values are indicated by an 11-row punch over the right-most digit of the field. This is known as an "overpunch" and is generally shown by means of a short line or bar in the appropriate position.

Incoming Data Record

According to everything you have learned so far, each of the two fields would be set up as PIC 99V99. Although the PICTURE entry of 99V99 is technically correct for positive numbers, it is *not* correct for fields whose contents *could become* negative. In the example shown above, the Credit Amount field would actually contain a *positive* 27 dollars. In order for the machine to handle negative values correctly, the programmer *must* insert an S before the 9's in the PICTURE entry: PIC S99V99. So, the general rule is that for any numeric field whose contents might become negative, the programmer must insert the S. Many data processing shops avoid the worry of which fields may become negative and which won't by requiring that *all* numeric fields be set up with an S. Our incoming card fields would be set up as follows.

```
03   MONTHLY-PAYMENT        PIC S99V99.
03   CREDIT-AMT             PIC S99V99.
```

When editing numeric fields to show whether the values are positive or negative, the programmer may choose the plus sign (+) or the minus sign (−) before or after the field and the debit or credit symbols (DB or CR) after the field. (The DB and CR "symbols" are simply the two letters indicated and take up two spaces on the output line.)

Numeric data—positive or negative values

Source field picture	Contents	Edit field picture	Result
PIC S99V99	2145	PIC +99.99	+21.45
PIC S99V99	214$\bar{5}$	PIC +99.99	−21.45
PIC S99V99	4619	PIC −99.99	b46.19
PIC S99V99	461$\bar{9}$	PIC −99.99	−46.19

Note that the plus sign edit character places *either* a plus *or* minus in the result field. However, the minus sign edit character places only the minus sign for a negative field.

PIC S999V99	38124	PIC $999.99+	$381.24+
PIC S999V99	3812$\bar{4}$	PIC $999.99+	$381.24−
PIC S999V99	97350	PIC $999.99−	$973.50b
PIC S999V99	9735$\bar{0}$	PIC $999.99−	$973.50−
PIC S999V99	48812	PIC ZZZ.99CR	488.12bb
PIC S999V99	4881$\bar{2}$	PIC ZZZ.99CR	488.12CR
PIC S999V99	09688	PIC ZZZ.99DB	b96.88bb
PIC S999V99	0968$\bar{8}$	PIC ZZZ.99DB	b96.88DB

Blanks can be inserted in the output field as the next example shows. It is particularly handy to make dates, account numbers, or social security numbers look more presentable.

Source field picture	Contents	Edit field picture	Result
PIC 9(6)	121585	PIC 99B99B99	12 15 85
PIC 9(9)	123456789	PIC 999B99B9999	123 45 6789

Let's set up a problem to see how editing works. Suppose we have a card file containing information on customers who subscribe to our magazine. In our problem all we want to do is read in the data and print a listing of the subscribers, as shown in Figure 4-2. An analysis of the output format shows that management wants several of the fields to appear in edited form. The dollars-and-cents fields are to contain a dollar sign and a decimal point; the sub-elements of the date field are to be separated by spaces; and the five-digit code field is to be broken into two parts separated by a hyphen.

Pseudocode specifications for the program are shown below.

Pseudocode Specification: SUBSCRIPTION LIST PROGRAM

```
CONTROL-ROUTINE
    PERFORM 010-OPENER
    PERFORM 020-READER UNTIL indicator = 1
    PERFORM 030-CLOSER
    STOP RUN

010-OPENER
    Open files
    Write heading line
    Read a record: at end move 1 to indicator

020-READER
    Move and edit incoming fields to output area
    Write main report line
    Read a record: at end move 1 to indicator

030-CLOSER
    Move end message to output area
    Write end message
    Close files
```

Our input format is straightforward except for the five-digit code field. We have broken it into two parts (three digits and two digits—lines 370 and 380) because COBOL does not have the capability of editing for hyphens. So, we will have to do it on our own, but fortunately this is not a big problem.

FIGURE 4-2

Subscription list program: I/O formats

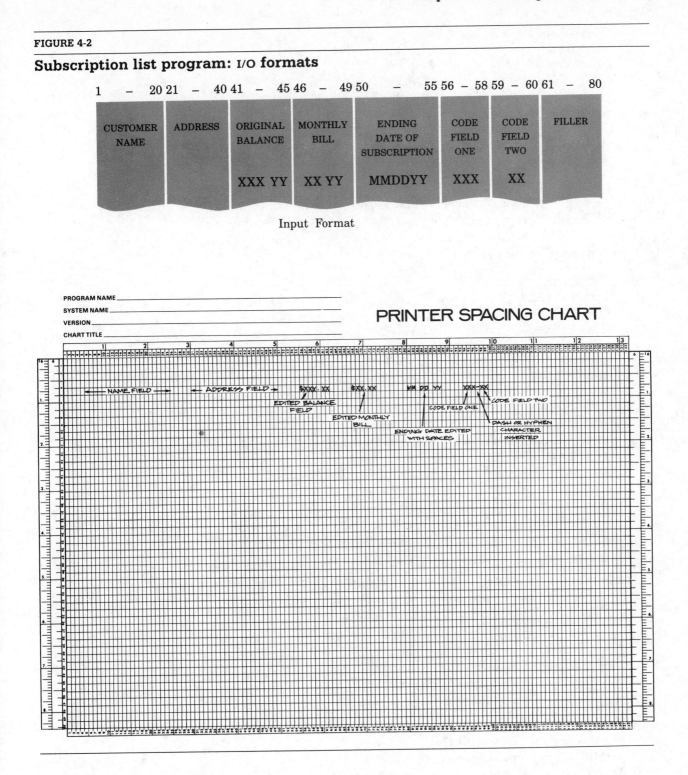

Input Format

PRINTER SPACING CHART

```
01    SUBSCRIPTION.
      03    NAME              PIC A(20).
      03    ADDRESS-IN        PIC X(20).
      03    ORIG-BALANCE      PIC 999V99.
      03    MO-BILL           PIC 99V99.
      03    ENDING-DATE       PIC 9(6).
      03    CODE-1            PIC 999.
      03    CODE-2            PIC 99.
      03    FILLER            PIC X(20).
```

The standard printer output line is as shown in previous examples, but we will need to set up a heading line and a main body line in WORKING-STORAGE. There will be quite a few entries in the heading-line in order to space the material across the page. The main-body-line record will follow the same pattern, but will contain edit fields.

```
01    MAIN-LINE.
      03    FILLER            PIC X.
      03    FILLER            PIC X(5) VALUE SPACES.
      03    NAME-OUT          PIC X(20).
      03    FILLER            PIC X(5) VALUE SPACES.
      03    ADDRESS-OUT       PIC X(20).
      03    FILLER            PIC X(5) VALUE SPACES.
      03    BALANCE-OUT       PIC $999.99.
      03    FILLER            PIC X(5) VALUE SPACES.
      03    MONTHLY-OUT       PIC $99.99.
      03    FILLER            PIC X(8) VALUE SPACES.
      03    END-DATE-OUT      PIC 99B99B99.
      03    FILLER            PIC X(5) VALUE SPACES.
      03    CODE-1-OUT        PIC 999.
      03    FILLER            PIC X VALUE '-'.
      03    CODE-2-OUT        PIC 99.
      03    FILLER            PIC X(19) VALUE SPACES.
```

Note that, in setting up the relationship between the heading-line characters and the body of the report, a printer spacing chart is an indispensable tool. Again, *editing* takes place simply *by moving* a field *into the field containing* the *edit characters*. Thus, the statement (line 930)

```
MOVE ORIG-BALANCE TO BALANCE-OUT.
```

will cause the ORIGINAL-BALANCE field to be edited into the format $xxx.xx. The 010-OPENER paragraph is shown below. Note how we can make use of the WRITE FROM and the ADVANCING PAGE formats.

```
010-OPENER.
      OPEN INPUT SUBSCRIPTION-FILE
          OUTPUT PRINTFILE.
      WRITE OUTPUT-LINE FROM HEADING-LINE
          AFTER ADVANCING PAGE.
      READ SUBSCRIPTION-FILE
          AT END MOVE 1 TO INDICATOR.
```

The heart of the move, print, read loop looks as follows:

```
020-READER.
    MOVE NAME TO NAME-OUT.
    MOVE ADDRESS-IN TO ADDRESS-OUT.
    MOVE ORIG-BALANCE TO BALANCE-OUT.
    MOVE MO-BILL TO MONTHLY-OUT.
    MOVE ENDING-DATE TO END-DATE-OUT.
    MOVE CODE-1 TO CODE-1-OUT.
    MOVE CODE-2 TO CODE-2-OUT.
    WRITE OUTPUT-LINE FROM MAIN-LINE
        AFTER ADVANCING 2 LINES.
    READ SUBSCRIPTION-FILE
        AT END MOVE 1 TO INDICATOR.
```

The CODE field presents some problems to us in that, as mentioned before, COBOL does not have the capability of inserting hyphens. Therefore, we will have to do our own editing by breaking up the field and creating a hyphen at the proper place (line 570). The MOVE statements are the same as usual.

```
    MOVE CODE-1 TO CODE-1-OUT.
    MOVE CODE-2 TO CODE-2-OUT.
```

Figure 4-3 shows the entire program, and Figure 4-4 shows the resulting output. Figure 4-5 illustrates the action as it takes place inside memory.

Calculating in COBOL

COBOL offers the programmer a set of four simple arithmetic statements (ADD, SUBTRACT, MULTIPLY, and DIVIDE) plus the composite COMPUTE statement. Before getting to these statements, however, we had better take care of a fairly persistent question that always seems to come up in beginning COBOL classes. The question that is frequently asked is, "How do I know the size of the results of arithmetic computation?" Obviously, you always know the size of incoming data fields, such as name, address, social security number, rate of pay, amount owed, and so on. Knowing that, the answer to the question asked above is really very simple. With one possible exception, you *always* know the size of the answers because the answers are generated the same way they are in regular arithmetic.

First, let's take care of the one occasion when a problem could arise. For example, if you were adding a two-digit field into a total area each time through a loop, you certainly would not make the total field only two digits long. But how long should it be? The most logical solution is that you inquire into the matter. Perhaps the operation was done manually before, and the size of the answer can be estimated very closely. Another possibility is to get a close guess as to the number of times the loop will be executed. Then, by assuming that each two-digit field will contain the maximum value of 99, you can easily determine the required size of the total field.

With the exception of the above case, you always know the size of the results. A three-digit field subtracted from a three-digit field *always* gives

FIGURE 4-3

Subscription program

```
000100 IDENTIFICATION DIVISION.
000110 PROGRAM-ID. SUBSCR.
000120*
000130 ENVIRONMENT DIVISION.
000140 CONFIGURATION SECTION.
000150 SOURCE-COMPUTER. - - -.
000160 OBJECT-COMPUTER. - - -.
000170 INPUT-OUTPUT SECTION.
000180 FILE-CONTROL.
000190     SELECT PRINTFILE ASSIGN TO - - -.
000200     SELECT SUBSCRIPTION-FILE ASSIGN TO - - -.
000210*
000220 DATA DIVISION.
000230 FILE SECTION.
000240 FD  PRINTFILE
000250     LABEL RECORD IS OMITTED
000260     DATA RECORD IS OUTPUT-LINE.
000270 01  OUTPUT-LINE                    PIC X(121).
000280 FD  SUBSCRIPTION-FILE
000290     LABEL RECORD IS OMITTED
000300     DATA RECORD IS SUBSCRIPTION.
000310 01  SUBSCRIPTION.
000320     03   NAME                      PIC A(20).
000330     03   ADDRESS-IN                PIC X(20).
000340     03   ORIG-BALANCE              PIC 999V99.
000350     03   MO-BILL                   PIC 99V99.
000360     03   ENDING-DATE               PIC 9(6).
000370     03   CODE-1                    PIC 999.
000380     03   CODE-2                    PIC 99.
000390     03   FILLER                    PIC X(20).
000400 WORKING-STORAGE SECTION.
000410 01  MISC-FIELDS.
000420     03   INDICATOR                 PIC 9 VALUE ZERO.
000430 01  MAIN-LINE.
000440     03   FILLER                    PIC X.
000450     03   FILLER                    PIC X(05) VALUE SPACES.
000460     03   NAME-OUT                  PIC X(20).
000470     03   FILLER                    PIC X(05) VALUE SPACES.
000480     03   ADDRESS-OUT               PIC X(20).
000490     03   FILLER                    PIC X(05) VALUE SPACES.
000500     03   BALANCE-OUT               PIC $999.99.
000510     03   FILLER                    PIC X(05) VALUE SPACES.
000520     03   MONTHLY-OUT               PIC $99.99.
000530     03   FILLER                    PIC X(08) VALUE SPACES.
000540     03   END-DATE-OUT              PIC 99B99B99.
000550     03   FILLER                    PIC X(05) VALUE SPACES.
000560     03   CODE-1-OUT                PIC 999.
000570     03   FILLER                    PIC X VALUE '-'.
000580     03   CODE-2-OUT                PIC 99.
```

FIGURE 4-3

continued

```
000590          03   FILLER                    PIC X(19) VALUE SPACES.
000600 01  HEADING-LINE.
000610          03   FILLER                    PIC X.
000620          03   FILLER                    PIC X(13) VALUE SPACES.
000630          03   FILLER                    PIC X(04) VALUE 'NAME'.
000640          03   FILLER                    PIC X(19) VALUE SPACES.
000650          03   FILLER                    PIC X(07) VALUE 'ADDRESS'.
000660          03   FILLER                    PIC X(12) VALUE SPACES.
000670          03   FILLER                    PIC X(07) VALUE 'BALANCE'.
000680          03   FILLER                    PIC X(05) VALUE SPACES.
000690          03   FILLER                    PIC X(07) VALUE 'MONTHLY'.
000700          03   FILLER                    PIC X(05) VALUE SPACES.
000710          03   FILLER                    PIC X(11) VALUE 'ENDING DATE'.
000720          03   FILLER                    PIC X(05) VALUE SPACES.
000730          03   FILLER                    PIC X(04) VALUE 'CODE'.
000740          03   FILLER                    PIC X(36) VALUE SPACES.
000750*
000760 PROCEDURE DIVISION.
000770 CONTROL-ROUTINE.
000780      PERFORM 010-OPENER.
000790      PERFORM 020-READER
000800          UNTIL INDICATOR = 1.
000810      PERFORM 030-CLOSER.
000820      STOP RUN.
000830 010-OPENER.
000840      OPEN INPUT SUBSCRIPTION-FILE
000850          OUTPUT PRINTFILE.
000860      WRITE OUTPUT-LINE FROM HEADING-LINE
000870          AFTER ADVANCING PAGE.
000880      READ SUBSCRIPTION-FILE
000890          AT END MOVE 1 TO INDICATOR.
000900 020-READER.
000910      MOVE NAME TO NAME-OUT.
000920      MOVE ADDRESS-IN TO ADDRESS-OUT.
000930      MOVE ORIG-BALANCE TO BALANCE-OUT.
000940      MOVE MO-BILL TO MONTHLY-OUT.
000950      MOVE ENDING-DATE TO END-DATE-OUT.
000960      MOVE CODE-1 TO CODE-1-OUT.
000970      MOVE CODE-2 TO CODE-2-OUT.
000980      WRITE OUTPUT-LINE FROM MAIN-LINE
000990          AFTER ADVANCING 2 LINES.
001000      READ SUBSCRIPTION-FILE
001010          AT END MOVE 1 TO INDICATOR.
001020 030-CLOSER.
001030      MOVE ' END OF PROGRAM' TO OUTPUT-LINE.
001040      WRITE OUTPUT-LINE
001050          AFTER ADVANCING 3 LINES.
001060      CLOSE SUBSCRIPTION-FILE PRINTFILE.
```

FIGURE 4-4

Output from subscription program

NAME	ADDRESS	BALANCE	MONTHLY	ENDING DATE	CODE
JONES, EDWIN	456 19TH ST LODI, CA	$043.76	$04.50	12 31 82	004-53
SMITH, SHIRLEY	PO BOX 48 SACTO, CA	$019.59	$05.00	06 15 82	009-00
NEWTON, JOHN	RT 15 RENO, NEV	$107.16	$24.00	08 30 84	038-62
CARDOZA, RAUL	1004 ELM ST S F, CA	$000.00	$09.50	05 30 82	014-00
FONG, ROBERT	274 FIR DR BRYTE, CA	$051.91	$08.00	02 28 83	112-53

END OF PROGRAM

FIGURE 4-5

Schematic: Subscription program action

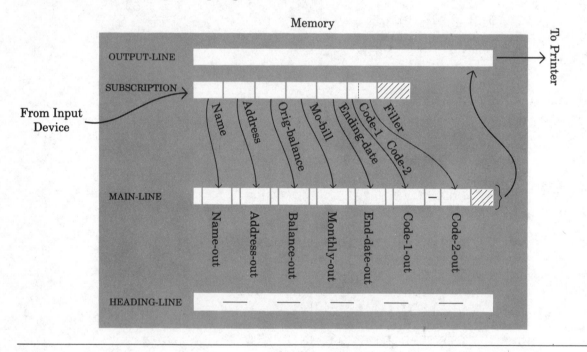

In a large computing environment, people are still the key. And they have to get together to solve problems.

a three-digit answer even though the left-most digit may be zero. In multiplication, the product is *always* equal to the sum of the lengths of the fields being multiplied, even though there may be leading zeros on the left.

Examples:

A *large* five-digit number multiplied by a *large* two-digit number.

$$
\begin{array}{rl}
987.50 & \text{PIC 999V99} \\
\underline{95} & \text{PIC 99} \\
4937\ 50 & \\
\underline{88875\ 0} & \\
93812.50 &
\end{array}
$$

A *small* value five-digit number multiplied by a *small* value two-digit number.

$$
\begin{array}{rl}
123.50 & \text{PIC 999V99} \\
\underline{15} & \text{PIC 99} \\
617\ 50 & \\
\underline{1235\ 0} & \\
01852.50 &
\end{array}
$$

Note that the product contains a nonsignificant digit (zero) on the left. Normally, when multiplying by hand we would not show this zero. However, it really is there and the computer system must account for *all* positions in the field since there is no way of knowing in advance the actual values that will be processed.

Division follows the same rules where the remainder is always the size of the divisor and the quotient is always the size of the dividend.

$$
\text{DIVISOR}\overline{)\text{DIVIDEND}}^{\displaystyle \text{QUOTIENT}}
$$

Examples:

A one-digit number divided into a three-digit number.

$$
\begin{array}{rl}
& \phantom{\text{PIC 9 }3)}085 \qquad \text{PIC 999} \\
\text{PIC 9}\ \ 3&\overline{)256} \qquad \text{PIC 999} \\
& \underline{24} \\
& 16 \\
& \underline{15} \\
& 1 \qquad\ \ \text{PIC 9}
\end{array}
$$

A two-digit number divided into a five-digit number.

$$
\begin{array}{rl}
& \phantom{\text{PIC 99 15}}007.08 \qquad \text{PIC 999V99} \\
\text{PIC 99}\ 15&\overline{)106.28} \qquad \text{PIC 999V99} \\
& \underline{105} \\
& 1\ 28 \\
& \underline{1\ 20} \\
& 08 \qquad\ \ \text{PIC 99}
\end{array}
$$

The programmer does *not* have to worry about the alignment of the data fields, since the system *automatically* aligns the fields on the decimal point during computations. In addition to the five basic arithmetic statements mentioned earlier, two options—ROUNDED and ON SIZE ERROR—may be used if needed.

The ADD statement

The first form of the ADD statement is

$$\underline{ADD} \left\{ \begin{array}{l} \text{identifier-1} \\ \text{literal-1} \end{array} \right\} \cdots \left\{ \begin{array}{l} \text{identifier-2} \\ \text{literal-2} \end{array} \right\} \cdots \underline{TO} \text{ identifier-n}$$

where the term "identifier" refers to a field that is an elementary numeric item.

```
ADD 1 TO COUNTER-B.
```

The contents of COUNTER-B are increased by one. The programmer would have set up the COUNTER-B field somewhere in the DATA DIVISION prior to the execution of this statement.

| 03 ∧ 5 | | 04 ∧ 5 |

COUNTER-B
before

COUNTER-B
after

```
ADD REG-PAY TO TOTAL-PAY.
```

The contents of REG-PAY remain unchanged in this operation.

| 098 ∧ 50 | | 0000 ∧ 00 |

REG-PAY
before

TOTAL-PAY
before

| 098 ∧ 50 | | 0098 ∧ 00 |

REG-PAY
after

TOTAL-PAY
after

Multiple fields and/or literals can be added in one ADD statement, as the next example, illustrates.

```
ADD REG-PAY OVER-TIME-PAY TO TOTAL-PAY.
```

The values contained in REG-PAY and OVER-TIME-PAY are unchanged. TOTAL-PAY is increased by the sum of the values in the first two fields. The system performs this operation by adding the values stored in REG-PAY and OVER-TIME-PAY in a special system work area. This amount is then added to TOTAL-PAY.

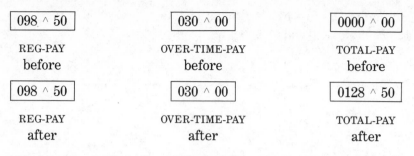

ADD 15.00, REG-PAY, OVER-TIME-PAY TO TOTAL-PAY.

This example is the same as the previous one, except that we have now included a literal value. Commas are shown in this example to illustrate that they may be used to provide better readability, but are *not* required.

A second version of the ADD statement allows the result of the computation to be transferred to another field by means of the GIVING option. In addition, either or both of the options ROUNDED or ON SIZE ERROR may be used.

$$\underline{\text{ADD}} \begin{Bmatrix} \text{identifier-1} \\ \text{literal-1} \end{Bmatrix} \cdots \begin{Bmatrix} \text{identifier-2} \\ \text{literal-2} \end{Bmatrix} \underline{\text{GIVING}} \text{ identifier-n}$$

[ROUNDED][ON SIZE ERROR imperative statement].

Note that TO and GIVING are *not* permitted in the same ADD statement. The identifier following GIVING may be a field containing numeric edit characters since GIVING is the equivalent of MOVE.

ADD FIELD-A FIELD-B GIVING GRAND-TOTAL.

The contents of FIELD-A and FIELD-B are unchanged. The contents of GRAND-TOTAL are destroyed and replaced by the sum of the values in FIELD-A and FIELD-B. As before, the summing operation is performed in the system work area.

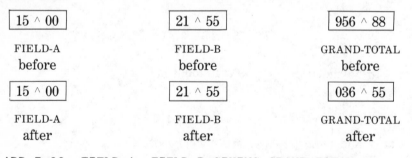

ADD 5.00, FIELD-A, FIELD-B GIVING GRAND-TOTAL.

The format is the same as the first example, except that a literal has been included along with optional commas.

ADD OLD-BAL SALES GIVING NEW-AMT ON SIZE ERROR PERFORM
   ERROR-ROUTINE.

The calculation part of the ADD statement is the same as before, but the SIZE ERROR option indicates what is to be done if a SIZE ERROR is encountered. This situation arises when the result of the addition is too large to fit into the NEW-AMT field. If the SIZE ERROR option were omitted, truncation—that is, loss of digits from the field—could result and the system would continue on to the next statement in sequence.

| 21 ∧ 25 | 40 ∧ 00 | 95 ∧ 72 |

OLD-BAL
before

SALES
before

NEW-AMT
before

and after

and after

| 61 ∧ 25 |

NEW-AMT
after

In the situation previously described there is no size error even though the total field (NEW-AMT) is really too small for the purpose. The second situation shows how a SIZE ERROR condition arises.

| 86 ∧ 00 | 40 ∧ 00 | 95 ∧ 72 |

OLD-BAL
before

SALES
before

NEW-AMT
before

and after

and after

| 26 ∧ 00 |

NEW-AMT
after

The inadequate size of the NEW-AMT field will be detected when the system recognizes that the digit carried to the left cannot fit in. The system then branches to ERROR-ROUTINE, which probably prints a message to the operator. Without SIZE ERROR the situation would go undetected and the 1 would be lost (truncated).

The ROUNDED option may be used with any of the COBOL arithmetic statements, as can SIZE ERROR. For example, in working with pay calculations, you know that the ultimate result must be a dollars-and-cents figure. Because of the intricacies of many pay-rate calculations, the intermediate steps may contain more than two digits to the right of the decimal point. When these values are finally moved (GIVING) to the final pay field, you will want to round the cents amount. If the third digit to the right of the decimal point is 5 or greater, you should round up to the next cent in the second digit position. The ROUNDED option does this by *rounding into the size of the receiving field.*

    ADD REG—PAY OT—PAY GIVING TOTAL—PAY ROUNDED.

| 098 ∧ 755 | 030 ∧ 100 | 8765 ∧ 43 |

REG-PAY
before

OT-PAY
before

TOTAL-PAY
before

and after

and after

and after

| 0128 ∧ 86 |

098.755
030.100
128.855

The answer will be rounded to 0128.86, since the third digit to the right of the decimal point is 5 or greater. Without the ROUNDED option, the answer would have been truncated to 0128.85.

```
ADD REG-PAY OT-PAY GIVING
    TOTAL-PAY ROUNDED ON SIZE ERROR PERFORM
        ERROR-ROUTINE.
```

The second example illustrates the use of both options in the same statement. In the previous example there was no size error, but suppose the TOTAL-PAY field had a picture of 99V99. The system could round as above, but the size error would occur because the left-most digit could not fit into the receiving field.

The SUBTRACT statement

The SUBTRACT statement follows the same general pattern as ADD in that you may use GIVING, ON SIZE ERROR, and ROUNDED when appropriate. The format is

$$\underline{\text{SUBTRACT}} \left\{ \begin{array}{l} \text{identifier-1} \\ \text{literal-1} \end{array} \right\} \ldots \left\{ \begin{array}{l} \text{identifier-2} \\ \text{literal-2} \end{array} \right\} \ldots \underline{\text{FROM}} \text{ identifier-n}$$

[ROUNDED][ON SIZE ERROR imperative statement].

```
SUBTRACT AMOUNT FROM TOTAL.
```

The value in AMOUNT is unchanged but the value of TOTAL is reduced by the value that was in AMOUNT.

143		568
AMOUNT		TOTAL
before		before

and after |425|

TOTAL
after

Note: In an earlier part of the book you saw that the PICTURE entry must contain an s in order for the system to store a negative result. Observe the following examples using the same SUBTRACT statement.

AMOUNT	TOTAL		Result
Value 143	original value 568	PIC 999	+425
Value 850	original value 300	PIC 999	+550
Value 850	original value 300	PIC S999	-550

```
SUBTRACT AMOUNT FROM TOTAL GIVING NEW-TOTAL.
```

In this case the original values of AMOUNT and TOTAL remain unchanged, but the result of the subtraction is moved into NEW-TOTAL. As with other examples, calculations are done in a work area on copies of the values in AMOUNT and TOTAL.

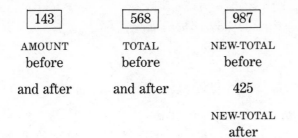

AMOUNT
before

and after

TOTAL
before

and after

NEW-TOTAL
before

425

NEW-TOTAL
after

SUBTRACT DISCOUNT FROM BILL GIVING INV—AMT ROUNDED.

The result of the subtraction is moved and rounded to the size of the receiving field (INV-AMT).

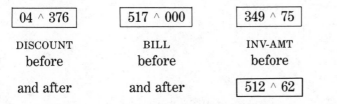

DISCOUNT
before

and after

BILL
before

and after

INV-AMT
before

512 ∧ 62

The answer was ROUNDED into INV-AMT, but was not rounded up since 4.376 from 517.000 equals 512.624. The last place was not large enough to round up to 63 cents.

The MULTIPLY statement

Unlike ADD and SUBTRACT, where you can add or subtract multiple fields with a single statement, you may only multiply two values at a time. The first format is

$$\underline{\text{MULTIPLY}} \begin{Bmatrix} \text{identifier-1} \\ \text{literal-1} \end{Bmatrix} \underline{\text{BY}}\ \text{identifier-2}$$

[ROUNDED][ON SIZE ERROR imperative statement].

MULTIPLY HOURS BY RATE.

The value in HOURS remains unchanged and the answer (product) replaces the original value stored in RATE.

MULTIPLY 10 BY BASE—RATE.

As in the first example, the answer replaces the previous value of BASE-RATE.

The following example is incorrect because a literal cannot be used in place of identifier-2.

MULTIPLY BASE—RATE BY 10.

The original version of MULTIPLY (MULTIPLY HOURS BY RATE) was correct, but it presents some problems if you recall our original rule that the size of the answer is equal to the sum of the sizes of the fields being multiplied. According to that rule, the answer could never fit identifier-2. For example, if HOURS had a PICTURE of 99 and RATE a PICTURE of 9V99, the product would be 999V99, which cannot be stored in the RATE field. One solution is to move RATE (PIC 9V99) to a larger field (RATE-RESULT PIC 999V99) so that we know there are two leading zeros on the left. Then we multiply HOURS BY RATE-RESULT and know that an answer of the correct size will be stored. A much easier solution is to use the GIVING option.

$$\text{\underline{MULTIPLY}} \begin{Bmatrix} \text{identifier-1} \\ \text{literal-1} \end{Bmatrix} \text{\underline{BY}} \begin{Bmatrix} \text{identifier-2} \\ \text{literal-2} \end{Bmatrix} \text{\underline{GIVING}} \text{ identifier-3}$$

[\underline{ROUNDED}][ON \underline{SIZE ERROR} imperative statement].

Examples:

```
MULTIPLY HOURS BY RATE GIVING GROSS.
```

The values of HOURS and RATE are unchanged as the multiplication is done in the system work area and moved into GROSS.

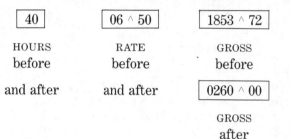

| 40 | 06 ∧ 50 | 1853 ∧ 72 |

HOURS   RATE   GROSS
before   before   before

and after   and after | 0260 ∧ 00 |

GROSS
after

```
MULTIPLY ORIG-BILL BY DISCOUNT-RATE GIVING
DISCOUNT-ROUNDED.
```

The values stored in ORIG-BILL and DISCOUNT-RATE are unchanged. The result of the calculation is moved into DISCOUNT-ROUNDED and rounding takes place if necessary.

| 245 ∧ 75 | ∧ 025 | 00 ∧ 00 |

ORIG-BILL   DISCOUNT-RATE   DISCOUNT-ROUNDED
before   before   before

and after   and after | 06 ∧ 14 |

DISCOUNT ROUNDED
after

```
MULTIPLY ORIG-BILL BY DISCOUNT-RATE GIVING
    DISCOUNT-ROUNDED ON SIZE-ERROR PERFORM CALC-ERROR.
```

The operation is the same as above except that an error routine is entered if a size error is detected. An abnormally large discount might generate an answer larger than the DISCOUNT-ROUNDED field.

The DIVIDE statement

DIVIDE follows the same general pattern as MULTIPLY in that you can only work with two values. The simple form is shown below, but the most useful version makes use of the GIVING option.

$$\text{DIVIDE} \begin{Bmatrix} \text{identifier-1} \\ \text{literal-1} \end{Bmatrix} \underline{\text{INTO}}\ \text{identifier-2}$$

[ROUNDED][ON SIZE ERROR imperative statement].

DIVIDE NBR-OF-SCORES INTO TOTAL-POINTS.

The value of NBR-OF-SCORES remains unchanged and the answer (quotient) replaces the original value of TOTAL POINTS.

DIVIDE 12 INTO YEARLY-SALES.

The action is the same as the first example except that a literal was used instead of an identifier (data field). Note that a literal cannot be used in place of the second field.

The most useful version of the DIVIDE statement allows you to use GIVING and either INTO or BY plus ROUNDED and ON SIZE ERROR.

$$\text{DIVIDE} \begin{Bmatrix} \text{identifier-1} \\ \text{literal-1} \end{Bmatrix} \begin{Bmatrix} \underline{\text{INTO}} \\ \underline{\text{BY}} \end{Bmatrix} \begin{Bmatrix} \text{identifier-2} \\ \text{literal-2} \end{Bmatrix} \underline{\text{GIVING}}\ \text{identifier-3}$$

[ROUNDED][ON SIZE ERROR imperative statement].

DIVIDE ITEMS-SOLD INTO DOLLAR-VALUE GIVING AVG-VALUE.

The values stored at ITEMS-SOLD and DOLLAR-VALUE are used as indicated in the computation, but remain unchanged. The answer replaces the value stored in AVG-VALUE.

23	963 ^ 85	587 ^ 68
ITEMS-SOLD	DOLLAR-VALUE	AVG-VALUE
before	before	before
and after	and after	041 ^ 90

DIVIDE DOLLAR-VALUE BY ITEMS-SOLD GIVING AVG-VALUE.

The BY version of this DIVIDE statement is exactly equivalent to the first example.

DIVIDE ITEMS-SOLD INTO DOLLAR-VALUE GIVING AVG-VALUE
      ROUNDED.

If the ROUNDED version is used, the answer moved into AVG-VALUE will be 041.91 because the third place after the decimal is a 6 and will round the zero-digit up to a 1. Note that although DIVIDE INTO without GIVING is permitted, the DIVIDE BY statement *must* contain the GIVING entry.

The DIVIDE statement also has a REMAINDER format that is supported on some COBOL compilers. As the name indicates, the remainder from the divide process is placed into the field designated after the word REMAINDER. It is the programmer's responsibility to make sure that all fields are of the proper size.

$$\text{DIVIDE} \begin{Bmatrix} \text{identifier-1} \\ \text{literal-1} \end{Bmatrix} \underline{\text{INTO}} \begin{Bmatrix} \text{identifier-2} \\ \text{literal-2} \end{Bmatrix} \underline{\text{GIVING}}\ \text{identifier-3 [ROUNDED]}$$

REMAINDER identifier-4 [ON SIZE ERROR imperative statement].

Examples:

```
DIVIDE NO-OF-TESTS INTO TOTAL-POINTS
    GIVING AVG-SCORE
    REMAINDER LEFT-OVER.

DIVIDE RUNNERS INTO TIME-CLOCK-VALUE
    GIVING RUN-TIME
    REMAINDER EXCESS-TIME
    ON SIZE ERROR
        PERFORM TIME-ERROR-ROUTINE.
```

If your system does not support the REMAINDER option, the following sequence may be used.

DIVIDE identifier-1 BY identifier-2

GIVING identifier-3.

COMPUTE identifier-4 = identifier-1 − (identifier-2 ∗ identifier-3)

Example:

```
DIVIDE FIELD-B BY FIELD-A GIVING FIELD-C.
COMPUTE REMAINDER-FIELD = FIELD-B - (FIELD-A * FIELD-C).
```

The COMPUTE statement

The last of the arithmetic statements is the composite statement COMPUTE, which allows you to do any of the previous arithmetic operations as specified by ADD, SUBTRACT, MULTIPLY, or DIVIDE plus exponentiation (raising to a power). The general form is

COMPUTE identifier-1 [ROUNDED]

= arithmetic expression [ON SIZE ERROR imperative statement].

The arithmetic operators used with COMPUTE are:

**	Exponentiation (raising to a power)
*	Multiplication
/	Division
+	Addition
−	Subtraction

When the arithmetic expression is calculated, the system follows a set pattern known as the "order of arithmetic operations." The order is:

1. All expressions in parentheses are evaluated first.
2. Exponentiation is performed next.
3. Multiplication and division are of the same rank and performed from left to right.
4. Addition and subtraction are of the same rank and performed from left to right.

The values stored in the fields used in the arithmetic expression are unchanged by the COMPUTE statement and the answer is *moved* to identifier-1. Each arithmetic operator must be preceded and followed by at least one space. The programmer must be aware of the order of operations in order to be certain that the desired arithmetic operation is carried out. Note the following examples.

Arithmetic operation	COBOL COMPUTE statement
TOTAL = AMT1 + AMT2	COMPUTE TOTAL = AMT1 + AMT2
$X = \dfrac{A + B}{C}$	COMPUTE X = (A + B) / C The parentheses are required in order to have the system calculate $\frac{A+B}{C}$. If the parentheses are omitted, COMPUTE X = A + B / C, the system will divide B by C and then add A to the result.
$X = \dfrac{A + B}{B - C}$	COMPUTE X = (A + B) / (B − C)
Rounding	COMPUTE X ROUNDED = (A + B) / (B − C)
Net pay rounded	COMPUTE NET-PAY ROUNDED = HOURS * RATE − DEDUCTIONS.

Assuming that we have come to this part of the program knowing that the hours-worked figure is greater than 40, we can compute NET-PAY (with time-and-a-half pay for hours in excess of 40) by the following COMPUTE statement:

```
COMPUTE NET-PAY
    = ((HOURS - 40) * (1.5 * RATE) + (40 * RATE)) - DEDUCTIONS.
```

COMMON ERRORS

Most of the statements presented in this chapter are easy to use and generally don't cause much of a problem for the programmer. However, some errors do seem to occur more often than others and are worth mentioning here.

The first error involves the use of the ADD statement and has been mentioned before. Remember that it is your responsibility to make sure that total areas are cleared to zero before attempting to do any arithmetic. The second error concerning ADD is the format of the statement itself. The rule is that you *cannot* have both TO and GIVING in the same ADD statement. The following is *incorrect*:

```
ADD A TO B GIVING C.
```

The severity of the diagnostic error message that the system gives to you depends upon the quality of the software. On some systems the level of the error is severe enough to prevent execution of your program. On other systems, the software will delete the TO, print a low-level warning message, and permit the execution of the program.

A second error that is extremely common concerns arithmetic operations on fields that contain edit characters. Common sense would tell you that such operations are not permitted. Note the following example:

```
AMOUNT                      PIC S999V99.
```

This is an arithmetic field—that is, one that can be manipulated arithmetically. The S and the V are *not* edit characters. They are there to inform the system of the nature or characteristics of the field.

```
AMOUNT-ED                   PIC    999.99.
TOTAL                       PIC  $999.99.
BALANCE-OUT                 PIC  Z,ZZZ.99.
PAY-AMT                     PIC    $$$.99.
```

All of the above are edit fields and *cannot* be worked on arithmetically. Observe that it is not a question of how many edit characters are contained in a field. If the field contains *any* edit characters, *it cannot be manipulated arithmetically.*

The programmer may MOVE into or give into (GIVING) or COMPUTE *into* the above fields, but cannot work on them with arithmetic statements. The statement

```
COMPUTE AMOUNT-ED = _____.
```

is correct as long as the fields used in the calculations (that is, to the right of the equal sign) are proper arithmetic fields. In the COMPUTE statement, the answer is calculated and then MOVEd to AMOUNT-ED.

PROGRAMMING TIPS

Generally, programmers are elated when their program runs to a natural conclusion—that is, without what is known as an "abend," which stands for "abnormal ending." But even a program that ends normally is not necessarily correct. You might very well end with beautifully printed pages of garbage. But whether your program abends or whether it outputs incorrect answers, the result is still the same in that it is your responsibility to make it work properly. How do you find your errors?

In the case of an abnormal ending, the system will print some type of error message indicating the point in your program at which the error occurred. That message, plus any printed output lines, will give you a good clue where to look. In my experience with beginning COBOL students, the single most common abend is found on an ADD statement. As mentioned in this chapter, the ADD statement itself is seldom in error. In at least 90% of the cases the error is in adding into a total area that was not initialized (cleared to zero) at the beginning of the program. Obviously, errors of this type will decrease as you become more familiar with the way COBOL works.

The second situation in which the program reaches a natural conclusion but generates incorrect answers is a little more difficult to correct. What should you look for? The best answer is to tell you to look for patterns in the output. Are the errors repeated exactly? If so, how many times before a change occurs? Are the answers off by the same amount for each record? Is the error amount cumulative from record to record?

If you cannot find an obvious pattern, look at the input data. Are your input specifications correct? Are your output specifications correct? Under what conditions does the error happen?

Suppose you try everything you can and the errors are still not apparent. Your alternatives are becoming fewer, and one of these involves desk checking the program line by line. By "desk checking" we mean that you "play" computer and try to figure out statement by statement exactly what the computer did (not what it *should have done*) in each case. Then, if that fails, seek outside help and, if no one can find the problem, you may have to reanalyze, redesign, and rewrite the program. A crucial point here: It is *your* responsibility to produce a program that will solve the problem.

To this point, there is an interesting saying that is used in programming to the effect that "there is always one more 'bug'." This is another way of saying that just because your program works "correctly," don't be surprised if it does not work correctly at a later date. A lengthy and involved program may not be able to be tested for every possible combination of events, and of course the bug will appear when that "one-in-a-million" set of circumstances arises. Thus, a "working" program is one that has only unobserved bugs. There is never time to do it right, but there is time to do it over.

Moral to the story: Do it right the first time.

An error always exists in that part of the program you are sure cannot possibly contain a mistake because it is so simple a process.

Corollary A: No one you ask will see the error.
Corollary B: Everyone who stops by with unsolicited advice will see it immediately.

It takes more time to find where to change a program than to make the change itself.

SELF-STUDY: QUESTIONS AND ANSWERS

1. With the WRITE statement must I always use either BEFORE or AFTER ADVANCING?

   Answer: No, unlike the AT END portion of the READ statement, the WRITE statement may be written without the ADVANCING portion. The format is:

       WRITE record name.

   However, there is a problem you should know about. On some systems, another rule says that "If you once use the ADVANCING option with a particular file, you must always use ADVANCING with that file." Since writing on the printer almost always involves some type of vertical spacing, the WRITE statement was shown this way.

2. Is C01 always used for the top printing line on a new page?

   Answer: No, although it is common to a great many machines, including most IBM computers. Check your computer to be sure.

3. Editing seems simple although there are a great many possibilities from which to choose. Does all editing take place when you move a numeric field to an edit field?

Answer: As far as the programmer is concerned, editing is very simple although the system is doing an enormous amount of work you don't see. Editing is accomplished by means of the MOVE statement or by the GIVING option with arithmetic statements. Certain specific computers may not accept all the possible combinations of editing that were shown, but usually it is easy to work around these problems. The most common editing features such as zero suppression, dollar signs, decimal points, and commas are well standardized.

4. Does it make any difference if I use multiple arithmetic statements such as ADD, SUBTRACT, and so on to solve a formula? Or should I use COMPUTE instead?

   Answer: Technically it makes no difference at all. The main thing is to solve the problem in the correct manner. There is some feeling that the use of COMPUTE in arithmetic operations is more "natural" than are the specific operations of ADD, SUBTRACT, MULTIPLY, and DIVIDE.

CHAPTER TERMS

abend	line counter
ADD	MULTIPLY
buffer (input buffer) area	ON SIZE ERROR
channels (printer control)	PAGE
COMPUTE	READ INTO
C01	ROUNDED
C12	SPECIAL-NAMES
DIVIDE	SUBTRACT
edit characters	truncation
editing (output editing)	WRITE FROM
exponentiation	zero suppression
floating dollar sign	

EXERCISES

1. Name one of the three reasons you might want to use READ INTO rather than just READ by itself.

2. TOP-OF-PAGE is/is not a reserved word.

3. In 74 ANS COBOL, PAGE is/is not a reserved word.

4. If a field had a value of 1234.569 and was moved to an edit field defined as $999,999.99, what would the output look like?

5. If a field has a value of $-123{^\wedge}45$ and is moved to an edit field defined as 999.99, what is the value after it is moved?

6. Use an ADD statement to add FIELD-A and FIELD-B to TOTAL.

7. Use an ADD statement to add FIELD-A and FIELD-B, the result to be placed into TOTAL.

8. What is wrong with this statement?

```
ADD SCORE-A SCORE-B TO TOTAL GIVING GRAND-TOTAL.
```

9. To check for a result that is too large for a result field, what change would you make to the following statement?

   ```
   ADD FIELD-A TO TOTAL.
   ```

10. What is wrong with this statement?

    ```
    SUBTRACT FROM FIELD-A GIVING NET-AMOUNT.
    ```

11. Evaluate the following expressions where A = 5, B = 10, C = 15.
    a. COMPUTE J = (A * B) + (B * C) / 10 * A   J =
    b. COMPUTE K = A * B + C * 8 − B * 4   K =
    c. COMPUTE L = A * (B + C) * (8 − B) * 4   L =

12. Given:

    ```
    01   FIELDS.
         03   FIELD-A        PIC 99V99.
         03   FIELD-B        PIC 999.99.
    ```

    What is wrong with the statement ADD FIELD-A TO FIELD-B?

13. Diagram the action of the WRITE FROM statement. Contrast this with a diagram of the READ INTO statement.

14. Although there is one exception we have not covered yet, the general rule is that the VALUE clause cannot be used in the FILE SECTION. Why is this? What is the logic behind this rule?

15. The text showed several examples in which a HEADING-LINE was set up in the WORKING-STORAGE SECTION (Figure 4-3). Each of the individual fields that made up the record called HEADING-LINE were FILLERS. Why weren't these fields given names? Explain.

16. In Figure 4-3 there is an incoming SUBSCRIPTION record containing the six-digit field ENDING-DATE. Make the necessary changes in the DATA DIVISION so that the field is subdivided into month, day, and year during input. Also change the necessary MAIN-LINE fields so that the ENDING-DATE is printed with a space between each of the subfields *without* using the blank (b) edit character.

17. In the WORKING-STORAGE SECTION of the Subscription Program (Figure 4-3), the INDICATOR field was established with an initial value of zero by means of the VALUE entry. What would have happened if the VALUE part of the entry had been omitted? What would have happened if the entry had been written as PIC 9 VALUE 5?

18. Every time we have used an indicator with PERFORM UNTIL, it has been set up as a numeric field. Could we have used an A or an X field instead? AT END could we have moved something other than a numeric character?

19. Write the WORKING-STORAGE entries for the following output (printer) records. Provide one extra position for carriage control.
    a. 120-character line containing the heading INCOME STATEMENT centered on the page.
    b. 132-character line containing the heading FOR THE YEAR 1984 indented 30 spaces from the left margin.
    c. Same as above, but indented 30 spaces from the right margin.

20. Write the WORKING-STORAGE entries for the following edited fields.
    a. Source field PIC 999V99: Output field to suppress leading zeros up to the decimal point and to include the decimal point.
    b. Same as above, but to have a floating dollar sign up to the decimal point.

   c. Source field PIC 9999V99: Output field to contain a decimal and a comma and to suppress leading zeros up to the decimal point.

   d. Same as above, but float the dollar sign up to the decimal point.

   e. Source field PIC S999V99: Output field to suppress leading zeros up to the decimal point and to include the decimal point and the CR symbol in case the field is negative.

   f. Same as above, except to provide for the printing of a trailing + or − sign in case the field is negative.

   g. Source field PIC S99999V99: Output field is to contain a fixed dollar sign, a comma, and a decimal point, no zero suppression, and is to provide for the printing of a DB symbol in case the field is negative.

   h. Source field PIC 9(9), which contains a social security number: Output is to break the number into its component parts (three digits, two digits, and four digits) by inserting a blank in the appropriate location.

21. Write complete output lines according to the following formats. You may assume that the printer line is 120 characters plus one position for carriage control. Space the fields appropriately across the page.

   a.

TOTALS	EDIT-1	EDIT-2
	$XXX.XX	$X,XXX.XX

     (fixed dollar sign; no zero suppression)

   b. Same as above with floating $.

   c. | XXX RECORDS WERE PROCESSED |

     (provide for zero suppression up to but not including the last digit)

   d. | GROSS PAY IS $XXXX.XX. NET PAY IS $XXX.XX |

     (provide for a floating dollar sign up to the decimal point)

   e. | SUBSCRIPTION EXPIRES ON XX XX XX. RENEW NOW. |

     (provide for blanks in the date field)

22. Indicate whether the following examples are correct or incorrect. If the statement is incorrect, make the necessary changes.

   a. ADD 1 TO TOTAL.

   b. ADD TOTAL TO 16.

   c. ADD 1 TO COUNT GIVING COUNT-A.

   d. ADD TAX-1 TAX-2 TAX-3 TAX-4 TO TOTAL-TAX.

   e. ADD TAX-1 TAX-2 TAX-3 GIVING TOTAL-TAX.

   f. ADD SALES-AMT AND TAX-AMOUNT GIVING TOTAL-AMT.

   g. ADD BAL-DUE, OLD-BAL GIVING NEW-BAL ROUNDED.

   h. ADD BAL-DUE ROUNDED TO OLD-BAL ROUNDED.

   i. ADD DISCOUNT TO OLD-DISC ROUNDED. ON SIZE ERROR PERFORM ERROR-MODULE.

   j. ADD $5.00 TO TOTAL.

   k. ADD 1 FIELD-A 17 TO NEW-RATE.

23. Indicate whether the following examples are correct or incorrect. If the statement is incorrect, make the necessary changes.

   a. SUBTRACT DISCOUNT FROM GROSS-SALES.

   b. SUBTRACT 1 FROM COUNT.

   c. SUBTRACT COUNT FROM 1.

   d. SUBTRACT 1 FROM COUNT GIVING TOTAL-COUNT.

   e. SUBTRACT FIELD-A FIELD-B GIVING ANSWER.

   f. SUBTRACT TAX-AMT FROM GROSS-PAY GIVING NEW-PAY ROUNDED.

g. SUBTRACT TAX-AMT ROUNDED FROM GROSS-PAY.

h. SUBTRACT FIRST-ANS FROM 15.75 GIVING BALANCE-DUE ROUNDED. ON SIZE ERROR PERFORM SIZE-ERROR-ROUTINE.

i. SUBTRACT LINES FROM TOTAL-LINES.

j. SUBTRACT ROUNDED DISCOUNT FROM BOOK-RATE.

24. Indicate whether the following examples are correct or incorrect. If the statement is incorrect, make the necessary changes.

   a. MULTIPLY .05 BY BASE-RATE.

   b. MULTIPLY BASE-RATE BY .05.

   c. MULTIPLY INTERMEDIATE-AMT BY CHANGE-RATE GIVING NEW-AMT.

   d. MULTIPLY FIELD-A, FIELD-B BY NEW GIVING TOTAL-NEW.

   e. MULTIPLY GRADE BY POINTS GIVING GRADE-POINTS ON SIZE ERROR WRITE OUTPUT-LINE FROM ERROR-1.

   f. DIVIDE UNITS INTO POINTS GIVING GPA.

   g. DIVIDE POINTS BY UNITS GIVING GPA.

   h. DIVIDE 12 INTO YRLY-TOTAL ROUNDED GIVING MO-TOTAL ROUNDED.

   i. DIVIDE YEARLY-TOTAL BY 12 GIVING MO-TOTAL ROUNDED.

   j. DIVIDE 150 BY 13 GIVING ANS ROUNDED.

25. Write the COMPUTE statement that would be used to solve the following equations. (*Note:* Some versions of COBOL do not permit raising to a power.)

   a. $X = \dfrac{A+B}{C}$

   b. $X = \dfrac{A}{C} + B$

   c. $X = A^2 + B^3$

   d. $X = 6AB + 4RQG$

   e. $X = \dfrac{6AB}{4QG}$

   f. Same as above, but round the answer.

   g. $X = \dfrac{A + A^2 + (A^3 - 15)}{T}$

   h. Same as Exercise 25a, but round the answer and perform an error message routine in case of a size error.

   i. Add 1 to the counter R.

26. Indicate the size of the following result or answer fields.

   a. PIC 99V99 multiplied by 99V99 gives a product size of _____ .

   b. PIC 999V99 multiplied by V999 gives a product size of _____ .

   c. PIC 999V99 divided by 999 gives a quotient of _____ and a remainder of _____ digits.

   d. PIC V9999 divided by 9V9 gives a quotient of _____ and a remainder of _____ digits.

27. Data file A in the appendix section of the text contains data that can be used for a variety of programs. Assume the data are records that have the following format.

Columns	Field description
1–9	Social security number
10–29	Employee name
30–34	Filler
35–36	Number of dependents
37–40	Insurance deduction amount in the format XX.XX
41–45	Credit union deduction in the format XXX.XX
46–50	Other deductions in the format XXX.XX
51–80	Filler

Write a program to produce the output according to the following requirements.

a. Advance the printer to the top of a new page before printing any output.

b. The output is to be spaced appropriately across the page.

c. The social security number field is to be output with the format XXX-XX-XXXX.

d. Provide for zero suppression completely through the dependents field.

e. The insurance and credit union amount fields are to be edited with a floating dollar sign and the decimal point.

f. The other deductions amount field is to be edited with a fixed dollar sign and zero suppression to the left of the decimal point.

EMPLOYEE LIST

NAME	SS–NUMBER	DEPENDENTS	INSURANCE	CREDIT UNION	OTHER DEDUCTIONS
____	XXX–XX–XXXX	XX	$XX.XX	$XXX.XX	$XXX.XX

28. This problem uses Data File A (see the appendix) to produce a payroll report.

Columns	Field description
1–9	Social security number
10–29	Name
30	Filler
31–34	Rate of pay in the format XX.XX
35–36	Filler
37–40	Insurance deduction amount in the format XX.XX
41–45	Credit union deduction amount in the format XXX.XX
46–50	Other deductions in the format XXX.XX
51–52	Hours worked
53–80	Filler

Specific output requirements are listed below and shown in the attached diagram.

a. Calculate Gross Pay by multiplying the hours field (columns 51 and 52) by rate of pay (columns 31–34 with a format of XXX.XX).

b. Provide for a floating dollar sign and decimal point for all dollar and cents fields.

c. Keep a running total of the Gross Pay, Total Deductions, and Net Pay fields so that totals can be printed at the end of the program.

d. Begin the output at the top of a new page and space it appropriately across the printer line.

PAYROLL REPORT

NAME	SS-NUMBER	GROSS PAY	TOTAL DEDUCTIONS	NET PAY
_____	XXX-XX-XXXX	XXXX.XX	XXX.XX	XXXX.XX
TOTALS		_____	_____	_____

Chapter 5
Conditional Operations in COBOL

LEARNING OBJECTIVES

1. To learn the format and use of the IF statement so that relational, sign, and class tests may be performed.

2. To see how multiple tests may be nested together and how COBOL handles tests involving AND, OR, and NOT.

3. To understand how the GO TO statement may be used in structured programming as part of a package of statements that includes PERFORM THRU and EXIT.

Like all programming languages, COBOL has the ability to compare or test values, and to take different paths through a program, depending upon the result of that test. Earlier in the text you were introduced to a general selection, or IFTHENELSE structure, which was diagrammed as follows:

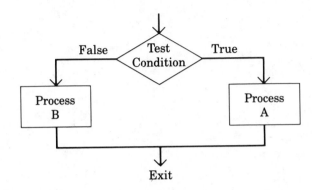

Perhaps the most important point of this diagram is that every selection structure has only one entry point and one exit point. As you will see in a moment, the test may be very simple or very complex, but the one-entry, one-exit point is always maintained.

The IF statement

The complete format of the IF statement is

$$\text{IF test-condition} \begin{Bmatrix} \text{statement-1} \\ \underline{\text{NEXT SENTENCE}} \end{Bmatrix} \begin{Bmatrix} \underline{\text{ELSE}} \text{ statement-2} \ldots \\ \underline{\text{ELSE NEXT SENTENCE}} \end{Bmatrix}$$

The IF statement can be used for three general types of tests: relational tests to determine the equality or inequality of two fields; a sign test to see whether a field is positive, negative, or zero; and a class test to determine whether a field is alphabetic or numeric.

Relational tests

A relational test is perhaps the most common form of testing in COBOL and involves the use of three basic conditions and their negation through the use of NOT.

COBOL wording	Relational operators
IS EQUAL TO	=
IS NOT EQUAL TO	NOT =
IS GREATER THAN	>
IS NOT GREATER THAN	NOT >
IS LESS THAN	<
IS NOT LESS THAN	NOT <

It is good programming practice to use the English wording for at least the greater than and less than conditions, for at least two reasons. (1) The English version is easier to understand. (At 3 o'clock in the morning, after having looked at the program for ten hours, the > and < symbols don't make much sense.) (2) Some printers don't have the > and < symbols.

The simplest version involves an abbreviated form of the IF statement that handles true tests only.

Example:

```
IF AMT-1 IS GREATER THAN MAX-AMT
    PERFORM 090-ERROR-ROUTINE.
MOVE ------.
```

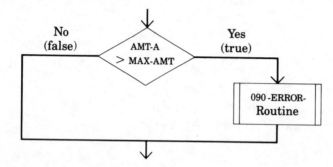

Note that the MOVE statement, which is our exit point from the structure, will *always* be executed:

```
IF   AMT-A IS EQUAL TO AMT-B
     ADD -----
     MOVE -----
     WRITE -----.
MOVE ZEROS TO COUNTER-A.
```

The second example illustrates two important points. First, multiple statements can be executed on the condition indicated. Second, each true condition statement was indented for ease of reading and the final MOVE ZEROS statement was brought back to the level of the IF. These actions make the program more readable and, therefore, lessen the chance of error.

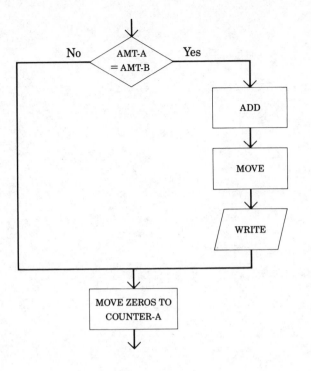

All relational tests result in a simple true or false condition, but it is important that you understand how the system derives its result. Numeric fields are compared on their algebraic values. For efficiency's sake, the length of the two fields should be the same, but a comparison of

2914 with 0001637

will correctly show that 2914 is larger. All numeric comparisons must, of course, take into account the location of the assumed decimal point.

Alphanumeric fields (X or A) are compared on the basis of the *collating sequence* of the permissible characters used on a particular machine. *Every* valid machine character has its place in the collating sequence so that it is permissible to compare any character against any other. The following statement is a valid comparison whose result will depend upon the machine used:

```
IF  FIELD-A IS GREATER THAN FIELD-B
    MOVE -----
    WRITE -----.
```

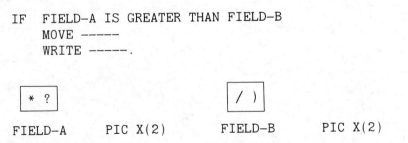

FIELD-A   PIC X(2)   FIELD-B   PIC X(2)

The most common form of the IF statement involves the use of the word ELSE to designate two sets of actions to be taken as a result of the test:

```
IF COUNTER IS LESS THAN 10
     MOVE FIELD-A TO FIELD-A-ED
     MOVE FIELD-B TO FIELD-B-ED
ELSE
     SUBTRACT AMOUNT FROM TEMP-TOTAL.
ADD 1 TO ITEM-COUNTER.
```

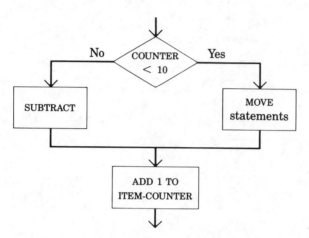

The MOVE statements are executed on the true condition of the test and the SUBTRACT statement is executed on the false condition. As before, the ADD statement is executed on *both* the true and false condition.

The term NEXT SENTENCE may be used when there are no actions to be taken for either the true or the false condition:

```
IF CLASS-CODE IS EQUAL TO 'SENIOR'
     NEXT SENTENCE
ELSE
     ADD 1 TO NOT-SENIOR-TOTAL.
MOVE -----.
```

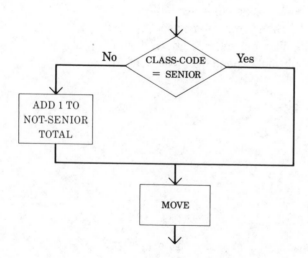

Obviously, more efficient coding would be to negate the test and return to the simple form of IF:

```
IF CLASS-CODE IS NOT EQUAL TO 'SENIOR'
    ADD 1 TO NOT-SENIOR-TOTAL.
```

In this context NEXT SENTENCE may seem useless, but later in the chapter you will see that it can become a very necessary entry.

Sign test

The sign test is a simple form of the IF statement that allows the programmer to determine whether a field is positive, negative, or zero.

$$\underline{IF} \begin{Bmatrix} \text{identifier} \\ \text{arithmetic expression} \end{Bmatrix} IS\ [\underline{NOT}] \begin{Bmatrix} \underline{POSITIVE} \\ \underline{NEGATIVE} \\ \underline{ZERO} \end{Bmatrix}$$

Examples:

```
IF BALANCE IS POSITIVE ------.
IF TOTAL IS NOT ZERO ------.
IF NBR-OF-ITEMS IS ZERO ------.
IF A + B - C IS NEGATIVE ------.
```

One common use of the sign test involves the testing of a divisor field just before a DIVIDE statement. In a particular situation it may be permissible for the divisor to be either positive or negative, but, of course, division by zero is not a permissible arithmetic operation.

Class test

The third general type of test that may be performed with the IF statement is the class test to see whether a field contains all numeric or all alphabetic characters.

$$\underline{IF}\ \text{identifier is}\ [\underline{NOT}] \begin{Bmatrix} \underline{ALPHABETIC} \\ \underline{NUMERIC} \end{Bmatrix}$$

Although the test appears simple, certain rules must be followed in order to get the correct results. A valid numeric field may contain only the digits 0 and 1 through 9 plus the appropriate internal coding to represent positive and negative values. A valid alphabetic field may contain only the alphabetic characters A through Z plus the space character.

Field type	IF NUMERIC test	IF ALPHABETIC test
PIC 9	Valid	Invalid
PIC A	Invalid	Valid
PIC X	Valid	Valid

Examples:

Field contents	PICTURE	Test	Result	Note
86<u>3</u>	S999	IF NUMERIC	True	
863	S999	IF NUMERIC	True	Bar indicates a negative field.
b97	S999	IF NUMERIC	False	Blank is not numeric.
b97	S999	IF NOT NUMERIC	True	
ABC	AAA	IF ALPHABETIC	True	
bBC	AAA	IF ALPHABETIC	True	
4BC	AAA	IF ALPHABETIC	False	Four is numeric.
,BC	AAA	IF NOT ALPHABETIC	True	Comma is not alphabetic.
XYZ	999	IF ALPHABETIC	Invalid	Invalid PICTURE entry.
123	XXX	IF NUMERIC	True	
123	XXX	IF ALPHABETIC	False	
bbb	XXX	IF ALPHABETIC	True	Blank is alphabetic.

The IF NUMERIC test cannot be applied to a *group* item containing numeric fields described with an S (for example, PIC S999). In order for the NUMERIC test to be considered true, the field contents must be numeric and a valid operational sign must be present. If the field description does *not* contain an S (for example, PIC 999), then the NUMERIC test is true when the field is numeric and an operational sign is *not* present.

The most common use of the class test is to validate input data. Many shops routinely run the records entered by data-entry operators through a validation program prior to performing any further processing of the data.

Nested IF's

The general format of IF statements allows them to be contained within other IF's. This characteristic is called *nesting* of IF statements and requires some extra attention by the programmer. Suppose we wish to process an employee record only if two conditions are met: the employee must have over 10 years with the company and be over 35 years old. One way of handling this is by means of the nested IF statement (another method will be presented later in the chapter):

```
IF EMPLOYEE-YRS IS GREATER THAN 10
    IF EMPLOYEE-AGE IS GREATER THAN 35
```

processing statements.

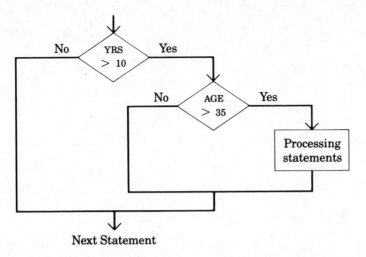

Next Statement

In the example, two conditions had to be true in order for processing to take place. Now, we will expand the problem by requiring that those over 35 will require one form of processing while those who are not over 35 will require a different set of processing steps:

```
IF EMPLOYEE-YRS IS GREATER THAN 10
    IF EMPLOYEE-AGE IS GREATER THAN 35
                --------⎫
                --------⎬    processing statements A

    ELSE
                --------⎫
                --------⎬    processing statements B
                --------.⎭
```

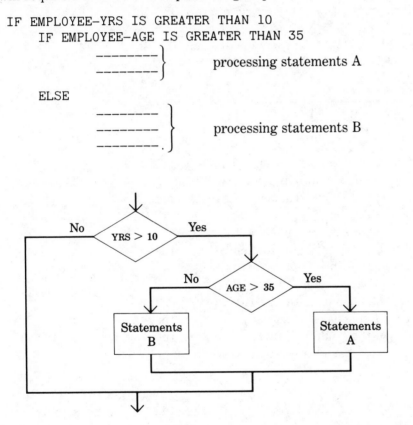

Several points are worth noting. First, we have a simple IF with an IF-ELSE nested within it. Second, a standard programming convention is to match IF's and ELSE's and to indent processing statements within the IF-ELSE. Let's add another facet to the problem. When an employee does not qualify, an appropriate message is to be written on the printer:

```
IF EMPLOYEE-YRS IS GREATER THAN 10
    IF EMPLOYEE-AGE IS GREATER THAN 35
                --------
                --------  }  processing statements A
                --------
    ELSE
                --------
                --------  }  processing statements B
                --------
    ELSE
        MOVE message to printer line
        WRITE message.
```

Theoretically, nesting of IF statements can continue indefinitely, but many shops have a rule that nesting be a maximum of three deep. Obviously, this rule aids in program maintenance and requires that your logic be thought out carefully before doing the coding.

During the nesting of IF-ELSE statements you may find the NEXT SEN-TENCE clause (discussed earlier) to be of great help. Remember that the function of NEXT SENTENCE is to transfer control out of that part of the IF to the next COBOL entry. Note the following example where, in a nested IF, no action is required on the true side of one of the imbedded IF's. The programmer is obligated to have a statement here in order to maintain the format of the IF. If we did not have the "dummy" NEXT SENTENCE, the programmer would have to insert some harmless statement on the true side of the test:

```
IF A = B
    MOVE ------
    IF C > D
        NEXT SENTENCE
    ELSE
        MOVE -------
        ADD -------
    ELSE
        MOVE -------
        WRITE -------.
```

Compound conditions—AND, OR, NOT

In our first example of a nested IF, an action was to take place if multiple conditions were met: An employee needed over 10 years of experience in the company and had to be older than 35. We coded it as follows:

```
IF EMPLOYEE-YRS IS GREATER THAN 10
    IF EMPLOYEE-AGE IS GREATER THAN 35
        ------
        ------
        ------.
```

Compound tests are permitted within a single IF by using AND or OR in the test. If AND is used, *both* tests must be true for the action to take place. With OR, if either or both conditions are met, the test is considered true. The test condition shown above can be recorded as follows:

```
IF EMPLOYEE-YRS IS GREATER THAN 10
    AND EMPLOYEE-AGE IS GREATER THAN 35
        ------
        ------
        ------.
IF TEST-GRADE-AVG IS GREATER THAN 92
    OR TERM-PAPER-GRADE IS EQUAL TO 'A'
        MOVE 'A' TO TERM-GRADE.
```

There are no limits to the number of ANDs and ORs that can be used in a test nor are there any limits on the mixing of different kinds of tests (relational; class; or sign). In general, however, the beginning programmer should avoid compound or tricky testing in favor of multiple simple tests:

```
IF HOURS-WORKED IS NUMERIC              (class test)
    AND HOURS-WORKED IS POSITIVE        (sign test)
    AND HOURS-WORKED IS GREATER THAN 40 (relational test)
        PERFORM 060-OVERTIME-ROUTINE.
```

In Warnier/Orr charts the AND condition is shown by the + symbol. The plus symbol by itself—that is, not circled—can be used for several purposes, but in its simplest use means "and," or a concurrent condition. For example, we may want to perform a paragraph only if two conditions are true at the same time. A situation of this type might be worded as follows: "If the employee is a day-shift worker AND has worked more than 5 years for the company, perform pay raise routine." Figure 5-1 shows both flowchart and Warnier/Orr formats for this condition:

```
IF WORK-CODE IS EQUAL TO 1 AND
    YEARS-WORKED IS GREATER THAN 5
        PERFORM PAY-RAISE-PROCESSING.
```

FIGURE 5-1

AND **logical testing**

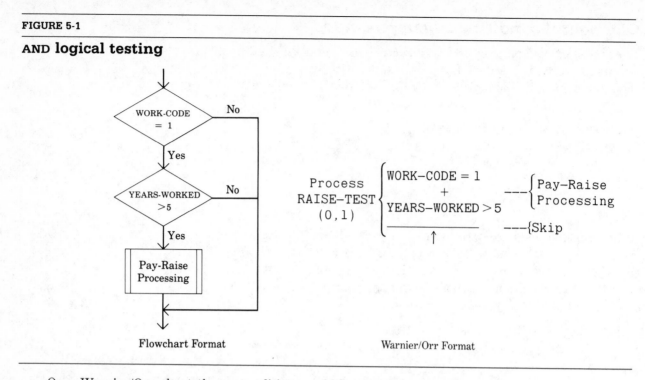

Flowchart Format   Warnier/Orr Format

On a Warnier/Orr chart the OR condition would be shown by a circle around the plus sign. The flowchart format shows that PAY-RAISE-PROCESS-ING is activated when *either* condition has been met (Figure 5-2).

The word NOT can be used to negate both simple and compound tests. Its use provides the programmer with a greater degree of flexibility in setting up logical tests. However, the programmer should be careful when NOT is used in compound conditions. Note the following table.

Condition X	Condition Y	X AND Y	X OR Y	NOT X
True	True	True	True	False
True	False	False	True	False
False	True	False	True	True
False	False	False	False	True

Examples:

```
IF EMPLOYEE-YRS IS NOT GREATER THAN 10
    OR EMPLOYEE-AGE IS NOT GREATER THAN 35.
IF TEST-GRADE-AVG IS NOT GREATER THAN 60
    AND TERM-PAPER-GRADE IS EQUAL TO 'F'
        MOVE 'F' TO TERM-GRADE.
```

When compound conditions are evaluated, the computer follows a pre-set *hierarchy of operations* as follows:

1. Arithmetic expressions within IF statements are evaluated first according to the hierarchy rules of the COMPUTE statement.

FIGURE 5-2

OR **logical testing**

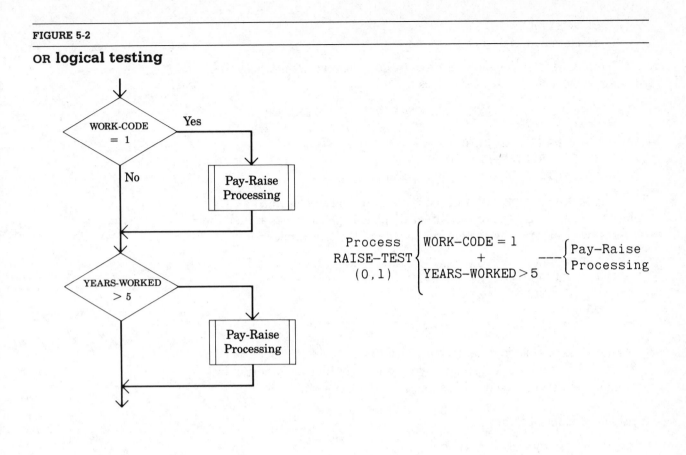

$$\text{Process} \atop \text{RAISE-TEST} \atop (0,1) \left\{ \begin{array}{c} \text{WORK-CODE} = 1 \\ + \\ \text{YEARS-WORKED} > 5 \end{array} \right. \text{---} \left\{ \begin{array}{c} \text{Pay-Raise} \\ \text{Processing} \end{array} \right.$$

Example:

```
IF A+B-C IS GREATER THAN AMT-B
   ------
   ------.
```

2. Relation conditions such as GREATER THAN, LESS THAN, and EQUAL TO are evaluated.
3. NOT conditions are evaluated.
4. AND conditions are evaluated.
5. OR conditions are evaluated.

Occasionally, these rules may cause the programmer some difficulty in setting up the IF statement to do exactly what he or she wants. A way out of the dilemma is to use parentheses in the formation of the IF statement. When parentheses are used, the system will evaluate the operations within the parentheses *first* (according to the above rules) before proceeding. If multiple sets of parentheses are used, the contents of the innermost pair are evaluated first.

For example, suppose we wish to produce a printed listing of those students who are classified as seniors and who have met at least one of the following tests:

1. are living on campus
2. are receiving student loans

3. are veterans
4. are classified as disabled

The following statement will produce an incorrect listing, because in the hierarchy, AND is evaluated before OR:

```
IF STUDENT-CODE = 'SR' AND ON-CAMPUS = 'YES' OR
    LOAN = 'YES' OR VET = 'YES' OR DISABLED = 'YES'
    MOVE NAME-FIELD TO ------
    WRITE PRINTER-RECORD
        AFTER ADVANCING 2 LINES.
```

Thus the STUDENT-CODE test and the CAMPUS test are performed as a set before the remaining OR's are evaluated. By placing parentheses around the OR tests, we can force the computer to evaluate the test properly.

```
IF STUDENT-CODE = 'SR' AND
    (ON-CAMPUS = 'YES' OR VET = 'YES'
    OR DISABLED = 'YES')
    MOVE ------
    WRITE ------.
```

Some versions of COBOL permit the use of *implied subjects* and/or *implied operators*. For the sake of portability of your program, it is better programming practice to use explicit subjects and operators.

Example: Explicit Subject

```
IF TEMP IS GREATER THAN 75 AND
    TEMP IS LESS THAN 90

    ------.
```

Example: Implied Subject

```
IF TEMP IS GREATER THAN 75 AND
    LESS THAN 90

    ------.
```

Example: Explicit Operator

```
IF A IS LESS THAN B
    AND A IS LESS THAN D

    ------.
```

Example: Implied Operator

```
IF A IS LESS THAN B AND D

    ------.
```

So far the emphasis has been on the valid uses of the IF statement. On occasion, a beginning programmer will inadvertently use an illegal combination that may or may not be detected during the compiling process. Let's take a look at two of these processes. The first involves a situation in which the programmer wishes to take certain actions on one side of the test (such as ADD and SUBTRACT), then use an IF statement, *and then continue on with the original set of instructions:*

```
IF A = B
    ADD -------
    SUBTRACT -------
    IF Q < R
        MOVE -------
        MOVE -------
    ADD -------
    MOVE -------
ELSE
    -------
    -------.
```

What the programmer intended is not what the computer will do. The ADD and the MOVE statements become part of the set of instructions to be activated on the true condition of Q < R. The way around the dilemma is to (a) restructure the program logic or (b) PERFORM the action of the IF condition:

```
IF A = B
    ADD -------
    SUB -------
    PERFORM 100-TESTER
    ADD -------
    MOVE -------
ELSE
    -------
    -------.
    .
    .
    .
100-TESTER.
    IF Q < R
        MOVE -------
        MOVE -------.
```

The same process should be used when you find it necessary to use a READ statement within an IF. Since READ is a conditional statement (AT END -------), it must be handled in the same way.

Condition names—Level 88 entries

The condition name test is really a variation of the relational test described earlier. Suppose we have a payroll operation in which workers paid hourly get an extra amount of pay for working the less desirable shifts, such as the swing shift or graveyard shift. We will read in the employee data record and immediately test a CODE-FIELD to see which shift the employee works (assume that Day Shift = 1, Swing Shift = 2, and Grave Shift is coded as a 3). Depending upon the value in the CODE-FIELD, we will want to branch to various places in the program. The COBOL coding required is shown in skeletal form:

```
FILE SECTION.
FD EMPLOYEE-FILE.
     ------
     ------
     ------
01 EMPLOYEE-PAY-RECORD.
     ------
     ------
     ------
     03  CODE-FIELD      PIC 9.
       .
       .
       .
PROCEDURE DIVISION
     IF CODE-FIELD IS EQUAL TO 1
         PERFORM DAY-SHIFT-ROUTINE.
     IF CODE-FIELD IS EQUAL TO 2
         PERFORM SWING-SHIFT-ROUTINE.
     IF CODE-FIELD IS EQUAL TO 3
         PERFORM GRAVE-SHIFT-ROUTINE.
       .
       .
       .
```

As you can see, the coding was very straightforward and should not cause any problem. However, we can modify it to use a *condition name test* instead. So far the rule has been that the VALUE entry is *not* permitted in the FILE SECTION. This rule is entirely logical since, in the FILE SECTION, you are only setting aside memory areas for the incoming or outgoing records. The WORKING-STORAGE SECTION, however, is an entirely different matter, since it is here that you want to create fields and records that contain specific values.

Condition names, or level 88's, as they are also called, are an exception to this rule. The VALUE clause *is* permitted with level 88's in both the FILE SECTION and the WORKING-STORAGE SECTION. In the revised example shown below, the level 88 entries are "saying" that if CODE-FIELD has a value of 1, you can refer to it by the name DAY-SHIFT. If it has a value of 2, you can refer to it by the name SWING-SHIFT, and so on:

```
FILE SECTION.
FD EMPLOYEE-FILE.
     ------
     ------
     ------
01  EMPLOYEE-PAY-RECORD.
     ------
     ------
     ------
     ------
```

```
03   CODE-FIELD      PIC 9.
     88   DAY-SHIFT VALUE 1.
     88   SWING-SHIFT VALUE 2.
     88   GRAVE-SHIFT VALUE 3.
 .
 .
 .

PROCEDURE DIVISION
 .
 .
 .
   IF DAY-SHIFT
       PERFORM DAY-SHIFT-ROUTINE.
   IF SWING-SHIFT
       PERFORM SWING-SHIFT-ROUTINE.
   IF GRAVE-SHIFT
       PERFORM GRAVE-SHIFT-ROUTINE.
 .
 .
 .
```

At this point, most beginning students wonder why they should bother using level 88's since these condition names really don't save any coding in your program. There are two reasons why they should be used: First, assuming that meaningful names have been chosen, they make the program easier to read. But a far more important reason is that they aid in program maintenance.

So far, you have seen only one situation involving three tests. But, suppose management decides to change the code values for day, swing, and graveyard shifts to D, S, and G. Under the original method, *all* PROCEDURE DIVISION statements that test the CODE-FIELD would have to be changed. Under the condition-name method, only the entries in the DATA DIVISION need be changed. Note that the PIC and the VALUE must correspond in terms of the type of data:

```
03   CODE-FIELD          PIC X.
     88 DAY-SHIFT         VALUE 'D'.
     88 SWING-SHIFT       VALUE 'S'.
     88 GRAVE-SHIFT       VALUE 'G'.
```

As mentioned earlier, level 88 entries may also be used in the WORKING-STORAGE SECTION. One of their most frequent uses is to indicate different conditions for switches such as last record indicators. So far, we have used this convention:

```
77   EOF-INDICATOR      PIC 9 VALUE ZERO.
 .
 .
 .
   PERFORM 020-READER
       UNTIL EOF-INDICATOR  = 1
 .
```

```
        READ INPUT-FILE
            AT END MOVE 1 TO EOF-INDICATOR.
```

Some programmers use level 88 entries to make their programs more readable:

```
    77   EOF-INDICATOR          PIC XXX VALUE 'OFF'.
         88   THERE-ARE-NO-MORE-RECORDS   VALUE 'YES'.
              .

              .

              .

         PERFORM 020-READER
             UNTIL THERE-ARE-NO-MORE-RECORDS.
              .

              .

              .

         READ INPUT-FILE
             AT END MOVE 'YES' TO EOF-INDICATOR.
```

Conditional statements and structured programming

So far we have been discussing the variations on a conditional statement—IF. Actually, the COBOL language contains several other statements that are really conditional in their operation, but that do not appear so on the surface. One conditional statement fairly apparent is READ. It is both an input statement and a conditional since the AT END portion is activated *if* a certain condition is true. Two other statements—EXAMINE and INSPECT—will be covered at the end of this chapter. Now, however, it is time to take a look at several statements that some DP shops use in very specific situations. The first of these—GO TO—is *not* conditional, but is sometimes used with a conditional action.

The GO TO statement is an *unconditional* branch statement used to transfer control to another point in the program. The format of the statement is very simple.

GO TO paragraph header.

Note that you cannot branch to a data area nor can you branch directly to a program statement. Instead, you must branch to the paragraph that contains the statement or statements you wish to execute. In recent years this COBOL statement has fallen into disrepute, although virtually every programming language has GO TO or a closely related statement. With the advent of top-down design and structured programming techniques, the use of GO TO has been nearly eliminated. The problem of the past use of GO TO was that programmers were under no obligation to thoroughly plan the program logic. Instead, if they came to a dead end, they could simply insert a GO TO, which, in effect, patches a poorly planned program. These programs became a thicket of GO TO statements that were nightmares to maintain.

A top-down, structured program, on the other hand, can be followed from beginning to end by reference to a control module that develops the program structure in an orderly fashion. With this approach the programmer does not have to make a conscious effort to eliminate GO TO's. These branch statements simply aren't there because the regular logic structures are sufficient.

As nice as all this sounds, you should be aware that not all programmers and managers agree on what constitutes a structured program. In general, they agree that a "good" program is correct, readable, and easily maintained. To some this means, among other things, *no* GO TO statements. However, other managers take a more liberal view, and permit the use of GO TO statements in those places where they think their use makes clearer and simpler code. Generally, this means limited use of GO TO in conjunction with the THRU variation of the PERFORM UNTIL statement. In all of this discussion, remember that the key point is to produce clear, understandable COBOL code.

Many data processing professionals feel that the READ-MOVE-WRITE sequence is more logical and natural than the "priming" READ followed by the MOVE-WRITE-READ sequence. Therefore, they are willing to permit the limited use of the GO TO statement to overcome the problem of how to skip over a series of program statements once the AT END situation is detected. In their method, the "priming" READ is eliminated entirely because of the combined action of a PERFORM THRU and a "downward" GO TO statement.

PERFORM THRU **and the** EXIT **statement**

The simple version of the PERFORM THRU statement follows:

<u>PERFORM</u> paragraph name <u>THRU</u> paragraph name.

Example:

```
PERFORM 050-READ-ROUTINE
    THRU 090-PRINT-ROUTINE.
```

In this example, the system performs (executes) all the paragraphs beginning with 050-READ-ROUTINE down through 090-PRINT ROUTINE. Any paragraphs within the range of the two named paragraphs are executed.

The UNTIL option simply adds a test to the operation by specifying that the paragraph will be executed repeatedly until a particular test is met.

Example:

```
PERFORM 050-READ-ROUTINE
    THRU 090-PRINT-ROUTINE
    UNTIL INDICATOR = 1.
```

The major drawback to the THRU version of PERFORM is that the whole operation—that is, the success of the whole program—depends upon the paragraphs being in the right place. For structured purists this is not tolerable because individual paragraphs, or modules, should be able to be located anywhere in the program.

The non-purist gets around this problem by stipulating that PERFORM THRU can only be used with another programming statement—EXIT. The

EXIT statement consists of just the single word— EXIT—and it *must* appear in a paragraph by itself. No other statement may appear in a paragraph that contains EXIT. Furthermore, managers who allow these coding variations generally permit only *downward* GO TO statements. We can now put all three of these ideas together (PERFORM THRU, EXIT, and a downward GO TO) to reconstruct our sample program that appeared earlier:

```
77  EOF-INDICATOR        PIC 9 VALUE ZERO.
*
PROCEDURE DIVISION.
CONTROL-ROUTINE.
    PERFORM 010-OPENER.
    PERFORM 020-READER
        THRU 020-EXIT
        UNTIL EOF-INDICATOR = 1.
    PERFORM 030-CLOSER.
    STOP RUN.
010-OPENER.
    OPEN INPUT STUDENT-FILE OUTPUT PRINTFILE.
020-READER.
    READ STUDENT-FILE
        AT END MOVE 1 TO EOF-INDICATOR
            GO TO 020-EXIT.
    MOVE STUDENT-RECORD TO LIST-LINE.
    WRITE LIST-RECORD AFTER ADVANCING 2 LINES.
020-EXIT. EXIT.
030-CLOSER.
    ------.
    ------.
```

Note what is happening in our revised program.

1. The control is still retained in the CONTROL-ROUTINE.
2. The 010-OPENER paragraph does *not* contain a "priming" READ statement.
3. The second PERFORM statement has been changed to PERFORM THRU UNTIL, which means that any and all paragraphs from 020-READER through 020-EXIT will be executed repeatedly until EOF-INDICATOR is equal to 1.
4. The 020-READER paragraph now contains a READ-MOVE-WRITE sequence plus a GO TO 020-EXIT statement that is executed when the AT END situation is detected.
5. When AT END is detected, the GO TO statement proceeds to the 020-EXIT paragraph, which contains the single statement EXIT. Control is then returned back to the PERFORM THRU UNTIL statement. The value of INDICATOR will be tested and, since it does equal 1, control passes to the next statement in sequence.

Those shops that permit this type of programming usually follow very explicit rules to prevent uncontrolled use of these statements. Normally, the EXIT paragraph must appear immediately after the PERFORMED paragraph—that is, with no intervening paragraphs. Also, the GO TO must only be *downward* and *always* to the exit paragraph.

When GO TO is permitted, there is a temptation to simply replace the GO TO statement with a PERFORM as follows:

```
020-READER.
    READ ------
        AT END PERFORM 030-CLOSER.
    MOVE ------.
    WRITE ------.
030-CLOSER.
    ------.
```

This strategy will work in the sense that it will get us out of the 020-READER loop. However, it destroys the top-down design idea in which we want all program control to be in the top of the program. It also "frustrates" the PERFORM UNTIL statement we set up earlier by branching out of the PERFORM without allowing it to test a condition.

Another temptation when making the transition from unstructured to structured programming is that of simply replacing a GO TO with PERFORM. A typical *unstructured* loop looks as follows:

```
020-READER.
    READ ------
        AT END ------.
    MOVE ------.
    WRITE ------.
    GO TO 020-READER.
```

If we replace the last GO TO with another PERFORM (PERFORM 020-READER), we are, in effect, PERFORMing ourselves. This technique is *"recursive"* and is not permitted, since it can lead to serious programming difficulties.

Character manipulation statements

For the most part, COBOL programs are written to handle data at the field or record level. From what has been presented in the text so far, it would be difficult for you to work at the *character* level. For example, suppose you had a five-digit numeric field that could possibly contain leading blanks. You would want to locate *and* replace these blanks with zeros prior to attempting any arithmetic work on this data. To do so would involve some cumbersome coding, only part of which is shown here:

```
03  AMOUNT-FIELD.
    05  FIRST-DIGIT      PIC 9.
    05  SECOND-DIGIT     PIC 9.
    05  THIRD-DIGIT      PIC 9.
    05  FOURTH-DIGIT     PIC 9.
    05  FIFTH-DIGIT      PIC 9.
         .
         .
         .

IF FIRST-DIGIT IS NOT NUMERIC
    MOVE ZERO TO FIRST-DIGIT.
```

```
    IF SECOND-DIGIT IS NOT NUMERIC
        MOVE ZERO TO SECOND-DIGIT.
            and so on.
```

Fortunately, COBOL has the character manipulation statements EXAMINE and/or INSPECT that allow the programmer to work with individual characters within a field. The general use of these statements is to permit easy data validation and character replacement and counting. The EXAMINE verb was available on 1968 COBOL compilers, and INSPECT—which is a more powerful version of EXAMINE—became available on the 1974 ANS compilers. Some systems support both verbs while others support only one. Check your COBOL manual to see which of these—and what options—are supported. Both will be presented here, since INSPECT is an extension of EXAMINE.

The EXAMINE statement

The EXAMINE statement has two formats:

Format 1:

$$\underline{\text{EXAMINE}} \text{ identifier } \underline{\text{TALLYING}} \begin{Bmatrix} \underline{\text{UNTIL FIRST}} \\ \underline{\text{ALL}} \\ \underline{\text{LEADING}} \end{Bmatrix} \text{literal-1}$$

[REPLACING BY literal-2]

The EXAMINE statement *automatically* creates a signed numeric field of an appropriate size (usually five digits), called TALLY (a reserved word), into which the system inserts the count of characters as designated by the selected option UNTIL-FIRST, ALL, or LEADING. TALLY is automatically reset to zero when another EXAMINE statement is executed. You may save the TALLY value by moving it to another field and you may perform arithmetic operations upon it.

EXAMINE statement	Field before EXAMINE	Field after EXAMINE	Tally

EXAMINE FIELD-A
  TALLYING LEADING SPACES
  REPLACING BY ZEROS.
	bb146	00146	2

Note: This format of the statement requires TALLY *even though the programmer may not need the stored* TALLY *value.*			

EXAMINE FIELD-A
  TALLYING
  UNTIL FIRST 'X'.
	JOEbXbSMITH	JOEbXbSMITH	4

Note: In this example, the EXAMINE *statement counts the number of characters up to but not including the first* X.			

EXAMINE FIELD-A
  TALLYING
  ALL 6.
	64632678	64632678	3

EXAMINE FIELD-A
  TALLYING ALL ','
  REPLACING BY '-'.
	1,234,567	1-234-567	2

```
EXAMINE FIELD-A
     TALLYING ALL
     LEADING ZEROS
     REPLACING WITH '*'.
MOVE TALLY TO
     TALLY-HOLD.
EXAMINE ------.
```

        | 0005.16 | | ***5.16 | 3

Note: The value of TALLY *was moved to a temporary holding area prior to execution of the next* EXAMINE *statement.*

Format 2 of the EXAMINE verb is similar to the first format except that TALLY is not used. An additional option, FIRST, allows greater flexibility.

Format 2:

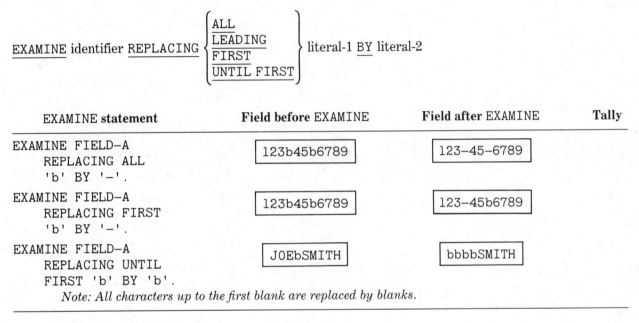

$$\underline{\text{EXAMINE}}\ \text{identifier}\ \underline{\text{REPLACING}}\ \left\{ \begin{array}{l} \underline{\text{ALL}} \\ \underline{\text{LEADING}} \\ \underline{\text{FIRST}} \\ \underline{\text{UNTIL FIRST}} \end{array} \right\}\ \text{literal-1}\ \underline{\text{BY}}\ \text{literal-2}$$

EXAMINE **statement**	**Field before** EXAMINE	**Field after** EXAMINE	**Tally**

EXAMINE FIELD-A
  REPLACING ALL
  'b' BY '-'.
	123b45b6789	123-45-6789	

EXAMINE FIELD-A
  REPLACING FIRST
  'b' BY '-'.
	123b45b6789	123-45b6789	

EXAMINE FIELD-A
  REPLACING UNTIL
  FIRST 'b' BY 'b'.
	JOEbSMITH	bbbbSMITH	

    Note: All characters up to the first blank are replaced by blanks.

The INSPECT statement

1974 ANS COBOL replaced the EXAMINE with the more versatile and more complex INSPECT statement. In general, it will do everything the EXAMINE statement would do, but features more powerful character manipulation capabilities. The two most important differences are listed below. The other differences are minor and can be observed in the specific formats.

1. Unlike EXAMINE, INSPECT does not automatically set up and initialize a TALLY field. Instead, the programmer must create, initialize, and designate a specific numeric field in which the tallying will take place.
2. The INSPECT statement permits the identification and replacement of strings of characters rather than the single character manipulation permitted by EXAMINE.

Format 1:

```
INSPECT identifier-1 TALLYING { identifier-2 FOR { { ALL      } { identifier-3 } [ { BEFORE } INITIAL { identifier-4 } ] } }
                                              { LEADING   } { literal-1    }   { AFTER  }         { literal-2    }
                                              { CHARACTERS }
```

```
INSPECT identifier-1 REPLACING { CHARACTERS BY { identifier-2 } [ { BEFORE } INITIAL { identifier-3 } ]                                              }
                               {               { literal-1    }   { AFTER  }         { literal-2    }                                               }
                               { { ALL     } { identifier-2 } BY { identifier-3 } [ { BEFORE } INITIAL { identifier-4 } ] }
                               { { LEADING } { literal-1    }    { literal-2    }   { AFTER  }         { literal-3    }
                               { { FIRST   }
```

```
INSPECT identifier-1 TALLYING { identifier-2 FOR { { ALL      } { identifier-3 } [ { BEFORE } INITIAL { identifier-4 } ] } }
                                              { LEADING   } { literal-1    }   { AFTER  }         { literal-2    }
                                              { CHARACTERS }

            REPLACING { CHARACTERS BY { identifier-5 } [ { BEFORE } INITIAL { identifier-4 } ]                                              }
                      {               { literal-3    }   { AFTER  }         { literal-2    }                                               }
                      { { ALL     } { identifier-5 } BY { identifier-6 } [ { BEFORE } INITIAL { identifier-7 } ] }
                      { { LEADING } { literal-3    }    { literal-4    }   { AFTER  }         { literal-5    }
                      { { FIRST   }
```

The versatility of the INSPECT statement is shown below.

INSPECT statement	Field before	Field after	Tally field

INSPECT FIELD-A TALLYING
    COUNTER FOR LEADING 'L'
    BEFORE INITIAL 'A'.
	ANALYST	ANALYST	COUNTER = 0

INSPECT FIELD-A TALLYING
    COUNTER FOR ALL 'L'
    REPLACING LEADING 'A'
    BY 'E' AFTER INITIAL 'L'.
	LATTER	LETTER	COUNTER = 1

INSPECT FIELD-A
    REPLACING ALL 'X' BY
    'b' BEFORE INITIAL 'N'.
	QXNZA	QbNZA	—

INSPECT FIELD-A TALLYING
    COUNT-1 FOR CHARACTERS
        BEFORE 'O'
    COUNT-2 FOR CHARACTERS
        AFTER 'O'.
	140678	140678	COUNT-1 = 2
			COUNT-2 = 3

INSPECT FIELD-A
    REPLACING ALL 'DRAT'
    BY 'GOSH'.
	DRATDARN	GOSHDARN	

INSPECT FIELD-A
    REPLACING CHARACTERS
    BY 'O' BEFORE INITIAL '1'.
	45136	00136	

Data validation

One of the more common operations in a data processing shop is input editing or validation of fields before the data are used for computational purposes. Often, a separate program is written just for this purpose and it will make extensive use of the IF NUMERIC and IF ALPHABETIC tests:

```
03  PART-ID.
    05  ID-NBR        PIC 9(4).
    05  ID-ALPHA      PIC X(3).
            .
            .
            .
IF  ID-NBR IS NOT NUMERIC OR
    ID-ALPHA IS NOT ALPHABETIC
        PERFORM 0100-RE-ENTRY-PROCESS.
```

The EXAMINE/INSPECT statements add further versatility to the validation process by allowing the identification and/or replacement of specific characters or strings of characters. One example of this occurs when data come to a DP shop from an outside source. We may be grateful to get the data (since our personnel won't have to duplicate the entry process that someone else has already done), but must convert them into a format we can use. Numeric amount fields may not have been keyed with leading zeros and now we must replace the blanks with zeros. Another possibility is that certain special characters need to be replaced in order to conform to our output formats.

```
INSPECT SALES-AMT REPLACING
    ALL 'b' BY '0'.
INSPECT AMT-OWED REPLACING
    ALL '-b' BY 'CR'.
```

Some of the more common input editing possibilities are listed below.

1. *Check for a numeric field.*

2. *Check for an alphabetic field.*

3. *Check for a missing or skipped field.* Normally a skipped field will contain blanks and the TALLY count of blanks will equal the field size.

4. *Test for any blanks in a field.* This differs from an all alphabetic test in that a space or blank is an alphabetic character. Thus, an alphabetic field that contains a blank would pass an IF test. However, any positive value in the TALLY field set up by an EXAMINE or INSPECT statement would indicate an error condition.

5. The *sign test* may be applicable when a field can only be positive and a negative condition indicates a mis-keyed value.

6. *Upper and lower limit checks.* Here you may be testing against specific values, such as 60, as the maximum permitted number of hours that could be worked in a week. Another possibility is to test against changing limits, such as a percentage of an amount contained within a field. For example, at the lower end it may be that commissions on sales under a certain amount are held until the next regular payroll processing.

7. *Reasonableness checks.* In addition to upper and lower limits checks, we may also perform a reasonableness check on calculated results such as intermediate and final totals to see if they fall within accepted norms. If not, we may wish to identify or in some way flag values that fall within our accepted limits, but that are unusual. In business terminology this would be known as "exception" reporting.

8. *Date checks.* Date fields (date of birth, date of application, date of payments, and so on) may be of critical importance to certain programs. For example, the date field in a driver's license application should be checked for the minimum legal driving age at which a person can apply. The same type of test could be used on social security transactions, senior citizens' benefits, and so on.

COMMON ERRORS

Most beginning COBOL students make relatively few errors involving IF. Those that are made, however, tend to be difficult to find. Recall that the format of the IF-ELSE statement is

IF test condition

—————————————— ⎫
—————————————— ⎬ executed if test is true
—————————————— ⎭

ELSE

—————————————— ⎫
—————————————— ⎬ executed if test is false
——————————————. ⎭

——————————————.   always executed.

One very common error involves the misplacement of the ending period. Note the following example:

```
IF COUNTER IS EQUAL TO TEST-VALUE
    MOVE MSSG-1 TO MSSG-AREA
    WRITE OUTPUT-LINE FROM MSSG-REC
        AFTER ADVANCING 2 LINES
ELSE
    MOVE VALUE-A TO VALUE-A-PACK
    COMPUTE ANS =  (VALUE-A - B + C) / D.
READ ------.
```

A flowchart of this operation is shown below.

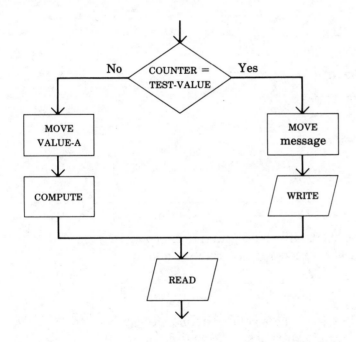

If the period that ends the IF-ELSE operation is misplaced at the end of the second MOVE statement,

```
IF ------
    MOVE ------
    WRITE ------
ELSE
    MOVE ------.
    COMPUTE ANS = (VALUE-A - B + C) / D
READ ------
```

then the logic of the operation is changed considerably as the following flowchart shows. Now the COMPUTE statement is executed *every* time— not on just the false condition of the IF test.

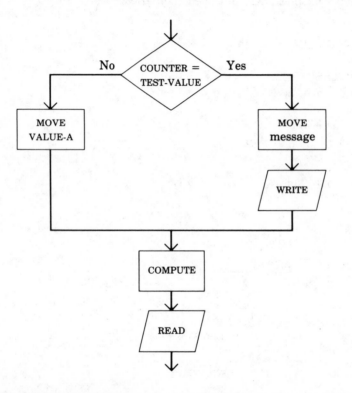

PROGRAMMING TIPS

When using the IF-ELSE statements, certain programming conventions should be followed in order to save you and the maintenance programmer a lot of extra work.

1. Limit nesting to a maximum of three levels.

2. Match all IF's and ELSE's and indicate the matching by indenting. (The indenting, of course, is for the sake of clarity when reading the program. To the compiler the indenting is meaningless.)

3. Use NEXT SENTENCE to fill out the non-action side of a test.

4. Avoid complex conditions in favor of simple tests whenever possible.

5. Be sure that the period ending the IF is placed in the correct spot.

6. If you have any doubt as to the action of an IF statement, diagram the logic rather than placing it in the program with the hope that it will work.

7. Use parentheses to clarify the order in which tests are evaluated.

8. Use explicit rather than implied subjects and operators.

9. When coding IF statements, end the statement with an extra heavy period mark—it may be worth its weight in gold.

10. Indent for clarity and ease of reading, but be consistent. Set up rules for indenting and follow them. Indenting is particularly important when using nested IF-ELSE statements so that the reader can properly associate the test options.

```
IF ------
    IF ------
        IF  ------
            ------
            ------
            ------
        ELSE
            ------
            ------
            ------
    ELSE
        ------
        ------
        ------
ELSE
    ------
    ------
    ------
```

The same rule holds true for simple COBOL statements within a paragraph. The following example may execute correctly, but is difficult to follow:

```
030-CALCULATION-LOOP.
    MOVE ------.
    MOVE ------.
        ADD ------.
    SUBTRACT ------.
        MOVE ------.
    MOVE ------.
        DIVIDE ------.
```

Since all the COBOL statements are of the same general level, they all should start in the same relative position:

```
030-CALCULATION-LOOP.
    MOVE ------.
    MOVE ------.
    ADD ------.
    SUBTRACT ------.
    MOVE ------.
    MOVE ------.
    DIVIDE ------.
```

When IF statements are used in the normal sequence of statements, they should be indented as indicated earlier and ELSE should appear on a line by itself:

```
030-CALCULATION-LOOP.
    MOVE ------.
    MOVE ------.
    ADD ------.
    IF (test)
        ------
        ------
    ELSE
        ------
        ------.
    SUBTRACT ------.
    MOVE ------.
```

Also, remember that the sequential READ statement is a conditional statement; that is, it contains a built-in IF in the form of AT END. This built-in testing feature means that the use of the READ statement within a regular IF is usually not permitted by the software. As mentioned earlier in the text, the problem can be avoided by PERFORMing the READ operation.

SELF-STUDY: QUESTIONS AND ANSWERS

1. Am I correct in saying the relational test simply compares two values to determine their arithmetic relationship?

   Answer: Yes. The relational test is a very simple comparison. For example, in the statement

   ```
   IF HOURS-WORKED IS GREATER THAN TEST-AMT
   ```

   the test is concerned solely with whether the value in the HOURS-WORKED field is greater than the value stored in the TEST-AMT field. Neither the system nor the programmer is concerned with *how much* the first field is greater than the second. The test is just as true if the comparison is 40.1 vs. 40.0 as it is if the test is 65.9 vs. 40.0. Also, remember that neither of the values is changed during the comparison testing.

2. How complex can the test be in an IF statement?

   Answer: The test may be as complex as you wish and may involve any combination of literals and data fields, but the result of the test is simply "true" or "false."

3. Why do you say to be careful using a compound condition in an IF statement?

Answer: Compound IF statements can present problems for the programmer unless they have been thought out thoroughly. It is easy to get into a situation where you think you know what is happening, but the machine is doing something entirely different. I suggest they be avoided unless you feel they are absolutely necessary. A good rule to follow is "if you can diagram—use it."

4. I understand that using condition names could save a lot of work if the test values were to be modified at a later date. However, in a class program this isn't going to happen. In that case, why should I use condition names?

Answer: You are right that in a classroom situation, the values are not likely to change. However, condition names (level 88's) should be used, because if appropriate names are chosen, it can make your program far more readable. And, of course, a more readable program is less likely to contain errors. However, you should resist the urge to use "cutesy" names just for the sake of being cute.

5. What if I get into a programming situation that requires the use of the GO TO statement? What do I do then?

Answer: If you have designed your program properly and if you understand how to use the programming structures shown in the text, you will not have any need for the GO TO statement. So you may have to rethink your approach to solving the problem. Remember, the GO TO statement tends to become a crutch that supports poor program design, because it allows you to escape from a badly designed section of code.

CHAPTER TERMS

class test	INSPECT statement
collating sequence	level 88's
condition names (level 88's)	limit tests
data validation	nested statements
EXAMINE statement	NEXT SENTENCE
EXIT statement	PERFORM THRU statement
GO TO statement	reasonableness test
hierarchy of operations	relational tests
IF statement	sign test
implied operator	TALLY field
implied subject	

EXERCISES

1. What are the 3 types of tests done in COBOL? Explain each.

2. Given FIELDA = 'ABCD', FIELDB = 'XYZ', FIELDC = '123.45':
   What is the result when this program segment is done?

   ```
   IF FIELDA IS NOT ALPHABETIC
       NEXT SENTENCE
   ELSE
       IF FIELDB IS EQUAL TO FIELDC
           (statements to print 'OK')
       ELSE
           IF FIELDC IS NOT NUMERIC
               (statements to print 'BAD')
           ELSE
               (statements to print 'ALL THE WAY THROUGH').
   Statements to print 'TEST CONCLUDED'.
   ```

3. What level of number is used to signify a conditional name?

4. Give two reasons why you might want to use conditional names.

5. Given:

   ```
   03   SWITCHES    PIC 9.
        88   DOG VALUE 1.
        88   CAT VALUE 2.
        88   MOUSE VALUE 3.
             .
             .
             .
   IF   DOG   (statements to print 'DOG').
   IF   CAT   (statements to print 'CAT').
   IF   MOUSE   (statements to print 'MOUSE').
   ```

   Change the program segment above so that SWITCHES uses 'D' to print 'DOG', 'C' for 'CAT', and 'M' to print out 'MOUSE'.

6. Write the COBOL statements to perform the following tests.
   a. PERFORM ROUTINE-1 if A-FIELD is not equal to zero.
   b. If A-FIELD is greater than LIMIT, you are to add 1 to COUNTER-A. Otherwise you are to subtract CONSTANT from COUNTER-B.
   c. If NAME-FIELD (PICTURE A) contains any numeric characters, you are to display the message "NAME-FIELD NOT ALPHABETIC" upon the console and ADD 1 TO COUNT-B. Otherwise you are to go on to the next statement, which is ADD 1 TO COUNT-C.
   d. If AMT-OF-PAY contains any non-numeric characters, you are to display the message 'DATA OF WRONG TYPE'. Otherwise you are to move BODY-LINE to OUTPUT-LINE and write it after advancing three lines. No matter what the result of the test, you are to execute the statement that multiplies the contents of SUB-TOTAL by RATE to get a rounded answer in ANSWER-1.

7. Write IF-ELSE statements for the following. If it is possible using either nested IF's or compound IF's, do them both ways.

	Condition	When true	When false

a.	A > B and
	C < D
		ADD 1 TO COUNT-A
		MOVE SPACES TO
		  AREA-B.
			ADD 1 TO COUNT-B
			MOVE ZEROS TO
			  COUNTER.

b.	A = B and A < D	no action	MOVE ------- ADD -------

c.	A NOT = B
	and
	C NOT = D
		READ FILE-A
		    AT END MOVE -------
		ADD -------
			READ FILE-B
			    AT END MOVE -------
			ADD -------

d.	A > B or
	B > C
		MOVE -------
		IF Z = Q
		    MOVE -------
		    ADD -------
		READ IN-FILE
		    AT END -------
			no action

e.	A NOT > B or
	X NOT > Y
		MOVE -------
		READ IN-FILE
		    AT END
		        ADD -------
		        SUBTRACT -------.
		MOVE -------
		ADD -------
			no action

8. Write the IF statement(s) that correspond to the following flowcharts.
   a.

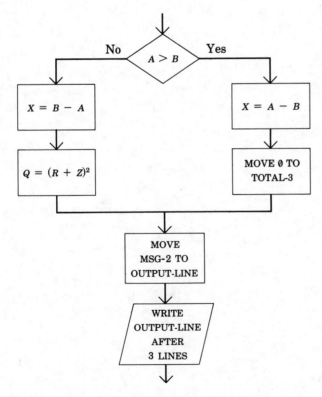

b.

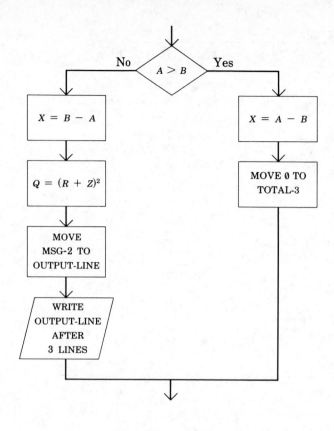

c.

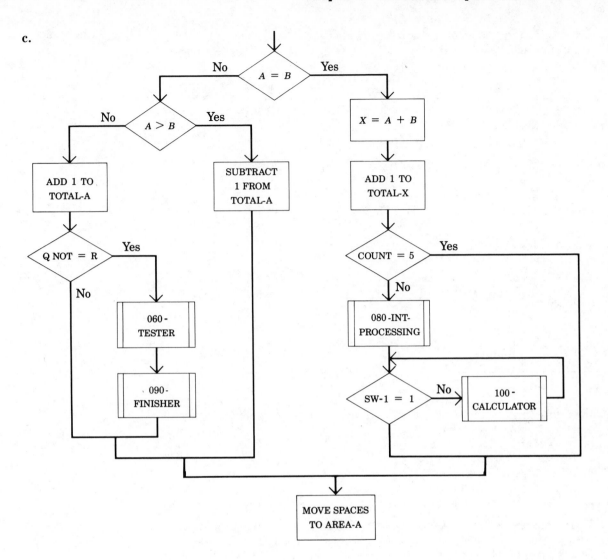

9. Indicate whether the following tests are valid or invalid and the result of the tests. If invalid, indicate why.

	Test	FIELD-A	CONTENTS
a.	IF FIELD-A IS NUMERIC	PIC 999	123
b.	IF FIELD-A IS NOT NUMERIC	PIC XXX	015
c.	IF FIELD-A IS NOT NUMERIC	PIC XXX	b63
d.	IF FIELD-A IS ALPHABETIC	PIC XXX	AbB
e.	IF FIELD-A IS NOT ALPHABETIC	PIC 999	415
f.	IF FIELD-A IS NOT NUMERIC	PIC ZZZ	unknown
g.	IF FIELD-A IS NUMERIC	PIC S999	+884
h.	IF FIELD-A IS NOT NUMERIC	PIC S999	-884

10. In the following IF statements, indicate the order in which the tests are evaluated.
   a. IF $A = B$ AND $C = D$
   b. IF $A = B$ AND $C = D$ OR $Q < R$.
   c. IF $A < B$ OR $C = D$ AND $Q = R$.
   d. IF $A < B$ OR ($C = D$ AND $Q = R$).
   e. IF $A = B$ AND C IS NOT $= Q$.
   f. IF $A = B$ AND C IS NOT $= Q$ OR $F < T$

11. Modify Exercise 27 from Chapter 4 (output format is the same) to print output lines only for those employees who have three or more dependents. (The Dependents field is in columns 35 and 36.) Also, after printing your total line, print the following:

   TOTAL RECORDS IN FILE XXX
   EMPLOYEES WITH 3 OR MORE DEPENDENTS XXX

12. Using Data File A, you are to perform an input editing operation in which you check a field to see if it contains the proper characters. The record format is:

Column	Field description
1–9	Social security number
10–29	Name
30–52	Filler
53–55	Work area field consisting of a two-digit section number and single alphabetic character for the work department
56–80	Filler

Write a program that checks the work area field to see that the first two characters are numeric and the last character is alphabetic. If the data fail either test, write a line on the printer as follows. (*Note:* You will be writing a line only for those records that contain an error.)

```
                    INPUT EDIT RUN

NAME     SOCIAL SECURITY NUMBER     WORK AREA CODE

   .                  .                   .
   .                  .                   .
   .                  .                   .


   TOTAL NUMBER OF ERRORS
```

13. Modify the previous problem to provide the following output:

```
                    INPUT EDIT RUN

   RECORD NUMBER     NAME     WORK AREA CODE
        X           ------        ------
        X           ------        ------
   TOTAL NUMBER OF ERRORS
```

Chapter 6
Handling Data (Part II)

LEARNING OBJECTIVES

1. To find out more about the MOVE statement and the MOVE variations that are possible.

2. To understand the way in which data are internally represented in DISPLAY, COMP-3 (packed), and COMP (binary) formats.

3. To learn ways in which program execution can take place more efficiently.

4. To see how the on-line processing statements DISPLAY and ACCEPT are used.

At this point you have been exposed to most of the statements in COBOL and you should be able to write fairly sophisticated programs. The statements you have encountered so far have fallen into five general categories: Input/Output, Arithmetic, Internal Data Movement, Program Control, and Testing. Some statements, such as READ (shown in parentheses), may fall into more than one category.

Input/Output	Arithmetic	Internal data movement	Program control	Testing
OPEN	ADD	MOVE	PERFORM	IF
CLOSE	SUBTRACT	(EXAMINE, INSPECT)	STOP RUN	(EXAMINE, INSPECT)
READ	MULTIPLY		GO TO	(READ)
WRITE	DIVIDE		EXIT	
	COMPUTE			

In this chapter we will pursue the intricacies of handling data and we will take a look at two statements (DISPLAY and ACCEPT) touched upon briefly before.

More about MOVE

MOVE is a "workhorse" statement in COBOL and its value and complexity tend to be under-appreciated. Before taking a look at more MOVE variations, let's review some of the features about it that you already know.

1. Numeric to numeric moves.
   a. Data are aligned on the indicated decimal point.
   b. Truncation of digits from the sending field may take place to the right or left or on both sides of the decimal point.
   c. The movement of shorter numeric fields may result in the padding of the receiving field with zeros on the left, on the right, or on both sides of the decimal point.
2. Numeric to edit field moves.
   a. The data are edited according to the format of the receiving edit field.
   b. It is the programmer's responsibility to provide the proper number of edit characters to account for all digits in the sending field.
3. Alphanumeric moves.
   a. Alphanumeric moves proceed from left to right.
   b. Excess characters from the sending field will be truncated on the right.
   c. A shorter sending field will result in the receiving field being padded with spaces to fill the excess positions on the right.
   d. Alphanumeric data may be sent by means of literals—that is, data within quotes.
4. The GIVING option of ADD, SUBTRACT, MULTIPLY, and DIVIDE is equivalent to MOVE.
5. The execution of the COMPUTE statement results in the movement of data to the designated field.

6. The READ INTO and WRITE FROM statements contain a built-in MOVE operation.

7. Data may be moved to several fields with a single MOVE statement.

Permissible MOVES

In previous discussions, the common (and valid) uses of the MOVE statement were emphasized. However, some types of moves are obviously invalid—such as trying to move numeric data to an alphabetic field. Other moves fall into an in-between area in which they may be permissible on one system but not on another. For the sake of portability, these move operations should *not* be used even if they work on your system.

Most of the move operations you have seen so far have involved the movement of one elementary data item to another elementary item. Simple group moves typically involve the movement of an output line to the area from which printing is to take place:

```
01  PRINTER-RECORD       PIC X(121).
WORKING-STORAGE SECTION.
      .
      .
      .

01  MAIN-REPORT-LINE.
    03  FILLER           PIC X.
    03  FILLER           PIC X(10) VALUE SPACES.
    03  NAME-OUT         PIC X(20).
    03  FILLER           PIC X(10) VALUE SPACES.
    03  ADDRESS-OUT      PIC X(20).
    03  FILLER           PIC X(10) VALUE SPACES.
    03  PHONE-NBR        PIC X(08).
    03  FILLER           PIC X(42) VALUE SPACES.
      .
      .
      .

PROCEDURE DIVISION.
      .
      .
      .
    MOVE MAIN-REPORT-LINE TO PRINTER-RECORD.
```

So, group moves are certainly permitted in COBOL. The rule concerning group moves is that the data are treated *alphanumerically* and that the move takes place *without* regard to the individual fields that are part of the group. Note the following example:

```
03  CUSTOMER-RECORD
    05  CUST-NBR-IN        PIC 9(05).
    05  CUST-NAME-IN       PIC X(30).
    05  CUST-ADDRESS-IN    PIC X(25).
      .
      .
```

```
WORKING-STORAGE SECTION.
        .
        .
        .
    03  CUSTOMER-RECORD-WS.
        05  CUST-NBR-WS          PIC 9(05).
        05  CUST-NAME-WS         PIC X(30).
        05  CUST-ADDRESS-WS      PIC X(25).
```

The statement

```
MOVE CUSTOMER-RECORD TO CUSTOMER-RECORD-WS.
```

will move the correct data because the length of each group is exactly the same (60 characters). The fact that the fields are mixed—that is, both 9s and xs—makes no difference. If the CUSTOMER-RECORD-WS fields were in a different order or were of different length, the proper values would *not* get into the various fields. Setting up the WORKING-STORAGE fields in the following manner will result in an *incorrect* group move even though the total lengths of the fields are the same as before:

```
03  CUSTOMER-RECORD-WS.
    05  CUST-ADDRESS-WS      PIC X(25).
    05  CUST-NBR-WS          PIC 9(05).
    05  CUST-NAME-WS         PIC X(30).
```

One other example should be mentioned here concerning group moves and the use of the figurative constant ZEROS. As shown in many examples so far, you are very likely to have various indicators, counters, totals, and so on, to set to zero in WORKING-STORAGE. Normally you would include the VALUE ZEROS entry for each of the fields because you wish to be certain of the field contents. Everything is fine so far, but suppose you use these fields in computations and then wish to reset them to zero before going on to the next part of your program. Instead of writing individual MOVE ZEROS statements, you could use a group MOVE. Let's assume we have the following fields in WORKING-STORAGE:

```
03  MISC-FIELDS.
    05  INDICATOR     PIC 9       VALUE ZERO.
    05  COUNTER       PIC 99      VALUE ZEROS.
    05  TOTAL-1       PIC 999V99  VALUE ZEROS.
```

The group move statement

```
MOVE ZEROS TO MISC-FIELDS
```

will work. However, there is an occasion, to be discussed a little later in this chapter, under which the move shown above will not work correctly. Figure 6-1 illustrates the outcome of various types of moves.

FIGURE 6-1

MOVE operations

		Receiving Field Type				
		Alphabetic PIC A	Numeric PIC 9	Alphanumeric PIC X	Edit PIC Z9	Group
Sending	PIC A	Valid	Invalid	Valid	Invalid	—
	PIC 9	Invalid	Valid	Valid for integer data	Valid	—
Field	PIC X	Valid if non-numeric	Invalid	Valid	Invalid	—
Type	PIC Z9	Invalid	Invalid	Valid	Invalid	—
	Group	Valid	Invalid	Valid	Invalid	Valid

Duplicate names and MOVE CORRESPONDING

The general practice in COBOL is to give each field a unique and meaningful name. In addition, it is helpful to identify the source of the field by attaching some identifier to the name, such as ID-NBR-DISK (for a disk input field), TOTAL-SALES-WS (for a WORKING-STORAGE entry), and so on. At the beginning level of programming, duplicate names normally are not used even though they are permissible in COBOL. The reason for this, of course, is that beginning programs seldom are long enough to cause any problem in the naming of fields. If duplicate names are used, the programmer must *qualify* them by indicating the record to which they belong. Note the following example of data fields within the input and output records:

```
01    STUDENT-RECORD.
      03   ID-NBR         PIC 9(05).
      03   NAME           PIC X(20).
      03   PHONE-NBR      PIC 9(07).
      03   ADDRESS-DATA   PIC X(30).
WORKING-STORAGE SECTION.
01    MAIN-REPORT-LINE.
      03   FILLER         PIC X(16)     VALUE SPACES.
      03   NAME           PIC X(20).
      03   FILLER         PIC X(10)     VALUE SPACES.
      03   ADDRESS-DATA   PIC X(30).
      03   FILLER         PIC X(10)     VALUE SPACES.
      03   ID-NBR         PIC 9(05).
      03   FILLER         PIC X(30)     VALUE SPACES.
```

Moving the three fields to the appropriate report line fields would involve three separate MOVE statements *with qualifiers:*

```
MOVE NAME OF STUDENT-RECORD TO
    NAME OF MAIN-REPORT-LINE.
MOVE ADDRESS-DATA OF STUDENT-RECORD TO
    ADDRESS-DATA OF MAIN-REPORT-LINE.
```

```
MOVE ID-NBR OF STUDENT-RECORD TO
    ID-NBR OF MAIN-REPORT-LINE.
```

The use of the qualifiers as shown above provides good documentation, but requires a lot of extra coding. MOVE CORRESPONDING, however, can simplify the whole process as the next example shows:

```
MOVE CORRESPONDING STUDENT-RECORD TO
    MAIN-REPORT-LINE.
```

The result of this statement is that the ID-NBR, NAME, and ADDRESS fields within STUDENT-RECORD are moved to the corresponding fields in the MAIN-REPORT-LINE record. Some special rules must be followed when using MOVE CORRESPONDING.

1. The references must be to group items, as shown in the previous example.
2. All data items with corresponding names are moved and FILLER fields are ignored.
3. As the example shows, the corresponding fields in the two records do not have to be in the same order for the move to take place.
4. Technically, the fields do not have to be equal in size, although the normal practice is to have fields of the same size. If, in our example, ID-NBR in MAIN-REPORT-LINE had a PICTURE of 9(3), truncation of the left-most digits would occur.
5. On some systems, the level numbers of the sending and receiving fields must be the same in order for the move to take place.

The MOVE CORRESPONDING statement should not be used casually since it does have some disadvantages.

1. The MOVE CORRESPONDING statement causes the compiler to generate MOVE statements for each elementary item of the same name in both groups. Simple MOVEs would result in more efficient internal operations.
2. The use of MOVE CORRESPONDING can make program maintenance difficult, since the addition or deletion of a field can have far-ranging consequences.
3. The MOVE CORRESPONDING statement moves *all* fields with corresponding names. Thus, in a particular circumstance, if you wish to move all the fields except one, each field would have to be moved individually.

Moving literal data

Our sample LISTER program included the following MOVE statement:

```
030-CLOSER.
    MOVE 'END-OF-PROGRAM' TO LIST-LINE.
    WRITE LIST-RECORD AFTER ADVANCING 3 LINES.
```

As you know, this variation of MOVE is permissible and results in the data within quotes being moved to the receiving area. The statement was appropriate at that place in the text, because it showed how a literal is formed and how it may be used. However, many programmers feel that the use shown does not represent the best programming technique. To understand this, you once more have to think in terms of program maintenance rather than your own (probably fairly short) program that may only be seen by yourself and your instructor.

A longer, production-type program is likely to have many places where literal data are moved to the printer, to the video screen, or to the operator console unit. What happens when a literal message needs to be changed? Under the method shown so far, the maintenance programmer must search through the program to find where that message was used. And, in some cases, the message may be used at multiple places in the program.

A far better technique is to put all such messages in WORKING-STORAGE where they can be easily located and modified:

```
WORKING-STORAGE SECTION.
        .
        .

        .
01   MESSAGES.
     03   MESSG-1-EOF     PIC X(14)
              VALUE 'END OF PROGRAM'.
     03   MSSG-2-ERROR    PIC X(19)
              VALUE 'ERROR IN NAME FIELD'.
        .

        .
PROCEDURE DIVISION.
        .

        .
     MOVE MSSG-1 TO LIST-LINE.
     WRITE LIST-RECORD AFTER ADVANCING 3 LINES.
```

The same advice holds true for numeric literals:

```
COMPUTE NEW-RATE = OLD-RATE * .07
```

A better approach is to use a variable whose value is defined by a VALUE entry in the DATA DIVISION. Under this method the maintenance programmer will not have to search through the PROCEDURE DIVISION statements to locate every numeric literal that exists in the program. When the next pay-rate change is authorized, the programmer need change only the VALUE entry:

```
WORKING-STORAGE SECTION.
01   CONSTANT-FIELDS.
     03   RATE-INCREASE    PIC V99 VALUE .07.
     03   ------
PROCEDURE DIVISION.
        .

        .
     COMPUTE NEW-RATE = OLD-RATE * RATE-INCREASE.
```

Data formats and the usage clause

One of the major advantages of COBOL is its ability to handle data in a variety of formats. For example, the data entering from a card reader or going out to a printer, whether numeric, alphabetic, or alphanumeric, are said to be DISPLAY format. On many computers (particularly IBM machines) this means that each character occupies one position or one *byte* of memory. By common definition a byte consists of eight binary or switchable elements, called *bits* (from the words binary digits). When numeric data are present, the rightmost four bits of each byte are used to represent the digits one through nine, while the leftmost four bits (called the zone portion) are used to represent the sign of the data.

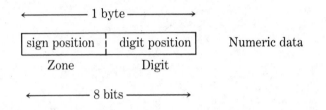

When alphabetic data are present, the zone portion is used to represent the code that indicates alphabetic characters (Figure 6-2).

Many computers are not truly byte-oriented machines, which is another way of saying that *internally* they may represent data in something other than the byte format. However, since the use of bytes is dominant today, even non-byte machines must be able to handle this format. Thus, manuals for a machine that may have a storage format of one million 32-bit *words* will speak of memory in terms of "4 million bytes," since a 32-bit word is the equivalent to 4 bytes.

Display, packed, and binary formats

What do display, packed, and binary formats mean to you as the programmer? So far, very little, since you can assume that your machine will operate on data that are in DISPLAY or byte format. All the examples so far have been of data in DISPLAY format. As a matter of fact, the system *assumes* DISPLAY unless told otherwise. For example, in the following entry, the first field takes up five bytes of memory and the second field takes up four bytes:

```
03   MONTHLY-PAYMENT      PIC S999V99.
03   AMOUNT-A             PIC S99V99.
```

The following is correct but unnecessary:

```
03   MONTHLY-PAYMENT      PIC S999V99
        USAGE IS DISPLAY.
03   AMOUNT-A             PIC S99V99
        USAGE IS DISPLAY.
```

FIGURE 6-2

Byte coding structure

Numeric Character	EBCDIC 8-bit Coding	
	Sign	Digit
0	1111	0000
1	1111	0001
2	1111	0010
3	1111	0011
4	1111	0100
5	1111	0101
6	1111	0110
7	1111	0111
8	1111	1000
9	1111	1001

Alphabetic Character	EBCDIC 8-bit Coding	
	Zone	Digit
A	1100	0001
B	1100	0010
C	1100	0011
D	1100	0100
E	1100	0101
F	1100	0110
G	1100	0111
H	1100	1000
I	1100	1001
J	1101	0001
K	1101	0010
L	1101	0011
M	1101	0100
N	1101	0101
O	1101	0110
P	1101	0111
Q	1101	1000
R	1101	1001
S	1110	0010
T	1110	0011
U	1110	0100
V	1110	0101
W	1110	0110
X	1110	0111
Y	1110	1000
Z	1110	1001

As a matter of fact, the words USAGE and IS are optional, so the entry

```
03   MONTHLY-PAYMENT     PIC S999V99 DISPLAY.
```

is correct, but still the word DISPLAY is not necessary.

The interesting part comes when you want to manipulate fields arithmetically. Suppose you set up a field for use as a counter. The WORKING-STORAGE entry

```
01   MISC-FIELDS.
     03   AMT-COUNTER     PIC 999V99 VALUE ZERO.
```

establishes the field *in* DISPLAY *format* because you did not specify otherwise. Later in your program it is very likely you will want to add to it by means of the statement

```
ADD AMOUNT-A TO AMT-COUNTER.
```

The statement is correct, and addition will take place exactly as indicated. However, the general rule is that the computer *cannot* do any arithmetic on fields that are in DISPLAY format. Obviously, we just showed an example where an arithmetic statement was used. The solution to the dilemma is that the system must first change the fields into a different format prior to doing the arithmetic. The steps the processor must go through are outlined as follows:

1. The fields are moved to a work area and the data values are converted to a different format.
2. Arithmetic is performed as indicated.
3. The answer is converted back into DISPLAY format and moved to the receiving field.

For the beginning programmer there is a great temptation to say "If the machine does all the work, why tell me about it?" The reason is that this method is inefficient in terms of machine time. With the effort of a few extra entries on your part, arithmetic operations can take place much more rapidly and efficiently. (Later we shall discuss the importance of machine efficiency.) For now all you have to do to gain some internal machine efficiency is to change the fields into a different format. The two general formats that provide for more efficient execution of arithmetic operations are called COMPUTATIONAL-3 ("packed" format)—or COMPUTATIONAL (binary format).

Most IBM machines use both the COMPUTATIONAL-3 (packed) and COMPUTATIONAL (binary) formats, while many non-IBM machines have only the binary representation. Check your machine about the formats it uses.

Suppose we have an incoming card record as shown in the next example. Note that all fields automatically are in DISPLAY format:

```
01  EMPLOYEE-REC.
    03  EMPLOYEE-NAME   PIC X(30).
    03  HOURS-WORKED    PIC S99V9.
    03  PAY-RATE        PIC S99V99.
    03  FILLER          PIC X(43).
```

The statement

```
MULTIPLY HOURS-WORKED BY PAY-RATE
    GIVING GROSS-PAY.
```

will cause the system to go through the conversion—arithmetic operations—process discussed earlier. You can gain some internal efficiency by converting these fields on your own rather than having the machine do it. To do so, all you have to do is MOVE the value to another field that is in the desired format:

```
WORKING-STORAGE SECTION.
77  -------
77  -------
01  WORK-FIELDS.
    03  HOURS-PACKED          PIC S99V9   COMP-3.
    03  PAY-RATE-PACKED       PIC S99V99  COMP-3.
    03  GROSS-PAY             PIC S9(4)V99.
```

COMP-3 and COMP are acceptable abbreviations for COMPUTATIONAL-3 and COMPUTATIONAL. The two fields we just set up are in packed format, and we have followed a common coding practice of identifying the fields as being in packed format. The MOVE statements will put the data into packed format in preparation for the MULTIPLY operation:

```
MOVE HOURS-WORKED TO HOURS-PACKED.
MOVE PAY-RATE TO PAY-RATE-PACKED.
MULTIPLY HOURS-PACKED BY PAY-RATE-PACKED GIVING
    GROSS-PAY.
```

Let's see how this format works. Suppose our incoming HOURS-WORKED field contained a value of 39.6. In byte format it would look as follows:

sign	3	sign	9	sign	6
zone	digit	zone	digit	zone	digit

HOURS-WORKED

It should be apparent that this format is wasteful of memory since there is no need for the sign of the *field* to be indicated within every *digit*. Packing is a method in which the system can take advantage of the byte structure to place *two* digits in each byte—one in the digit portion and one in the zone portion. Actually, this is not exactly correct since a half byte must be used to indicate the sign of the field. Note how this is done.

HOURS-WORKED

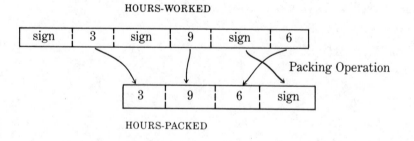

Packing Operation

HOURS-PACKED

Several points are worth noting:

1. The sign of the field (positive or negative) occupies the right half of the rightmost byte. (By the way, a half byte is called a "nibble.")
2. The HOURS-PACKED field is correctly described as PIC 99V9, even though it will occupy only two bytes of storage. (The software is entirely capable of calculating that three digits in DISPLAY format can be stored in packed format in a two-byte area.)
3. If the sending field contains an even number of digits, the system will fill in a zero at the left to pad out the field.

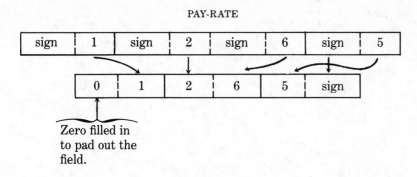

Zero filled in
to pad out the
field.

The same general process is followed for COMPUTATION (binary data).
Again, note that the PIC entries remain the same:

```
01   WORK-FIELDS.
     03   HOURS-BIN        PIC 99V9   COMP.
     03   PAY-RATE-BIN     PIC 99V99 COMP.
     .
     .
     .
     MOVE HOURS-WORKED TO HOURS-BIN.
     MOVE PAY-RATE TO PAY-RATE-BIN.
     MULTIPLY HOURS-BIN BY PAY-RATE-BIN
             GIVING GROSS-PAY.
```

In both of the examples above, if GROSS-PAY were *not* going to be worked
upon arithmetically, the field should be in DISPLAY format. If it is going to
be worked upon, it should be set up in either packed or binary format.
When a field is converted to binary, the conversion is to either 16 bits (2
bytes), 32 bits (4 bytes), or 64 bits (8 bytes), including the sign. Numeric
fields of 1 to 4 digits require 2 bytes in binary format, 5 to 9 digits require
4 bytes, and 10 to 18 digits require 8 bytes. The following table illustrates
the storage requirements of various size fields. Check the manual on your
machine to see how it handles the various data formats.

Number of digits in DISPLAY format	Number of bytes required in packed format	Number of bytes required in binary format
1	1	2
2	2	2
3	2	2
4	3	2
5	3	4
6	4	4
7	4	4
8	5	4
9	5	4
10	6	8
11	6	8
12	7	8
13	7	8
14	8	8
15	8	8
16	9	8
17	9	8
18	10	8

Programming considerations

At this point we need to address the matter of "efficiency." From the preceding discussion, it is apparent that your program can be made to run faster—that is, more efficiently—if you put the fields into the proper arithmetic format. The question is, is it worth the effort, since COBOL will perform these chores anyway?

From a broader viewpoint, efficiency can be defined at least two ways: programmer efficiency and machine efficiency. Computers are fast; humans are not. In the long run it may be more "efficient" to produce an internally inefficient program that is written in a reasonable amount of time.

Now the intention is not to forget machine efficiency entirely, but it is important for the programmer and the supervisor to weigh the two kinds of efficiency. From a practical standpoint, however, there is a middle position that can be taken. First, write the program as you normally would. Then examine it to find the main loop(s) (probably the main processing loop) that will be executed most frequently in the program. If you do decide to optimize your program for machine efficiency, this is the place at which to devote your time. Don't spend your time trying to optimize the whole program; it may not be worth the effort.

Note that what may be efficient on one machine may not be efficient on another. This consequence stems partially from the fact that although the binary format is the accepted COBOL standard, some machines (particularly IBM and IBM look-alikes) may not work efficiently in this format under all conditions. The problem is further compounded because some machines do not support packed format, or, if they do, they require extra internal machine effort to simulate it. That result brings us full circle—to the conclusion that the most portable program will use the one format that is used by all machines, DISPLAY format.

Today, there is little standardization of the internal data representation on microcomputers. Thus, it is possible to find that DISPLAY, COMPUTATIONAL-3, and COMPUTATIONAL formats on these machines do not exactly fit the formats described in this section.

Now, we can get back to an idea discussed earlier in this chapter—group MOVE's. There you saw that it was permissible to say MOVE ZEROS TO MISC-FIELDS:

```
01   MISC-FIELDS.
     03   INDICATOR        PIC 9 VALUE ZERO.
     03   COUNTER          PIC 99 VALUE ZEROS.
     03   TOTAL-1          PIC 999V99 VALUE ZEROS.
```

This operation worked *only* because each of these fields was in DISPLAY format. Group moves are made alphanumerically without regard to the format of the individual fields or subfields. Therefore, if any of the fields had been in COMP or COMP-3 formats, correct zeros would *not* have been moved. Then, either incorrect answers would result or the program would abort when the programmer tried to do arithmetic on these fields.

However, efficiency can be enhanced by means of a few simple entries. As shown earlier, every time a DISPLAY field containing an even number of digits is converted to packed format the system is required to generate a leading zero. A better plan is to set up the field with an odd number of digits to begin with (if this is possible). The format

```
01   MISC-FIELDS.
     03   TOTAL-1          PIC 99V99 COMP-3 VALUE ZERO.
```

is not as efficient as

```
     03   TOTAL-1          PIC 999V99 COMP-3 VALUE ZERO.
```

In addition, the reserved word SYNC or SYNCHRONIZED can be used to gain additional internal efficiency. Some computers, particularly IBM, require that data values stored in memory be aligned on specific memory boundaries. These boundaries are locations that are evenly divisible by 2, 4, or 8. These boundaries are especially important in binary operations, and if the programmer does not specify correct boundary alignment, the machine must generate the appropriate code. Boundary alignment is specified by the words SYNC or SYNCHRONIZED, as shown below:

```
WORKING-STORAGE SECTION.
01   MISC-FIELDS.
     03   TOTAL-AREA       PIC 999V99 COMP SYNC.
```

SYNC should *not* be used with packed (COMP-3) items nor should it be used within the incoming or outgoing record areas. Check your machine to see what effect this clause has on internal efficiency.

On-line processing statements

In Chapter 2 you saw an example of on-line, screen-oriented processing using the DISPLAY and ACCEPT statements. The operation of these statements varies greatly, depending upon whether you are on a microcomputer or on a larger machine. In the discussion that follows, you will first see how these statements are used on the minicomputers and mainframe computers. Then, some of the commonly found implementations on microcomputers will be discussed. Since the exact operation of these statements is highly dependent upon the version of COBOL used, you should check your system manual first.

The DISPLAY statement

The DISPLAY statement is used to output a *small amount* of data to an output device.

$$\underline{\text{DISPLAY}} \left\{ \begin{matrix} \text{identifier-1} \\ \text{literal-1} \end{matrix} \right\} \ldots \left\{ \begin{matrix} \text{identifier-n} \\ \text{literal-n} \end{matrix} \right\} \ldots [\underline{\text{UPON}}\ \text{mnemonic-name}]$$

On batch-oriented systems the statement

```
DISPLAY 'END OF PROGRAM'
```

will direct the output to the system printer, while on terminal-oriented systems the output will be to the user's terminal device. As indicated by the statement format, combinations of literals and identifiers may be used in the output message, and numeric fields must be in DISPLAY format. However, the system does not automatically add space between the items. The programmer is responsible to do so either by including it within the literal or by using the figurative constant SPACE:

```
DISPLAY 'THE ANSWER ISb' FIELD-A.
```

or

```
DISPLAY 'THE ANSWER IS' SPACE FIELD-A.
```

If the UPON option is used, most systems require that the named device be specified in the SPECIAL-NAMES area. Some systems use the reserved word CONSOLE to specify the designated system operator console device:

```
DISPLAY 'END OF FIRST RUN' UPON CONSOLE.
```

or

```
SPECIAL-NAMES.
    CONSOLE IS SYS-VIDEO.
      .
      .
      .
    DISPLAY 'END OF FIRST RUN' UPON SYS-VIDEO.
```

Perhaps the most important characteristic of the DISPLAY statement is that it is designed for *low-volume* output. It is *not* designed to take the place of the WRITE statement, which handles high-volume output. Note that with DISPLAY, you are not obligated to set up a file (SELECT . . . FD . . . 01). If WRITE and DISPLAY both are on the same output device, particularly if the statements are intermixed, there is a possibility that the output may not be in the same order that was anticipated.

There are two major uses of DISPLAY: first, as shown above, to transmit messages to the operator console, and second, as an aid in debugging a program. In complex programs involving many loops, it is sometimes difficult to tell exactly where the program failed. DISPLAY statements can be inserted to print short messages that help trace the path of the program up to the point of failure. Then, when the program is corrected, the DISPLAY statements are removed:

```
DISPLAY 'COUNTER =' COUNTER-A.
DISPLAY 'SWITCH ONE EQUALS' SWITCH-ONE.
```

Traditionally, microcomputer systems have made far heavier use of the video screen than other systems. Indeed, some systems do not even have a printer, which means that virtually all communication is done via the screen. On these systems, the DISPLAY and ACCEPT statements have been expanded to include a rich set of options. One of the most common options is that of allowing the output data to be displayed on a particular line (normally lines 1 through 24 from top to bottom of the screen). If LINE is not specified, the data are displayed on the next line below the current position of the screen *cursor* or *pointer:*

```
DISPLAY 'WELCOME TO COBOL' LINE 13.
```

Another very handy option allows the programmer to ERASE the contents of the screen before displaying the current message. As with other possibilities you will see, the options may be combined within a single statement:

```
DISPLAY 'WELCOME TO COBOL' LINE 13 ERASE.
```

Another option, called POSITION, allows the programmer to position the output data to a specific column or position across the screen. If the position is omitted, output begins at the leftmost screen position:

```
DISPLAY 'HI', LINE 9, POSITION 7.
```

Some machines allow the programmer to specify that the displayed message blink on and off:

```
DISPLAY 'HI', LINE 9, POSITION 7, BLINK.
```

Other options include:

REVERSE—causes the message to be displayed in reverse video format.
BEEP—causes the system to emit a "beep" sound prior to the display of the data.
HIGH/LOW—indicates the specified light intensity of the displayed material. (If HIGH or LOW is not specified, the system assumes HIGH.)
SIZE—specifies the physical size of the displayed material and overrides the PICTURE entry that may be associated with the field. If

you are displaying a figurative constant such as ZERO, use the SIZE option. DISPLAY ZEROS, SIZE 10.

UNIT—The UNIT phrase, if used, *must* appear first in the DISPLAY statement. (In theory, all other entries may be written in any order, but you are urged to experiment with the various combinations.) In a multi-terminal system the UNIT phrase directs the displayed material to a specific device. If UNIT is omitted, the output is always to the unit that executed the program.

```
DISPLAY ACCT-NBR SIZE 6 BLINK.
DISPLAY FIELD-01 LINE 3 POSITION 6 REVERSE.
DISPLAY 'HI' LINE 12 FIELD-1 POSITION 23.
```

The ACCEPT statement

The ACCEPT statement is a close "cousin" of the DISPLAY statement and, as you saw in Chapter 2, ACCEPT is used to enter a low volume of data from the designated device. It has two formats:

Format 1:

$$\underline{\text{ACCEPT}} \text{ identifier } [\underline{\text{FROM}} \text{ mnemonic name}]$$

Format 2:

$$\underline{\text{ACCEPT}} \text{ identifier } \underline{\text{FROM}} \left\{ \begin{array}{l} \text{DATE} \\ \text{DAY} \\ \text{TIME} \end{array} \right\}$$

Format 1 is commonly used with on-line systems where data are entered into the specified field from the user console. The FROM option is more commonly used for batch processing systems to enter data from the system console. In either case, ACCEPT is most often preceded by a DISPLAY statement that delivers a prompt message to the user:

```
WORKING-STORAGE SECTION.
77  CLASS-CODE          PIC 99.
      .
      .
      .
PROCEDURE DIVISION.
      .
      .
      .

    DISPLAY 'ENTER A TWO-DIGIT CLASS CODE'.
    DISPLAY 'WHERE 01 IS A FRESHMAN; 02 IS A SOPHOMORE'.
    DISPLAY '03 IS A JUNIOR AND 04 IS A SENIOR'.
    ACCEPT CLASS-CODE.
```

If the mnemonic is used, it must first be defined in the SPECIAL-NAMES area.

```
SPECIAL-NAMES.
    CONSOLE IS VIDEO-SCREEN.
    .
    .
    .
WORKING-STORAGE SECTION.
77  STARTING-DATE       PIC 9(6).
    .
    .
    .
PROCEDURE DIVISION.
    .
    .
    .
    DISPLAY 'ENTER STARTING DATE IN FORMAT MMDDYY'.
    ACCEPT STARTING-DATE FROM VIDEO-SCREEN.
```

When entering numeric data, it is imperative that the data values be entered with strict regard to the format in which they were established. For example, if COUNTER-MAX were established as

```
77  COUNTER-MAX         PIC 999.
```

then an entry value of 43 *must* be entered as 043, *not* as 43. The same is true for dollar and cents fields as shown below:

```
77  PAY-RATE            PIC 999V99.
```

A rate of $9.50 per hour is entered as 00950. Although the ACCEPT statement can contain multiple operands, you are advised to ACCEPT only one data item at a time.

The second format of the ACCEPT statement enables the programmer to access today's date which is available within the system software. Note that the DATE, DAY, and TIME fields are pre-defined, which means that the programmer *cannot* create these fields in the DATA DIVISION. The most commonly used one is DATE, which is six digits long in the format YYMMDD:

```
WORKING-STORAGE SECTION.
01  MISC-FIELDS.
    03  DATE-IN.
        05  YEAR-IN     PIC 99.
        05  MONTH-IN    PIC 99.
        05  DAY-IN      PIC 99.
    .
    .
    .
    ACCEPT DATE-IN FROM DATE.
```

On microcomputer systems the ACCEPT statement is likely to have many of the same options that are available with DISPLAY (LINE, POSITION, SIZE, ERASE, HIGH, LOW, BLINK, REVERSE), plus a few others. Check your system to see what is available.

COBOL can be used on microcomputers also!

Manipulating data on-line

At this point we can put together an on-line program that will allow us to create a file of data on-line—that is, by means of values entered through use of the DISPLAY and ACCEPT statements. In this example, we wish to create an inventory file containing records with the following format.

part name	part number	cost price	retail	markup

The first three fields will be entered by ACCEPTing the values from the console, while the last two values will be calculated by the program. The retail price will be calculated as the cost price plus a markup, in this case 80% of the cost price. Thus an item costing $2.00 would have a retail price of $2.00 + 80% × 2.00 = $3.60.

The file will be written to magnetic storage media (tape or disk) as designated by the ASSIGN part of the SELECT entry. Figure 6-3 illustrates the process while Figure 6-4 shows the program.

One of the most important points of this example is seeing how easy it is to create a sequential file on disk or tape. Creating the file involves three parts of our COBOL program.

1. First, the system must, in some way, be informed of the *external name* you wish to associate with the file you are creating. The *internal file name* is INVENTORY-FILE, but the system must have some way of linking the internal file name and the device to which the file is ASSIGNed to the external file name. Unfortunately, the method by which this is done is highly dependent upon the machine being used. Some of the more common methods are shown below, but check the manual on your system for specific details.

FIGURE 6-3

Schematic: Creating a file on-line

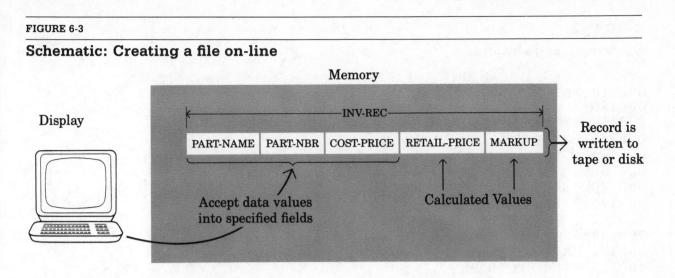

On some systems, the external file name is indicated by a file description such as shown in the program:

```
SELECT INVENTORY-FILE ASSIGN TO disk device.
        .
        .
        .

FD  INVENTORY-FILE
    LABEL RECORD IS STANDARD
    VALUE OF FILE-ID IS 'INV-FILE'
```

or

```
VALUE OF FILE IS 'INV-FILE'
        .
        .
        .
```

On many microcomputers, the external file name is indicated within the SELECT:

```
SELECT INVENTORY-FILE
       ASSIGN TO ------ 'INV-FILE'.
```

Many IBM and IBM look-alike systems use the SELECT entry for this purpose but require further entries outside of the program:

```
SELECT INVENTORY-FILE
       ASSIGN TO SYSXXX-UT-XXXX-S.
```

Normally, the program entry above would require the assignment of an external file name by means of a job control entry via some input device.

2. The next part of the file creation process occurs when the file is OPENed as OUTPUT. At this point the system "knows" that the file is being created and, therefore, to create (write) the file label 'INV-FILE' in a STANDARD bit format. In addition, since the file was opened as output, the system "authorizes" the use of the WRITE statement for that file.

FIGURE 6-4

Creating a sequential file

```
000100 IDENTIFICATION DIVISION.
000110 PROGRAM-ID. LOADER1.
000120*
000130 ENVIRONMENT DIVISION.
000140 CONFIGURATION SECTION.
000150 SOURCE-COMPUTER. - - -.
000160 OBJECT-COMPUTER. - - -.
000170 INPUT-OUTPUT SECTION.
000180 FILE-CONTROL.
000190      SELECT INVENTORY-FILE ASSIGN TO - - -.
000200*
000210 DATA DIVISION.
000220 FILE SECTION.
000230 FD  INVENTORY-FILE
000240      LABEL RECORD IS STANDARD
000250      VALUE OF FILE-ID IS 'INV-FILE'
000260      DATA RECORD IS INV-RECORD.
000270 01  INV-RECORD.
000280     03   PART-NAME              PIC X(10).
000290     03   PART-NBR               PIC 9(05).
000300     03   COST-PRICE             PIC 999V99.
000310     03   RETAIL-PRICE           PIC 999V99.
000320     03   MARKUP                 PIC 999V99.
000330 WORKING-STORAGE SECTION.
000340 01  MISC-FIELDS.
000350     03   EOF-INDICATOR          PIC 9 VALUE ZERO.
000360     03   EIGHTY-PERCENT         PIC V99 VALUE .80.
000370*
000380 PROCEDURE DIVISION.
000390 CONTROL-MODULE.
000400      OPEN OUTPUT INVENTORY-FILE.
000410      PERFORM 010-ENTER-DATA
000420          UNTIL EOF-INDICATOR = 1.
000430      CLOSE INVENTORY-FILE.
000440      STOP RUN.
000450 010-ENTER-DATA.
000460      DISPLAY 'ENTER 10 CHARACTER PART NAME'.
000470      ACCEPT PART-NAME.
000480      DISPLAY 'ENTER 5 DIGIT PART NUMBER'.
000490      ACCEPT PART-NBR.
000500      DISPLAY 'ENTER 5 DIGIT COST PRICE'.
000510      ACCEPT COST-PRICE.
000520      COMPUTE MARKUP ROUNDED = COST-PRICE * EIGHTY-PERCENT.
000530      COMPUTE RETAIL-PRICE = COST-PRICE  + MARKUP.
000540      WRITE INV-RECORD.
000550      DISPLAY 'IF LAST RECORD, ENTER 1; ELSE ENTER ZERO'.
000560      ACCEPT EOF-INDICATOR.
```

Had the file been OPENed as INPUT, the system would have looked for the file with a label of 'INV-FILE' and would have authorized the use of the READ statement for that file.

3. The third part of the process takes place when the data records are written to the file by means of the WRITE statement. The CLOSE statement *writes* the End-of-File marker, since this is an OUTPUT file.

Throughout the text you will see the use of VALUE OF FILE-ID IS whenever magnetic media files are used. In essence this should be considered as a sort of "generic" entry that will undoubtedly be different on your machine. You should, however, realize the use and importance of this line in the program. A few other points about the program are worth noting.

1. In line 360 our value of 80% was created as a constant that, in accordance with the chapter material, avoids the problem of using a literal in the COMPUTE statement.
2. Values are entered via DISPLAY (as a prompt message) and ACCEPT and COMPUTE statements are used to fill in the rest of the fields in INV-RECORD.
3. The INV-RECORD is written to auxiliary storage via the WRITE statement. Since output is *not* to the printer, the AFTER ADVANCING clause is omitted.
4. An indicator (EOF-INDICATOR) is used to get out of the enter-and-write loop.

COMMON ERRORS

The statements presented in this chapter tend to cause very few errors. The MOVE statement is normally not a problem since most versions of COBOL will flag an illegal MOVE operation during the compiling process. Conceivably you could get into trouble with MOVE CORRESPONDING as some systems will not move sub-fields properly.

```
01   RECORD-A.
     03   FIELD-A        PIC 999.
     03   NAME-IN.
          05   FIRST-NAME PIC X(10).
          05   LAST-NAME  PIC X(10).
     03   FIELD-B        PIC XXX.
01   RECORD-A-OUT.
     03   FILLER         PIC X.
     03   FILLER         PIC X(10) VALUE SPACES.
     03   NAME-OUT.
          05   LAST-NAME  PIC X(10).
          05   FILLER     PIC X(5) VALUE SPACES.
          05   FIRST-NAME PIC X(10).
     03   FILLER         PIC X(10) VALUE SPACES.
     03   FIELD-A        PIC 999.
     03   FILLER         PIC X(10) VALUE SPACES.
     03   FIELD-B        PIC XXX.
     03   FILLER         PIC X(59) VALUE SPACES.
```

The statement

```
MOVE CORRESPONDING RECORD-A TO RECORD-A-OUT
```

may not move the NAME fields in the arrangement just presented.

Another source of error was discussed in the chapter, but you should be reminded about it again. Resist the urge to make changes in the PIC entry when fields are converted to packed (or binary format). A seven-digit DISPLAY field is described as

```
FIELD-A                    PIC 9(7)
```

and a seven-digit packed field will have the same PIC entry. Remember that PIC tells the system the number of *digits* in the field and the location of the assumed decimal point. DISPLAY, COMP-3, or COMP tells the format, which is independent of the PIC:

```
FIELD-A                    PIC 9(7) COMP-3.
```

PROGRAMMING TIPS

For a moment, let's continue an earlier discussion about what to do when your program won't work. Recall that what the whole thing may boil down to is the laborious task of desk checking—that is, playing computer with your program statements. Obviously, you should not have to do this with every statement—only those in the module(s) you suspect of causing the problem. Application of appropriate "horse sense" logic will allow you to narrow down the area of search. If you still cannot find the error, this is a good time to insert DISPLAY statements at strategic points in the module(s). For example, you may suspect that a counter used to control a program loop is not working properly. To see what is happening you may wish to display the value of the counter *before and after* exiting from the module in question.

Another possibility is that a module seems to be executed more often than it should be. In this case, set up an extra counter and add one to it each time the module is executed. Then, at the appropriate time, DISPLAY the counter value.

Sometimes a specific field will not contain the size of answer you were expecting. DISPLAY statements can be used to record the field contents before and after or even in between a series of arithmetic operations. Use DISPLAY to isolate the source of the error. (Also, don't forget to remove the DISPLAY statements once the error has been found and corrected.)

One of the convenient features of top-down program design is that your *general* program logic can be tested without getting bogged down in the details of lesser or lower modules. Suppose we have the example of a payroll application where we are interested in overtime pay calculations. At this point in our coding we are concerned about the calculations in module B200 and reach the point where we will test to see if overtime pay should be included. Should we stop work on module B300 and code the overtime module A400 and then come back to the higher level module? Should we even be concerned about A400 now? Probably not; we can take care of the situation by using a *stub* module. Note that in the following example we will PERFORM a module that has not yet been written fully. The module will really be a stub of the real module and will contain only a DISPLAY statement:

```
B300-PAY-CALCULATIONS.
    ------
    ------
    IF HOURS-WORKED IS GREATER THAN 40
        PERFORM A-400-OVERTIME-PAY
    ELSE
        ------
    .
    .
    .
A-400-OVERTIME-PAY.
    DISPLAY 'A-400 OVERTIME PAY MODULE EXECUTED'.
```

With this arrangement, and knowing our sample data, we can verify our program logic—that we have entered the lower level module whenever HOURS-WORKED was greater than 40. After we are satisfied that the B300-PAY-CALCULATIONS module is working, then we can drop down to code the A-400 module.

The chapter discussed the various formats that numeric data may take and the effect these formats may have on internal efficiency. Some other points of efficiency are listed below.

Make binary items less than five digits if possible; if not, make them less than nine, as this is a more efficient format on IBM or byte-oriented machines.

When using VALUE with numeric fields, indicate a positive number with a plus sign and include the S in the PICTURE entry.

Example:

```
03  PI PIC S9V99 VALUE +3.14 COMP.
```

Except where COMP is desired, numeric fields should be specified as COMP-3 and include S in the PIC entry. In addition, it is more efficient to specify an odd number of digits when using COMP-3.

SELF-STUDY: QUESTIONS AND ANSWERS

1. COBOL allows the use of literals in MOVE, IF, and arithmetic statements and yet you indicate that these literal values should be set up in WORKING-STORAGE, not created in the PROCEDURE DIVISION. This procedure seems like a lot of extra effort for something that COBOL does easily.

Answer: You are right that it probably is easier to use literals now in your program, rather than do as I suggested. For classroom programs or short programs in general, literals are perfectly acceptable. For long programs or those where the literal data may need to be changed frequently, they should be established as indicated. It may save a great amount of program maintenance in the future.

2. You said something to the effect that the programmer should be careful in intermixing WRITE and DISPLAY statements because the system might not produce correct data. Why is this a problem?

Answer: Input and output operations actually are very complex activities on modern computers. In order to make printing more efficient, many systems use temporary storage areas, called buffers. If the DISPLAY statement is intermixed with WRITE, the movement of data records to and from the buffer areas may be interrupted with the result that output may not be what was expected. The problem does not arise when data are displayed to an on-line terminal.

3. Creating a data file as shown in the chapter seemed very simple. It seems like there should be a different WRITE statement for this purpose.

Answer: You are correct that the operation, as far as the programmer is concerned, is simple. As far as the WRITE statement goes, remember that it is a general output statement that can be used with a variety of devices.

4. When I do use the COMPUTE statement, do all the fields have to be of the same USAGE format—such as all DISPLAY—or all COMPUTATIONAL-3?

Answer: No, the fields used in any arithmetic operation can be of a mixture of USAGE formats. However, as discussed in the chapter, the system must convert those fields that are in DISPLAY format to a format usable in arithmetic operations. You can provide for greater machine efficiency by doing these conversions yourself prior to executing the specific arithmetic operation of COMPUTE, ADD, and so on.

CHAPTER TERMS

ACCEPT
binary data format
bits
buffer
byte
COMPUTATIONAL (binary)
COMPUTATIONAL-3 (packed)

DISPLAY
duplicate names
group moves
MOVE CORRESPONDING
nibble
packed data format
qualifiers (duplicate names)
SYNCHRONIZED (SYNC)

EXERCISES

1. Given:

```
01  DATA1.
    03  FIELD-A     PIC XX.
    03  FIELD-B     PIC XXXX.
01  DATA2.
    03  FIELD-A     PIC XX.
    03  FIELD-C     PIC XXXX.
```

To move data as indicated, fill in this statement.

MOVE FIELD-A _____ _____ TO FIELD-A _____ _____ .

2. Do the same as in Exercise 1 without using qualifiers.

3. Why might it be better to put constants in the WORKING-STORAGE SECTION rather than in the main line code?

4. Data which are defined as PIC 999 are 3 numeric characters in _____ format.

5. Packed format is noted by the entry _____ .

6. What is wrong with this statement?

```
03  FIELD-C     PIC 9V999 COMP-3 SYNC.
```

7. The DISPLAY *statement* should be used for _____ volume of data output.

8. Complete this statement.

```
ACCEPT DAY-MONTH-YEAR FROM _____ .
```

9. True/False—The storage required for PIC 9(9) and PIC 9(9) COMP-3 is the same.

10. True/False—The storage required for PIC 9(9) COMP and PIC 9(9) COMP-3 is the same.

11. Write the WORKING-STORAGE entries for the following fields where arithmetic manipulations are going to be performed.
    a. A three-position total area called NO-OF-SALES; display format.
    b. A five-position total area called COUNTER-1; display format.
    c. A seven-position total area for the storage of dollar and cents data; packed format.
    d. A six-position total area for the storage of dollar and cents data; binary format.
    e. An eight-position total area for the storage of dollar and cents data; display format.
    f. A six-position dollar and cents area in packed format into which a data value will be moved.

12. Write the WORKING-STORAGE entries for the following fields.
    a. A field called KONSTANT that contains the value 763.714 in packed format.
    b. A field called FUDGE-AMT that contains the value 21.65 in binary format.
    c. A field called ONE-AMT that contains the value 9 in packed format.
    d. A three-digit field that contains the value 6 in binary format.
    e. An alphanumeric field containing the message BAD INPUT DATA.
    f. A four-position numeric area in binary format into which a data value will be moved.

13. Indicate how many bytes of storage the following fields will occupy.
    a. A six-digit packed field
    b. A seven-digit packed field
    c. A two-digit packed field
    d. A five-digit binary field
    e. An eight-digit binary field
    f. A three-digit binary field.

14. Write the code that will allow the following input fields to be efficiently manipulated in arithmetic operations for your machine.
    a. FIELD-A   PIC 99.
       FIELD-B   PIC 99V9.
    b. FIELD-A   PIC V9999.
       FIELD-B   PIC 9999V99.
    c. FIELD-A   PIC 9.
       FIELD-B   PIC 9V9.

15. Write DISPLAY statements for the following output.
    a. 'GOLLY' to be displayed on the video screen.
    b. 'GOLLY' to be displayed on the printer.
    c. 'ANSWER A IS' FIELD-A to be displayed on line 16, starting at position four.
    d. Same as part c above, but provide for erasing the previous contents of the screen.
    e. Assume the screen width is 80 characters. Display the words GONZALES COMPANY centered on a 24-line screen.

16. Write the code to display the following values on the system console device.
    a. FIELD-A   PIC 999V99 COMP-3.
    b. FIELD-B   PIC 999V9 COMP.

17. The chapter loader program (Figure 6-3) provided for the entry of the part name, part number, and cost price. Write the coding that will test to see that the data values were entered correctly. Allow for a second "try" at entering each of the values before aborting the entry process. Be sure that your DISPLAY statements explain the process completely since new people may be involved in the data entry process.

Chapter 7
Control Breaks and Programmed Switches

CHAPTER OUTLINE

Control breaks
    Minor breaks
    Higher level breaks
Summary or group printing
Programmed switches
Group indication
Common errors
Programming tips
Self-study: Questions and answers
Chapter terms
Exercises

LEARNING OBJECTIVES

1. To learn some of the different formats that printed reports can take using control break processing.

2. To learn how to set up the program logic to handle minor and intermediate control breaks.

3. To understand the difference between—and to program for—detail and group printed reports.

4. To see how programmed switches can be used to prepare group indicated reports.

5. To see how the REDEFINES entry is used.

$\mathbf{A}$ great many report-type problems involve simple totals (running totals) that are accumulated during the execution of each program loop and printed in the ending stage of the program. Some types of reports, however, require that in addition to final totals, subtotals be accumulated and printed at various points within the body of the report. This subtotaling and printing activity is triggered by what are known as *control breaks*.

Control breaks

In order to understand how control breaks work, we will set up the following situation. Suppose you have been asked to prepare a sales report using a disk data file that has the following record format:

Filler	Sales Department	Filler	Sales Amount XXX.XX
1–5	6–7	8–9	10–14

You are to prepare a report that lists the sales by department number (you may assume that the data records have already been sorted into ascending order based on Sales Department number). In addition to a straight sales listing, however, your program is to print a subtotal for each department plus a final total of all departments. Figure 7-1 shows how the output should look.

FIGURE 7-1

Printed output format

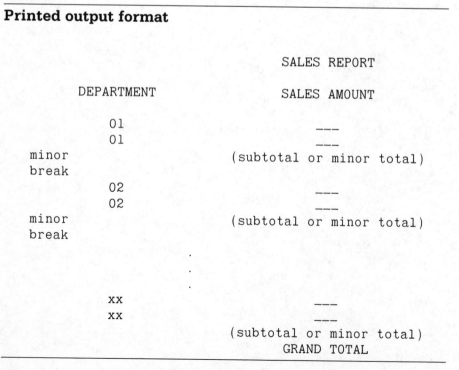

The actual data records we will use and the control breaks that will be generated are shown in Figure 7-2. Note that a control break can occur even if the department group contains only a single record (as in the case of departments 03 and 09). In addition, a control break always occurs after the last record in the file. When a break is detected, the program will print what is called a *minor total*, which is the total of the sales in that particular department.

Minor breaks

Obviously, we need something that will allow us to break out of the traditional Read-Total-Print pattern used in traditional listing-type programs. Our break will be based on the department number field and, since there is only one level of break, it is called a *minor* break. The strategy to be used in our control break problem is one of comparing the department number of the *previous* record against the department number of the *current* record. To do this means we will have to set up a field (OLD-DEPT-NBR) in WORKING-STORAGE specifically for this purpose. As usual, we will use an

FIGURE 7-2

Control breaks

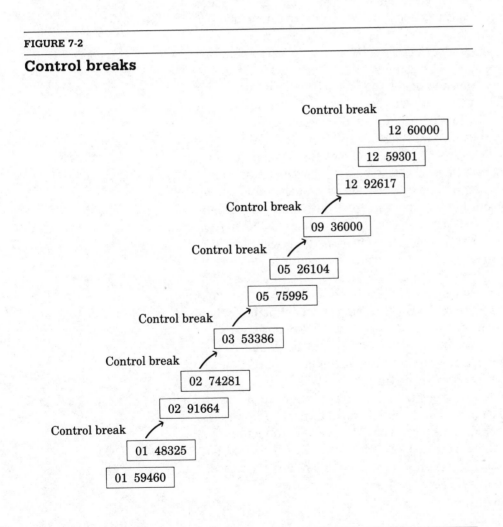

EOF-INDICATOR field (often called a *flag* or *switch*) plus fields in which to accumulate the minor and final totals:

```
WORKING-STORAGE SECTION.
01   MISC-FIELDS.
     03   EOF-INDICATOR     PIC X(03) VALUE 'OFF'.
     03   OLD-DEPT-NBR      PIC 9(02).
     03   MINOR-TOTAL       PIC 9(05)V99 VALUE ZERO.
     03   GRAND-TOTAL       PIC 9(06)V99 VALUE ZERO.
```

As indicated earlier, our strategy is straightforward: Simply compare the current and previous department number values to see whether a minor break routine that will print the department subtotal should be executed. There is one catch in the plan and that concerns the first record. Against what are we to compare it? The incoming record will place the department number in the field called DEPARTMENT; but if we try to compare it against OLD-DEPT-NBR, our program will come to an abnormal end (*abend*) because the OLD-DEPT-NBR field would not contain valid characters. Even if we had said VALUE zero for this field, we would not be improving the situation, because the comparison would be 00 against 01 and that *would* trigger a minor break process. The solution lies in the A100-OPENER paragraph. Here we execute our regular priming READ and move the department number from the first record to the OLD-DEPT-NBR field in WORKING-STORAGE. Our comparison in the main processing module A200-MAIN-PROCESSING for this first record will always result in an equal condition. But this is all right at this point, since we do *not* want to trigger the minor break routine. From then on, however, we *do* want to trigger the break routine whenever an unequal department comparison is detected. Pseudocode, Warnier/Orr, and flowchart specifications are shown in Figures 7-3–7-5.

The logic in the main processing module follows the normal process-write-read pattern, with one exception. The MOVE DEPARTMENT TO OLD-DEPT-NBR statement in the A100-OPENER paragraph took care of the department number comparison problem for the first record. However, every time a regular record is processed the current department number must be moved to WORKING-STORAGE, in preparation for the comparison that will take place when the *next* record is processed. This arrangement results in the department number from the first record being moved to OLD-DEPT-NBR *twice*, but it is a small price to pay for setting up the logic for the rest of the comparisons.

The minor break routine, triggered by the unequal department number comparison, will move the minor total to the print line. Then, since we wish to accumulate a final total, the MINOR-TOTAL value will be added to the GRAND-TOTAL field. This act of adding totals into a higher level total is known as *rolling totals*. Immediately after rolling the total we will clear the MINOR-TOTAL field in preparation for summing the values from the group of entries in the next department. The final point to notice is that after the B100-MINOR-BREAK-ROUTINE is PERFORMed, control returns to the MOVE statement in the A200-MAIN-PROCESSING module. This point is critical because if we did not return there, the first record of each new group would not get processed.

The file description for our incoming disk file is as follows:

```
FD  SALES-FILE
    LABEL RECORD IS STANDARD
    VALUE OF FILE-ID IS 'SALES DATA'
    DATA RECORD IS SALES-REC.
```

Since the file is on magnetic media, we have used VALUE OF FILE-ID IS 'SALES DATA' to tell the system the external name of the data file being used. (Note: There are at least three ways that this information can be conveyed to the system. Your system may use a method other than that shown.) Figures 7-6 and 7-7 show the complete program and the output.

FIGURE 7-3

Pseudocode: Minor break problem

```
CONTROL-MODULE
    PERFORM A100-OPENER
    PERFORM A200-MAIN-PROCESSING UNTIL end of file indicator = ON
    PERFORM B100-MINOR-BREAK-ROUTINE
    PERFORM A300-CLOSER
    STOP RUN


A100-OPENER
    Open the files
    Write a heading line
    Read first record, at end move ON to end of file indicator
    Move department number to storage


A200-MAIN-PROCESSING
    IF incoming department number is not = storage department number
        PERFORM B100-MINOR-BREAK-ROUTINE
    ENDIF
    Move incoming department number to storage
    Add to minor total
    Move fields to print area
    Write a report line on the printer
    Read a new record at end move ON to end of file indicator


B100-MINOR-BREAK-ROUTINE
    Move minor total to print area
    Add minor total to grand total
    Clear minor total area
    Write a minor total line on the printer


A300-CLOSER
    Move grand total to print area
    Write a grand total line on the printer
    Close the files
```

FIGURE 7-4

Warnier/Orr diagram—Control break problem

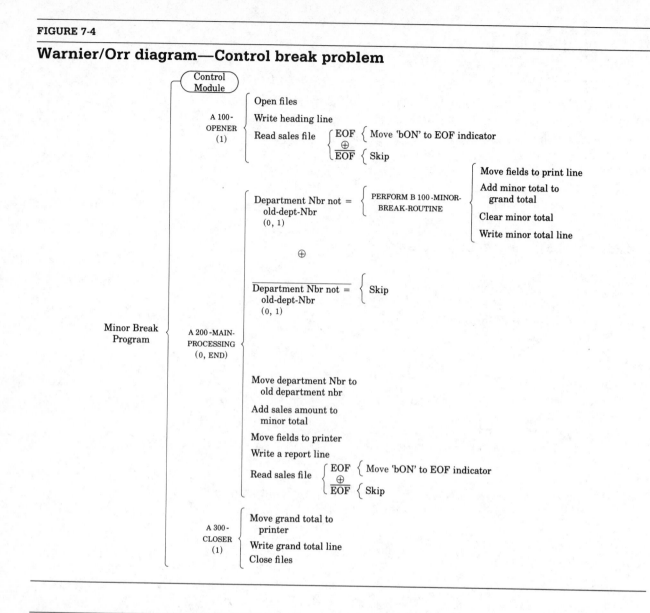

Higher level breaks

In the previous program we used the change in department numbers to activate the printing of minor totals. A report may have several levels of totals, and our next example illustrates how you can deal with both a minor-level and an intermediate-level break. We will start by revising the incoming data to include a sales territory number in columns 1 through 3 (Figure 7-8). As before, the success or failure of the program rests on the fact that the data records are sorted into groups by department number *within* the territory number. Our strategy will be much the same as before, except now a change in territory number will trigger the printing of *both* a minor

FIGURE 7-5

Flowchart: Minor break problem

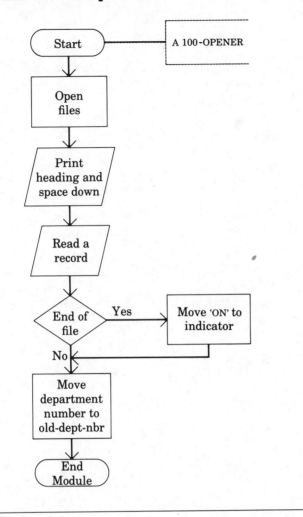

continued

and an intermediate total. An intermediate total will be the sum of the minor totals within that control group. Whenever a minor break is detected, the department total will be printed and rolled into an intermediate total field. Whenever an intermediate break is detected, a minor total will be printed and followed by an intermediate total. In addition, our program will print a single asterisk next to the minor total value and two asterisks next to each intermediate total. A pattern of this type is commonly used in business so that various levels of totals can be recognized quickly.

FIGURE 7-5

continued

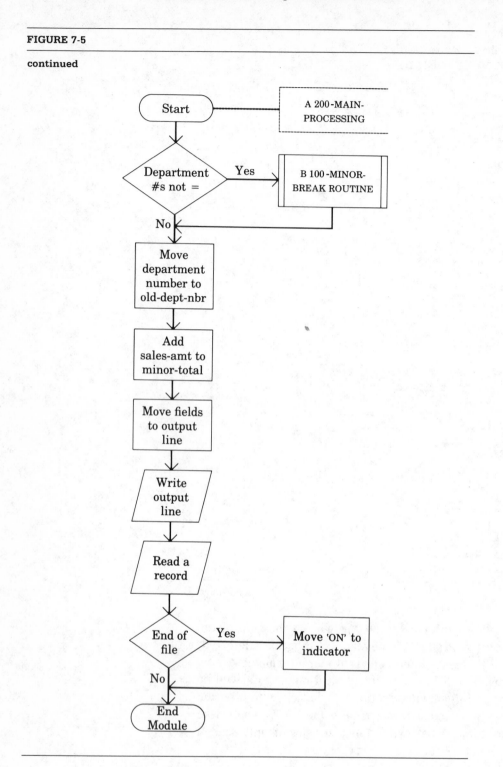

FIGURE 7.5

continued

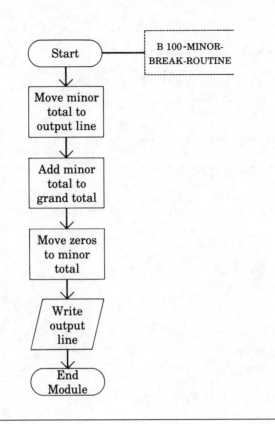

In modifying the previous program to take care of the possibility of both a minor and an intermediate break, we will have to expand our logic slightly. One thing we must do is set up an OLD-TERRITORY-NBR field in WORKING-STORAGE and move in the territory number from the first record (A100-OPENER). A second point is after the last record has been processed and control returned to the CONTROL-MODULE, we will have to perform *both* the minor and intermediate break routines. Also, our testing statement in the A200-MAIN-PROCESSING routine will have to be expanded to take care of testing for changes in either or both the territory and department numbers. One easy way to do this is by means of a nested IF statement:

```
IF TERRITORY IS NOT EQUAL TO OLD-TERRITORY-NBR
    PERFORM B200-INTERMEDIATE-BREAK
ELSE
    IF DEPARTMENT IS NOT EQUAL TO OLD-DEPT-NBR
        PERFORM B100-MINOR-BREAK-ROUTINE.
```

FIGURE 7-6

Minor control break

```
000100 IDENTIFICATION DIVISION.
000110 PROGRAM-ID.   BREAK1.
000120*****************************************
000130*                                        *
000140*   THIS PROGRAM PROVIDES FOR A DETAIL   *
000150*   PRINTED REPORT WITH A MINOR TOTAL    *
000160*   WHENEVER A CHANGE IN DEPARTMENT      *
000170*   NUMBER IS ENCOUNTERED.  A FINAL      *
000180*   OR GRAND TOTAL IS ALSO PRINTED.      *
000190*                                        *
000200*****************************************
000210 ENVIRONMENT DIVISION.
000220 CONFIGURATION SECTION.
000230 SOURCE-COMPUTER. - - -.
000240 OBJECT-COMPUTER. - - -.
000250 INPUT-OUTPUT SECTION.
000260 FILE-CONTROL.
000270      SELECT SALES-FILE ASSIGN TO - - -.
000280      SELECT PRINT-FILE ASSIGN TO - - -.
000290*
000300 DATA DIVISION.
000310 FILE SECTION.
000320 FD   SALES-FILE
000330      LABEL RECORD IS STANDARD
000340      VALUE OF FILE-ID IS 'SALES-DATA'
000350      DATA RECORD IS SALES-REC.
000360 01   SALES-REC               PIC X(14).
000370 FD   PRINT-FILE
000380      LABEL RECORD IS OMITTED
000390      DATA RECORD IS PRINT-LINE.
000400 01   PRINT-LINE              PIC X(121).
000410 WORKING-STORAGE SECTION.
000420 01   MISC-FIELDS.
000430      03   EOF-INDICATOR      PIC X(03) VALUE 'OFF'.
000440      03   OLD-DEPT-NBR       PIC 9(02).
000450      03   MINOR-TOTAL        PIC 9(05)V99 VALUE ZERO.
000460      03   GRAND-TOTAL        PIC 9(06)V99 VALUE ZERO.
000470 01   SALES-REC-WS.
000480      03   FILLER             PIC X(05).
000490      03   DEPARTMENT         PIC 9(02).
000500      03   FILLER             PIC X(02).
000510      03   SALES-AMT          PIC 999V99.
000520 01   HEAD-LINE.
000530      02   FILLER             PIC X.
000540      03   FILLER             PIC X(31) VALUE SPACES.
000550      03   FILLER             PIC X(10) VALUE 'DEPARTMENT'.
000560      03   FILLER             PIC X(10) VALUE SPACES.
000570      03   FILLER             PIC X(12) VALUE 'SALES AMOUNT'.
000580      03   FILLER             PIC X(57) VALUE SPACES.
000590 01   REPORT-LINE.
000600      03   FILLER             PIC X.
000610      03   FILLER             PIC X(35) VALUE SPACES.
000620      03   DEPARTMENT-PR      PIC 9(02).
000630      03   FILLER             PIC X(17) VALUE SPACES.
000640      03   SALES-AMT-PR       PIC $$$$.99.
```

FIGURE 7-6

continued

```
000650        03   FILLER              PIC X(59) VALUE SPACES.
000660 01  MINOR-TOTAL-LINE.
000670        03   FILLER              PIC X.
000680        03   FILLER              PIC X(10) VALUE SPACES.
000690        03   FILLER              PIC X(16) VALUE 'DEPARTMENT TOTAL'.
000700        03   FILLER              PIC X(25) VALUE SPACES.
000710        03   MINOR-TOTAL-PR      PIC $(6).99.
000720        03   FILLER              PIC X(59) VALUE SPACES.
000730 01  GRAND-TOTAL-LINE.
000740        03   FILLER              PIC X.
000750        03   FILLER              PIC X(10) VALUE SPACES.
000760        03   FILLER              PIC X(11) VALUE 'FINAL TOTAL'.
000770        03   FILLER              PIC X(31) VALUE SPACES.
000780        03   GRAND-TOTAL-PR      PIC $(7).99.
000790        03   FILLER              PIC X(59) VALUE SPACES.
000800 PROCEDURE DIVISION.
000810 CONTROL-MODULE.
000820      PERFORM A100-OPENER.
000830      PERFORM A200-MAIN-PROCESSING
000840          UNTIL EOF-INDICATOR IS EQUAL TO 'ON'.
000850      PERFORM B100-MINOR-BREAK-ROUTINE.
000860      PERFORM A300-CLOSER.
000870      STOP RUN.
000880 A100-OPENER.
000890      OPEN INPUT SALES-FILE OUTPUT PRINT-FILE.
000900      WRITE PRINT-LINE FROM HEAD-LINE
000910          AFTER ADVANCING PAGE.
000920      MOVE SPACES TO PRINT-LINE.
000930      WRITE PRINT-LINE AFTER ADVANCING 2 LINES.
000940      READ SALES-FILE INTO SALES-REC-WS
000950          AT END MOVE 'ON' TO EOF-INDICATOR.
000960      MOVE DEPARTMENT TO OLD-DEPT-NBR.
000970 A200-MAIN-PROCESSING.
000980      IF DEPARTMENT IS NOT EQUAL TO OLD-DEPT-NBR
000990          PERFORM B100-MINOR-BREAK-ROUTINE.
001000      MOVE DEPARTMENT TO OLD-DEPT-NBR.
001010      ADD SALES-AMT TO MINOR-TOTAL.
001020      MOVE DEPARTMENT TO DEPARTMENT-PR.
001030      MOVE SALES-AMT TO SALES-AMT-PR.
001040      WRITE PRINT-LINE FROM REPORT-LINE
001050          AFTER ADVANCING 1 LINE.
001060      READ SALES-FILE INTO SALES-REC-WS
001070          AT END MOVE 'ON' TO EOF-INDICATOR.
001080 B100-MINOR-BREAK-ROUTINE.
001090      MOVE MINOR-TOTAL TO MINOR-TOTAL-PR.
001100      ADD MINOR-TOTAL TO GRAND-TOTAL.
001110      MOVE ZEROS TO MINOR-TOTAL.
001120      WRITE PRINT-LINE FROM MINOR-TOTAL-LINE
001130          AFTER ADVANCING 2 LINES.
001140      MOVE SPACES TO PRINT-LINE.
001150      WRITE PRINT-LINE AFTER ADVANCING 2 LINES.
001160 A300-CLOSER.
001170      MOVE GRAND-TOTAL TO GRAND-TOTAL-PR.
001180      WRITE PRINT-LINE FROM GRAND-TOTAL-LINE
001190          AFTER ADVANCING 3 LINES.
001200      CLOSE SALES-FILE PRINT-FILE.
```

FIGURE 7-7

Output: Minor break program

	DEPARTMENT	SALES AMOUNT
	01	$594.60
	01	$483.25
MINOR TOTAL		$1077.85
	02	$916.64
	02	$742.81
MINOR TOTAL		$1659.45
	03	$533.86
MINOR TOTAL		$533.86
	05	$759.95
	05	$261.04
MINOR TOTAL		$1020.99
	09	$360.00
MINOR TOTAL		$360.00
	12	$926.17
	12	$593.01
	12	$600.00
MINOR TOTAL		$2119.18
FINAL TOTAL		$6771.33

FIGURE 7-8

Revised data

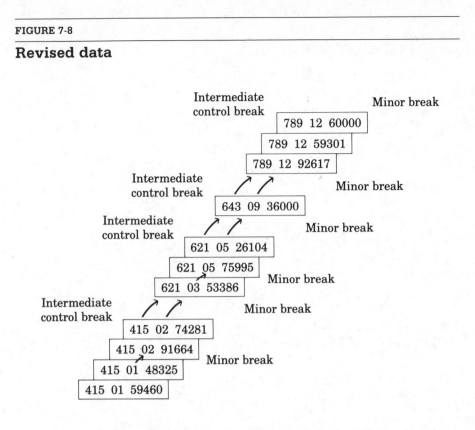

With this arrangement, the program first tests for the intermediate level change, and if there is such a change, the second IF statement is ignored (false condition). The B200-INTERMEDIATE-BREAK paragraph will PERFORM the minor break routine since, by definition in the problem, every intermediate break automatically represents a minor break as well. If an intermediate break is *not* encountered, the nested IF is executed to see if a minor break is called for. If neither break is indicated, the Department and Territory numbers are moved to storage and regular detail line processing takes place. Figures 7-9 and 7-10 illustrate this logic in pseudocode and flowchart formats.

The B100-MINOR-BREAK-ROUTINE will contain only one slight change: The MINOR-TOTAL value will be added to or rolled into the INTERMEDIATE-TOTAL field rather than into a final total as before. The B200-INTERMEDIATE-BREAK paragraph starts by PERFORMing the minor total routine; it then duplicates the actions of the minor break routine at a higher or intermediate level. Figures 7-11 and 7-12 show the program and resulting output.

FIGURE 7-9

Pseudocode specifications: INTERMEDIATE BREAK

```
CONTROL-MODULE
    PERFORM A100-OPENER
    PERFORM A200-MAIN-PROCESSING UNTIL end of file indicator = ON
    PERFORM B200-INTERMEDIATE-BREAK
    PERFORM A300-CLOSER
    STOP RUN


A100-OPENER
    Open the files
    Write a heading line
    Read a disk record at end move ON to end of file indicator
    Move department number to storage
    Move territory number to storage


A200-MAIN-PROCESSING
    IF territory number is not = stored territory number
        PERFORM B200-INTERMEDIATE-ROUTINE
    ELSE
        IF department number is not = stored department number
        PERFORM B100-MINOR-BREAK-ROUTINE
        ENDIF
    ENDIF
    Move department number to storage
    Move territory number to storage
    Add to minor total
    Move disk fields to print area
    Write a report line on the printer
    Read a disk record at end move ON to end of file indicator


B100-MINOR-BREAK-ROUTINE
    Move minor total to print area
    Add minor total to intermediate total
    Clear minor total area
    Write a minor total line on the printer


B200-INTERMEDIATE-BREAK
    PERFORM B100-MINOR-BREAK-ROUTINE
    Move intermediate total to print area
    Add intermediate total to grand total
    Clear intermediate total area
    Write intermediate total on the printer
```

FIGURE 7-10

Flowchart: Intermediate-level break

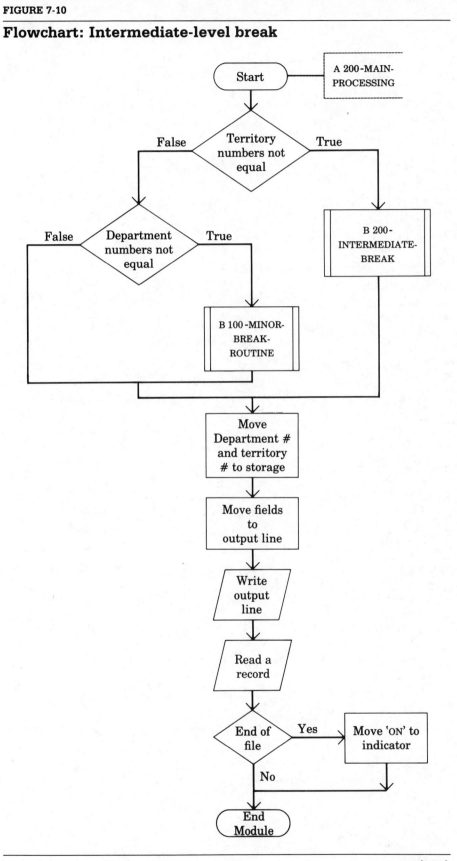

continued

FIGURE 7-10

continued

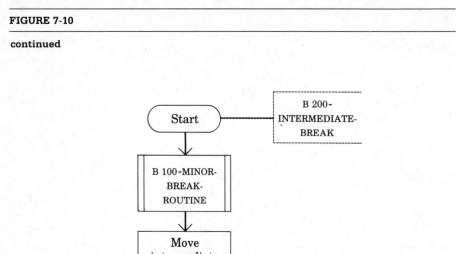

continued

FIGURE 7-10

continued

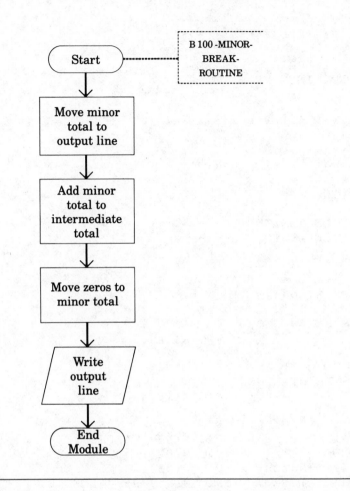

FIGURE 7-11

Intermediate-level break

```
000100 IDENTIFICATION DIVISION.
000110 PROGRAM-ID. BREAK2.
000120**************************************
000130*                                    *
000140*   THIS PROGRAM DETAIL PRINTS A SALES  *
000150*   REPORT WITH MINOR, INTERMEDIATE,    *
000160*   AND FINAL TOTALS.                    *
000170*                                    *
000180**************************************
000190 ENVIRONMENT DIVISION.
000200 CONFIGURATION SECTION.
000210 SOURCE-COMPUTER. - - -.
000220 OBJECT-COMPUTER. - - -.
000230 INPUT-OUTPUT SECTION.
000240 FILE-CONTROL.
000250     SELECT SALES-FILE ASSIGN TO - - -.
000260     SELECT PRINT-FILE ASSIGN TO - - -.
000270 DATA DIVISION.
000280 FILE SECTION.
000290 FD  SALES-FILE
000300     LABEL RECORD IS STANDARD
000310     VALUE OF FILE-ID IS 'SALES-DATA'
000320     DATA RECORD IS SALES-REC.
000330 01  SALES-REC                 PIC X(14).
000340 FD  PRINT-FILE
000350     LABEL RECORD IS OMITTED
000360     DATA RECORD IS PRINT-LINE.
000370 01  PRINT-LINE                PIC X(121).
000380 WORKING-STORAGE SECTION.
000390 01  MISC-FIELDS.
000400     03   EOF-INDICATOR        PIC X(03) VALUE 'OFF'.
000410     03   OLD-DEPT-NBR         PIC 9(02).
000420     03   OLD-TERRITORY-NBR    PIC 9(03).
000430     03   MINOR-TOTAL          PIC 9(05)V99 VALUE ZERO.
000440     03   INTERMEDIATE-TOTAL   PIC 9(06)V99 VALUE ZERO.
000450     03   GRAND-TOTAL          PIC 9(06)V99 VALUE ZERO.
000460 01  SALES-REC-WS.
000470     03   TERRITORY            PIC 9(03).
000480     03   FILLER               PIC X(02).
000490     03   DEPARTMENT           PIC 9(02).
000500     03   FILLER               PIC X(02).
000510     03   SALES-AMT            PIC 999V99.
000520 01  HEAD-LINE.
000530     03   FILLER               PIC X.
000540     03   FILLER               PIC X(43) VALUE SPACES.
000550     03   FILLER               PIC X(09) VALUE 'TERRITORY'.
000560     03   FILLER               PIC X(10) VALUE SPACES.
000570     03   FILLER               PIC X(10) VALUE 'DEPARTMENT.
000580     03   FILLER               PIC X(10) VALUE SPACES.
000590     03   FILLER               PIC X(12) VALUE 'SALES AMOUNT'.
000600     03   FILLER               PIC X(26) VALUE SPACES.
000610 01  REPORT-LINE.
000620     03   FILLER               PIC X.
000630     03   FILLER               PIC X(46) VALUE SPACES.
000640     03   TERRITORY-PR         PIC 9(03).
```

FIGURE 7-11

continued

```
000650        03   FILLER                    PIC X(17) VALUE SPACES.
000660        03   DEPARTMENT-PR             PIC 9(02).
000670        03   FILLER                    PIC X(16) VALUE SPACES.
000680        03   SALES-AMT-PR              PIC $$$$.99.
000690        03   FILLER                    PIC X(29) VALUE SPACES.
000700 01  MINOR-TOTAL-LINE.
000710        03   FILLER                    PIC X.
000720        03   FILLER                    PIC X(54) VALUE SPACES.
000730        03   FILLER                    PIC X(16) VALUE 'DEPARTMENT TOTAL'.
000740        03   FILLER                    PIC X(17) VALUE SPACES.
000750        03   MINOR-TOTAL-PR            PIC $(6).99.
000760        03   FILLER                    PIC X VALUE SPACE.
000770        03   FILLER                    PIC X VALUE '*'.
000780        03   FILLER                    PIC X(27) VALUE SPACES.
000790 01  INTERMEDIATE-TOTAL-LINE.
000800        03   FILLER                    PIC X(54) VALUE SPACES.
000810        03   FILLER                    PIC X(15) VALUE
000820                                          'TERRITORY TOTAL'.
000830        03   FILLER                    PIC X(12) VALUE SPACES.
000840        03   INT-TOTAL-PR              PIC $(07).99.
000850        03   FILLER                    PIC X VALUE SPACE.
000860        03   FILLER                    PIC X(02) VALUE '**'.
000870        03   FILLER                    PIC X(26) VALUE SPACES.
000880 01  GRAND-TOTAL-LINE.
000890        03   FILLER                    PIC X.
000900        03   FILLER                    PIC X(54) VALUE SPACES.
000910        03   FILLER                    PIC X(11) VALUE 'FINAL TOTAL'.
000920        03   FILLER                    PIC X(16) VALUE SPACES.
000930        03   GRAND-TOTAL-PR            PIC $(7).99.
000940        03   FILLER                    PIC X(29) VALUE SPACES.
000950 PROCEDURE DIVISION.
000960 CONTROL-MODULE.
000970        PERFORM A100-OPENER.
000980        PERFORM A200-MAIN-PROCESSING
000990           UNTIL EOF-INDICATOR IS EQUAL TO ' ON'.
001000        PERFORM B200-INTERMEDIATE-BREAK.
001010        PERFORM A300-CLOSER.
001020        STOP RUN.
001030 A100-OPENER.
001040        OPEN INPUT SALES-FILE OUTPUT PRINT-FILE.
001050        WRITE PRINT-LINE FROM HEAD-LINE
001060           AFTER ADVANCING PAGE.
001070        MOVE SPACES TO PRINT-LINE.
001080        WRITE PRINT-LINE AFTER ADVANCING 2 LINES.
001090        READ SALES-FILE INTO SALES-REC-WS
001100           AT END MOVE ' ON' TO EOF-INDICATOR.
001110        MOVE DEPARTMENT TO OLD-DEPT-NBR.
001120        MOVE TERRITORY TO OLD-TERRITORY-NBR.
001130 A200-MAIN-PROCESSING.
001140        IF TERRITORY IS NOT EQUAL TO OLD-TERRITORY-NBR
001150           PERFORM B200-INTERMEDIATE-BREAK
001160        ELSE
001170           IF DEPARTMENT IS NOT EQUAL TO OLD-DEPT-NBR
001180              PERFORM B100-MINOR-BREAK-ROUTINE.
001190        MOVE DEPARTMENT TO OLD-DEPT-NBR.
```

continued

FIGURE 7-11

continued

```
001200        MOVE TERRITORY TO OLD-TERRITORY-NBR.
001210        ADD SALES-AMT TO MINOR-TOTAL.
001220        MOVE DEPARTMENT TO DEPARTMENT-PR.
001230        MOVE TERRITORY TO TERRITORY-PR.
001240        MOVE SALES-AMT TO SALES-AMT-PR.
001250        WRITE PRINT-LINE FROM REPORT-LINE
001260            AFTER ADVANCING 1 LINE.
001270        READ SALES-FILE INTO SALES-REC-WS
001280            AT END MOVE ' ON' TO EOF-INDICATOR.
001290 B100-MINOR-BREAK-ROUTINE.
001300        MOVE MINOR-TOTAL TO MINOR-TOTAL-PR.
001310        ADD MINOR-TOTAL TO INTERMEDIATE-TOTAL.
001320        MOVE ZEROS TO MINOR-TOTAL.
001330        WRITE PRINT-LINE FROM MINOR-TOTAL-LINE
001340            AFTER ADVANCING 1 LINE.
001350        MOVE SPACES TO PRINT-LINE.
001360        WRITE PRINT-LINE AFTER ADVANCING 2 LINES.
001370 B200-INTERMEDIATE-BREAK.
001380        PERFORM B100-MINOR-BREAK-ROUTINE.
001390        MOVE INTERMEDIATE-TOTAL TO INT-TOTAL-PR.
001400        ADD INTERMEDIATE-TOTAL TO GRAND-TOTAL.
001410        MOVE ZEROS TO INTERMEDIATE-TOTAL.
001420        WRITE PRINT-LINE FROM INTERMEDIATE-TOTAL-LINE
001430            AFTER ADVANCING 1 LINE.
001440        MOVE SPACES TO PRINT-LINE.
001450        WRITE PRINT-LINE AFTER ADVANCING 2 LINES.
001460 A300-CLOSER.
001470        MOVE GRAND-TOTAL TO GRAND-TOTAL-PR.
001480        WRITE PRINT-LINE FROM GRAND-TOTAL-LINE
001490            AFTER ADVANCING 2 LINES.
001500        CLOSE SALES-FILE PRINT-FILE.
```

FIGURE 7-12

Output: Intermediate break program

TERRITORY	DEPARTMENT	SALES AMOUNT
415	01	$594.60
415	01	$483.25
	MINOR TOTAL	$1077.85 *
415	02	$916.64
415	02	$742.81
	MINOR TOTAL	$1659.45 *
	INTERMEDIATE TOTAL	$2737.30 **
621	03	$533.86
	MINOR TOTAL	$533.86 *
621	05	$759.95
621	05	$261.04
	MINOR TOTAL	$1020.99 *
	INTERMEDIATE TOTAL	$1554.85 **
643	09	$360.00
	MINOR TOTAL	$360.00 *
	INTERMEDIATE TOTAL	$360.00 **
789	12	$926.17
789	12	$593.01
789	12	$600.00
	MINOR TOTAL	$2119.18 *
	INTERMEDIATE TOTAL	$2119.18 **
	FINAL TOTAL	$6771.33

Summary or group printing

Both program examples used in this chapter have produced *detail* printed reports—that is, one line for each record plus whatever total lines were required. Reports of this kind are very common, but management may not wish to see all the line-by-line details. Since a manager's time is valuable, he or she may wish to see only a *group* or *summary* printed report. Instead of one line per record, we would produce a report with *one* line *per group* or, in our case, one line for each of the totals. Two immediate advantages of this procedure are that the report is faster to print and that it takes less paper. Then, if the manager notices some numbers that seem out of the ordinary, a detail printed report may be requested for a closer look at particular sales areas.

The main difference between this program and the previous one is that we will omit the detail printing statements although the record-by-record totaling activities must still be included. Figure 7-13 illustrates the logic by means of a Warnier/Orr diagram and Figures 7-14 and 7-15 show the program and the output.

FIGURE 7-13

Warnier/Orr diagram: Group printing

Group
Print
Program

Control Module

A-100 - OPENER (1)

Open files

Write heading

Read sales-file   EOF { Move 'ON' to last-record-indicator
⊕
$\overline{EOF}$ { Skip

A-200 - MAIN-PROCESSING (0, END)

Move department number to storage

Move territory number to storage

Territory nbr not = old-territory-nbr (0,1)   PERFORM B 200 -INTERMEDIATE-BREAK

PERFORM B 100-MINOR-BREAK-ROUTINE { Move fields to print line / Add minor total to intermediate total / Clear minor total / Write minor total line

Move fields to print line

Add intermediate total to grand total

Clear intermediate total

Write intermediate total line

⊕

Territory nbr not = old-territory-nbr (0, 1)

Department nbr not = old-dept-nbr (0, 1)   PERFORM B 100-MINOR-BREAK-ROUTINE { Move fields to print line / Add minor total to intermediate total / Clear minor total / Write minor total line

⊕

$\overline{Department\ nbr\ not\ =}$ old-dept-nbr (0, 1) { Skip

Move department nbr to old-dept-nbr

Move territory nbr to old-territory-nbr

Add sales-amt to minor-total

Read sales-file   EOF { Move 'ON' to last-record-indicator
⊕
$\overline{EOF}$ { Skip

B-200 - INTERMEDIATE-BREAK (1)

PERFORM B 100-MINOR-BREAK-ROUTINE { Move fields to print line / Add minor total to intermediate total / Clear minor total / Write minor total line

Move fields to print line

Add intermediate total to grand total

Clear intermediate total

Write intermediate total line

A-300 - CLOSER (1)

Move grand total to print line

Write grand total line

FIGURE 7-14

Group printing

```
000100 IDENTIFICATION DIVISION.
000110 PROGRAM-ID. GROUP2.
000120*****************************************
000130*                                        *
000140*   THIS PROGRAM GROUP PRINTS A SALES    *
000150*   REPORT WITH MINOR, INTERMEDIATE,     *
000160*   AND FINAL TOTALS.                     *
000170*                                        *
000180*****************************************
000190 ENVIRONMENT DIVISION.
000200 CONFIGURATION SECTION.
000210 SOURCE-COMPUTER. - - -.
000220 OBJECT-COMPUTER. - - -.
000230 INPUT-OUTPUT SECTION.
000240 FILE-CONTROL.
000250     SELECT SALES-FILE ASSIGN TO - - -.
000260     SELECT PRINT-FILE ASSIGN TO - - -.
000270 DATA DIVISION.
000280 FILE SECTION.
000290 FD  SALES-FILE
000300     LABEL RECORD IS STANDARD
000310     VALUE OF FILE-ID IS 'SALES-DATA'
000320     DATA RECORD IS SALES-REC.
000330 01  SALES-REC                   PIC X(14).
000340 FD  PRINT-FILE
000350     LABEL RECORD IS OMITTED
000360     DATA RECORD IS PRINT-LINE.
000370 01  PRINT-LINE                  PIC X(121).
000380 WORKING-STORAGE SECTION.
000390 01  MISC-FIELDS.
000400     03   EOF-INDICATOR          PIC X(03) VALUE 'OFF'.
000410     03   OLD-DEPT-NBR           PIC 9(02).
000420     03   OLD-TERRITORY-NBR      PIC 9(03).
000430     03   MINOR-TOTAL            PIC 9(05)V99 VALUE ZERO.
000440     03   INTERMEDIATE-TOTAL     PIC 9(06)V99 VALUE ZERO.
000450     03   GRAND-TOTAL            PIC 9(06)V99 VALUE ZERO.
000460 01  SALES-REC-WS.
000470     03   TERRITORY              PIC 9(03).
000480     03   FILLER                 PIC X(02).
000490     03   DEPARTMENT             PIC 9(02).
000500     03   FILLER                 PIC X(02).
000510     03   SALES-AMT              PIC 999V99.
000520 01  HEAD-LINE.
000530     03   FILLER                 PIC X.
000540     03   FILLER                 PIC X(43) VALUE SPACES.
000550     03   FILLER                 PIC X(09) VALUE 'TERRITORY'.
000560     03   FILLER                 PIC X(10) VALUE SPACES.
000570     03   FILLER                 PIC X(10) VALUE 'DEPARTMENT'.
000580     03   FILLER                 PIC X(10) VALUE SPACES.
```

FIGURE 7-14

continued

```
000590      03   FILLER                PIC X(12) VALUE 'SALES AMOUNT'.
000600      03   FILLER                PIC X(26) VALUE SPACES.
000610 01   MINOR-TOTAL-LINE.
000620      03   FILLER                PIC X.
000630      03   FILLER                PIC X(10) VALUE SPACES.
000640      03   FILLER                PIC X(16) VALUE
000650                                     'DEPARTMENT TOTAL'.
000660      03   FILLER                PIC X(20) VALUE SPACES.
000670      03   TERRITORY-PR-M        PIC 9(03).
000680      03   FILLER                PIC X(17) VALUE SPACES.
000690      03   DEPARTMENT-PR-M       PIC 9(02).
000700      03   FILLER                PIC X(16) VALUE SPACES.
000710      03   MINOR-TOTAL-PR        PIC $(6).99.
000720      03   FILLER                PIC X(27) VALUE SPACES.
000730 01   INTERMEDIATE-TOTAL-LINE.
000740      03   FILLER                PIC X.
000750      03   FILLER                PIC X(10) VALUE SPACES.
000760      03   FILLER                PIC X(15) VALUE
000770                                     'TERRITORY TOTAL'.
000780      03   FILLER                PIC X(21) VALUE SPACES.
000790      03   TERRITORY-PR-I        PIC 9(03).
000800      03   FILLER                PIC X(34) VALUE SPACES.
000810      03   INT-TOTAL-PR          PIC $(07).99.
000820      03   FILLER                PIC X(27) VALUE SPACES.
000830 01   GRAND-TOTAL-LINE.
000840      03   FILLER                PIC X.
000850      03   FILLER                PIC X(10) VALUE SPACES.
000860      03   FILLER                PIC X(30) VALUE
000870                   'FINAL TOTAL OF ALL TERRITORIES'.
000880      03   FILLER                PIC X(43) VALUE SPACES.
000890      03   GRAND-TOTAL-PR        PIC $(7).99.
000900      03   FILLER                PIC X(27) VALUE SPACES.
000910 PROCEDURE DIVISION.
000920 CONTROL-MODULE.
000930      PERFORM A100-OPENER.
000940      PERFORM A200-MAIN-PROCESSING
000950          UNTIL EOF-INDICATOR IS EQUAL TO ' ON'.
000960      PERFORM B200-INTERMEDIATE-BREAK.
000970      PERFORM A300-CLOSER.
000980      STOP RUN.
000990 A100-OPENER.
001000      OPEN INPUT SALES-FILE OUTPUT PRINT-FILE.
001010      WRITE PRINT-LINE FROM HEAD-LINE
001020          AFTER ADVANCING PAGE.
001030      MOVE SPACES TO PRINT-LINE.
001040      WRITE PRINT-LINE AFTER ADVANCING 2 LINES.
001050      READ SALES-FILE INTO SALES-REC-WS
001060          AT END MOVE ' ON' TO EOF-INDICATOR.
001070      MOVE DEPARTMENT TO OLD-DEPT-NBR.
```

continued

FIGURE 7-14

---

continued

```
001080      MOVE TERRITORY TO OLD-TERRITORY-NBR.
001090 A200-MAIN-PROCESSING.
001100      IF TERRITORY IS NOT EQUAL TO OLD-TERRITORY-NBR
001110          PERFORM B200-INTERMEDIATE-BREAK
001120      ELSE
001130          IF DEPARTMENT IS NOT EQUAL TO OLD-DEPT-NBR
001140              PERFORM B100-MINOR-BREAK-ROUTINE.
001150      MOVE DEPARTMENT TO OLD-DEPT-NBR.
001160      MOVE TERRITORY TO OLD-TERRITORY-NBR.
001170      ADD SALES-AMT TO MINOR-TOTAL.
001180      READ SALES-FILE INTO SALES-REC-WS
001190          AT END MOVE ' ON' TO EOF-INDICATOR.
001200 B100-MINOR-BREAK-ROUTINE.
001210      MOVE OLD-DEPT-NBR TO DEPARTMENT-PR-M.
001220      MOVE OLD-TERRITORY-NBR TO TERRITORY-PR-M.
001230      MOVE MINOR-TOTAL TO MINOR-TOTAL-PR.
001240      ADD MINOR-TOTAL TO INTERMEDIATE-TOTAL.
001250      MOVE ZEROS TO MINOR-TOTAL.
001260      WRITE PRINT-LINE FROM MINOR-TOTAL-LINE
001270          AFTER ADVANCING 1 LINE.
001280      MOVE SPACES TO PRINT-LINE.
001290      WRITE PRINT-LINE AFTER ADVANCING 2 LINES.
001300 B200-INTERMEDIATE-BREAK.
001310      PERFORM B100-MINOR-BREAK-ROUTINE.
001320      MOVE OLD-TERRITORY-NBR TO TERRITORY-PR-I.
001330      MOVE INTERMEDIATE-TOTAL TO INT-TOTAL-PR.
001340      ADD INTERMEDIATE-TOTAL TO GRAND-TOTAL.
001350      MOVE ZEROS TO INTERMEDIATE-TOTAL.
001360      WRITE PRINT-LINE FROM INTERMEDIATE-TOTAL-LINE
001370          AFTER ADVANCING 1 LINE.
001380      MOVE SPACES TO PRINT-LINE.
001390      WRITE PRINT-LINE AFTER ADVANCING 2 LINES.
001400 A300-CLOSER.
001410      MOVE GRAND-TOTAL TO GRAND-TOTAL-PR.
001420      WRITE PRINT-LINE FROM GRAND-TOTAL-LINE
001430          AFTER ADVANCING 2 LINES.
001440      CLOSE SALES-FILE PRINT-FILE.
```

FIGURE 7-15

Output: Group printing

	TERRITORY	DEPARTMENT	SALES AMOUNT
DEPARTMENT TOTAL	415	01	$1077.85
DEPARTMENT TOTAL	415	02	$1659.45
TERRITORY TOTAL	415		$2737.30
DEPARTMENT TOTAL	621	03	$533.86
DEPARTMENT TOTAL	621	05	$1020.99
TERRITORY TOTAL	621		$1554.85
DEPARTMENT TOTAL	643	09	$360.00
TERRITORY TOTAL	643		$360.00
DEPARTMENT TOTAL	789	12	$2119.18
TERRITORY TOTAL	789		$2119.18
FINAL TOTAL OF ALL TERRITORIES			$6771.33

Programmed switches

By definition, a *switch* is any field used to convey control information within the program. In the text, switches have been used extensively with the UNTIL version of the PERFORM statement to execute a block of code until a particular condition is met. For the sake of illustration, the switches have been given various names (INDICATOR or EOF-INDICATOR) that would help to identify these fields as switches. Since switches are used so frequently, a good habit to get into is that of naming and handling them in a standard, or preset, way. For example, you can always include the letters SW or the name SWITCH with the main characters as in OLD-MSTR-SWITCH or EOF-SW. For numerically defined switch fields, 0 normally indicates the OFF condition while 1 indicates ON. For those switches defined as X or A, YES (or Y) should indicate ON while NO (or N) should indicate OFF. It is also very likely that the shop where you work will have a standard way of handling switches.

Alphabetic or alphanumerically defined switches have the advantage of providing for better documentation than would numeric switches. Note the following example:

```
03  TAPE-EOF-SW            PIC X(3) VALUE 'NO '.

    PERFORM 010-READ-MODULE
        UNTIL TAPE-EOF-SW IS EQUAL TO 'YES'.
```

The example shown above is better than using a numeric switch, but can be improved upon by using conditional names (level 88 entries) discussed in Chapter 5. With conditional names the switch values can be defined in a more meaningful way:

```
02  DISK-EOF-SW            PIC X(3) VALUE 'NO '.
    88 OUT-OF-DISK-RECORDS VALUE 'YES'.
          .
          .
          .

    PERFORM 030-READ-MODULE
        UNTIL OUT-OF-DISK-RECORDS.
```

Switches, however, are not limited to use with PERFORM. You can use them anytime you wish for whatever needs you have. One common use of a programmed switch is to set it to a particular value in one part of the program and then test that value in another part of the same program. In effect, a programmed switch (also known as a "flag") is a method of communicating or passing information from one part of the program to another. A simple example will illustrate this point. Recall that the first program in this chapter printed a minor total whenever a control break in the department number was detected. The key to *not* generating a control break on the first record was that in the A100-OPENER routine we read a record and moved the department number from the incoming record to OLD-DEPT-NBR. Then, when the department number from the first record was tested in the A200-MAIN-PROCESSING paragraph we knew that a minor break would not be generated. We can do the same thing, however, by means of a programmed switch. To make the change we will set up a switch in WORKING-STORAGE (appropriately called SWITCH since this is not a reserved word) and give it a beginning value of ON:

```
03  SWITCH              PIC X(03) VALUE ' ON'.
```

Then, we will remove the MOVE DEPARTMENT TO OLD-DEPT-NBR statement from the A100-OPENER paragraph, since it will no longer be needed. The value of the switch will then be tested in a nested IF statement when we come to the main processing routine:

```
IF  SWITCH IS NOT EQUAL TO ' ON'
    IF DEPARTMENT IS NOT EQUAL TO OLD-DEPT-NBR
        PERFORM B100-MINOR-BREAK-ROUTINE.
```

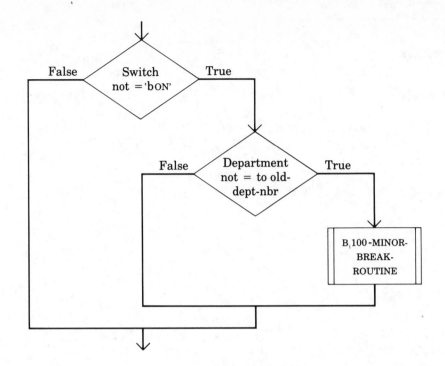

Since SWITCH was initially set to 'bON' in WORKING-STORAGE, the test IF SWITCH IS NOT EQUAL TO 'bON' will be false and the department comparison will be ignored. So far, so good; but if we leave SWITCH in the ON condition, the department number test will never be made and minor breaks will never be detected. To take care of this we will turn the switch off right after the IF statement, by moving 'OFF' TO SWITCH.

Pseudocode for the revised A200-MAIN-PROCESSING module is shown below. Figure 7-16 shows the pertinent parts of the program.

```
A200-MAIN-PROCESSING
    IF  switch is not = 'ON'
        IF incoming department number is not = stored
            department number
            PERFORM B100-MINOR-BREAK-ROUTINE
        ENDIF
    ENDIF
    Move OFF to switch
    Move incoming department number to storage
    Add to minor total
    Move fields to print area
    Write a report line on the printer
    Read a record at end move ON to end of file indicator
```

FIGURE 7-16

Control break using a switch

```
WORKING-STORAGE SECTION.
01  MISC-FIELDS.
    03  SWITCH              PIC X(03) VALUE ' ON'.
    03  EOF-INDICATOR       PIC X(03) VALUE 'OFF'.
    03  OLD-DEPT-NBR        PIC 9(02).
    03  MINOR-TOTAL         PIC 9(05)V99 VALUE ZERO.
    03  GRAND-TOTAL         PIC 9(06)V99 VALUE ZERO.
               .
               .
               .

PROCEDURE DIVISION.
               .
               .
               .


A200-MAIN-PROCESSING.
    IF SWITCH IS NOT EQUAL TO ' ON'
        IF DEPARTMENT IS NOT EQUAL TO OLD-DEPT-NBR
            PERFORM B100-MINOR-BREAK-ROUTINE.
    MOVE 'OFF' TO SWITCH.
    MOVE DEPARTMENT TO OLD-DEPT-NBR.
    ADD SALES-AMT TO MINOR-TOTAL.
    MOVE DEPARTMENT TO DEPARTMENT-PR.
    MOVE SALES-AMT TO SALES-AMT-PR.
    WRITE PRINT-LINE FROM REPORT-LINE
        AFTER ADVANCING 1 LINE.
    READ SALES-FILE INTO SALES-REC-WS
        AT END MOVE ' ON' TO EOF-INDICATOR.
```

Group indication

Group indication is the term used to describe a detail printed report in which a *complete* output line is printed only for the first record of each group. The output from the previous programs was not group-indicated because we printed a department number and/or a territory number each time a record was processed. In this example we will use a data file that contains the department number in columns 1 and 2, a filler in 3–5, and the sales amount in columns 5–9. Thus, the problem will only involve a minor break (one level of breaks), detail printing (one line per record), and group indication (print the department number only for the first occurrence of a new department group). Managers often request group-indicated reports because detail reports have a "cluttered" look.

The previous program can be modified for this purpose by using a second switch that will "tell" the program when to print the department number and when not to. Naturally, we will want to print the department number for the first record that is read, but after that we want to print the number only for the first record of a new group. The first step is to set up our switch in WORKING-STORAGE:

```
03   GRP-INDICATE-SWITCH      PIC X(03) VALUE ' ON'.
```

The REPORT-LINE contains the field DEPARTMENT-PR and we will use the GRP-INDICATE-SWITCH to move either the department number or SPACES to that area depending upon whether it is ON or OFF. To do this we will remove the MOVE DEPARTMENT TO DEPARTMENT-PR statement from the A200-MAIN-PROCESSING module and replace it with the following:

```
IF GRP-INDICATE-SWITCH IS EQUAL TO ' ON'
    MOVE DEPARTMENT TO DEPARTMENT-PR
ELSE
    MOVE SPACES TO DEPARTMENT-PR.
MOVE 'OFF' TO GRP-INDICATE-SWITCH.
```

The logic is as follows. First, the switch was set to ON in WORKING-STORAGE so that the department number will be moved to the output area and printed for the first record. Immediately after that we will turn off the switch so that succeeding records will *not* have the department number printed. Those statements take care of the first record and all succeeding records of that group, but after a minor break is detected we will want to repeat the ON-for-one-record process. This is accomplished by turning the switch on again at the end of the minor break routine.

Although the logic expressed in the previous paragraph is correct, there is still one small problem. Remember that we wanted to move either the department number or spaces to DEPARTMENT-PR depending upon a switch setting. The problem is DEPARTMENT-PR is defined as PIC 9(02) and spaces cannot be moved to a numeric field. The solution is to use the REDE-FINES clause to give a different name and format to the same area:

```
03   DEPARTMENT        PIC 9(02).
03   DEPT-SPACE-PR REDEFINES DEPARTMENT
                     PIC X(02).
```

The rules for using REDEFINES are simple. The entry containing REDE-FINES must immediately follow the area being redefined and the level numbers must be the same. REDEFINES can be used at the group level, as the following example shows, and in both the FILE SECTION and WORKING-STOR-AGE SECTION. Note that the total number of characters in each definition must be the same.

```
03   SENIOR-STUDENT.
     05   GRADE-AVERAGE      PIC 9V99.
     05   CAMPUS             PIC X(10).
     05   COLLEGE-MAJOR      PIC 99.
03   GRAD-STUDENT REDEFINES SENIOR-STUDENT.
     05   ADVISOR-NAME       PIC X(15).
```

The original field *may* contain a VALUE entry, but the redefining field *cannot*. Of the following examples, the first one is permissible, but the second is *not*.

Examples:

```
03   SWITCH-THREE          PIC 9 VALUE 1.
03   INDICATOR REDEFINES SWITCH-THREE    PIC X.
```

(Incorrect)

```
03   SWITCH-THREE          PIC 9 VALUE 1.
03   EOF-FLAG REDEFINES SWITCH-THREE    PIC X VALUE 'N'.
```

The revised IF statement is shown below while Figures 7-17 and 7-18 show the pseudocode and a flowchart of the main processing module. The complete program and output are shown in Figures 7-19 and 7-20.

```
IF GRP-INDICATE-SWITCH IS EQUAL TO ' ON'
    MOVE DEPARTMENT TO DEPARTMENT-PR
ELSE
    MOVE SPACES TO DEPT-SPACE-PR.
```

FIGURE 7-17

Pseudocode: Group indication

```
A200-MAIN-PROCESSING
    IF  switch is not = to ON
         IF incoming department number is not = storage
           department number
             PERFORM B100-MINOR-BREAK-ROUTINE
         ENDIF
    ENDIF
    Move OFF to switch
    Move incoming department number to storage
    Add to minor total
    IF group indicate switch is = ON
         Move department number to print area
    ELSE
         Move spaces to department number print area
    ENDIF
    Move OFF to group indicate switch
    Move fields to print area
    Write a report line on the printer
    Read a record at end move ON to end of file switch

B100-MINOR-BREAK-ROUTINE
    Move minor total to print area
    Add minor total to grand total
    Clear minor total
    Write a minor total line on the printer
    MOVE ON to group indicate switch
```

FIGURE 7-18

Flowchart: Group indication

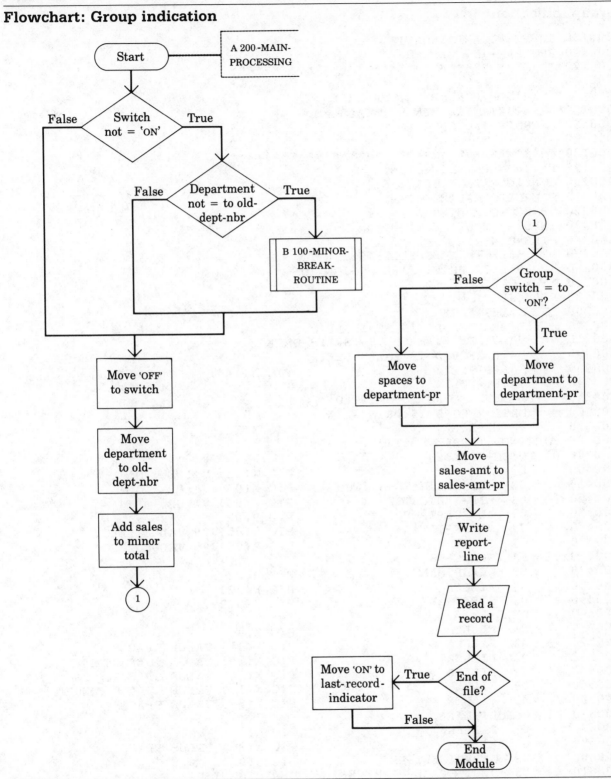

FIGURE 7-19

Group indication

```
000100 IDENTIFICATION DIVISION.
000110 PROGRAM-ID. GRPIND.
000120*****************************************
000130*                                        *
000140*   THIS REPORT PRINTS A SALES           *
000150*   REPORT WITH MINOR TOTALS AND         *
000160*   GROUP INDICATION.                    *
000170*                                        *
000180*****************************************
000190 ENVIRONMENT DIVISION.
000200 CONFIGURATION SECTION.
000210 SOURCE-COMPUTER. - - -.
000220 OBJECT-COMPUTER. - - -.
000230 INPUT-OUTPUT SECTION.
000240 FILE-CONTROL.
000250      SELECT SALES-FILE ASSIGN TO - - -.
000260      SELECT PRINT-FILE ASSIGN TO - - -.
000270 DATA DIVISION.
000280 FILE SECTION.
000290 FD   SALES-FILE
000300      LABEL RECORD IS STANDARD
000310      VALUE OF FILE-ID IS 'SALES-DATA'
000320      DATA RECORD IS SALES-REC.
000330 01   SALES-REC                    PIC X(14).
000340 FD   PRINT-FILE
000350      LABEL RECORD IS OMITTED
000360      DATA RECORD IS PRINT-LINE.
000370 01   PRINT-LINE                   PIC X(121).
000380 WORKING-STORAGE SECTION.
000390 01   MISC-FIELDS.
000400      03   SWITCH                  PIC X(03) VALUE ' ON'.
000410      03   GRP-INDICATE-SWITCH     PIC X(03) VALUE ' ON'.
000420      03   EOF-INDICATOR           PIC X(03) VALUE 'OFF'.
000430      03   OLD-DEPT-NBR            PIC 9(02).
000440      03   MINOR-TOTAL             PIC 9(05)V99 VALUE ZERO.
000450      03   GRAND-TOTAL             PIC 9(06)V99 VALUE ZERO.
000460 01   SALES-REC-WS.
000470      03   DEPARTMENT              PIC 9(02).
000480      03   FILLER                  PIC X(02).
000490      03   SALES-AMT               PIC 999V99.
000500 01   HEAD-LINE.
000510      03   FILLER                  PIC X.
000520      03   FILLER                  PIC X(31) VALUE SPACES.
000530      03   FILLER                  PIC X(10) VALUE 'DEPARTMENT'.
000540      03   FILLER                  PIC X(10) VALUE SPACES.
000550      03   FILLER                  PIC X(12) VALUE 'SALES AMOUNT'.
000560      03   FILLER                  PIC X(57) VALUE SPACES.
000570 01   REPORT-LINE.
000580      03   FILLER                  PIC X.
000590      03   FILLER                  PIC X(35) VALUE SPACES.
000600      03   DEPARTMENT-PR           PIC 9(02).
000610      03   DEPT-SPACE-PR REDEFINES DEPARTMENT-PR
000620                                   PIC X(02).
000630      03   FILLER                  PIC X(17) VALUE SPACES.
000640      03   SALES-AMT-PR            PIC $$$$.99.
```

FIGURE 7-19

continued

```
000650         03   FILLER              PIC X(59) VALUE SPACES.
000660  01  MINOR-TOTAL-LINE.
000670         03   FILLER              PIC X.
000680         03   FILLER              PIC X(10) VALUE SPACES.
000690         03   FILLER              PIC X(16)
000700                                  VALUE 'DEPARTMENT TOTAL'.
000710         03   FILLER              PIC X(25) VALUE SPACES.
000720         03   MINOR-TOTAL-PR      PIC $(6).99.
000730         03   FILLER              PIC X(59) VALUE SPACES.
000740  01  GRAND-TOTAL-LINE.
000750         03   FILLER              PIC X.
000760         03   FILLER              PIC X(10) VALUE SPACES.
000770         03   FILLER              PIC X(11) VALUE 'FINAL TOTAL'.
000780         03   FILLER              PIC X(30) VALUE SPACES.
000790         03   GRAND-TOTAL-PR      PIC $(7).99.
000800         03   FILLER              PIC X(59) VALUE SPACES.
000810  PROCEDURE DIVISION.
000820  CONTROL-MODULE.
000830         PERFORM A100-OPENER.
000840         PERFORM A200-MAIN-PROCESSING
000850             UNTIL EOF-INDICATOR  IS WQUAL TO ' ON'.
000860         PERFORM B100-MINOR-BREAK-ROUTINE.
000870         PERFORM A300-CLOSER.
000880         STOP RUN.
000890  A100-OPENER.
000900         OPEN INPUT SALES-FILE OUTPUT PRINT-FILE.
000910         WRITE PRINT-LINE FROM HEAD-LINE
000920             AFTER ADVANCING PAGE.
000930         MOVE SPACES TO PRINT-LINE.
000940         WRITE PRINT-LINE AFTER ADVANCING 2 LINES.
000950         READ SALES-FILE INTO SALES-REC-WS
000960             AT END MOVE ' ON' TO EOF-INDICATOR.
000970  A200-MAIN-PROCESSING.
000980         IF SWITCH IS NOT EQUAL TO ' ON'
000990             IF DEPARTMENT IS NOT EQUAL TO OLD-DEPT-NBR
001000                 PERFORM B100-MINOR-BREAK-ROUTINE.
001010         MOVE 'OFF' TO SWITCH.
001020         MOVE DEPARTMENT TO OLD-DEPT-NBR.
001030         ADD SALES-AMT TO MINOR-TOTAL.
001040         IF GRP-INDICATE-SWITCH IS EQUAL TO ' ON'
001050             MOVE DEPARTMENT TO DEPARTMENT-PR
001060         ELSE
001070             MOVE SPACES TO DEPT-SPACE-PR.
001080         MOVE 'OFF' TO GRP-INDICATE-SWITCH.
001090         MOVE SALES-AMT TO SALES-AMT-PR.
001100         WRITE PRINT-LINE FROM REPORT-LINE
001110             AFTER ADVANCING 1 LINE.
001120         READ SALES-FILE INTO SALES-REC-WS
001130             AT END MOVE ' ON' TO EOF-INDICATOR.
001140  B100-MINOR-BREAK-ROUTINE.
001150         MOVE MINOR-TOTAL TO MINOR-TOTAL-PR.
001160         ADD MINOR-TOTAL TO GRAND-TOTAL.
001170         MOVE ZEROS TO MINOR-TOTAL.
001180         WRITE PRINT-LINE FROM MINOR-TOTAL-LINE
001190             AFTER ADVANCING 2 LINES.
```

continued

FIGURE 7-19

```
001200      MOVE SPACES TO PRINT-LINE.
001210      WRITE PRINT-LINE AFTER ADVANCING 2 LINES.
001220      MOVE ' ON' TO GRP-INDICATE-SWITCH.
001230 A300-CLOSER.
001240      MOVE GRAND-TOTAL TO GRAND-TOTAL-PR.
001250      WRITE PRINT-LINE FROM GRAND-TOTAL-LINE
001260          AFTER ADVANCING 3 LINES.
001270      CLOSE SALES-FILE PRINT-FILE.
```

COMMON ERRORS

We have already mentioned one common error when working with control breaks: Forgetting to process the first record of a new group. The control field is used to trigger the break, but after the printing of minor totals the program must return to process the data from the record that caused the break.

Another common error involves the totaling process in the control break paragraph(s). Most beginners have no difficulty with the idea of rolling a minor total into an intermediate or final total. What they tend to forget, however, is to clear the minor total area in preparation for the next data group.

A third opportunity for error occurs after the last data record has been processed. Usually the programmer is quite aware that a final total must be printed, but he or she will often forget that the ending process requires the performance of all lesser control breaks.

PROGRAMMING TIPS

When working with the control breaks it is important for the programmer to have a clear idea about the setup of the control break fields and their contents. A simple diagram containing representative values can be made up to help in the design process. This mock-up must contain all the control break possibilities, even if you are assured that some possibilities cannot occur.

For example, does your logic take care of the one-record group? Would a one-record group be processed correctly if it were the first record? Would it be processed correctly if it were the last record in the file? "Walk" your program through the sample data to see if the breaks are handled properly. Actually, this is not as bad as it sounds. Although it would be nice to do this "desk check" or "walk through" statement-by-statement, you can con-

FIGURE 7-20

Output: Group indicate problem

	DEPARTMENT	SALES AMOUNT
	01	$95.16
		$231.42
		$533.00
		$795.00
		$462.91
MINOR TOTAL		$2117.49
	02	$803.77
		$659.83
		$428.05
		$714.55
		$988.09
		$613.12
MINOR TOTAL		$4207.41
	03	$794.68
		$865.97
		$903.64
		$456.89
		$681.92
MINOR TOTAL		$3703.10
FINAL TOTAL		$10028.00

centrate your efforts on the really important statements that set up, change, or test various switches or control fields.

Programmed switches are a very valuable programming tool and should be studied until they are thoroughly understood. Once their importance and use are grasped, they can be used anywhere in the program. As mentioned earlier, a standard format for the switch ON and OFF condition should be developed and used consistently. If possible, use PIC X for switches (such as End-of-File switches) instead of numeric fields, since it saves extra computer instructions during compare operations. In addition, specify the same USAGE for items involved in moves, comparisons, and arithmetic operations.

It has been mentioned before, but bears repeating—use comments throughout the program. This rule can be expanded to include extra spacing before paragraphs, starting each COBOL DIVISION on a new page, and inserting comments so they are visible. An excellent way to do this is by means of a box made up of asterisks.

```
* * * * * * * * * * * * * * * * * * * * * * * * * * *

*   THE NEXT PARAGRAPH CALCULATES THE OVERTIME PAY      *

*   AMOUNT AND ADDS IT TO THE REGULAR PAY CALCULATED    *

*   PREVIOUSLY IN THE 050-REGULAR-PAY ROUTINE           *

* * * * * * * * * * * * * * * * * * * * * * * * * * *
```

Comments can be especially useful in control break and group indication problems where the conditions of switches may be changed at various locations in the program.

SELF-STUDY: QUESTIONS AND ANSWERS

1. How many levels of totals can you have?

   Answer: Technically there is no limit to the number of totals one could have in a particular problem. However, three levels (minor, intermediate, major) plus a final one are all you are likely to run across.

2. Instead of looking for a change in department numbers, couldn't we check either for a blank record between each group or for a particular value, such as all 9s?

   Answer: Yes, you could do this, and the blank record technique was used extensively with the punched-card operations years ago. The problem is, even though the technique is entirely logical, its success is dependent upon the dummy record being placed between the control groups *every* time. To do so is both time consuming and prone to error. If the dummy record were omitted, the control break would not be detected. Therefore, the more certain method is to compare the values in the control break fields.

3. The chapter programs to detail print and group print are very similar. Could they be combined into a single program and triggered by an entry when the program is executed?

   Answer: Yes, they could. A problem of that type is included in the exercises at the end of the chapter.

4. Since detail printing and detail printing with group indication are so similar, I assume they also could be combined into a single program.

   Answer: Exactly right. Several types of control break and printing programs might be combined into one complex program.

5. Is there any limit to the number of programmed switches I may have in one program?

   Answer: No, there isn't. But regardless of the number, be sure to label them for ease of understanding, and follow a set pattern of values to represent ON and OFF.

6. Is it possible to have an intermediate break and yet not have a minor break?

   Answer: Theoretically it would be possible, although it would not be a very common occurrence. Depending upon the situation, it might be legitimate or it might be an error condition. You could have a situation as follows:

```
    TERRITORY            DEPARTMENT              AMOUNT

       500                   01                 _____
       500                   01                 _____
                         MINOR TOTAL            _____
       500                   02                 _____
       500                   02                 _____
                         MINOR TOTAL            _____
                      INTERMEDIATE TOTAL        _____
       600                   01                 _____
       600                   01                 _____
                         MINOR TOTAL            _____
                      INTERMEDIATE TOTAL        _____
       700                   01                 _____
       700                   01                 _____
```

   Normally the intermediate break (700 vs. 600) would be used to force a minor-level control break even though the department numbers had not changed.

CHAPTER TERMS

control breaks

detail printing

flag (switch)

group indication

group printing (summary printing)

intermediate break (intermediate total)

LABEL RECORD IS STANDARD

minor break (minor total)

REDEFINES

rolling totals

summary printing (group printing)

switch (programmed switch)

VALUE OF FILE-ID

EXERCISES

1. Note the following output

```
        XXX  01    172
        XXX  01    925
        XXX  01    263
              A  1360
        XXX  07    123
        XXX  07    265
              A   388
              B  1748
        YYY  03    129
               .
               .
               .
```

   In the output above, A is called a _____ control break and B is called a
   _____ control break.

2. Which should you check for first, intermediate break or minor break and why?

3. What type of report is this?

```
        XXX  01    555
             03    999
                  1554
        YYY  02    321
             07    888
                  1109
                  2653
```

4. Passing information from one part of a program to another is done by means
   of a _____ .

5. Which of the following is *not* allowed?

```
    03   FIELDS.
         05    LAST-NAME.       PIC X(04) VALUE 'LAST'.
         05    MIDDLE-INIT      PIC X(01) VALUE 'I'.
         05    FIRST-NAME.      PIC X(09) VALUE 'FIRSTNAME'.
    03   FULL-NAME REDEFINES    FIELDS.
         05    TOTAL-NAME       PIC X(14).
```

   or

```
    03   FIELDS.
         05    LAST-NAME        PIC X(04).
         05    MIDDLE-INIT      PIC X(01).
         05    FIRST-NAME       PIC X(09).
    03   FULL-NAME REDEFINES    FIELDS.
         05    TOTAL-NAME       PIC X(14) VALUE 'LASTIFIRSTNAME'.
```

6. Define or explain what the term "control break" means. What is meant by
   "rolling" a total?

7. When working with control breaks, what is the problem concerning the first
   data record? Explain and/or draw diagrams to show how the control break field
   is handled.

8. How does an intermediate break differ from a minor-level break? How does a
   major-level break differ from an intermediate-level break?

9. What is the difference between a detail printed report and a group or summary printed report?

10. What is meant by the term "group indication"? Can a summary report be group indicated? If so, explain or diagram your answer.

11. What is a programmed switch? How does it differ from the end-of-file indicator you have been using so far?

12. For the next few problems you will use data records with the following format:

Columns 1–2 Region	Columns 3–5 Territory	Columns 6–7 Department	Columns 8–12 Sales Amount (PIC 99V99)
01	415	01	59460
01	415	01	48325
01	415	02	91664
01	415	02	74281
01	621	03	53386
01	621	05	75995
02	643	09	36000
02	789	12	92617
02	789	12	59301
02	789	12	60000

Write a program that detail prints a sales report with minor, intermediate, major, and final totals. Use the Department field for the minor break, Territory for the intermediate break, and Region for the major break. Edit your output for floating dollar signs, commas, and one asterisk for the minor total, two for intermediate, and three for the major level total.

13. Modify your program from the previous exercise to include an ending routine that verifies that the lower-level totals correspond to the grand total figure. If they do not, print an appropriate error message.

14. Use the data from Exercise 12 to group-print a report with a total for each Region group and each Territory. Output will be as follows.

```
                      SALES REPORT


   REGION           TERRITORY         DEPARTMENT       SALES AMOUNT

     01                 415                01            -------
     01                 415                02            -------
                 TOTAL  TERRITORY          415            -------
     01                 621                03            -------
     01                 621                05            -------
                 TOTAL  TERRITORY          621            -------
     02                 643
                        etc.



            FINAL TOTAL     ALL REGIONS          _____
```

15. Modify the program you wrote for Exercise 12 to group-indicate the Region and Territory numbers. In addition, group-indicate the dollar sign in the Sales Amount field so that it prints only for the first sales figure of each group.

16. Modify Exercise 12 to provide for the printing of *either* a group printed or a detail printed report depending upon the value of a switch that will be entered via the DISPLAY and ACCEPT statement. In addition, your program is to allow for at least two re-entries of the switch value in case the user strikes an incorrect key.

Chapter 8
Working with Tables of Data

CHAPTER OUTLINE

LEARNING OBJECTIVES

1. To understand why tables are needed and why they are so useful in solving certain types of problems.

2. To learn how to create various types of tables.

3. To learn two major ways of placing data into tables.

4. To see how table data can be accessed and used.

$\mathbf{U}$ntil now, all the examples and problems have followed the same basic pattern of read-calculate-print. Data records have been read-in from files and processed one record at a time. The critical point in each of these problems has been that each record of data can be processed *completely* by one execution of the processing loop. A payroll program that reads a record, processes the data to produce a paycheck, and then branches back to read another record is a classic example of this type of program logic.

However, some problems can make this standard approach very awkward. For example, suppose a standardized college entrance test has been given at several locations throughout the state. Further, we will assume that a maximum of 10 people were allowed to take the test at each site and that all 10 positions were taken. (This latter point is important and will be discussed in detail later.) Our input data has the following format:

SITE NBR   SCORES PIC 99V9

PIC 99	1st score	2nd score	3rd score	etc.	10th score

Our program is to read in a record as shown above and find the highest score, the lowest score, and the average score achieved at that testing site. Output will look as follows:

```
SITE#   HIGHEST SCORE   LOWEST SCORE   AVERAGE SCORE

  1       _____         _____        _____
  2       _____         _____        _____
etc.
```

Based on what you have learned so far, we would give a unique name to each of the scores and process the data accordingly:

```
FD   SCORES-FILES
     _____

     _____
     DATA RECORD IS SCORES.
01   SCORES.
     03   SITE-NBR       PIC 99.
     03   SCORE-1        PIC 99V9.
     03   SCORE-2        PIC 99V9.
     03   SCORE-3        PIC 99V9.
      .
      .
      .
     03   SCORE-10       PIC 99V9.
```

Calculating the total score and finding the average is the easiest part of the problem but would be cumbersome:

```
ADD SCORE-1 SCORE-2 SCORE-3...SCORE-10 TO TOTAL-SCORES.
DIVIDE TOTAL-SCORES BY 10 GIVING AVG-SCORE.
```

or

```
COMPUTE TOTAL-SCORES = (SCORE-1 + SCORE-2 + etc.)
```

Finding the highest or lowest score becomes even more cumbersome since it would involve multiple IF's and MOVE's:

```
IF SCORE-1 IS GREATER THAN
        .
        .
        .
```

At this point it may seem that the method depicted above is not too difficult. Try to imagine the programming that would be necessary to handle groups of 100 or even 200 scores! A far easier way to handle the problem is to set up a table area for the incoming data.

Creating tables

The idea of a table is quite simple. A table is nothing more than a series of adjacent or contiguous memory positions into which the data values are placed. The actual allocating of memory space is done by the OCCURS clause, which has the following format:

OCCURS integer TIMES

We can now modify our program by creating a table area for our incoming scores:

```
FD   SCORES-FILE
     ------
     ------
     DATA RECORD IS SCORES.
01   SCORES.
     03   SITE-NBR          PIC 99.
     03   SCORE-DATA        PIC 99V9 OCCURS 10 TIMES.
```

The above entry reserves 30 positions of memory (just as our original entries did—SCORE-1 SCORE-2 . . . SCORE-10) and can be visualized in either of two ways:

SITE- NBR	SCORE-DATA	SCORE-DATA	. . .	SCORE-DATA

or as

SCORE-DATA
SCORE-DATA
SCORE-DATA
.
.
.
SCORE-DATA

At this point we do face one small problem. That is, although our original method was cumbersome, each field could be referenced because each had a unique name. With the second method, there are 10 places called SCORE-DATA. We solve the dilemma by using what is known as a *subscript*. The subscript refers to the location of a data element within a table.

SCORE-DATA table

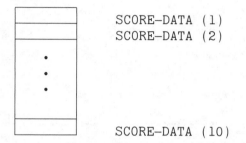

```
                        SCORE-DATA (1)
                        SCORE-DATA (2)
                  .
                  .
                  .


                        SCORE-DATA (10)
```

Certain rules must be followed when using tables.

1. The OCCURS clause *cannot* be written at the 01 level.

2. The subscript value may be a constant value, such as SCORE-DATA (5), or it may be a variable, such as SCORE-DATA (COUNT). In this case, if COUNT had a value of 4, reference would be made to the fourth element in the table called SCORE-DATA. (*Note:* Some versions permit the use of arithmetic expressions as subscripts. Example: TABLE (COUNT + 1). Check your system to see if this structure is permitted.)

3. It is incorrect to try to access a position that is outside the range of the table. The entries SCORE-DATA (0); SCORE-DATA (15)—when there are only 10 elements in the table; or SCORE-DATA (3.5) are errors. (*Note:* In the case of the last example, the system will drop the fractional portion and go to the third element of the SCORE-DATA table.) Obviously, you are not likely to make such an error if you are using real values in the subscripts. In actual practice you will be using variables almost all the time and the same rule holds true: The value of the subscript variable must meet the rules discussed above.

4. The OCCURS clause names the table and reserves an area for table data. It does *not* put any data into that area. It is the programmer's responsibility to place data into the table correctly.

5. ANS 74 COBOL allowed the entry to be written without a space between the table name and the subscript.

```
SCORE-DATA(3)
```

Now, with the data in table format, our program will be much easier to write and will take advantage of the looping capability of the computer.

```
77   COUNTER          PIC 999 VALUE 1.
77   TOTAL-SCORES     PIC 9999V9 VALUE ZERO.
77   LARGEST          PIC 99V9.
77   SMALLEST         PIC 99V9.
```

```
     PERFORM COUNT-SCORES
          UNTIL COUNTER IS GREATER THAN 10.
     COMPUTE AVG = TOTAL-SCORES / 10
     MOVE SCORE-DATA (1) TO LARGEST SMALLEST.
     MOVE 2 TO COUNTER.
     PERFORM FIND-LARGEST-SMALLEST
          UNTIL COUNTER IS GREATER THAN 10.
          .
          .
          .
 COUNT-SCORES.
     ADD SCORE-DATA (COUNTER) TO TOTAL-SCORES.
     ADD 1 TO COUNTER.
 FIND-LARGEST-SMALLEST.
     IF SCORE-DATA (COUNTER) IS GREATER THAN LARGEST
          MOVE SCORE-DATA (COUNTER) TO LARGEST.
     IF SCORE-DATA (COUNTER) IS LESS THAN SMALLEST
          MOVE SCORE-DATA (COUNTER) TO SMALLEST.
     ADD 1 TO COUNTER.
          .
          .
          .
```

A few points are worth noting about the program segment shown above.

1. The program set up the field (COUNTER) that will be used as a subscript to work our way through the table elements.
2. The subscript (COUNTER) was set to 1 before the loop was entered since a zero subscript normally is not permitted.
3. On the first execution of COUNT-SCORES, the COUNTER value was 1, which means that the first element in the table (SCORE-DATA) was added to the total.
4. The programmer adds one to the COUNTER value in order to work through the table.
5. The test is for "greater than 10" in order to process the tenth record.
6. The FIND-LARGEST-SMALLEST paragraph follows the same pattern as COUNT-SCORES. Note that the strategy was to move the first value in the table to LARGEST and SMALLEST, assuming that these would be the correct answers. Then, the subscript was set to 2, to start the process of comparing the other table values against these values. If larger or smaller values are found, they are moved into the reserved fields. Note the ease of this method, as opposed to that of trying to work with individually named fields.

Note that the advantage of using tables is that it gives us an easy way to handle multiple data elements of the same size and type. The routine to find the largest and smallest scores will follow the same pattern in which the subscript is used to work our way through the table.

Using PERFORM with tables

Throughout the text you have seen that the PERFORM statement was a vital part of structured programming. The three forms of the statement—PERFORM, PERFORM UNTIL, and PERFORM THRU (used in conjunction with the EXIT statement)—gave you several control variations. Two additional variations of PERFORM are especially useful with tables. The first of these is quite simple and is called the TIMES option.

The PERFORM TIMES format

The TIMES variation of the PERFORM statement is extremely simple and has the following format:

$$\underline{\text{PERFORM}} \text{ procedure name} \begin{Bmatrix} \text{identifier} \\ \text{integer} \end{Bmatrix} \underline{\text{TIMES}}.$$

The integer option could be used in our previous example by saying

```
PERFORM COUNT-SCORES
    10 TIMES.
```

Of course, this version will work only if we know in advance the exact number of repetitions required. Also, note that the programmer still has to set up the subscript value and add to it.

The identifier option tells the system to PERFORM the paragraph a specific number of times depending upon the current value of a variable. A statement of this type is very valuable when we wish to execute a loop a different number of times each time the program is run.

```
PERFORM 090-PROCESSING COUNT-A TIMES.
```

The PERFORM VARYING format

Perhaps the most useful format of PERFORM with tables is the version that uses VARYING. A simplified version is shown below:

$$\underline{\text{PERFORM}} \text{ procedure name}$$
$$\underline{\text{VARYING}} \text{ identifier-1} \underline{\text{FROM}} \begin{Bmatrix} \text{identifier-2} \\ \text{literal-1} \end{Bmatrix}$$
$$\underline{\text{BY}} \begin{Bmatrix} \text{identifier-3} \\ \text{literal-2} \end{Bmatrix} \underline{\text{UNTIL}} \text{ condition}.$$

Our previous example can now be written using the PERFORM VARYING.

```
PERFORM COUNT-SCORES
    VARYING COUNTER FROM 1 BY 1
        UNTIL COUNTER IS GREATER THAN 10.
        .
        .
        .

COUNT-SCORES.
    ADD SCORE-DATA (COUNTER) TO TOTAL-SCORES.
```

Identifier-1 (our COUNTER field) must be established in the DATA DIVI-SION by the programmer. The "FROM 1" part of the statement sets COUNTER to this initial value by moving a 1 value into the field. The "BY 1" portion automatically adds 1 to COUNTER *after* the loop has been executed. The test condition may be any test the programmer wishes, but here we wish to stop executing the loop when COUNTER is greater than 10. The value of COUNTER is 1 *during* the first execution of the loop, but is automatically incremented by 1 at the end of the first pass through the loop. The software then tests the value of COUNTER against the test condition to see if the paragraph should be PERFORMED again. At the *conclusion* of the tenth pass through the loop, COUNTER is automatically incremented by 1. Again the software tests COUNTER against the test condition and, since 11 is greater than 10, exits from the PERFORM to the next statement in sequence. If we had said "UNTIL COUNTER IS EQUAL TO 10," the loop would only have been executed nine times.

As the format indicates, combinations of identifier fields and/or literals may be used:

```
PERFORM MAIN-LOOP
    VARYING LOOP-COUNTER FROM 1
    BY 1 UNTIL TEST-AMT-A IS GREATER THAN
    TEST-AMT-B.
PERFORM PROCESS-ROUTINE
    VARYING CONTROL-VALUE FROM 6
    BY AMT-A UNTIL CONTROL-VALUE
    IS EQUAL TO MAIN-CONTROL-VALUE.
```

Large systems must have access to hundreds of data files.

Loading a table externally

Although we just finished reading data into a table, the table contained only the data from one record. We often run across problems that require the pertinent fields to be placed into a table before any processing can take place.

Now let's set up a second example of how tables can make life easier. We will assume that our company has an outside sales force of seven people. The month has just ended and the sales data are stored in a file (SALES-INFO). Right now each record consists of a *single* field—MONTHLY-SALES PIC 9(4)V99. You are asked to write a program that prints the total sales for the month, the average sales amount, and the amount by which each area differs (plus or minus) from the average.

SALES FOR MONTH

TOTAL SALES	------			
AVERAGE SALES	------			
SALES AREA 1	------	DIFFERENCE	------	(+)
SALES AREA 2	------	DIFFERENCE	------	(−)
etc.				

A problem of this type is particularly suitable to the use of tables, since all the data must be processed once to find the average before the difference amount for the various areas can be calculated and printed. Our approach will be quite simple.

1. Read and store all the data values in a table.
2. Access the table to total the values and find the average.
3. Access the table a second time to calculate and print out the sales and difference amounts.

Our incoming record format will be quite simple, since each record contains only one field. A single, seven-element table will be set up in the WORKING-STORAGE SECTION using OCCURS:

```
FD  SALES-FILE
    LABEL RECORD IS STANDARD
    VALUE OF FILE-ID IS 'SALES-INFO'
    DATA RECORD IS SALES-REC.
01  SALES-REC.
    03  SALES-IN            PIC 9(4)V99.
FD  PRINT-FILE
      .
      .
      .
WORKING-STORAGE SECTION.
01  STORAGE-AREAS.
    03  EOF-INDICATOR       PIC 9 VALUE ZERO.
    03  TOTAL-SALES         PIC 9(6)V99 VALUE ZEROS.
    03  AVG-SALES           PIC 9(4)V99.
    03  COUNTER             PIC 9 VALUE ZERO.
    03  NBR-OF-SALES-AREAS  PIC 9 VALUE 7.
    03  TABLE-AREA.
        03  SALES           PIC 9(4)V99 OCCURS 7 TIMES.
```

Placing the values into the table is again done by the READ statement in conjunction with MOVE. Figure 8-1 illustrates this action.

```
PROCEDURE DIVISION.

    CONTROL-ROUTINE.
        PERFORM 010-OPEN-ROUTINE.
        PERFORM 020-LOAD-TABLE
            UNTIL EOF-INDICATOR = 1.
                .
                .
                .

    010-OPEN-ROUTINE.
        OPEN INPUT SALES-FILE, OUTPUT PRINTFILE.
        READ SALES-FILE
            AT END MOVE 1 TO EOF-INDICATOR.
    020-LOAD-TABLE.
        MOVE SALES-IN TO SALES (COUNTER).
        ADD 1 TO COUNTER.
        READ SALES-FILE
            AT END MOVE 1 TO EOF-INDICATOR.
    030-PROCESSING-ROUTINE.
                .
                .
                .
```

Note the following points in the program (Figure 8-2).

1. The table (SALES) was set up in WORKING-STORAGE and the incoming values were MOVEd into table elements one through seven.
2. The programmer set up the subscript field (COUNTER) with a beginning value of 1 and added to it each time through the 020-LOAD-TABLE paragraph.
3. The TIMES option of PERFORM was used to control the number of times the 040-CALC-TOTAL paragraph was executed. As with the 020-LOAD-TABLE paragraph, the programmer was responsible for setting and adding to the subscript.
4. The 060-PRINT-SALES paragraph was controlled by the VARYING option of PERFORM. Since this version of PERFORM set the subscript to an initial value of 1, the 030-RESET-SUBSCRIPT paragraph was *not* used. Incrementing and testing of the subscript value was handled by the PERFORM. Therefore, ADD 1 TO COUNTER was not needed within the 060-PRINT-SALES paragraph.

So far we have placed data into a table using two methods: (1) by the READ statement and (2) by READ followed by MOVE. For those of you working with an on-line, video-screen-oriented system, the ACCEPT statement can serve the same purpose as READ. A modified version of the pertinent sections of the previous program illustrates

FIGURE 8-1

Reading data into a table

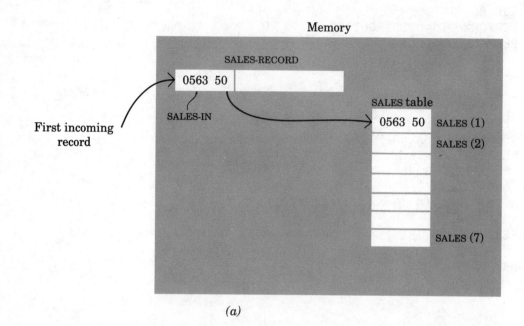

(a)

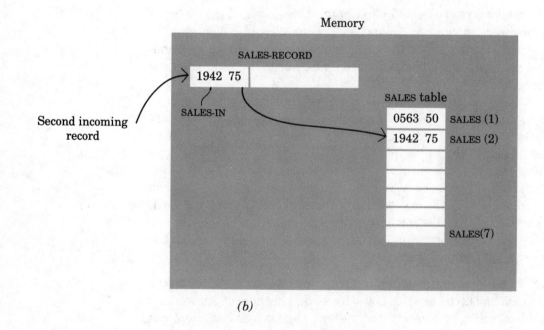

(b)

FIGURE 8-2

Table program

```
000100 IDENTIFICATION DIVISION.
000110 PROGRAM-ID.  TBL.
000120*
000130 ENVIRONMENT DIVISION.
000140 CONFIGURATION SECTION.
000150 SOURCE-COMPUTER. - - -.
000160 OBJECT-COMPUTER. - - -.
000170 INPUT-OUTPUT SECTION.
000180 FILE-CONTROL.
000190     SELECT SALES-FILE ASSIGN TO - - -.
000200     SELECT PRINTFILE ASSIGN TO - - -.
000210*
000220 DATA DIVISION.
000230 FILE SECTION.
000240 FD  SALES-FILE
000250     LABEL RECORDS ARE STANDARD
000260     VALUE OF FILE-ID IS 'SALES'
000270     DATA RECORD IS SALES-REC.
000280 01  SALES-REC.
000290     03  SALES-IN            PIC 9(4)V99.
000300 FD  PRINTFILE
000310     LABEL RECORDS ARE OMITTED
000320     DATA RECORD IS LIST-RECORD.
000330 01  LIST-RECORD.
000340     03  FILLER              PIC X.
000350     03  LIST-LINE           PIC X(120).
000360 WORKING-STORAGE SECTION.
000370 01  STORAGE-AREAS.
000380     03  EOF-INDICATOR       PIC 9 VALUE ZERO.
000390     03  TOTAL-SALES         PIC 9(6)V99 VALUE ZEROS.
000400     03  AVG-SALES           PIC 9(4)V99 VALUE ZEROS.
000410     03  COUNTER             PIC 99 VALUE 01.
000420     03  NBR-OF-SALES-AREAS  PIC 9 VALUE 7.
000430 01  TABLE-AREA.
000440     03  SALES               PIC 9(4)V99 OCCURS 7 TIMES.
000450 01  HD-LINE.
000460     03  FILLER              PIC X.
000470     03  FILLER              PIC X(20) VALUE SPACES.
000480     03  FILLER              PIC X(15) VALUE 'SALES FOR MONTH'.
000490     03  FILLER              PIC X(85) VALUE SPACES.
000500 01  SALES-TOT-LINE.
000510     03  FILLER              PIC X.
000520     03  FILLER              PIC X(11) VALUE 'TOTAL SALES'.
000530     03  FILLER              PIC X(10) VALUE SPACES.
000540     03  TOTAL-SALES-OUT     PIC $ZZZ,ZZZ.99.
000550     03  FILLER              PIC X(88) VALUE SPACES.
000560 01  AVG-SALES-LINE.
000570     03  FILLER              PIC X.
000580     03  FILLER              PIC X(13) VALUE 'AVERAGE SALES'.
```

continued

FIGURE 8-2

continued

```
000590        03   FILLER                 PIC X(10) VALUE SPACES.
000600        03   AVG-SALES-OUT          PIC $Z,ZZZ.99.
000610        03   FILLER                 PIC X(88) VALUE SPACES.
000620 01   SALES-LINE.
000630        03   FILLER                 PIC X.
000640        03   FILLER                 PIC X(12) VALUE 'SALES: AREA '.
000650        03   AREA-CODE              PIC 9.
000660        03   FILLER                 PIC X(8) VALUE SPACES.
000670        03   SALES-OUT              PIC $Z,ZZZ.99.
000680        03   FILLER                 PIC X(5) VALUE SPACES.
000690        03   FILLER                 PIC X(12) VALUE 'DIFFERENCE  '.
000700        03   DIFFERENCE-OUT         PIC $Z,ZZZ.99+.
000710        03   FILLER                 PIC X(63) VALUE SPACES.
000720*
000730 PROCEDURE DIVISION.
000740 CONTROL-ROUTINE.
000750        PERFORM 010-OPEN-ROUTINE.
000760        PERFORM 020-LOAD-TABLE
000770            UNTIL EOF-INDICATOR = 1.
000780        PERFORM 030-RESET-SUBSCRIPT.
000790        PERFORM 040-CALC-TOTAL 7 TIMES.
000800        PERFORM 050-PRINT-AVG.
000810        PERFORM 060-PRINT-SALES
000820            VARYING COUNTER FROM 1 BY 1
000830            UNTIL COUNTER IS GREATER THAN 7.
000840        PERFORM 070-CLOSER.
000850        STOP RUN.
000860*
000870 010-OPEN-ROUTINE.
000880        OPEN INPUT SALES-FILE OUTPUT PRINTFILE.
000890        WRITE LIST-RECORD FROM HD-LINE
000900            AFTER ADVANCING PAGE.
000910        READ SALES-FILE
000920            AT END MOVE 1 TO EOF-INDICATOR.
000930*
000940 020-LOAD-TABLE.
000950        MOVE SALES-IN TO SALES (COUNTER).
000960        ADD 1 TO COUNTER.
000970        READ SALES-FILE
000980            AT END MOVE 1 TO EOF-INDICATOR.
000990*
001000 030-RESET-SUBSCRIPT.
001010        MOVE 1 TO COUNTER.
001020*
001030 040-CALC-TOTAL.
001040        ADD SALES (COUNTER) TO TOTAL-SALES.
001050        ADD 1 TO COUNTER.
001060*
001070 050-PRINT-AVG.
001080        COMPUTE AVG-SALES = TOTAL-SALES / NBR-OF-SALES-AREAS.
```

FIGURE 8-2

continued

```
001090        MOVE AVG-SALES TO AVG-SALES-OUT.
001100        WRITE LIST-RECORD FROM AVG-SALES-LINE
001110            AFTER ADVANCING 2 LINES.
001120*
001130 060-PRINT-SALES.
001140        MOVE COUNTER TO AREA-CODE.
001150        MOVE SALES (COUNTER) TO SALES-OUT.
001160        COMPUTE DIFFERENCE-OUT = SALES (COUNTER) - AVG-SALES.
001170        WRITE LIST-RECORD FROM SALES-LINE
001180            AFTER ADVANCING 2 LINES.
001190*
001200 070-CLOSER.
001210        CLOSE SALES-FILE PRINTFILE.
```

```
CONTROL-ROUTINE.
    -------
    PERFORM 020-LOAD-TABLE
        UNTIL EOF-INDICATOR = 1.
    .
    .
    .
020-LOAD-TABLE.
    DISPLAY 'PLEASE ENTER 7 DIGIT SALES VALUE'.
    ACCEPT SALES (COUNTER).
    ADD 1 TO COUNTER.
    DISPLAY 'IF LAST RECORD, ENTER 1; ELSE'.
    DISPLAY 'ENTER A ZERO'.
    ACCEPT EOF-INDICATOR.
```

The DISPLAY statement may be used to produce output on the contents of a variable, including table values, to the video screen. For example, the statement

```
DISPLAY SALES (6)
```

would display output on the contents of the sixth element of the SALES table. In this case, the output will be in straight numeric format. If the value had been moved to an edit field first, the displayed output would contain the appropriate edit characters. If SALES (6) contains 141762, then this is exactly what would show on the screen. However, if we had done the following,

```
03  SALES-OUT          PIC $Z,ZZZ.99.
    .
    .
    .
MOVE SALES (6) TO SALES-OUT.
DISPLAY SALES-OUT.
```

the output would now show

```
$1,417.62
```

Loading a table internally

The second method of getting data into a table is by creating the data internally within the program. This technique involves a slight refinement in the use of the VALUE clause you have used previously. We will start by defining or creating seven data values in the WORKING-STORAGE SECTION.

```
WORKING-STORAGE SECTION.
    01   SALES-VALUES.
         03   FILLER      PIC 9(4)V99 VALUE 0563.50.
         03   FILLER      PIC 9(4)V99 VALUE 1942.75.
         03   FILLER      PIC 9(4)V99 VALUE 6873.00.
         03   FILLER      PIC 9(4)V99 VALUE 0045.21.
         03   FILLER      PIC 9(4)V99 VALUE 4976.58.
         03   FILLER      PIC 9(4)V99 VALUE 3214.16.
         03   FILLER      PIC 9(4)V99 VALUE 8765.52.
```

Unfortunately, just defining these values won't put them into a table. It would seem that we should be able to work in the OCCURS clause with the above entry. However, the rule is that "VALUE cannot be used with OCCURS." This rule is entirely logical, since VALUE defines a *single* value while OCCURS sets aside room for multiple elements. We can get around this problem by using the REDEFINES clause. Right below our last entry we will do the following:

```
         .
         .

         .
         03   FILLER       PIC 9(4)V99 VALUE 8765.52.
    01   TABLE-DATA REDEFINES SALES-VALUES.
         03   SALES        PIC 9(4)V99 OCCURS 7 TIMES.
```

This use of REDEFINES follows the same pattern that was discussed earlier when REDEFINES was first mentioned. In this case, the seven entries under SALES-VALUES simply lay out 42 digits [seven times a PIC OF 9(4)V99] in memory. At this point it is *not* a table. The REDEFINES and OCCURS entries now "tell" the system that this area is to be redefined as a table with the name SALES.

A second way of placing data into a table internally is by means of arithmetic statements and the MOVE statement:

```
COMPUTE ANSWER-TABLE (X) = (AMT-A + AMT-B) / AMT-C.
ADD FIELD-1 FIELD-2 GIVING TOTAL-T (COUNTER).
MOVE AMT-X TO AMT-X-TABLE (1).
```

One of the most important points to understand is that once data values are placed in a table, they can be treated just like any other field in COBOL. Many beginning programmers seem to feel that data are read out of a table, but this is not so. *There simply is no such concept as reading out of a table.*

Working with tables

In our sales table problem we had a unique situation in which the incoming record contained only one field. The more likely case is that the record would contain multiple fields such as sales amount, salesperson's name, and sales product group such as hardware, automotive, household, and so on:

Sales amount	Name	Product group
PIC 9(4)V99	PIC X(20)	PIC X(20)

With this new data, our output will be revised to include the salesperson's name and the product group.

```
                    SALES FOR MONTH


TOTAL SALES _____
AVERAGE SALES _____
SALES AREA 1 ___    DIFFERENCE ___    JOE SMITH   HOUSEHOLD
SALES AREA 2 ___    DIFFERENCE ___    NORMA LEE   HARDWARE
                    and so on
```

We now have need for three tables: the sales amount as before, salesperson's name, and the product group. This additional requirement does not pose any great difficulty as COBOL can handle any number of tables, subject only to the limits of available memory. One possibility is to create three separate tables as shown below:

```
01   TABLE-AREAS.
     03   SALES           PIC 9(4)V99 OCCURS 7 TIMES.
     03   NAME            PIC A(20) OCCURS 7 TIMES.
     03   PRODUCT-GROUP   PIC X(20) OCCURS 7 TIMES.
```

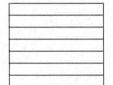

```
        PERFORM 020-LOAD-TABLE
            UNTIL EOF-INDICATOR = 1.
          .

          .

          .

020-LOAD-TABLE.
     MOVE SALES-IN TO SALES (COUNTER).
     MOVE NAME-IN TO NAME (COUNTER).
     MOVE PRODUCT-GRP-IN TO PRODUCT-GROUP (COUNTER).
     ADD 1 TO COUNTER.
     READ SALES-FILE
         AT END MOVE 1 TO EOF-INDICATOR.
```

Tables with multiple fields

A second possibility, however, is that the programmer can create a single table that contains *multiple* fields. Note the following DATA DIVISION entry:

```
01   TABLE-DATA.
     03   TABLES OCCURS 7 TIMES.
          05   SALES           PIC 9(4)V99.
          05   NAME            PIC A(20).
          05   PRODUCT-GROUP   PIC X(20).
```

Since the OCCURS entry was written at the 03 level and the 05 level entries are subordinate to it, the single table now contains room for seven SALES values, seven NAME entries, and seven PRODUCT-GROUP entries. Also note that our multi-field table can consist of mixed data types: numeric, alphabetic, and alphanumeric. A schematic of the table is shown below.

← TABLES (1) →		
SALES (1)	NAME (1)	PRODUCT-GROUP (1)
← TABLES (2) →		
SALES (2)	NAME (2)	PRODUCT-GROUP (2)
← TABLES (7) →		
SALES (7)	NAME (7)	PRODUCT-GROUP (7)

An interesting part of this arrangement is that we can access various parts of the table separately and in groups. As you can see from the diagram, SALES (2) accesses only the data from the second element in the SALES column and NAME (2) accesses the second element in the NAME column. TABLE (2), however, accesses *all* values in the second position: SALES (2), NAME (2), and PRODUCT-GROUP (2). Figure 8-3 illustrates the action of a single table that contains multiple fields.

FIGURE 8-3

Multifield table

```
000100 IDENTIFICATION DIVISION.
000110 PROGRAM-ID. MULTI.
000120*
000130 ENVIRONMENT DIVISION.
000140 CONFIGURATION SECTION.
000150 SOURCE-COMPUTER. - - -.
000160 OBJECT-COMPUTER. - - -.
000170 INPUT-OUTPUT SECTION.
000180 FILE-CONTROL.
000190     SELECT SALES-FILE ASSIGN TO - - -.
```

FIGURE 8-3

continued

```
000200*
000210 DATA DIVISION.
000220 FILE SECTION.
000230 FD  SALES-FILE
000240     LABEL RECORD IS STANDARD
000250     VALUE OF FILE-ID IS 'SALES1'
000260     DATA RECORD IS SALES-RECORD.
000270 01  SALES-RECORD.
000280     03  SALES-IN          PIC 9(4)V99.
000290     03  NAME-IN           PIC X(20).
000300     03  PRODUCT-GRP-IN    PIC X(20).
000310 WORKING-STORAGE SECTION.
000320 01  TABLE-DATA.
000330     03  TABLES OCCURS 7 TIMES.
000340         05  SALES         PIC 9(4)V99.
000350         05  NAME          PIC X(20).
000360         05  PRODUCT-GROUP PIC X(20).
000370 01  OTHER-FIELDS.
000380     03  COUNTER           PIC 9 VALUE 1.
000390     03  EOF-INDICATOR     PIC 9 VALUE ZERO.
000400*
000410 PROCEDURE DIVISION.
000420 CONTROL-ROUTINE.
000430     PERFORM 010-OPEN-ROUTINE.
000440     PERFORM 020-LOAD-TABLE
000450         VARYING COUNTER FROM 1 BY 1
000460         UNTIL COUNTER IS GREATER THAN 7.
000470     PERFORM 030-PROCESSING-ROUTINE.
000480     STOP RUN.
000490 010-OPEN-ROUTINE.
000500     OPEN INPUT SALES-FILE
000510         OUTPUT PRINT-FILE.
000520     READ SALES-FILE
000530         AT END MOVE 1 TO EOF-INDICATOR.
000540 020-LOAD-TABLE.
000550     MOVE SALES-RECORD TO TABLES (COUNTER).
000560     ADD 1 TO COUNTER.
000570     READ SALES-FILE
000580         AT END MOVE 1 TO EOF-INDICATOR.
000590 030-PROCESSING-ROUTINE.
000600     DISPLAY SALES (4).
000610     DISPLAY NAME (4).
000620     DISPLAY PRODUCT-GROUP (4).
000630     DISPLAY TABLES (4).
000640     CLOSE SALES-FILE.


04521
SAM JOHNSON
HARDWARE
004521SAM JOHNSON          HARDWARE
```

In the example, we were able to move the entire incoming data record (SALES-RECORD) to table *only because every* field in the record was going into the table. If some of the fields in the incoming record were not going to be used in the problem, there would be no reason to put them in a table, since this would be both a waste of effort and a waste of memory.

The last DISPLAY statement illustrates the organization of our multi-field table by printing the contents of the fourth element across.

It is also possible to load a multi-field table internally using VALUE and REDEFINES as before. Suppose we wish to create a table with the following format.

PIC X(6)	PIC 9(3)	PIC A
BLUE	123	A
GREEN	456	B
BLACK	789	C
ORANGE	987	D

One method is shown below.

```
WORKING-STORAGE SECTION.
01   MULTI-DATA.
     03   FILLER          PIC X(6) VALUE 'BLUE '.
     03   FILLER          PIC 9(3) VALUE 123.
     03   FILLER          PIC A VALUE 'A'.
     03   FILLER          PIC X(6) VALUE 'GREEN '.
     03   FILLER          PIC 9(3) VALUE 456.
     03   FILLER          PIC A VALUE 'B'.
     03   FILLER          PIC X(6) VALUE 'BLACK'.
     03   FILLER          PIC 9(3) VALUE 789.
     03   FILLER          PIC A VALUE 'C'.
     03   FILLER          PIC X(6) VALUE 'ORANGE'.
     03   FILLER          PIC 9(3) VALUE 987.
     03   FILLER          PIC A VALUE 'D'.
01   MULTI-TABLE REDEFINES MULTI-DATA.
     03   TABLES OCCURS 4 TIMES.
          05   COLOR-T     PIC X(6).
          05   NBR-T       PIC 9(3).
          05   ALFA-T      PIC A.
```

A shorter method can be used to save a few keystrokes, but may lead to difficulties when the table data need to be revised. In either case, the action of the system is the same: the FILLER entries lay out the data values in consecutive memory locations and OCCURS redefines the area in terms of a specific table format:

```
WORKING-STORAGE SECTION.
01   MULTI-DATA.
     03   FILLER          PIC X(10) VALUE 'BLUEbb123A'.
     03   FILLER          PIC X(10) VALUE 'GREENb456B'.
     03   FILLER          PIC X(10) VALUE 'BLACKb789C'.
     03   FILLER          PIC X(10) VALUE 'ORANGE987D'.
```

```
01   MULTI-TABLE REDEFINES MULTI-DATA.
     03   TABLES OCCURS 4 TIMES.
          05   COLOR-T     PIC X(6).
          05   NBR-T       PIC 9(3).
          05   ALFA-T      PIC A.
```

Generally, "hard coding" of table data should be avoided in favor of table values read in from a file. The hard-coding method requires recompiling the program every time a change is made, while the file data can be changed without modifying program code.

Clearing a table

Another point to be considered is that of clearing a table. As you know, the function of the OCCURS entry is to reserve a designated amount of memory. Note that OCCURS does *not* clear this area to zeros or spaces. Normally this is not a problem since tables are reserved specifically for the entry of data values into that area. Some versions of COBOL *automatically* clear table areas prior to execution of the program.

Since you cannot assume that every system does this, your best approach is to assume that the area is filled with garbage. A single element can be cleared with a MOVE statement:

```
MOVE ZEROS TO AMT-A (X)
MOVE SPACES TO ADDRESS-TABLE (9)
```

Most systems permit the clearing of an entire table with a MOVE as shown below:

```
01   NUMERIC-TABLES.
     03   AMT-A          PIC 999V99 OCCURS 20 TIMES.
     03   AMT-B          PIC 9999V99 OCCURS 35 TIMES.
       .
       .
       .
     MOVE ZEROS TO NUMERIC-TABLES.
```

Table size considerations

So far in this chapter, all examples have illustrated table handling activities in which the number of data elements were known in advance. Thus, we could set the OCCURS value to a specific size and even use PERFORM TIMES or PERFORM VARYING based on this knowledge. What do you do when the number of table elements is unknown? Several possibilities need to be discussed.

One solution is obvious: Make the table too large. Assuming that you have a rough idea of the number of data elements, you can specify a larger table. Thus, if you estimate 75 elements, setting the table to 100 (OCCURS 100 TIMES) may not be unreasonable. However, setting the table to a very large size may not be possible because of the memory limitations of a particular machine. Tables can consume large amounts of memory very quickly as the example below indicates. It will require $1000 \times 49 = 49,000$ bytes of memory.

```
03  TABLES OCCURS 1000 TIMES.
    05  NAME          PIC X(20).
    05  ADDRESS       PIC X(20).
    05  SS-NBR        PIC 9(9).
```

However, by investigating the characteristics of the data file you should be able to keep the excess positions to a minimum. Presumably, you will load your table in a loader routine and then go back to access the data elements in one or more processing routines. At this point you face a slight problem—you must be careful not to try to access a table element that is beyond the point at which the last data value was loaded.

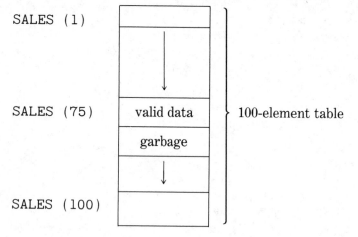

One way to handle this is to count the number of records being moved to the table (your subscript provides this information) and use this in later processing loops:

```
PERFORM MAIN-PROCESSING TABLE-COUNT TIMES.
```

or

```
PERFORM MAIN-PROCESSING
    VARYING SUB FROM 1
    BY 1 UNTIL SUB IS GREATER THAN TABLE-COUNT.
```

What if you make your table size too small? On most systems you will get a run-time error message that will indicate something like "SUBSCRIPT OUT OF RANGE".

A second *apparent* solution to the problem of the table size lies in the OCCURS entry. It would seem that if we can state

```
03  SALES   PIC 999V99 OCCURS 100 TIMES.
```

we should be able to use a variable for the table size:

```
03  SALES   PIC 999V99 OCCURS X TIMES.
```

Then, during the running of the program we could input the table size needed via an ACCEPT statement. This would give us a handy way of dealing with tables that vary in size from run to run:

```
DISPLAY 'PLEASE ENTER TABLE SIZE'.
ACCEPT X.
```

Unfortunately, this approach won't work for one very simple reason: the OCCURS entry appears in the DATA DIVISION and the table size is generated during the *compilation* of your program. The ACCEPT statement is acted upon during the *execution* of the program and, therefore, we cannot change the table size. In the next chapter you will see a variation of the OCCURS entry that *seems* to solve our dilemma. Although it offers some interesting programming applications, the rules stated above still hold true.

Table lookup operations

Previous examples have shown how the programmer can set up various types of tables and how the subscript can be manipulated in order to get to specific elements within the table. The term "table lookup" is often applied to the job of searching a table to find specific values. Perhaps the simplest form of table lookup is that of searching for either a specific value or, more likely, for values that fall within a certain range. For example, we may wish to print a listing of all salespeople with sales over $3000:

```
01    TABLES.
      03    SALES-DATA OCCURS 100 TIMES.
            05    SALES-AMT        PIC 9(5)V99.
            05    SALESPERSON      PIC X(20).
            .
            .
            .

      PERFORM SALES-SEARCH
            VARYING SUB FROM 1 BY 1
            UNTIL SUB IS GREATER THAN 100.
SALES-SEARCH.
      IF    SALES-AMT (SUB) IS GREATER THAN 3000.00
            MOVE _____
            MOVE _____.
```

A more sophisticated—and far more useful—variation would allow for the entry of the search value through a terminal:

```
77    SEARCH-VALUE            PIC 9(5)V99.
            .
            .
            .

      DISPLAY 'PLEASE ENTER SALES SEARCH'.
      DISPLAY 'VALUE IN FORMAT XXXXX.XX'.
      ACCEPT SEARCH-VALUE.
            .
            .
            .

SALES-SEARCH.
      IF SALES-AMT (SUB) IS GREATER THAN SEARCH-VALUE
            MOVE _____
            MOVE _____.
```

A more imaginative form of table lookup can be shown with an example that involves payroll processing. Imagine a situation in which we have a great many employees (such as in governmental agencies) but relatively few different pay rates. If the employee personnel record contains a pay rate field, then a blanket raise given to all employees would require that the rate field be modified in *every* record. A more efficient way to do this is to have a *pay code* field within each employee record. The actual pay rate may be kept in a pay table that is created internally or brought in from a separate file. When end-of-the-pay-period processing is done, the pay code field points the way to the pay rate for the individual. If a blanket pay raise is granted, only the pay rate table needs to be changed, *not* all the individual records.

In this example we will have five pay classifications with five different rates. The classifications and rates will be stored in a one-dimensional multi-field table by means of VALUE and REDEFINES:

```
WORKING-STORAGE SECTION.
01   PAY-DATA.
     03   FILLER          PIC X(11) VALUE 'TRAINEE    '.
     03   FILLER          PIC 99V99 VALUE 05.45.
     03   FILLER          PIC X(11) VALUE 'REGULAR    '.
     03   FILLER          PIC 99V99 VALUE 06.50.
     03   FILLER          PIC X(11) VALUE 'LEAD WORKER'.
     03   FILLER          PIC 99V99 VALUE 07.80.
     03   FILLER          PIC X(11) VALUE 'FOREPERSON '.
     03   FILLER          PIC 99V99 VALUE 09.75.
     03   FILLER          PIC X(11) VALUE 'SUPERVISOR '.
     03   FILLER          PIC 99V99 VALUE 11.85.
01   TABLES REDEFINES PAY-DATA
     03   PAY-TABLE OCCURS 5 TIMES.
          05   PAY-CLASS  PIC X(11)
          05   PAY-RATE   PIC 99V99.
```

TRAINEE	05ᴧ45
REGULAR	06ᴧ50
LEAD WORKER	07ᴧ80
FOREPERSON	09ᴧ75
SUPERVISOR	11ᴧ85

Technically, the table just described consists of two parts: an *argument* and a *function*. The argument—PAY-CLASS in this case—is a known value that will help us find the function—the value we are looking for, which, in this case, is the PAY-RATE data.

In the example just set up, we would read in an employee record as shown,

Name	SS-NBR	Pay classification	-------

and use the pay classification as our *search argument* to find the matching pay classification *argument* in the table that will take us to the associated

function (PAY-RATE) (Figure 8-4). The coding to perform our table lookup
makes use of the IF statement and a subscript to work through the table.

```
FD   EMPLOYEE-FILE
     _____
     _____
     DATA RECORD IS EMPLOYEE-REC.
01   EMPLOYEE-REC.
     03   NAME-IN.        _____
     03   SS-NBR-IN       _____
     03   PAY-CLASS-IN    PIC X(11).
     _____
          .
          .
          .
WORKING-STORAGE SECTION.
77   SUBSCRIPT           PIC 9 VALUE 1 COMP.
01   PAY-DATA.
     03   FILLER         PIC X(11) VALUE 'TRAINEE    '.
     03   FILLER         PIC 99V99 VALUE 05.45.
     03   FILLER         PIC X(11) VALUE 'REGULAR    '.
     03   FILLER         PIC 99V99 VALUE 06.50.
     03   FILLER         PIC X(11) VALUE 'LEAD WORKER'.
     03   FILLER         PIC 99V99 VALUE 07.80.
     03   FILLER         PIC X(11) VALUE 'FOREPERSON '.
     03   FILLER         PIC 99V99 VALUE 09.75.
     03   FILLER         PIC X(11) VALUE 'SUPERVISOR'.
     03   FILLER         PIC 99V99 VALUE 11.85.
01   TABLES REDEFINES PAY-DATA.
     03   PAY-TABLE OCCURS 5 TIMES.
          05   PAY-CLASS  PIC X(11).
          05   PAY-RATE   PIC 99V99.
          .
          .
          .
     READ EMPLOYEE-FILE _____.
          .
          .
     PERFORM LOCATE-PAY-DATA
          UNTIL PAY-CLASS-IN IS EQUAL TO PAY-CLASS (SUBSCRIPT)
          OR SUBSCRIPT IS GREATER THAN 5.
          .
          .
LOCATE-PAY-DATA.
     IF PAY-CLASS (SUBSCRIPT) IS EQUAL TO PAY-CLASS-IN
          PERFORM PAYROLL-CALCULATIONS.
     ELSE
          ADD 1 TO SUBSCRIPT.
          .
          .
PAYROLL-CALCULATIONS.
     MULTIPLY PAY-RATE (SUBSCRIPT) BY _____.
```

FIGURE 8-4

Table lookup

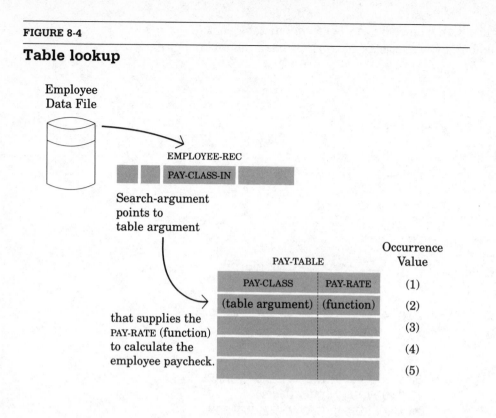

A few points are worth noting.

1. Although our example had only one function (PAY-RATE), the table could have contained other functions that would have been needed in payroll processing. For instance, we could have set up a table item for organizational dues for each of the pay classifications. These data could have been actual dollar amounts or they could be codes that become the search argument to locate dollar amounts stored in another table.

2. The search argument and the argument were established as alphanumeric values to show that it is not always necessary to work with numeric values.

3. The subscript value acted as a *pointer* to allow us to search or "IF" our way through the table. As before, it is the programmer's responsibility to set up and manipulate the subscript.

4. A subscript contains what is known as an *occurrence value*, which indicates the position of the data element within the table. Thus, an occurrence, or subscript, value of one refers to the first element in the table, while an occurrence value of seven refers to the seventh element in the table.

5. On most systems, subscript values are handled in binary (COMP) format and you can increase machine efficiency by setting up the subscript with that usage.

In any operation involving tables, the programmer should code a routine that checks the subscript to see that it is within the permissible range. This includes *both* ends of the range to see if the subscript has reached zero or a negative number and to see if it has exceeded the occurrence size set by the OCCURS entry. Obviously, this should be done prior to any processing that makes use of the current subscript value.

COMMON ERRORS

There are very few errors that one can make with tables and most of these are relatively easy to detect. Perhaps the single most common error involves the subscript value. Certain common sense rules apply to the subscript when referencing table data.

1. The subscript cannot be zero since there is no zero position in the table.
2. The same rule applies to the other end of the table data: The subscript cannot exceed the maximum number of elements as established by the OCCURS clause.
3. Negative subscripts are also forbidden, as are fractional subscript values such as 3.5. In the latter case, the system would go to the third element in the table.

Errors of the type described above will not be detected during the compilation of your program. Instead, they are execution, or run-time, errors that depend upon the value you have given to the subscript. It is up to the programmer to establish the beginning value of the subscript, to increment it properly, and to reset it when necessary. One very common error is forgetting to reset the subscript value after exiting from one loop and before entering into the next loop. In the same manner, the programmer must remember to increment the subscript value when working within the loop.

Another type of error is really one of understanding exactly how tables work. Most beginners have no problem with reading in a record and moving the data to appropriate tables, as shown in various examples throughout this chapter. After the data are in tables, however, many programmers try to READ the data "out" of the table so that they can be manipulated. This idea, of course, is entirely wrong, since the data have already been read in and placed in the table. READ implies the idea of bringing data into memory from some outside source such as cards, tape, or disk. Therefore, you do not READ the data "out" of tables; instead, you access them in the same general way you have always accessed data that are in memory. The only difference now is that the reference to the data must contain a subscript.

PROGRAMMING TIPS

There seems to be a tendency on the part of many beginning programmers to feel that the use of tables somehow falls outside of any known programming techniques. Just the opposite is true since tables fit with everything you have learned so far, plus they offer you the opportunity of developing additional programming techniques. Tables open a whole new way of thinking about how a problem can be solved.

In the traditional approaches to problem solving on the computer, you were obligated to perform all actions on the data record during the one time it was in memory. Thus, the sequential nature of the file handling forced you to a relatively narrow set of techniques. Tables free you from this limitation by allowing you to access table elements in a multitude of ways. Professional programmers make extensive use of tables to save time and effort, and so should you.

Remember that subscripts are usually handled by the system in binary format. Setting up the subscript in this format takes very little effort and will greatly improve program efficiency.

Tables can use a large amount of memory and it is possible to exceed *available* memory very quickly. Some memory-saving and efficiency considerations are listed below.

Set up numeric fields as COMP-3 (packed) or COMP (binary) to conserve storage.

Don't clear large tables (to zero or whatever value is appropriate) unless absolutely necessary.

Don't store FILLER fields in tables.

Comment: The size of an average application (such as payroll, accounts receivable, and so on) on a large mainframe computer is:

55 programs;
23,000 source statements;
6 master files;
13 million bytes in the database;
26 predefined user reports.*

SELF-STUDY: QUESTIONS AND ANSWERS

1. I don't understand when one is supposed to use tables and when one is not.

   Answer: This answer may sound as though the question is being evaded, but it really isn't. The answer is that you have to determine when or when not to use tables. The general rule is that if you can completely process a record by accessing it once—as in a read-calculate-print loop—then tables are not needed. If an analysis of the problem shows that you cannot do all of the processing on a record at one time, then tables would seem to be a likely method. Another way of looking at this is for you to

---

*"Software Maintenance Management," Lientz, B. P., and Swanson, E. B., Addison-Wesley Publishing Company, 1980, as reported in *Datamation* magazine, January 1984.

decide which is the most efficient method in terms of machine time and programmer time.

2. What are the limitations on the use of tables?

Answer: The first and most obvious limitation is the size of memory. You would be amazed how fast memory can be used up by tables, particularly by table data in DISPLAY format. This is why we will store in tables only the pertinent data fields from the incoming record. It would be a total waste of your time and of computer memory to store unneeded or FILLER fields.

3. What do I do when I want to use a table but don't know how many elements there will be?

Answer: You have hit upon one of the major problems concerning tables. Assuming you have a rough idea of the number of items, you can make that table larger than necessary. For example, if you think there may be 80 or 90 elements to deal with, you could play it safe by saying OCCURS 100 TIMES. This is a perfectly acceptable way of programming since you are under no obligation to use all the space allotted. During the read-in phase of your program you can set up a counter and actually count the elements as they come in. Then, future loops in your pattern can be executed "counter" times. This method is not as strange as it may seem because you might have a situation where the number of elements within the table varies with each execution of the program.

The problem with making the OCCURS entry too large is that it allocates memory that might be used for more important reasons. You can guess fairly close on the OCCURS and then, if your guess was too small, make the table larger. The fact that the table was too small will be detected by a run-time error; it will not be detected during compilation of your program.

CHAPTER TERMS

argument	PERFORM VARYING
clearing a table	REDEFINES
function	search argument
multi-field table	subscript
occurrence value	table loading
OCCURS	table lookup
PERFORM TIMES	tables

EXERCISES

1. What is the definition of a table?

2. Given: 03 DATA-FIELD PIC 999V99 OCCURS 100 TIMES . What does this statement do?

3. How would you access the 37th position in the above table?

4. What is wrong with this statement?

   ```
   01  TABLE-DATA      PIC 9(07)V99 OCCURS 10 TIMES.
   ```

5. In the statement

   ```
   ADD DATA-ARRAY (COUNT) TO TOTAL(COUNT).
   COUNT is called _____ .
   ```

6. Use PERFORM VARYING to write a program statement that adds the values in the odd locations of a table to a field called TOTAL.

   ```
   Assume  DATA-FIELD is a table 100 elements long.
        010-ADDER.
             ADD DATA-FIELD (COUNT) TO TOTAL.
   ```

7. Do the same for the even table positions.

8. Do every 5th position starting at 5 until a data value less than zero is encountered.

9. Modify the previous statement to make sure that the table action does not go beyond the end of the table.

10. How many times would this loop be performed?

    ```
    PERFORM DATA-TEST VARYING X FROM 1 BY 3
        UNTIL X IS EQUAL TO 28.
    ```

11. Why is it usually better to load a table from a file than have it internally loaded?

12. Rather than placing an employee's payrate in a file, what might be better to store there? Why?

13. What is wrong with this statement?

    ```
    ADD DATA-FIELD (-6) TO TOTAL
    ```

14. Define or explain the following terms. (Use diagrams if this will help.)
    a. table
    b. subscript
    c. search argument
    d. argument
    e. function
    f. pointer

15. Write the COBOL entries to set up the following tables.
    a. A table called RETURNS that consists of 50, four-digit numeric values in DISPLAY format.
    b. A table called SALES-AMT consisting of 50 packed numeric values in the format 9999V99.
    c. A 70-element alphabetic table consisting of EMPLOYEE-NAMES PIC A(20).
    d. A 60-element table called TABLE-INFO that consists of two fields: AMOUNT-IN PIC 9(4) and ITEM-DESCRIPTION PIC X(30).
    e. Same as part d above, but AMOUNT-IN is to be in packed format.
    f. A 10-element table called TABLE-DATA that consists of four fields: SS-NBR PIC 9(9) packed format, E-NAME PIC X(30), RATE PIC S99V999 packed format, and HOURS PIC S99.

16. Write the COBOL entries to do the following. Use the table names you set up in the previous exercise. Assume that a field called COUNTER has been established with a beginning value of 1.
    a. Clear the RETURNS table to zero. (Exercise 15a)
    b. Fill the RETURNS table with nines. (Exercise 15a)
    c. Move zeros to the numeric fields in the tables you set up in Exercise 15f above.

17. Write the statements to do the following calculations.
    a. Calculate and place the answer to the following in the location ANS (5) (use COMPUTE): $A^2 + B^2$.
    b. Calculate the answer to the above formula and place the answer in the Jth element of the ANS table (use COMPUTE).
    c. Sum the values found in the first three elements of the SALES table and place the answer in TOTAL.
    d. Add 6 to the value found in ANS (7) (use ADD).
    e. Add 1.3 to the value found in the Xth element of the table called AMOUNT (use the COMPUTE statement).

18. Create internally a four-element table called TABLE-1 that contains the following values 6.75, 9.42, 8.56, and 1.49.

19. Assume that incoming records have the following format:

Columns	Field description
1–5	Part number PIC 9(5)
6–8	Bin number PIC 9(3)
9–14	Cost price PIC 9(4)V99
15–18	Quantity on hand 9(4)
19–22	Orders 9(4)

    a. Write the program segment to set up the above numeric fields in five separate tables. Assuming that there are 40 records, place the numeric values in the tables.
    b. Change Exercise 19a to use a single, multi-field table.

20. Using the tables from Exercise 19a above, write the PROCEDURE DIVISION entries to sum the ORDERS amounts from the table, and print the total in edited format. Do not use PERFORM VARYING.

21. Change Exercise 20 so you *do* use PERFORM VARYING.

22. Create a multi-field, four-element table as shown below.

PIC X(20)	PIC 9(9)	PIC X(9)
NAME (1)	SS–NBR (1)	SCHOOL–CLASS (1)
NAME (4)	SS–NBR (4)	SCHOOL–CLASS (4)

Write the PROCEDURE DIVISION coding to use DISPLAY and ACCEPT statements to enter the data values into each element *separately*. (School class will be FRESHMAN, SOPHOMORE, JUNIOR, or SENIOR.)

For exercises 23, 24, and 25, enter 10 unique three-digit values into a table called NUMBERS by any method you choose (REDEFINES, READ, or ACCEPT). Write complete programs as follows.

23. Write a program that prints the average value, the highest value, and the lowest value.

24. Write a program that not only prints out the average value, the highest value, and the lowest value, but also prints the table location of the highest and lowest values.

25. Write a program that takes the data from the table and creates a second 10-position table with the values in ascending order. Output is to be as follows:

    ```
    ORIGINAL TABLE            SORTED TABLE


      ───────                   ───────
      ───────                   ───────
      and so on                 and so on
    ```

26. Assume you have two 10-element tables [TABLE-A and TABLE-B, PIC X(20)], each of which contains employee names. Write the PROCEDURE DIVISION entries to create a new table (TABLE-B) that contains the names in interspersed order as shown below.

    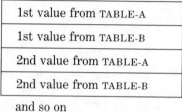

    | 1st value from TABLE-A |
    | 1st value from TABLE-B |
    | 2nd value from TABLE-A |
    | 2nd value from TABLE-B |

    and so on

27. Assume you have a 10-element table [TABLE-A, PIC X(20)] that contains employee names. Delete or remove the names from the fourth and seventh elements in the table and move all the remaining names up so that the top end of the table is completely filled.

28. Revise the previous problem so that your program will consolidate the names in the table no matter how many empty elements are encountered.

Chapter 9
More About Tables

CHAPTER OUTLINE

LEARNING OBJECTIVES

1. To acquaint you with the world of multidimensional tables—how they are set up and how the elements are accessed.

2. To learn how to use the special table handling statements available in COBOL—SET and SEARCH.

3. To understand the difference between a subscript and an index value in table handling.

4. To see how the OCCURS DEPENDING entry can be useful in situations where the number of table values is variable.

The table handling features discussed in Chapter 8 were fairly straightforward and can go a long way toward relieving many programming headaches. Since tables are used so frequently, COBOL offers several advanced features that can further lighten the burden of the programmer. The first of these is the ability to work with multidimensional tables.

Multidimensional tables

So far you have encountered only one-dimensional tables—that is, a table organized in such a way that you can have access to particular table elements by means of a single subscript. Even the multi-field table described earlier fell into this category. COBOL, however, allows you to create two- and three-dimensional tables. To illustrate a two-dimensional table, we will expand our original sales data problem to include sales data for seven salespeople for a three-month period. Each record will have the format shown below.

Sales Month 1	Sales Month 2	Sales Month 3

Our table will be set up as shown below:

```
01  TABLE-DATA.
    03  SALES OCCURS 7 TIMES.
        05  MONTH OCCURS 3 TIMES    PIC 9(4)V99.
```

At first glance our two-dimensional tables appear to be the same as a single-dimensional table that contains multiple fields. However, there are two important differences. First, *two* OCCURS entries are needed and they *must be at different levels*. Second, to get to a single element within the table, *two* subscripts are required.

MONTH (1,1)	MONTH (1,2)	MONTH (1,3)
MONTH (2,1)	MONTH (2,2)	MONTH (2,3)
MONTH (7,1)	MONTH (7,2)	MONTH (7,3)

Reference to the positions within the two-dimensional table is made by using the field name with the *highest*-level number—MONTH in this case. Since this is the most subordinate, or lowest ranking, entry and since there is an OCCURS above it, reference to MONTH requires a double subscript, such as MONTH (5,2). The first value in the subscript refers to the position *down* the table, and the second number refers to the position *across* the table. (COBOL also allows the use of three-dimensional tables that use three subscripts—down, across, and in—to reference the data elements.) Figure 9-1 illustrates the loading of a two-dimensional table and accessing data values by means of a double subscript.

A few extra points about the program should be noted.

1. All references to *individual* elements within the table were to MONTH and always included a double subscript.

2. The first value of the subscript referenced the down position while the second value referenced the across position.

3. In loading the table we had to move across in order to place the individual sales values into table positions 1-1, 1-2, and 1-3. In order to place the second set of sales figures into the proper positions, we had to increment the first subscript (DOWN) by 1 *and* reset the second subscript (ACROSS) back to 1. By doing so the second set of values was moved into the correct table positions of 2-1, 2-2, and 2-3. This process continued until the last set of values was moved into 7-1, 7-2, and 7-3.

4. In the 030-PROOF-ROUTINE reference was made to SALES with a *single* subscript. This reference is correct because SALES, as set up in the DATA DIVISION, has only one OCCURS associated with it. MONTH, on the other hand, must always be referenced with a double subscript, because it has two OCCURS associated with it.

Figure 9-1 showed how external data can be loaded into a two-dimensional table. It is also possible to create a two-dimensional table internally. (As noted before, "hard coding" of a table is not the preferred method—reading it in from a file gives greater flexibility.)

Suppose we wish to create the two-dimensional file (via VALUE and REDEFINES) shown below. Note that this is a two-dimensional table—*not* a multi-field one-dimensional table—that has three elements down and two elements across.

73∧1	66∧3
97∧5	85∧2
81∧6	91∧4

```
WORKING-STORAGE SECTION.
01  SCORES-DATA.
    03  ABC.
        05  FILLER      PIC 99V9 VALUE 73.1.
        05  FILLER      PIC 99V9 VALUE 66.3.
    03  XYZ.
        05  FILLER      PIC 99V9 VALUE 97.5.
        05  FILLER      PIC 99V9 VALUE 85.2.
    03  PDQ.
        05  FILLER      PIC 99V9 VALUE 81.6.
        05  FILLER      PIC 99V9 VALUE 91.4.
01  TABLE-DATA REDEFINES SCORES-DATA.
    03  SCORES-TABLE OCCURS 3 TIMES.
        05  SCORES PIC 99V9 OCCURS 2 TIMES.
```

FIGURE 9-1

Two-dimensional table

```
000100 IDENTIFICATION DIVISION.
000110 PROGRAM-ID. TWODEE.
000120*
000130 ENVIRONMENT DIVISION.
000140 CONFIGURATION SECTION.
000150 SOURCE-COMPUTER. - - -.
000160 OBJECT-COMPUTER. - - -.
000170 INPUT-OUTPUT SECTION.
000180 FILE-CONTROL.
000190      SELECT SALES-FILE ASSIGN TO - - -.
000200*
000210 DATA DIVISION.
000220 FILE SECTION.
000230 FD   SALES-FILE
000240      LABEL RECORD IS STANDARD
000250      VALUE OF FILE-ID IS 'SALES-DATA'
000260      DATA RECORD IS SALES-RECORD.
000270 01   SALES-RECORD.
000280      03   SALES-IN-ONE          PIC 9(4)V99.
000290      03   SALES-IN-TWO          PIC 9(4)V99.
000300      03   SALES-IN-THREE        PIC 9(4)V99.
000310 WORKING-STORAGE SECTION.
000320 01   TABLE-DATA.
000330      03   SALES OCCURS 7 TIMES.
000340           05   MONTH OCCURS 3 TIMES
000350                               PIC 9(4)V99.
000360 01   OTHER-FIELDS.
000370      03   EOF-INDICATOR         PIC 9 VALUE ZERO.
000380      03   TOTALS                PIC 9(6)V99 VALUE ZEROS.
000390      03   TOTALS-ED             PIC ZZZZZZ.99.
000400      03   COUNTER               PIC 9 VALUE 1.
000410      03   DOWN-T                PIC 9 VALUE ZERO.
000420      03   ACROSS                PIC 9 VALUE ZERO.
000430*
000440 PROCEDURE DIVISION.
000450 CONTROL-ROUTINE.
000460      PERFORM 010-OPEN-ROUTINE.
000470      PERFORM 020-LOAD-TABLE 7 TIMES.
000480      PERFORM 030-PROOF-ROUTINE.
000490      PERFORM 040-ADD-ROUTINE
000500           VARYING COUNTER FROM 1 BY 1
000510             UNTIL COUNTER IS EQUAL TO 8.
000520      PERFORM 050-PRINT-TOTAL.
000530      STOP RUN.
000540 010-OPEN-ROUTINE.
000550      OPEN INPUT SALES-FILE.
000560      READ SALES-FILE
000570           AT END MOVE 1 TO EOF-INDICATOR.
000580 020-LOAD-TABLE.
```

FIGURE 9-1

continued

```
000590        ADD 1 TO DOWN-T.
000600        PERFORM 025-LOAD-ROUTINE.
000610        READ SALES-FILE
000620            AT END MOVE 1 TO EOF-INDICATOR.
000630        MOVE ZERO TO ACROSS.
000640 025-LOAD-ROUTINE.
000650        ADD 1 TO ACROSS.
000660        MOVE SALES-IN-ONE TO MONTH (DOWN-T, ACROSS).
000670        ADD 1 TO ACROSS.
000680        MOVE SALES-IN-TWO TO MONTH (DOWN-T, ACROSS).
000690        ADD 1 TO ACROSS.
000700        MOVE SALES-IN-THREE TO MONTH (DOWN-T, ACROSS).
000710 030-PROOF-ROUTINE.
000720        DISPLAY MONTH (1, 1).
000730        DISPLAY MONTH (3, 3).
000740        DISPLAY MONTH (7, 1).
000750        DISPLAY MONTH (7, 2).
000760        DISPLAY MONTH (7, 3).
000770        DISPLAY SALES (7).
000780 040-ADD-ROUTINE.
000790        ADD MONTH (COUNTER, 1) TO TOTALS.
000800 050-PRINT-TOTAL.
000810        MOVE TOTALS TO TOTALS-ED.
000820        DISPLAY TOTALS-ED.
000830        CLOSE SALES-FILE.
```

```
056350
859744
876552
645367
718600
876552645367718600
 26380.72
```

The statement

DISPLAY SCORES (2,1) will show a value of $97_\wedge 5$

and the statement

DISPLAY SCORES (3,2) will show a value of $91_\wedge 4$.

What if we had wanted the table to be two down and three across?

$73_\wedge 1$	$66_\wedge 3$	$97_\wedge 5$
$85_\wedge 2$	$81_\wedge 6$	$91_\wedge 4$

Although it would reflect somewhat sloppy programming, the FILLER entries could remain as they were originally, since their only purpose is to lay out the data in memory. The OCCURS, along with REDEFINES, tells the system the format the table will take:

```
01  TABLE-DATA REDEFINES SCORES-DATA.
    03  SCORES-TABLE OCCURS 2 TIMES.
        05  SCORES PIC 99V9 OCCURS 3 TIMES.
```

In the first example, the system interpreted the table data as

73∧1	66∧3	97∧5	85∧2	81∧6	91∧4	Data
1,1	1,2	2,1	2,2	3,1	3,2	Table Position

In the second example, the system interpreted the data as

73∧1	66∧3	97∧5	85∧2	81∧6	91∧4	Data
1,1	1,2	1,3	2,1	2,2	2,3	Table Position

Retrieving data from a table can be done in one of three ways:

1. Searching through a table via IF (or the SEARCH statement that will be covered later in this chapter) to find the data element or elements that satisfy your test requirements.
2. By means of a direct-access approach that lets you go immediately to the specific element desired.
3. By means of a *binary* searching method that uses the SEARCH ALL statement.

You have seen how the subscript can be manipulated to work through the table elements. But some applications lend themselves to a more direct approach. Assume we have a two-dimensional table that contains the high temperature for each day of the year. It consists of 12 elements down (months) and 31 elements across, which represent the days of the month. (We will assume for now that each month has 31 days.)

```
01  MISC-FIELDS.
    03  DATE-ENTRY.
        05  MONTH-SUB      PIC 99.
        05  DAY-SUB        PIC 99.
    03  DAY-TEMP-ED        PIC Z99.99.
    03  DATE-ENTRY-ED      PIC 99/99.
01  TABLE-DATA.
    03  MONTH OCCURS 12 TIMES.
        05  DAY-TEMP OCCURS 31 TIMES PIC 999V9.
```

1,1	1,2	1,3	⋯	1,31
2,1	2,2		⋯	2,31
3,1			⋯	3,31
12,1	12,2		⋯	12,31

Access to the table can be made by requesting the user to enter the month and day of the temperature that he or she is requesting. Note that there is no "searching" involved since the entry data provide the subscript values for accessing the table.

```
            .
            .
            .
DISPLAY 'ENTER 2 DIGIT MONTH CODE'.
ACCEPT MONTH-SUB.
(statements to test that the value entered does not exceed the allowable
range)
            .
            .
            .
DISPLAY 'ENTER 2 DIGIT DAY CODE'.
ACCEPT DAY-SUB.
(statements to test that the value entered does not exceed the allowable
range)
            .
            .
            .
MOVE DAY-TEMP (MONTH-SUB, DAY-SUB) TO DAY-TEMP-ED.
MOVE DATE-ENTRY TO DATE-ENTRY-ED.
DISPLAY 'HIGH TEMPERATURE FOR ' DATE-ENTRY-ED.
DISPLAY 'WAS ' DAY-TEMP-ED.
```

In this case we moved the data to edited fields in order to provide better looking output. The data values in the temperature table could have been stored in edited format. However, this is normally not done as numeric table data are often stored for the purpose of arithmetic manipulation.

Now let's expand the scope of the data and place it into a three-dimensional table. Instead of having just high temperature for a single year, we will store the high temperature for an entire decade—10 years.

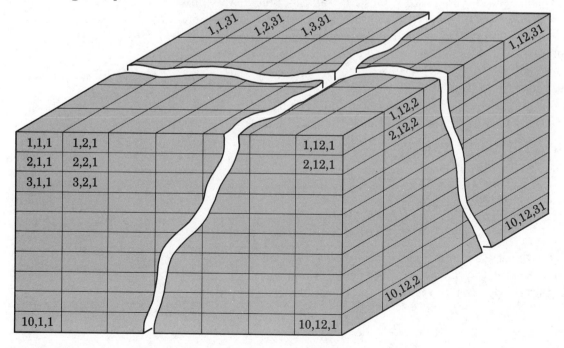

```
01    MISC-FIELDS.
      03    DATE-ENTRY.
            05    YEAR-SUB        PIC 99.
            05    MONTH-SUB       PIC 99.
            05    DAY-SUB         PIC 99.
      03    DAY-TEMP-ED           PIC Z99.99.
      03    DATE-ENTRY-ED         PIC 99/99/99.
01    TABLE-DATA.
      03    YEAR OCCURS 10 TIMES.
            05    MONTH OCCURS 12 TIMES.
                  07    DAY-TEMP OCCURS 31 TIMES PIC 999V9.

DISPLAY 'ENTER 2 DIGIT YEAR CODE'.
ACCEPT YEAR-SUB.
```
(statements to test that the value entered does not exceed the allowable
range)

```
DISPLAY _____
ACCEPT MONTH-SUB.
      .
      .
      .
DISPLAY _____
ACCEPT DAY-SUB.
      .
      .
      .
MOVE DAY-TEMP (YEAR-SUB, MONTH-SUB, DAY-SUB) TO
DAY-TEMP-ED.
MOVE DATE-ENTRY TO DATE-ENTRY-ED.
DISPLAY 'HIGH TEMPERATURE FOR ' DATE-ENTRY-ED.
DISPLAY 'WAS ' DAY-TEMP-ED.
```

Another interesting possibility is that a table need not contain "data"
in the normal sense. So far, our tables have all contained data values that
could be worked upon—payroll data, sales data, and so on. However, subscripts themselves can be stored in table form. Then, when accessed, they
can point the way to actual data stored in a second table. We will revise our
previous example to show this (however, there are other, better ways this
problem could be solved).

We will start by having a one-dimensional, multi-field table that contains the high temperature, low temperature, and noon temperature for
every day of the year:

```
01    TEMP-TABLE.
      03    TEMP-DATA OCCURS 365 TIMES.
            05    HIGH-T    PIC 999V9.
            05    LOW-T     PIC 999V9.
            05    NOON-T    PIC 999V9.
```

The difficulty is that our values are stored on a 1 to 365 basis, but the
user will ask for the data in terms of month and day such as 0914 for
September 14. One solution is to create a two-dimensional table that con-

tains the day of the year that each month and day figure represents. (As before, we will assume that each month has exactly 31 days.)

```
01   MISC-FIELDS.
     03   DAY-SUB        PIC 99.
     03   MONTH-SUB      PIC 99.
     03   TEMP-SUB       PIC 999.
01   DATE-TABLE.
     03   MONTH-T OCCURS 12 TIMES.
          05   DAY-T OCCURS 31 TIMES PIC 999.
```

With this arrangement the value stored in DAY-T (2,7), February 7, would be 38 (31 days for January plus seven days of February). These table values will be used as subscripts to access our TEMP-TABLE:

```
        .
        .
        .

DISPLAY 'ENTER 2 DIGIT MONTH CODE'.
ACCEPT MONTH-SUB.

        .
        .
        .

DISPLAY 'ENTER 2 DIGIT DAY CODE'.
ACCEPT DAY-SUB.

        .
        .
        .

MOVE DAY-T (MONTH-SUB, DAY-SUB) TO TEMP-SUB.
MOVE TEMP-DATA (TEMP-SUB) TO _____.
(statements for further processing of the temperature values)
```

Finally, for those of you who have given the above example some thought, the following three-dimensional table is permitted:

```
01   TABLE-DATA.
     03   YEAR OCCURS 10 TIMES.
          05   MONTH OCCURS 12 TIMES.
               07   DAY-TEMPS OCCURS 31 TIMES.
                    09   HIGH-T   PIC 999V9.
                    09   LOW-T    PIC 999V9.
                    09   NOON-T   PIC 999V9.
```

Special COBOL statements for tables

Since table searching is such a common task, COBOL has several special statements or entries that allow this searching with a little more ease and grace.

As you know, table elements can only be referenced by means of a pointing device (a subscript) that is controlled by the programmer. When the COBOL SEARCH verb is used, what we called a subscript before is now known as an *index*. Actually, the use of the COBOL SEARCH verb involves three separate components: an INDEXED BY entry and the use of the SET and the SEARCH statements.

As before, the process starts by establishing a table with the OCCURS entry. In this case, assume we have need for a 10-element, multi-field table called STUDENT-RECORDS that contains the fields S-NUMBER, S-NAME, S-MAJOR, and S-GRADE-AVG. The table will be set up the same as it was before with one minor addition—an INDEXED BY entry:

```
03   STUDENT-RECORDS OCCURS 10 TIMES
                             INDEXED BY TABLE-INDEX.
     05   S-NUMBER          PIC 9(9).
     05   S-NAME            PIC A(30).
     05   S-MAJOR           PIC A(20).
     05   S-GRADE-AVG       PIC 9V99.
```

This table contains unsorted data fields—that is, data fields not in alphabetic or numeric sequence. The point is important, as COBOL has different search techniques depending on whether the table data are or are not in sorted order. The INDEXED BY entry alerts the system that the variable TABLE-INDEX will be used as the index or pointer when we reference the STUDENT-RECORDS table. However, the programmer *does not* set up TABLE-INDEX in the DATA DIVISION. To do so would result in an error, because the COBOL software does this on its own. Furthermore, the programmer is restricted to the use of certain special COBOL statements that can be used with this index variable.

How does an index value differ from a subscript value? The difference is subtle, but is important to your understanding of how COBOL works. Let's go back to the seven-element, one-dimensional SALES table that we used earlier:

```
77   COUNTER           PIC 9 VALUE 1 COMP.
     .
     .
     .
     03   SALES  PIC 9(4)V99 OCCURS 7 TIMES.
```

The table that this entry created occupied a total of 42 bytes (seven elements times six bytes):

SALES (1)	------------------------------	SALES (7)

subscript value or occurrence number

A subscript value, whether used as a literal

```
MOVE SALES (3) TO _____
```

or as a variable

```
MOVE SALES (COUNTER) TO _____
```

represents an occurrence number. An index, on the other hand, represents a *displacement* from the start of the table and requires far less internal processing by the machine than do subscript values.

In the table shown above, the subscript values range from one to seven. Index values are calculated as shown below.

Start of table. This byte has a displacement of zero from the beginning of the table and is equivalent to a subscript of one.

The second element in the table has a displacement of six bytes from the beginning of the table and is equivalent to a subscript of two.

Subscript value	Index displacement
1	0
2	6
3	12
4	18
5	24
6	30
7	36

Fortunately, the programmer does not have to worry about the displacement shown above. Instead, you are able to treat the table index in much the same way you would treat a subscript, with two minor differences:

1. A subscript field is created by the programmer—a table index *cannot* be created by the programmer. The system will automatically set up the field—all you do is give it a name.
2. A subscript field can be manipulated by standard COBOL statements such as ADD, SUBTRACT, MOVE, and so on. Table index fields can *only* be manipulated by special statements such as SET, SEARCH, and PERFORM VARYING.

The SET statement

The SET statement is used to control the value of the index variable. Two general formats are used: one to establish the initial value of the index and one to change that value. Abbreviated versions of the SET statement formats are shown below.

Format 1:

SET index-name-1 [index-name-2] TO $\left\{\begin{array}{l}\text{index-name-3}\\\text{data-item-3}\\\text{integer-3}\end{array}\right\}$

Example:

```
SET TABLE-INDEX TO 1.
```

TABLE-INDEX, as defined in our previous entry

```
03   STUDENT-RECORDS OCCURS 10 TIMES
                    INDEXED BY TABLE-INDEX.
```

is initialized to a value of 1.

```
SET TABLE-INDEX TO COUNT-INDEX.
```

In the above example the value currently in the field called COUNT-INDEX is moved to TABLE-INDEX. The field called COUNT-INDEX must be specifically established as an index field:

```
03   COUNT-INDEX USAGE IS INDEX.
     .
     .
     .
SET TABLE-INDEX TO COUNT-INDEX.
```

If COUNT-INDEX is not an index field, the value in COUNT-INDEX must be a positive integer value. When the value from COUNT-INDEX is moved to TABLE-INDEX, it is converted into the proper displacement amount.

Format 2:

$$\underline{SET} \text{ index-name-1} \left\{ \begin{array}{l} \underline{UP\ BY} \\ \underline{DOWN}\ BY \end{array} \right\} \text{integer-1}$$

Examples:

```
SET TABLE-INDEX UP BY 1.
SET TABLE-INDEX DOWN BY 1.
```

The SEARCH statement

The SEARCH verb has two general formats: one involving tables containing *unsorted* or unordered data elements (SEARCH) and another involving sorted data values (SEARCH ALL). In both cases, SEARCH can only be used with an OCCURS entry that uses INDEXED BY. The most commonly used version of SEARCH is shown below.

$$\underline{SEARCH} \text{ table name} \left[\underline{VARYING} \left\{ \begin{array}{l} \text{index name} \\ \text{data item name} \end{array} \right\} \right]$$
$$[\underline{AT}\ \underline{END} \text{ imperative statement-1...}]$$

$$\underline{WHEN} \text{ condition-1} \left\{ \begin{array}{l} \text{imperative-statement-2} \\ \underline{NEXT\ SENTENCE} \end{array} \right\}$$
$$\left[\underline{WHEN} \text{ condition-2} \left\{ \begin{array}{l} \text{imperative-statement-3} \\ \underline{NEXT\ SENTENCE} \end{array} \right\} \right]...$$

1. "Condition" can be a relation, class, sign, or conditional name test.

2. Imperative statements *cannot* include a conditional such as PER-FORM UNTIL, IF, or READ.

Let's see how the SEARCH statement works. We will assume that the STUDENT-RECORDS table has been loaded with data. Now, we want to read in a record containing a student identification number and search the table to find the matching table data. The program in skeletal form is shown in Figure 9-2.

The SEARCH operation involves the following steps.

1. The SET statement is used to establish the initial value of the index *before* entering the search routine.
2. Execution of the SEARCH statement causes the system to begin a *sequential* search through the table starting with the first element.
3. The condition set by WHEN is evaluated. (It should be apparent that WHEN is really an IF statement that has been adapted for use with SEARCH.)
   a. If the condition is *not* met, the index is *automatically* incremented and the search is repeated.
   b. If the condition *is* met, the statements following WHEN, down to the ending period, are executed; *the index is* not *incremented; and the search is ended.*
4. The AT END is optional, although it is usually included. If omitted, control passes to the next statement after the SEARCH. If AT END is included, the statements following AT END up to WHEN are executed and control then passes to the next statement after SEARCH. Note that in this example the SEARCH statement ends with the period ending the MOVE S-GRADE-AVG TO _____.
5. The AT END condition is signaled when the value of the index exceeds the size of the table as set up with the OCCURS entry.
6. The search value could have been entered via the ACCEPT statement rather than from a file. Figure 9-3 illustrates the general logic of the SEARCH operation.

Our example searched the table once since only one SEARCH-VALUE was provided. Repeated searching of the table would follow the same pattern and would require a triggering mechanism to exit from the program. Figure 9-4 shows this operation using search values brought in by means of the ACCEPT statement.

The key element that makes the repetitive execution of the SEARCH-ROUTINE work is that the value of the index is reset to one each time a new search operation is initiated. A point worth noting, although you may not have need for it now, is that the index can be set to any beginning value you desire, not just one. In a long table you may know that the matching table data could not be in the first 300 positions. Rather than waste 300 compare operations every time the table is searched, you could set TABLE-INDEX to a specific starting place in the table.

```
SET TABLE-INDEX TO 300.
```

An even better plan that would make the program far more flexible would be to enter the starting search point by means of ACCEPT.

FIGURE 9-2

SEARCH operation

```
        .
        .
        .
    FD  INPUT-FILE
        ------
        ------
    01  IN-REC
        03  SEARCH-VALUE        PIC 9(9).
        .
        .
        .
    WORKING-STORAGE SECTION.
    01  MISC-FIELDS.
        ------
        ------
    01  TABLE-AREA.
        03  STUDENT-RECORDS OCCURS 10 TIMES
                    INDEXED BY TABLE-INDEX.
            05  S-NUMBER        PIC 9(9).
            05  S-NAME          PIC A(30).
            05  S-MAJOR         PIC A(20).
            05  S-GRADE-AVG     PIC 9V99.
        .
        .
        .
    PROCEDURE DIVISION.
        .
        .
        .
        READ INPUT-FILE                     (to read in the value for which you
            AT END ------.                   are searching)
        .
        .
        PERFORM SEARCH-ROUTINE.
        .
        .
        .
    SEARCH-ROUTINE.
            SET TABLE-INDEX TO 1.
            SEARCH STUDENT-RECORDS
                AT END
                    MOVE 'MATCH NOT FOUND' TO ------
                    MOVE SEARCH-VALUE TO ------
                WHEN S-NUMBER (TABLE-INDEX)
                    IS EQUAL TO SEARCH-VALUE
                    MOVE S-NAME (TABLE-INDEX) TO ------
                    MOVE S-MAJOR (TABLE-INDEX) TO ------
                    MOVE S-GRADE-AVG (TABLE-INDEX) TO ------.
            WRITE OUTPUT-LINE ------.
```

FIGURE 9-3

SEARCH logic

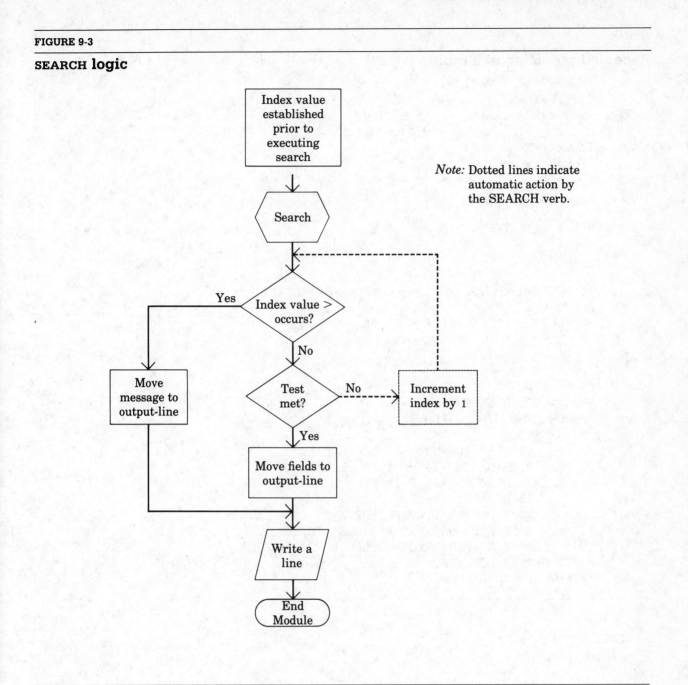

FIGURE 9-4

Repeated searching of a table

```
WORKING-STORAGE SECTION.
01  MISC-FIELDS.
    03  SEARCH-VALUE        PIC 9(9).
    _____
01  TABLE-AREA
        (entries as before)
    .
    .
    .

PROCEDURE DIVISION.
    .
    .
    .
    ACCEPT SEARCH-VALUE  (this is our "priming" ACCEPT)
    PERFORM SEARCH-ROUTINE
        UNTIL SEARCH-VALUE = ZEROS.
    .
    .
    .

SEARCH-ROUTINE.
    SET TABLE-INDEX TO 1.
    SEARCH STUDENT-RECORDS
        AT END
            MOVE 'MATCH NOT FOUND' TO _____
            MOVE SEARCH-VALUE TO _____
        WHEN S-NUMBER (TABLE-INDEX)
            IS EQUAL TO SEARCH-VALUE
            MOVE S-NAME (TABLE-INDEX) TO _____
            MOVE S-MAJOR (TABLE-INDEX) TO _____
            MOVE S-GRADE-AVG (TABLE-INDEX) TO _____.
    WRITE OUTPUT-LINE FROM _____.
    ACCEPT SEARCH-VALUE.
```

As shown in the SEARCH format, multiple testing conditions (WHEN) are permitted. If multiple tests are used, the action is equivalent to the execution of an IF with OR in that the search will stop if *either* condition is met. The flowchart of this operation is shown in Figure 9-5.

```
SEARCH-ROUTINE.
    SET TABLE-INDEX TO 1.
    SEARCH STUDENT-RECORDS
        AT END
            MOVE 'MATCH NOT FOUND' TO _____
            MOVE SEARCH-VALUE TO _____
        WHEN S-NUMBER (TABLE-INDEX)
            IS EQUAL TO SEARCH-VALUE
            MOVE S-NAME (TABLE-INDEX) TO _____
            MOVE S-MAJOR (TABLE-INDEX) TO _____
            MOVE S-GRADE-AVG (TABLE-INDEX) TO _____
        WHEN S-NUMBER (TABLE-INDEX)
            IS EQUAL TO ZERO
            MOVE 'ZERO STUDENT NUMBER' TO _____.
    WRITE OUTPUT-LINE.
```

Complex conditions within WHEN may be set by use of AND or OR and follow the same general rules that are used for IF statements. Remember that AND means that both conditions must be true while OR means that either condition may be true in order to satisfy the test:

```
01  _____.
    03   TEMPERATURE-TABLE
            OCCURS 365 TIMES
            INDEXED BY I-FIELD.
        05   TEMP    PIC 999.
        05   DATE-T  PIC 9(6).
    .
    .
    .

SEARCH TEMPERATURE-TABLE
    WHEN TEMP (I-FIELD) IS LESS THAN 32

    OR TEMP (I-FIELD) IS GREATER THAN 100
        DISPLAY TEMP (I-FIELD)
        DISPLAY DATE-T (I-FIELD).
```

FIGURE 9-5

Multiple test conditions

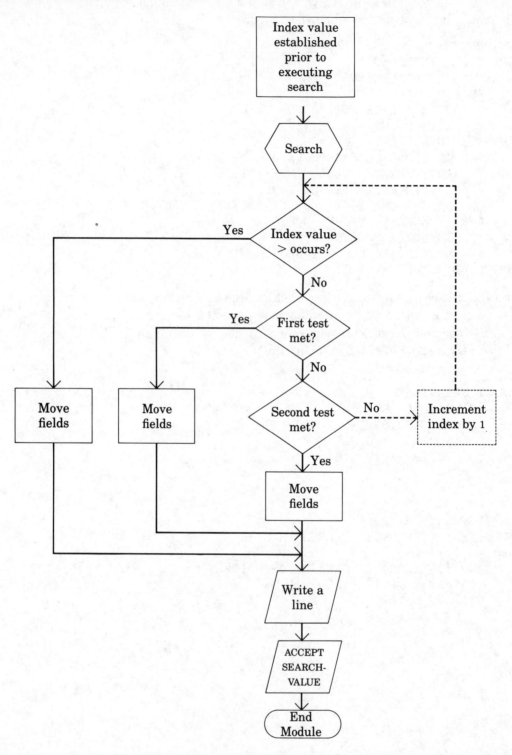

As you can see from the previous examples, the SEARCH statement not only offers you some interesting testing options, but also provides for greater internal efficiency than using IF. However, in one case, "IFing" your way through a table is a little easier than using SEARCH. The case in question arises when we wish to search through a table to find multiple occurrences of a value. For example, finding *all* sales that are greater than $3000 is quite easy using IF and a subscript:

```
        .
        .
        .
    03   SUBSCRIPT    PIC VALUE 1.
        .
        .
        .
    03   SALES        PIC 9(4)V99 OCCURS 7 TIMES.
        .
        .
        .
PROCEDURE DIVISION.
        .
        .
        .
    PERFORM 040-TABLE-SEARCH
        UNTIL SUBSCRIPT IS GREATER THAN 7.
        .
        .
        .
040-TABLE-SEARCH.
    IF   SALES (SUBSCRIPT) IS GREATER THAN 3000.00
        DISPLAY SALES (SUBSCRIPT).
    ADD 1 TO SUBSCRIPT.
```

The skeletal program shown above will continue the search through the entire table while the SEARCH statement is designed to stop the searching action the *first time* the condition is met. However, we can get around this problem.

1. The SET statement that initializes the index to 1 must be taken out of the search module and placed in a module by itself.
2. The 040-TABLE-SEARCH module is entered from the PERFORM and the table is searched until the first matching condition is found and DISPLAYED. At this point the search operation stops but the SET X UP BY 1 statement increments the index to the next table position after the match.
3. Control returns to the PERFORM where the index is tested to see if it has exceeded seven. If it has not, the search is started *at the current value of the index.* Figures 9-6 and 9-7 show the logic and the program.

Our examples have shown the use of SEARCH with a one-dimensional table and its associated index, but the same process holds true for multilevel tables. If SEARCH is to be used with a two-dimensional table, the programmer must specify two index variables. In the two-dimensional table program (Figure 9-1) at the beginning of the chapter you saw the following:

```
01   TABLE-DATA.
     03   SALES OCCURS 7 TIMES.
          05   MONTH OCCURS 3 TIMES  PIC 9(4)V99.
01   OTHER-FIELDS.
     03   DOWN-T          PIC 9 VALUE ZERO.
     03   ACROSS          PIC 9 VALUE ZERO.
```

Addressing a single element at the lowest level (MONTH) was done by means of *two* subscripts:

```
DISPLAY MONTH (DOWN-T, ACROSS)
```

The higher-level element (SALES) required only a single subscript:

```
DISPLAY SALES (COUNTER)
```

If indexes are used, our table would look as follows:

```
01   TABLE-DATA.
     03   SALES OCCURS 7 TIMES
               INDEXED BY INDEX-D.
          05   MONTH OCCURS 3 TIMES
               INDEXED BY INDEX-A    PIC 9(4)V99.
```

FIGURE 9-6

Flowchart: Continued searching of a table

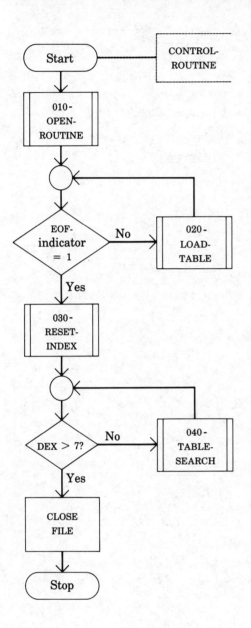

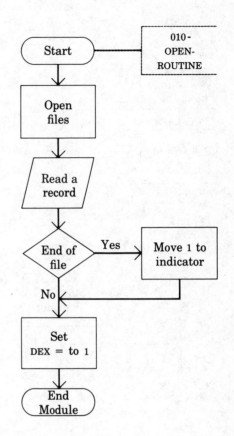

continued

FIGURE 9-6

continued

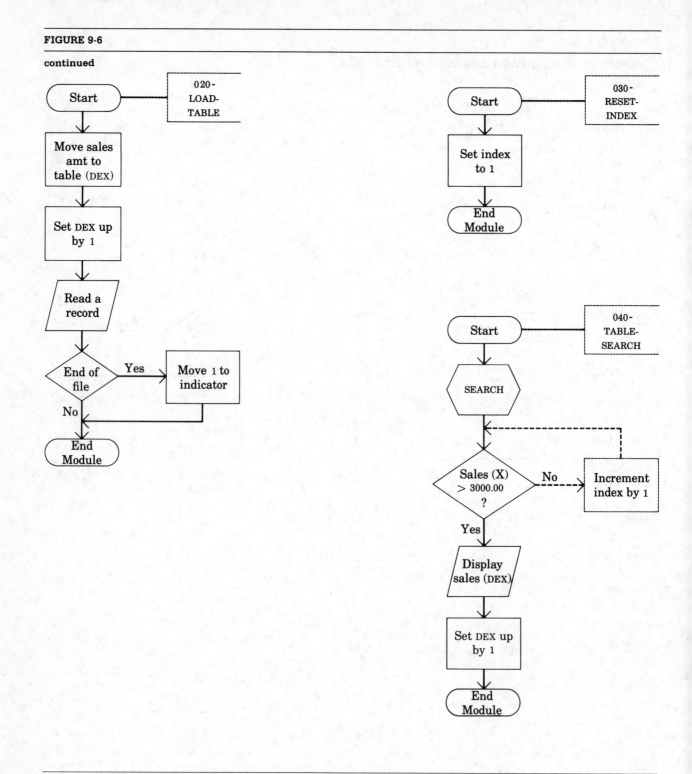

FIGURE 9-7

Continued SEARCH example

```
000100 IDENTIFICATION DIVISION.
000110 PROGRAM-ID.  FINDIT.
000120*
000130 ENVIRONMENT DIVISION.
000140 CONFIGURATION SECTION.
000150 SOURCE-COMPUTER. - - -.
000160 OBJECT-COMPUTER.- - -.
000170 INPUT-OUTPUT SECTION.
000180 FILE-CONTROL.
000190     SELECT SALES-FILE ASSIGN TO - - -.
000200*
000210 DATA DIVISION.
000220 FILE SECTION.
000230 FD  SALES-FILE
000240     LABEL RECORD IS STANDARD
000250     VALUE OF FILE-ID IS 'SALES-DATA'
000260     DATA RECORD IS SALES-RECORD.
000270 01  SALES-RECORD.
000280     03  SALES-IN               PIC 9(4)V99.
000290 WORKING-STORAGE SECTION.
000300 01  TABLE-DATA.
000310     03  SALES-TABLE OCCURS 7 TIMES INDEXED BY DEX.
000320         05  SALES          PIC 9(4)V99.
000330 01  OTHER-FIELDS.
000340     03  EOF-INDICATOR      PIC 9 VALUE ZERO.
000350*
000360 PROCEDURE DIVISION.
000370 CONTROL-ROUTINE.
000380     PERFORM 010-OPEN-ROUTINE.
000390     PERFORM 020-LOAD-TABLE
000400         UNTIL EOF-INDICATOR = 1.
000410     PERFORM 030-RESET-INDEX.
000420     PERFORM 040-TABLE-SEARCH
000430         UNTIL DEX IS GREATER THAN 7.
000440     CLOSE SALES-FILE.
000450     STOP RUN.
000460 010-OPEN-ROUTINE.
000470     OPEN INPUT SALES-FILE.
000480     READ SALES-FILE
000490         AT END MOVE 1 TO EOF-INDICATOR.
000500     SET DEX TO 1.
000510 020-LOAD-TABLE.
000520     MOVE SALES-IN TO SALES (DEX).
000530     SET DEX UP BY 1.
000540     READ SALES-FILE
000550         AT END MOVE 1 TO EOF-INDICATOR.
000560 030-RESET-INDEX.
000570     SET DEX TO 1.
000580 040-TABLE-SEARCH.
000590     SEARCH SALES-TABLE
000600         WHEN SALES (DEX) IS GREATER THAN 3000.00
000610             DISPLAY SALES (DEX)
000620             SET DEX UP BY 1.
```

Accessing the elements would follow the same pattern as before. MONTH can *only* be addressed by the use of two indexes,

```
DISPLAY MONTH (INDEX-D, INDEX-A)
```

and SALES can only be indexed by a single index value.

```
DISPLAY SALES (INDEX-D)
```

The VARYING version of the SEARCH statement is a little more complex but offers the programmer more flexibility when working with indexes. For example, suppose we have the following tables.

```
03   ID-TABLE     PIC 9(9) OCCURS 50 TIMES
                     INDEXED BY Q.
03   NAME-TABLE   PIC X(20) OCCURS 50 TIMES
                     INDEXED BY Z.
              .
              .
              .

SEARCH ID-TABLE VARYING Q
     WHEN _____
```

As explained earlier, during the execution of the SEARCH process, the value of the index associated with ID-TABLE (Q in this case) will automatically be incremented according to the rules of SEARCH. With the VARYING option, Z, which is the index to a *different* table (NAME-TABLE), will be set to the same value as Q. Thus, immediately upon finding the desired value in ID-TABLE, the programmer can use Z to get to the corresponding position in NAME-TABLE.

If, as shown in the original SEARCH statement format, data item name is used, certain rules must be followed. Data item name must be declared as an index item

```
03   ABC     PIC 99 USAGE IS INDEX.
```

or it must be an elementary numeric item that can only contain integer values.

```
03   XYZ     PIC 99.
```

When using index values, the programmer must treat them with some degree of respect. For example, suppose we have the following table:

```
03   SALES-AMT   PIC 999V99 OCCURS 10 TIMES
                     INDEXED BY T.
```

The following entries are *incorrect:*

1. SUBTRACT AMT-A FROM SALES-AMT (7).
   Why? You cannot use a constant in place of the index T. Instead, the correct entry would be

   ```
   SUBTRACT AMT-A FROM SALES-AMT (T).
   ```

2. MOVE T TO INDEX-HOLD.

Why? An index value cannot be processed by a MOVE statement. Instead, use the SET statement.

    SET INDEX—HOLD TO T.

3. SUBTRACT 1 FROM T.

Why? An index value cannot be processed by regular arithmetic statements. Instead, use SET.

    SET T DOWN BY 1.

The SEARCH ALL statement

As you know, the SEARCH statement is used with tables whose contents are *unordered;* that is, the data items are not in any sequence. Since the search process involves a straight sequential search of the table items beginning with the first element, the most frequently needed items should appear early in the table. If all table items are likely to be needed with the same frequency, then a straight sequential search to find a particular element may become very inefficient. A solution to our problem lies in the use of the SEARCH ALL statement.

The SEARCH ALL statement *must* be used on a *sorted table*—that is, a table whose argument (or key field) has been sorted into ascending or descending sequence. (The topic of sorting will be covered in a later chapter.) Normal procedure would be to use it on large tables where the frequency of use of the elements is evenly distributed throughout the table.

With SEARCH ALL the system performs a "binary search" rather than a straight sequential search. In a binary search the system first goes to the middle entry in the table and compares the value found there against the test value. It is important for you to note here that the comparison can only be for equality; testing for greater than or less than is not permitted. The result of the test "tells" the system whether the desired element is now in the first half or second half of the table. Knowing this, the system then goes to the middle of that half and performs another comparison, and so on until the item is located.

Format:

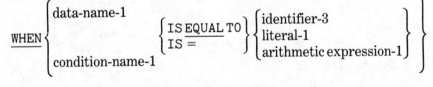

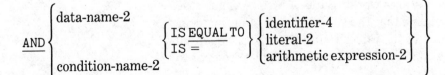

$$\left\{ \begin{array}{l} \text{imperative statement-2} \\ \underline{\text{NEXT SENTENCE}} \end{array} \right\}$$

An optional entry in the OCCURS clause is used to tell the system the name of the table field on which the table is ordered and the nature of the order:

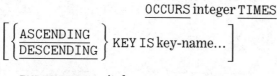

$$\underline{\text{OCCURS}} \text{ integer } \underline{\text{TIMES}}$$

$$\left[\left\{ \begin{array}{l} \underline{\text{ASCENDING}} \\ \underline{\text{DESCENDING}} \end{array} \right\} \text{KEY IS key-name...} \right]$$

$$\underline{\text{INDEXED BY}} \quad \text{index-name}$$

As an example, suppose our SALES-TABLE includes multiple fields—SALES, REGION, and TABLE-ID. The ASCENDING KEY entry tells the system the name of the field on which the table data were sorted. As you can see from the example, SALES-TABLE is in ascending order according to the TABLE-ID field. Note that this is a single-dimensional table consisting of three fields. Each field may be accessed by a single subscript.

```
WORKING-STORAGE SECTION.
01   TABLE-DATA.
     03   SALES-TABLE   OCCURS 1000 TIMES
                        INDEXED BY DEX
                        ASCENDING KEY IS TABLE-ID.
          05   SALES      PIC 9(4)V99.
          05   REGION     PIC 999.
          05   TABLE-ID   PIC 9(4).
```

SALES-TABLE

SALES (1)	REGION (1)	TABLE-ID (1)
SALES (2)	REGION (2)	TABLE-ID (2)
. . .	. . .	. . .
SALES (1000)	REGION (1000)	TABLE-ID (1000)

To perform a binary search on the SALES-TABLE we would program as follows:

```
SEARCH ALL SALES-TABLE
    WHEN ID-NBR-INPUT IS EQUAL TO TABLE-ID (DEX)
    DISPLAY SALES (DEX)
    DISPLAY REGION (DEX).

------.
```

Now, let's see how the binary search works. Suppose we ACCEPT a value for ID-NBR-INPUT. We further assume that the TABLE-ID entry that matches this value is in the 743rd position of the table. Using a straight sequential search, the system would have to make 742 comparisons before coming to the matching element in the table. A binary comparison, however, is far more efficient as you will see by the following outline:

1. The system goes to the middle of the table and compares the ID-NBR-INPUT value against the value found in TABLE-ID (500). The comparison will show that ID-NBR-INPUT is greater than the value in TABLE-ID, so the system now goes to the *middle* (position 750) of the *second half* of the table (positions 501 to 1000) to continue the comparison.

2. The value at TABLE-ID (750) is compared with the ID-NBR-INPUT value and the comparison now shows that ID-NBR-INPUT (743) is less than the value in TABLE-ID (750). The system now goes to the middle of the table elements between 500 and 750—that is, TABLE-ID (625).

3. Comparisons continue in this manner until the system gets to TABLE-ID (743), which contains a value equal to the value of ID-NBR-INPUT. Using this method, it will take a maximum of 10 comparisons to find any matching value in the table.

4. As indicated in the SEARCH-ALL statement, the system will then display the values found at SALES (743) and REGION (743) and proceed to the next statement.

5. The AT END part of a SEARCH ALL statement will be activated when a matching condition is not found—that is, when none of the comparisons is equal.

The OCCURS DEPENDING entry

The OCCURS DEPENDING entry is one that, although not used too often, can have some interesting and very useful applications. The first example in Chapter 8 concerned testing sites that recorded the test scores. Our program had to find the average score, the highest score, and the lowest score and print these answers. As trivial as this problem sounds, the whole program was dependent upon knowing in advance that the data record would always contain 10 scores. A teacher is likely to have a similar situation in which each student is *supposed* to take six tests during the semester. In fact, by the end of the semester, any given student may have taken from zero to six tests. The problem comes in processing the test scores because the missed test fields are likely to contain blanks. Thus, if a student has taken only five tests, the statement

```
ADD SCORE-DATA (COUNTER) TO TOTAL-SCORES
```

when COUNTER has a value of six, will result in a program abend:

STUDENT NAME	Test 1	Test 2	Test 3	Test 4	Test 5	garbage

By modifying the data record slightly, we can make use of OCCURS DEPENDING. Right after the STUDENT NAME field we will insert a number of TESTS-TAKEN field:

STUDENT NAME	Number of TESTS-TAKEN	Test 1	Test 2	------	Test 6

The format of the OCCURS DEPENDING is

```
OCCURS integer-1 TO integer-2 TIMES
DEPENDING ON data-name-1
```

Our example can be modified as follows:

```
FD   STUDENT-TESTS
     -------

     -------
     DATA RECORD IS TEST-REC.
01   TEST-REC.
     03   NAME-IN        PIC X(20).
     03   TESTS-TAKEN    PIC 9.
     03   TESTS-TABLE    PIC 99V99
                         OCCURS 0 TO 6 TIMES
                         DEPENDING ON TESTS-TAKEN.
     .
     .

     .
     PROCEDURE DIVISION.
     .
     .

     .
     PERFORM SUM-SCORES
         VARYING SUB FROM 1 BY 1
         UNTIL SUB IS GREATER THAN TESTS-TAKEN.
or   (PERFORM SUM-SCORES TESTS-TAKEN TIMES)
```

An important point to recognize is that the *table size* is *not* variable; it is always set at the maximum—six in this case. The number of entries placed into the table *is* variable and depends upon the value contained in the TESTS-TAKEN field.

Although the entry

```
OCCURS 0 TO 6 TIMES
```

seems appropriate for our problem, '74 COBOL does not permit the integer-1 field to be zero. In that case we would use

```
OCCURS 1 TO 6 TIMES
```

and make sure that the first test score field contains valid data—zeros if necessary.

The data-name-1 field that indicates the number of table elements to be used does *not* have to come in with the table data as shown in the example. The major requirement is that the designated field contain the desired value *before* table processing starts. For example, we may have a situation that requires a large table but the number of entries will vary from run to run. With jobs of this type we often know the exact number of elements that will be used. Under this arrangement we can enter the table size information via an ACCEPT statement before actually working on the table:

```
WORKING-STORAGE SECTION.
01  MISC-FIELDS.
        03   EOF-INDICATOR        PIC XXX VALUE 'OFF'.
        03   TABLE-SIZE           PIC 9999 VALUE COMP.
            .
            .
            .

01  TABLES.
        03   SALES-TABLE OCCURS 1 TO 1000 TIMES
                        DEPENDING ON TABLE-SIZE.
            05   _____
            05   _____
        .
        .
        .
PROCEDURE DIVISION.
        .
        .
        .
        PERFORM 050-SET-TABLE-SIZE.
        PERFORM 060-LOAD-TABLE
            VARYING COUNTER FROM 1 BY 1
            UNTIL COUNTER IS GREATER THAN TABLE-SIZE.
        .
        .
        .
050-SET TABLE-SIZE.
        DISPLAY 'PLEASE ENTER 4 DIGIT TABLE SIZE'.
        DISPLAY 'NOT IN EXCESS OF 1000. IF SIZE'.
        DISPLAY 'IS UNKNOWN, ENTER 1000'.
        ACCEPT TABLE-SIZE.
```

As with all table handling operations, you should incorporate a routine in your program to see if the subscript or index has exceeded the allowable range. In this case, our test will be made against the value contained in the variable called TABLE-SIZE.

COMMON ERRORS

The previous chapter mentioned that a common error was that of not handling the subscript properly and of trying to "READ out of" a table. In advanced table handling applications there seem to be three errors that come to the surface fairly frequently.

1. NOT understanding the difference between a one-dimensional, multi-field table and a two-dimensional table. Along with this goes the lack of understanding of how the subscript can be used to access either a specific item in the table or to access an entire row across. Hopefully, the text made these points clear.
2. Some programmers become "enamored" with the SET statement and try to use it on non-index fields. Theoretically, this should not work, although, on some systems, it is permissible.

3. Another common error is in not understanding that the SEARCH statement *automatically* increments the index. If you put in a statement that increments the index at the wrong place, the net effect is that the index will go up by two, not one.

PROGRAMMING TIPS

When working with multidimensional tables—that is, two- or three-dimensional tables—you have need for multiple subscripts or indexes. A wise programmer pays close attention to these values to be sure they don't "wander" outside the allowable range. Most programmers seem to think of a subscript/index in terms of *upper* or *lower* limits in reference to elements or positions *down* the table. However, a two-dimensional table has the same limitations for the subscript/index going *across* the table.

Theoretically, the system should abort the job whenever the subscript or index goes beyond the boundaries set by the OCCURS. This does not always happen and it is possible to access a table element that really doesn't exist, such as SALES (-5). See what your manual says about this and then write a short program that tries to access elements beyond both the upper and lower boundaries. If your system permits this (it shouldn't!), try to determine what data it picked up. Usually it will be from other areas in the WORKING-STORAGE SECTION that appear just before or just after your table area.

When working with sorted tables and SEARCH ALL, the rule is that no duplicate values are permitted in the key field. If duplicate values are included, the system does not halt or indicate an error, but there is no assurance as to which of the duplicate values will be retrieved.

In terms of efficiency:

Avoid clearing a large table unless it is absolutely necessary.
Generally, indexing is more efficient than subscripting.
When using tables, there may be relatively few values that are needed over and over. If possible, place these values at the beginning of the table so that they are found quickly by the SEARCH statement.
Use SEARCH if a table has fewer than 50 entries. If the table is sorted and contains over 50 entries, use SEARCH ALL.

SELF-STUDY: QUESTIONS AND ANSWERS

1. Can you give me another example of the use of two-dimensional tables?

Answer: Certainly. One of the most common uses of tables is the calculation of payroll. Probably, the master payroll file will *not* contain an employee's actual salary amount. Instead, as in the case of many governmental workers, we will store the employee's job class and job step. For example, we may have five salary steps within the Clerk I category and another five steps for Clerk II, Supervisor I, and so on. The weekly or monthly payroll calculations are made by getting the employee job class and job step from the master record and using this information to access a salary amount in a two-dimensional salary table. The nice feature about this method is that across-the-board pay changes can be made on the relatively few elements in the pay table rather than on the individual employee master pay record.

2. Must I use SEARCH and SEARCH ALL with tables?

Answer: The answer to your question is both yes and no. No, you don't have to use the SEARCH statement because it is very easy to implement the SEARCH and SET actions by other simple COBOL statements such as MOVE, ADD, SUBTRACT, and IF.

The second part of the answer is that since SEARCH ALL is a binary rather than a sequential search, it would be very much to your benefit to take advantage of the actions of the SEARCH ALL verb. Coding for a binary search using IF is fairly cumbersome and inefficient.

3. When using SEARCH ALL, you said that the table must be in order, either ascending or descending. Do the values have to be in 1-2-3 order or can there be gaps?

Answer: The answer is that the values must be in sequence and gaps are permitted. If gaps in sequence were not allowed, the SEARCH ALL statement would have little use since data seldom are in strict 1-2-3 order.

CHAPTER TERMS

binary search
displacement
hard coding
index
multidimensional tables
OCCURS DEPENDING
SEARCH

SEARCH ALL
sequential search
SET
sorted table
subscript
WHEN (with SEARCH)

EXERCISES

1. Define or explain the following terms.
   a. subscript
   b. index
   c. occurrence value
   d. two-dimensional table
   e. displacement
   f. sequential or serial search
   g. binary search

2. What, besides data, might be stored in a table?

3. If the COBOL verb SEARCH is used, what other tablehandling entries must be used elsewhere in the program?

4. When using the SEARCH verb, a subscript is then called an _____ .

5. When using INDEXED BY, the field must/must not be defined in the WORKING-STORAGE SECTION.

6. The SET statement is used to control the value of an _____ .

7. What is wrong with this statement?

```
SEARCH ALL TABLE-DATA
    AT END DISPLAY 'OOPS'
    WHEN FIELD-D IS GREATER THAN INPUT-VALUE
        DISPLAY 'GREATER'.
```

8. Given:

```
03  TABLE-DATA.
    05  NUMBER      PIC 99.
    05  DATA-IN     PIC X(9) OCCURS 1 TO 10 TIMES
                        DEPENDING ON NUMBER.
```

If NUMBER is equal to 8, how many slots or positions will be allotted by the system for the DATA-IN table?

9. Set up a two-dimensional, ten-year temperature table consisting of 365 elements down by ten elements across (PIC 999V9) that will be accessed by means of subscripts.
   a. DISPLAY the temperature for the 312th day of the 7th year.
   b. DISPLAY the temperature for the Xth day of the Rth year.
   c. Change the temperature table so that it consists of 10 elements down and 365 elements across.

10. Revise Exercise 9 to use indexes.

11. For this problem, use Data Set A in Appendix D. Assume that the file consists of at least 25 records but not more than 40 records. Record format is as follows.

Field	Characters	Type
Filler	9	------
Name	20	Alphabetic
YTD SALES	7	Numeric dollars and cents, display format
Filler		To remainder of record

Write a program that reads in the data and stores it in a one-dimensional, multi-field table. Then, using IF, go through the table and print the names of all those salespeople whose sales were between $2000 and $5000. Do *not* use the SEARCH statement.

12. Modify Exercise 11 to use indexes and the special COBOL statements for tables. (*Note:* The table data will not be in sorted order.)

13. Again, as in Exercise 11, you are to store the data values in a table. Then, your program is to ACCEPT or read in, from a separate file, the following names.

```
WALSH JUDITH
MOORE SAMUEL
KANDER ED
BRONSON PATTY
```

As each name is entered, IF your way through the table and print out the sales amount for that person. Provide for the condition of an unmatched name, print an appropriate error message, and continue the input/search/print action. Your program is to terminate when a name field of all *X*'s is entered.

14. Revise Exercise 13 to use SET, SEARCH, and INDEXED BY.

15. Further revise Exercise 11 to account for the fact that the first nine characters of the record contain the salesperson's social security number. This field is in ascending order and is to be accessed by means of the SEARCH ALL statement. READ or ACCEPT the following social security numbers:

    010116104
    410954321
    366492891
    666666666
    230965777
    784321592

As each social security number is matched, print the person's name, number, and sales amount. Total the sales values and print this at the end of the program. Also, as before, provide for a number that is not in the table and print an appropriate message. Your program is to terminate when a social security number of all nines is encountered.

16. Assume that the following data are contained within a two-dimensional table. Note that the positions for the seventh elements down and the seventh elements across are unfilled.

```
01  _____.
    03  DOWN-T  OCCURS 7 TIMES.
        05  ACROSS-T OCCURS 7 TIMES    PIC 999.
```

01	02	03	04	05	06	
10	20	30	40	50	60	
02	04	06	07	10	12	
20	40	60	80	10	00	
04	08	16	32	64	28	
40	06	00	80	01	00	

Write the program segment that will: (a) Total each row across and place the average of the values in this row in the seventh position; and (b) total each column down and place the average in the seventh position. (c) Position 7,7 will not be filled.

Chapter 10
Sorting

CHAPTER OUTLINE

LEARNING OBJECTIVES

1. To understand the nature of both internal and external sorting.

2. To learn one internal sorting method—''bubble'' sorting.

3. To recognize the power and versatility of the SORT verb.

4. To understand the use of the two basic formats of SORT: SORT with USING and GIVING; and SORT with INPUT and OUTPUT PROCEDURE.

One of the most common operations performed in any data processing installation is sorting. By *sorting*, of course, we mean changing the order of the data records (as they now exist) to a different order that will make further processing more efficient. For example, it may be desirable to take an unordered student enrollment file and put it into ascending order based on the student identification number field or student name field. Sorting can be either numeric or alphabetic and can place a file into descending order if that is appropriate to the application.

As indicated above, we can base our sort operation upon a single field (known as the *key field*), but multiple fields can be used as well. Customer charge amounts that had been accumulated for the past week might have to be sorted into ascending customer number order *within* the date-charged field. Sorting can be as simple or as complex as you wish, but it is a very common programming task with which you should be familiar. Before getting to the sorting capabilities of COBOL, let's consider a few more aspects of this operation.

Sorting falls into two general categories—*internal* sorts and *external* sorts. Internal sorts are performed on data that are in table form, as discussed in Chapters 8 and 9. External sorts are performed on tape and disk files and involve a great amount of input/output activity to put the records into the desired order. First, we will take a look at how table sorting is accomplished and then look at the second method, which makes use of the COBOL SORT statement.

Internal sorting

Table data may be sorted by several different techniques including a "bubble" sort, a selection sort, and a "shell" sort. All of the techniques involve testing of the data items and a movement or an exchange operation to put them in order. As the table size increases, the number of machine operations to perform the sort can grow at an alarming rate. Therefore, internal sorts should be kept to under 100 items and, preferably, to the 20- to 30-item range.

To show you how a bubble sort works, assume we have the following one-dimensional table that contains 6 two-digit values. Our task is to write a program that sorts these values into ascending order.

16
21
14
36
10
31

A bubble sort is appropriately named, since the technique involves the process of "bubbling up" the lowest value to the top of the table. The process involves multiple passes through the data, since only one value can be bubbled up to the top on each pass.

Pass 1

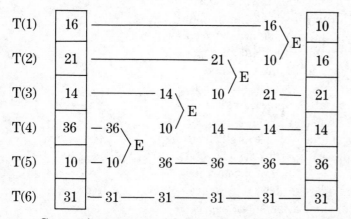

Comparison starts with T(6) versus T(5). IF T(6) is smaller than T(5), an exchange takes place. If not, the values remain in their respective slots. Then T(5) is compared to T(4), and the process is repeated until the lowest value is in the top slot. In this particular case, four exchanges took place during the five comparisons.

Pass 2

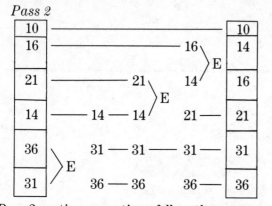

Pass 2 sorting operations follow the same pattern as before with one exception—there is one fewer comparison to be made since the top value is already in the correct place. As you can see, each succeeding pass requires one fewer comparison than the previous pass. In our example, the data were such that the values were placed into the correct order at the end of the second pass by means of three more exchanges. The worst possible condition would occur when the data happen to be in exactly the reverse of the order desired.

Coding for the bubble sort is shown below in skeletal form. Note that we will need to use a PERFORM within a PERFORM—in effect, a nested PERFORM—in order to generate multiple passes through the table:

```
PERFORM BUBBLE-SORT
     VARYING COUNTER FROM 1 BY 1
     UNTIL COUNTER IS GREATER THAN 6.
          .
          .
```

```
BUBBLE-SORT.
    PERFORM INNER-SORT.
        VARYING L FROM 6 BY -1
        UNTIL L IS EQUAL TO 1.
INNER-SORT.
    COMPUTE N = L - 1.
    IF TABLE-DATA (L) IS LESS THAN TABLE-DATA (N)
        MOVE TABLE-DATA (N) TO TEMP
        MOVE TABLE-DATA (L) TO TABLE-DATA (N)
        MOVE TEMP TO TABLE-DATA (L).
```

A field called COUNTER is used to keep track of the number of passes through the table. Another counter, L, acts as the subscript to access the table elements. Note that L is started at 6 and decremented by 1 each time. On the first pass, the first comparison is made between TABLE-DATA (6) and TABLE-DATA (5). A temporary subscript (N) is COMPUTEd to the value of L minus 1, since some versions of COBOL do not permit arithmetic operations within a subscript. If arithmetic is permitted, the COMPUTE statement could be removed, and the IF statement modified to

```
IF TABLE-DATA (L) IS LESS THAN TABLE-DATA (L - 1)
```

when the fifth and fourth items of the table are compared, an exchange takes place with the use of a temporary holding area called TEMP.

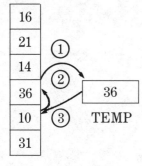

Although the program works correctly and does result in a sorted table, the sort logic is very inefficient. The INNER-SORT always involves five comparisons.

```
PERFORM INNER-SORT
    VARYING L FROM 6 BY -1
    UNTIL L IS EQUAL TO 1.
```

As you know, each pass through the table requires one fewer comparison since the lowest was moved to the top.

PASS 1	PASS 2	PASS 3	PASS 4	PASS 5
5 comparisons	4 comparisons	3 comparisons	2 comparisons	1 comparison
6-5	6-5	6-5	6-5	6-5
5-4	5-4	5-4	5-4	
4-3	4-3	4-3		
3-2	3-2			
2-1				

We can implement this by changing the test in the PERFORM INNER-SORT statement to read

```
PERFORM INNER-SORT
     VARYING L FROM 6 BY -1
     UNTIL L IS EQUAL TO COUNTER.
```

Figures 10-1 and 10-2 show the program logic and the program that creates the table, DISPLAYS the contents in original form, sorts the data, and DISPLAYS the table in sorted order.

FIGURE 10-1

Logic: Bubble sort

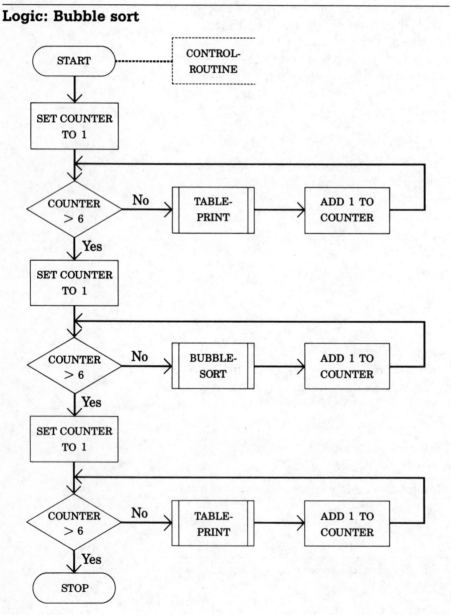

FIGURE 10-1

continued

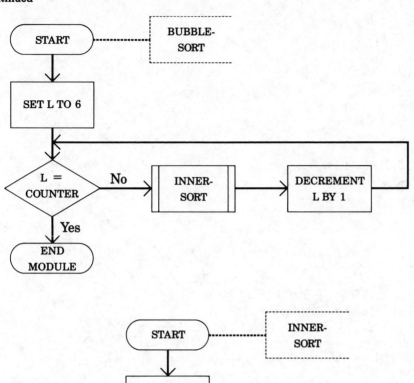

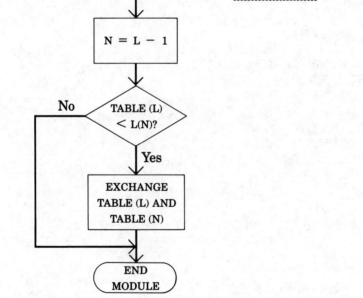

FIGURE 10-2

Bubble sort

```
000100 IDENTIFICATION DIVISION.
000110 PROGRAM-ID. BUBBLE.
000120*
000130 ENVIRONMENT DIVISION.
000140 CONFIGURATION SECTION.
000150 SOURCE-COMPUTER. - - -.
000160 OBJECT-COMPUTER.- - -.
000170*
000180 DATA DIVISION.
000190 WORKING-STORAGE SECTION.
000200 01   MISC-FIELDS.
000210      03   COUNTER            PIC 9.
000220      03   L                  PIC 9.
000230      03   TEMP               PIC 99.
000240      03   N                  PIC 9.
000250 01   DATA-AREA.
000260      03   FILLER             PIC 9(12)
000270                  VALUE 162114361031.
000280 01   TABLE-AREA REDEFINES DATA-AREA.
000290      03   TABLE-DATA         PIC 99 OCCURS 6 TIMES.
000300*
000310 PROCEDURE DIVISION.
000320 CONTROL-ROUTINE.
000330      PERFORM TABLE-PRINT
000340          VARYING COUNTER FROM 1 BY 1
000350          UNTIL COUNTER IS GREATER THAN 6.
000360      PERFORM BUBBLE-SORT
000370          VARYING COUNTER FROM 1 BY 1
000380          UNTIL COUNTER IS GREATER THAN 6.
000390      PERFORM TABLE-PRINT
000400          VARYING COUNTER FROM 1 BY 1
000410          UNTIL COUNTER IS GREATER THAN 6.
000420      STOP RUN.
000430*
000440 TABLE-PRINT.
000450      DISPLAY TABLE-DATA (COUNTER).
000460*
000470 BUBBLE-SORT.
000480      PERFORM INNER-SORT
000490          VARYING L FROM 6 BY -1
000500          UNTIL L IS EQUAL TO COUNTER.
000510*
000520 INNER-SORT.
000530      COMPUTE N = L - 1.
000540      IF TABLE-DATA (L) IS LESS THAN TABLE-DATA (N)
000550          MOVE TABLE-DATA (N) TO TEMP
000560          MOVE TABLE-DATA (L) TO TABLE-DATA (N)
000570          MOVE TEMP TO TABLE-DATA (L).
```

The program shown in Figure 10-2 is more efficient than our original attempt, but it can still be improved. In some cases, the table data may be fairly close to being in sorted order. For example, in our original table there was no need to continue on through passes 3, 4, and 5 since sorting was complete at the conclusion of the second pass. Figure 10-3 is a modified version of the previous program that incorporates two counters: one to keep track of the number of exchanges and one to keep track of the number of comparisons (IF-COUNTER). With the data shown, the DISPLAYed output are the following:

```
NBR OF EXCHANGES    07
NBR OF IF TESTS     15
```

Our program logic can be modified to allow us to exit from the sorting process once the table has been placed into sorted order (Figure 10-4).

1. An EXCHANGE-SWITCH is set up with an initial value of ' ON' based on the fact that every table—even one that is already in sorted order—will require one pass or set of comparisons.
2. At the start of each pass, the EXCHANGE-SWITCH is set to OFF.
3. Whenever an exchange is made, ' ON' is moved to the switch.
4. The PERFORM BUBBLE-SORT statement has been modified to check for the end of sorting activities:

```
PERFORM BUBBLE-SORT
    VARYING COUNTER FROM 1 BY 1
    UNTIL NO-MORE-EXCHANGES
```

5. Note that the table must be passed through one time after the last exchange has taken place in order to verify that there are no more exchanges. Output from this program is

```
NBR OF EXCHANGES    07
NBR OF IF TESTS     12
```

FIGURE 10-3

Revised bubble sort

```
000100 IDENTIFICATION DIVISION.
000110 PROGRAM-ID. BUBBLE1.
000120*
000130 ENVIRONMENT DIVISION.
000140 CONFIGURATION SECTION.
000150 SOURCE-COMPUTER. MICRO.
000160 OBJECT-COMPUTER. MICRO.
000170*
000180 DATA DIVISION.
000190 WORKING-STORAGE SECTION.
000200 01  MISC-FIELDS.
000210     03  COUNTER            PIC 9.
000220     03  L                  PIC 9.
000230     03  TEMP               PIC 99.
000240     03  N                  PIC 9.
000250     03  EXCHANGE-COUNTER   PIC 99 VALUE ZEROS.
000260     03  IF-COUNTER         PIC 99 VALUE ZERO.
000270 01  DATA-AREA.
000280     03  FILLER             PIC 9(12)
000290              VALUE 162114361031.
000300 01  TABLE-AREA REDEFINES DATA-AREA.
000310     03  TABLE-DATA         PIC 99 OCCURS 6 TIMES.
000320*
000330 PROCEDURE DIVISION.
000340 CONTROL-ROUTINE.
000350     PERFORM TABLE-PRINT
000360         VARYING COUNTER FROM 1 BY 1
000370         UNTIL COUNTER IS GREATER THAN 6.
000380     PERFORM BUBBLE-SORT
000390         VARYING COUNTER FROM 1 BY 1
000400         UNTIL COUNTER IS GREATER THAN 6.
000410     PERFORM TABLE-PRINT
000420         VARYING COUNTER FROM 1 BY 1
000430         UNTIL COUNTER IS GREATER THAN 6.
000440     DISPLAY "NBR OF EXCHANGES ", EXCHANGE-COUNTER.
000450     DISPLAY "NBR OF IF TESTS ", IF-COUNTER.
000460     STOP RUN.
000470*
000480 TABLE-PRINT.
000490     DISPLAY TABLE-DATA (COUNTER).
000500*
000510 BUBBLE-SORT.
000520     PERFORM INNER-SORT
000530         VARYING L FROM 6 BY -1
000540         UNTIL L IS EQUAL TO COUNTER.
000550*
000560 INNER-SORT.
000570     ADD 1 TO IF-COUNTER.
000580     COMPUTE N = L - 1.
000590     IF TABLE-DATA (L) IS LESS THAN TABLE-DATA (N)
000600         MOVE TABLE-DATA (N) TO TEMP
000610         MOVE TABLE-DATA (L) TO TABLE-DATA (N)
000620         MOVE TEMP TO TABLE-DATA (L)
000630         ADD 1 TO EXCHANGE-COUNTER.
```

FIGURE 10-4

Bubble sort further revised

```
000100 IDENTIFICATION DIVISION.
000110 PROGRAM-ID. BUBBLE2.
000120*
000130 ENVIRONMENT DIVISION.
000140 CONFIGURATION SECTION.
000150 SOURCE-COMPUTER. MICRO.
000160 OBJECT-COMPUTER. MICRO.
000170*
000180 DATA DIVISION.
000190 WORKING-STORAGE SECTION.
000200 01  MISC-FIELDS.
000210     03  COUNTER            PIC 9.
000220     03  L                  PIC 9.
000230     03  TEMP               PIC 99.
000240     03  N                  PIC 9.
000250     03  EXCHANGE-SWITCH    PIC XXX VALUE " ON".
000260         88 NO-MORE-EXCHANGES    VALUE "OFF".
000270     03  EXCHANGE-COUNTER   PIC 99 VALUE ZEROS.
000280     03  IF-COUNTER         PIC 99 VALUE ZERO.
000290 01  DATA-AREA.
000300     03  FILLER             PIC 9(12)
000310                 VALUE 361621141031.
000320 01  TABLE-AREA REDEFINES DATA-AREA.
000330     03  TABLE-DATA         PIC 99 OCCURS 6 TIMES.
000340*
000350 PROCEDURE DIVISION.
000360 CONTROL-ROUTINE.
000370     PERFORM TABLE-PRINT
000380         VARYING COUNTER FROM 1 BY 1
000390         UNTIL COUNTER IS GREATER THAN 6.
000400     PERFORM BUBBLE-SORT
000410         VARYING COUNTER FROM 1 BY 1
000420         UNTIL NO-MORE-EXCHANGES.
000430     PERFORM TABLE-PRINT
000440         VARYING COUNTER FROM 1 BY 1
000450         UNTIL COUNTER IS GREATER THAN 6.
000460     DISPLAY "NBR OF EXCHANGES ", EXCHANGE-COUNTER.
000470     DISPLAY "NBR OF IF TESTS ", IF-COUNTER.
000480     STOP RUN.
000490*
000500 TABLE-PRINT.
000510     DISPLAY TABLE-DATA (COUNTER).
000520*
000530 BUBBLE-SORT.
000540     MOVE "OFF" TO EXCHANGE-SWITCH.
000550     PERFORM INNER-SORT
000560         VARYING L FROM 6 BY -1
000570         UNTIL L IS EQUAL TO COUNTER.
000580*
000590 INNER-SORT.
000600     ADD 1 TO IF-COUNTER.
000610     COMPUTE N = L - 1.
000620     IF TABLE-DATA (L) IS LESS THAN TABLE-DATA (N)
000630         MOVE TABLE-DATA (N) TO TEMP
000640         MOVE TABLE-DATA (L) TO TABLE-DATA (N)
000650         MOVE TEMP TO TABLE-DATA (L)
000660         MOVE " ON" TO EXCHANGE-SWITCH
000670         ADD 1 TO EXCHANGE-COUNTER.
```

External sorting

Larger files are said to be sorted externally because the process makes extensive use of disk or tape files. Different methods may be used, but the technique often involves building "strings" of sorted records. For example, two records are read into memory, sorted into order, and then written onto an output tape or disk file. Later, these strings of two records are sorted and merged into a string of four. The process continues until the entire file is sorted and the elements merged together, a task that normally involves the use of three or more tape or disk files.

Fortunately, you will not have to worry about the various sorting techniques, since COBOL has a special SORT feature to do the job. The SORT statement in COBOL is extremely powerful, but very easy to use. The programmer indicates the name of the (input) file to be sorted, the file where the sorting will take place (the sort work file), and the name of the (result) file that will contain the new, sorted records. In addition to identifying the files as outlined above, the programmer also specifies the key field or fields on which the sort will take place. For our example we will use the PAY-DATA file (Data File A). The file actually is in ascending order according to the employee identification number field (positions 1 through 9). However, in this case we will assume that we wish the file to be in alphabetic order based on the name field (positions 10 through 29). Figure 10-5 shows the file in its original condition—in order by the identification number field.

FIGURE 10-5

PAY-DATA file

ID NUMBER	NAME
010114101	SMITH ELBERT
010116104	BARNHART STANLEY
050124101	WALSH JUDITH
050125395	PEARSON SAMUEL
060443916	LEE KIMBERLY
140133010	CHICANE HERB
190456301	HARKELRODE CLARA
220133512	KOCHINIS ANGELO
230965777	RUSE WAYNE
270134109	MOORE SAMUEL
304165298	BILBERRY DALTON
320135004	MARTIN SUSAN
346945678	FUJIMOTO KEN
350214101	STOLL GEORGE
365593864	EVANS ROBERT
410954321	GARCIA FRAN
555438619	DEE ELLIS
666666666	BRONSON PATTY
684836197	ROSSI JACK
745678432	JOHNSON PAM

To set up the operation, we need to specify the input file, the sort file where sorting will take place, and the result or sorted file:

```
SELECT INPUT-FILE
     ASSIGN TO _____.
```

This is our payroll data file that is on disk (or tape) and that will be used as the input data to the COBOL sort routine. Sorting, however, does not in any way hurt the INPUT-FILE. The SORT software will copy the contents of the file onto the sort work file prior to starting the sort operation:

```
SELECT SORT-FILE
     ASSIGN TO _____.
```

This is a disk file onto which a copy of the INPUT-FILE will be written. The SORT verb will then cause this file to be sorted in accordance with instructions specified in the PROCEDURE-DIVISION. Some systems have a special designation for this file that further specifies it as a sort work file:

```
ASSIGN TO SYSXXX-DA-XXXX-S-SORTWK1
```

After the sorting is complete, the newly sorted records will be written onto a tape file (RESULT-FILE). And, of course, we will need a printer file to print the results of the sort process:

```
SELECT RESULT-FILE
     ASSIGN TO _____.
SELECT PRINTER-FILE
     ASSIGN TO _____.
```

The DATA DIVISION entries are just what you would expect for the INPUT-FILE:

```
FD   INPUT-FILE
     LABEL RECORDS ARE STANDARD
     VALUE OF FILE-ID IS 'PAY-DATA'
     DATA RECORD IS PAY-DATA-IN.
01   PAY-DATA-IN.
     03  ID-NBR          PIC 9(9).
     03  NAME            PIC X(20).
     03  FILLER          PIC X(51).
```

The entry for SORT-FILE, however, has one small but very important change. Instead of the "FD" entry, we will not show it as FD (File Description) but as SD for Sort Description. This designation alerts the software that this is the file that will be acted upon by the SORT statement:

```
SD   SORT-FILE
     DATA RECORD IS SORT-RECORD.
01   SORT-RECORD.
     03  ID-NBR-SORT-FILE    PIC 9(9).
     03  NAME-SORT-FILE      PIC X(20).
     03  FILLER              PIC X(51).
```

Note that the LABEL RECORD IS entry is missing. Since this is a work file, the entry is not only not required, but also is usually *not permitted* by most systems. The sorted records will be written automatically to the RESULT-FILE, which is described with an FD entry:

```
FD   RESULT-FILE
     LABEL RECORDS ARE STANDARD
     VALUE OF FILE-ID IS 'SORTED-PAY'
     DATA RECORD IS SORTED-RECORDS.
01   SORTED-RECORDS.
     03  ID-NBR-RESULT-FILE    PIC 9(9).
     03  NAME-RESULT-FILE      PIC X(20).
     03  FILLER                PIC X(51).
```

The new file may be given whatever name the programmer chooses as designated by the VALUE OF FILE-ID entry.

The SORT statement: USING/GIVING

The SORT statement has two basic formats, the first of which is called SORT USING/GIVING.

$$\underline{\text{SORT}} \text{ file-name } \underline{\text{ON}} \left\{ \begin{array}{c} \underline{\text{ASCENDING}} \\ \underline{\text{DESCENDING}} \end{array} \right\} \text{KEY data-name-1 [data name-2]} \dots$$

$$\left[\text{ON} \left\{ \begin{array}{c} \underline{\text{ASCENDING}} \\ \underline{\text{DESCENDING}} \end{array} \right\} \text{KEY data-name-3 [data-name-4]} \dots \right] \dots$$

$$\underline{\text{USING}} \text{ file-name-1}$$
$$\underline{\text{GIVING}} \text{ file-name-2.}$$

In the example we have set up, file-name is our SORT-FILE as described with an SD entry; file-name-1 is the INPUT-FILE; and file-name-2 is the RESULT-FILE that will contain the data records in sorted order. The sort itself will take place on the NAME-SORT-FILE field and the results are to be in ASCENDING order based on this key (field):

```
SORT SORT-FILE ON ASCENDING KEY NAME-SORT-FILE
    USING INPUT-FILE
    GIVING RESULT-FILE.
```

Pseudocode specifications for the sort operation are shown in Figure 10-6 while the programs and output are shown in Figures 10-7 and 10-8. If we had specified DESCENDING in the SORT statement, the listing would have been in reverse alphabetical order.

FIGURE 10-6

SORT ASCENDING

```
CONTROL-ROUTINE
    PERFORM SORT-ROUTINE
    PERFORM 010-STARTING-PROCEDURE
    PERFORM 020-READ-AND-WRITE UNTIL end of file
     indicator = 1
    PERFORM 030-END-ROUTINE
    STOP RUN

SORT-ROUTINE
    Sort ascending name field
    Open the files

010-STARTING-PROCEDURE
    Write heading line
    Read sorted record at end move 1 to end of file indicator

020-READ-AND-WRITE
    Move fields to print area
    Write report line on printer
    Read sorted record at end move 1 to end of file indicator

030-END-ROUTINE
    Close the files
```

FIGURE 10-7

Sorting program

```
000100 IDENTIFICATION DIVISION.
000110 PROGRAM-ID. SORTING.
000120*
000130 ENVIRONMENT DIVISION.
000140 CONFIGURATION SECTION.
000150 SOURCE-COMPUTER. - - -.
000160 OBJECT-COMPUTER. - - -.
000170 INPUT-OUTPUT SECTION.
000180 FILE-CONTROL.
000190       SELECT INPUT-FILE ASSIGN TO - - -.
000200       SELECT SORT-FILE ASSIGN TO - - -.
000210       SELECT RESULT-FILE ASSIGN TO - - -.
000220       SELECT PRINTER-FILE ASSIGN TO - - -.
000230*
000240 DATA DIVISION.
000250 FILE SECTION.
000260 FD  INPUT-FILE
000270       VALUE OF FILE-ID IS 'PAY-DATA'
000280       LABEL RECORDS ARE STANDARD
000290       DATA RECORD IS PAY-DATA-IN.
000300 01  PAY-DATA-IN.
000310       03   ID-NBR                    PIC 9(9).
000320       03   NAME                      PIC X(20).
000330       03   FILLER                    PIC X(51).
000340 SD  SORT-FILE
000350       DATA RECORD IS SORT-RECORD.
000360 01  SORT-RECORD.
000370       03   ID-NBR-SORT-FILE          PIC 9(9).
000380       03   NAME-SORT-FILE            PIC X(20).
000390       03   FILLER                    PIC X(51).
000400 FD  RESULT-FILE
000410       LABEL RECORDS ARE STANDARD
000420       VALUE OF FILE-ID IS 'SORTED-PAY'
000430       DATA RECORD IS SORTED-RECORDS.
000440 01  SORTED-RECORDS.
000450       03   ID-NBR-RESULT-FILE        PIC 9(9).
000460       03   NAME-RESULT-FILE          PIC X(20).
000470       03   FILLER                    PIC X(51).
000480 FD  PRINTER-FILE
000490       LABEL RECORDS ARE OMITTED
000500       DATA RECORD IS OUTPUT-LINE.
000510 01  OUTPUT-LINE                      PIC X(121).
000520 WORKING-STORAGE SECTION.
000530 01  MISC-FIELDS.
000540       03   EOF-INDICATOR        PIC 9 VALUE ZERO.
000550 01  HEADING-LINE.
000560       03   FILLER               PIC X(10) VALUE SPACES.
000570       03   FILLER               PIC X(9) VALUE 'ID NUMBER'.
```

FIGURE 10-7

continued

```
000580      03  FILLER                  PIC X(14) VALUE SPACES.
000590      03  FILLER                  PIC X(4) VALUE 'NAME'.
000600      03  FILLER                  PIC X(84) VALUE SPACES.
000610 01  DATA-OUT.
000620      03  FILLER                  PIC X(10) VALUE SPACES.
000630      03  ID-NBR-OUT              PIC 9(9).
000640      03  FILLER                  PIC X(10) VALUE SPACES.
000650      03  NAME-OUT                PIC X(20).
000660      03  FILLER                  PIC X(72) VALUE SPACES.
000670*
000680 PROCEDURE DIVISION.
000690 CONTROL-ROUTINE.
000700      PERFORM SORT-ROUTINE.
000710      PERFORM 010-STARTING-PROCEDURE.
000720      PERFORM 020-READ-AND-WRITE
000730          UNTIL EOF-INDICATOR = 1.
000740      PERFORM 030-END-ROUTINE.
000750      STOP RUN.
000760 SORT-ROUTINE.
000770      SORT SORT-FILE ON ASCENDING KEY
000780          NAME-SORT-FILE
000790              USING INPUT-FILE
000800              GIVING RESULT-FILE.
000810      OPEN INPUT RESULT-FILE
000820          OUTPUT PRINTER-FILE.
000830 010-STARTING-PROCEDURE.
000840      WRITE OUTPUT-LINE FROM HEADING-LINE
000850          AFTER ADVANCING PAGE.
000860      MOVE SPACES TO OUTPUT-LINE.
000870      WRITE OUTPUT-LINE AFTER ADVANCING 2 LINES.
000880      READ RESULT-FILE
000890          AT END MOVE 1 TO EOF-INDICATOR.
000900 020-READ-AND-WRITE.
000910      MOVE ID-NBR-RESULT-FILE TO ID-NBR-OUT.
000920      MOVE NAME-RESULT-FILE TO NAME-OUT.
000930      WRITE OUTPUT-LINE FROM DATA-OUT
000940          AFTER ADVANCING 1 LINE.
000950      READ RESULT-FILE
000960          AT END MOVE 1 TO EOF-INDICATOR.
000970 030-END-ROUTINE.
000980      CLOSE RESULT-FILE, PRINTER-FILE.
```

FIGURE 10-8

SORT output

```
ID NUMBER           NAME

010116104           BARNHART STANLEY
304165298           BILBERRY DALTON
666666666           BRONSON PATTY
140133010           CHICANE HERB
555438619           DEE ELLIS
365593864           EVANS ROBERT
346945678           FUJIMOTO KEN
410954321           GARCIA FRAN
190456301           HARKELRODE CLARA
745678432           JOHNSON PAM
220133512           KOCHINIS ANGELO
060443916           LEE KIMBERLY
320135004           MARTIN SUSAN
270134109           MOORE SAMUEL
050125395           PEARSON SAMUEL
684836197           ROSSI JACK
230965777           RUSE WAYNE
010114101           SMITH ELBERT
350214101           STOLL GEORGE
050124101           WALSH JUDITH
```

If you haven't already done so, take a close look at the sorting operation that was just shown. We "triggered" into the operation by setting up the appropriate files and by using the SORT verb. Notice what the system does for us.

1. The SORT software *automatically* OPENs the input file and the sort work file. As a matter of fact, we *cannot* open these files—to do so would be an error.
2. The contents of the input file—that is, the file to be sorted—are copied onto the sort work file.
3. The sort work file is sorted according to the specifications given in the SORT statement (ASCENDING KEY or DESCENDING KEY).
4. The input file is closed and the output file is opened.
5. The sorted contents of the sort work file are copied onto the result file.
6. The work file and the output file are closed at the end of the SORT operation.

Figure 10-9 diagrams the basic SORT operation as described above. Note that after the SORT statement was executed, the RESULT-FILE was OPENed in the same way that you would handle any regular input file.

However, there is one additional point you should be aware of. We specified a single sort work file (SORT-FILE) for the sort operation. But, as described earlier in the chapter, the process of sorting commonly requires the use of *several* files. The sort software takes care of this by perhaps using

FIGURE 10-9

SORT operations

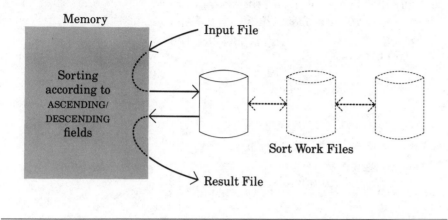

several files for the actual sort process, but usually requires you to set up only one file as we did in this program.

As indicated earlier, records may be sorted on the basis of multiple fields simply by specifying these fields in the SORT statement. The fields must be listed according to the desired order of sorting. For example, to sort customer charge records into ascending date order *within* ascending customer number order, we would specify the following:

```
SORT
    ON ASCENDING KEY CUSTOMER-NBR
        ASCENDING KEY DATE-FIELD
    USING _____
    GIVING _____.
```

The SORT operations described so far are very simple for the programmer to use, but are very inflexible in that the data records cannot be manipulated either on the way into memory from the input file or on the way out to the result file. The INPUT and OUTPUT PROCEDURE options of the SORT statement allow the programmer to manipulate data fields within the records before or after the sort operation.

The SORT statement: INPUT/OUTPUT PROCEDURE

The USING/GIVING version of the SORT statement is extremely powerful and easy to use, but, in return for the ease of use, the programmer has little or no control over the action of the sort. The second version of SORT—with INPUT and OUTPUT PROCEDURE—gives the programmer far greater control over the system action, but in return, the programmer must pay a price. In this case, the programmer is responsible for taking care of many of the actions that were automatic with the USING/GIVING option.

In general, the INPUT PROCEDURE allows the programmer to intercept the data records on their way in from the unsorted file. At this point the programmer may wish to manipulate (insert, modify, or delete) fields in the record prior to releasing the record out to the sort work file. Another, and perhaps more common, activity performed within the input procedure is selecting which of the incoming records will be released to the work file for sorting.

OUTPUT PROCEDURE is essentially the reverse of the INPUT PROCEDURE. Here, the programmer can intercept the records from the work file and manipulate the data prior to returning them to the sorted result file. The SORT format using INPUT and OUTPUT PROCEDURE follows.

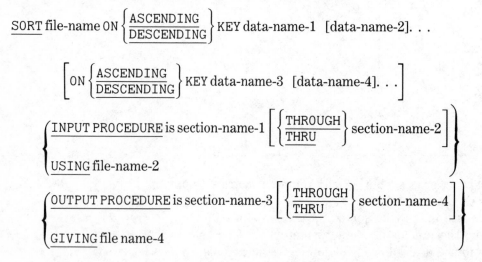

This version of SORT differs from the previous version in several ways.

1. INPUT PROCEDURE may be used in place of USING and OUTPUT PRO-CEDURE may be used in place of GIVING. Thus, it is not necessary to use *both* INPUT PROCEDURE and OUTPUT PROCEDURE in the SORT statement although this option is possible.
2. If INPUT and/or OUTPUT PROCEDURE are used, they must refer to a *section name* within the PROCEDURE DIVISION rather than a para-graph name. This requirement will be illustrated in an example that shows the use of section names within a program.
3. Two special statements—RELEASE and RETURN—must be used with this format of SORT.

To see how INPUT PROCEDURE works, assume we have an unsorted inventory file (INV-FILE) with the following format:

Item Name	Item Code	Manufacturing Plant Name	Plant Code
PIC X (20)	PIC 9(5)	PIC X(20)	PIC X(5)

Example:

Widget	68413	San Francisco	WESTb

Our task is to produce a new file (NEW-FILE) of those items produced by our western plants sorted into ascending order based on the Item Code field. The record format for NEW-FILE will have a slightly different format that will leave out the Plant Code field:

Item Name	Item Code	Manufacturing Plant Name

In the problem described above, we will want to make use of the SORT INPUT PROCEDURE, and, since no special output procedures are required, we can use the GIVING format described earlier. Our file description entries follow.

```
FD  INPUT-FILE
    LABEL RECORD IS STANDARD
    VALUE OF FILE-ID IS 'INV-FILE'
    DATA RECORD IS INV-REC.
01  INV-REC.
    03   ITEM-NAME IN       PIC X(20).
    03   ITEM-CODE-IN       PIC 9(05).
    03   PLANT-NAME-IN      PIC X(20).
    03   PLANT-CODE-IN      PIC X(05).
SD  SORT-FILE
    DATA RECORD IS SORT-REC.
01  SORT-REC.
    03   ITEM-NAME-S        PIC X(20).
    03   ITEM-CODE-S        PIC 9(05).
    03   PLANT-NAME-S       PIC X(20).
FD  RESULT-FILE
    LABEL RECORD IS STANDARD
    VALUE OF FILE-ID IS 'NEW-FILE'
    DATA RECORD IS RESULT-REC.
01  RESULT-REC.
    03   ITEM-NAME          PIC X(20).
    03   ITEM-CODE          PIC 9(05).
    03   PLANT-NAME         PIC X(20).
```

The SORT statement follows the general format of the first version but will include INPUT PROCEDURE instead of USING:

```
SORT SORT-FILE
    ON ASCENDING KEY ITEM-CODE-S
    INPUT PROCEDURE IS 0100-INPUT-PROCESSING
    GIVING RESULT-FILE.
```

According to the format of the SORT verb, 0100-INPUT-PROCESSING *must* be a section name. A section name acts as a higher-level paragraph name that may contain one or more paragraph headers. In addition, on most systems one extra point must be observed by the programmer. If *any* paragraph of the PROCEDURE DIVISION is sectioned, *all* paragraphs of the PROCEDURE DIVISION must fall within a section name. Our PROCEDURE DIVISION entries follow.

```
PROCEDURE DIVISION.
MAIN-PROCESSING-CONTROL SECTION.
CONTROL-ROUTINE.
    SORT SORT-FILE
        ON ASCENDING KEY ITEM-CODE-S
        INPUT PROCEDURE IS 0100-INPUT-PROCESSING
        GIVING RESULT-FILE.
    CLOSE INPUT-FILE,RESULT FILE.
    STOP RUN.
```

```
0100-INPUT-PROCESSING SECTION.
0100-INPUT-PARA-1.
    OPEN INPUT INPUT-FILE.
    READ INPUT-FILE
        AT END MOVE 1 TO EOF-INDICATOR.
    PERFORM 0100-INPUT-PARA-2
        UNTIL EOF-INDICATOR = 1.
    GO TO 0100-INPUT-PARA-EXIT.
0100-INPUT-PARA-2.
    IF PLANT-CODE-IN IS EQUAL TO 'WESTb'
        MOVE ITEM-NAME-IN TO ITEM-NAME-S
        MOVE ITEM-CODE-IN TO ITEM-CODE-S
        MOVE PLANT-NAME-IN TO PLANT-NAME-S
        RELEASE SORT-REC.
    READ INPUT-FILE
        AT END MOVE 1 TO EOF-INDICATOR.
0100-INPUT-PARA-EXIT.
    EXIT.
```

Several important points should be noted.

1. Since INPUT PROCEDURE is used, the programmer is responsible for opening and closing the file that holds the incoming data and for writing records to the work file.

2. All paragraphs within the PROCEDURE DIVISION fall within a section name (MAIN-PROCESSING-CONTROL SECTION and 0100-INPUT-PROCESS-ING SECTION).

3. The INPUT PROCEDURE transfers control to the 0100-INPUT-PROCESS-ING SECTION, which uses a priming read to read a record from the INPUT-FILE.

4. The 0100-INPUT-PARA-2 tests the plant code field and only those records meeting the test are moved to the SORT-REC area.

5. The RELEASE statement is a special form of WRITE that can and must be used *only* with INPUT PROCEDURE. The WEST plant code records are RELEASEd (written) to the SORT-FILE.

6. When the end of the INPUT-FILE is detected, the system executes the downward GO TO that takes it out of the 0100-INPUT-PROCESSING SECTION and back to the GIVING RESULT-FILE part of the SORT verb. The downward GO TO (to an EXIT paragraph) is necessary because of the way in which the system handles sections. Escape from a section can only be accomplished by going to (GO TO) or by executing all statements within the section. Without the downward GO TO, the system, upon detecting the end of the file, would drop down and execute the 0100-INPUT-PARA-2 one more time. Therefore, the EXIT paragraph was coded in to provide an escape mechanism.

7. When control returns to the GIVING clause, the system automatically sorts the file into ascending order on the basis of the item code field and writes the file onto the RESULT-FILE.

Let's expand the problem to include the use of the OUTPUT PROCEDURE option. The way the program was originally set up, the sorted records were simply written to the RESULT-FILE. Now, we will intercept the sorted records on their way to the RESULT-FILE and modify one of the fields. The records coming out of the SORT-FILE represent WEST manufactured products that have been sorted on the Item Code field. We need to modify the Item Code field by adding a product sequence number at the tail end of the Item Code. For example, if the first Item Code is

10632

we want it to be stored as

10632001

and the next item will be 002, then 003, and so on. RESULT-REC will be modified to accommodate these changes:

```
01   RESULT-REC.
     03   ITEM-NAME      PIC X(20).
     03   ITEM-CODE
          05   CODE-NBR   PIC 9(05).
          05   SEQ-NBR    PIC 999.
     03   PLANT-NAME     PIC X(20).
```

Our SORT verb will be modified as follows:

```
SORT SORT-FILE
    ON ASCENDING KEY ITEM-CODE-S
    INPUT PROCEDURE IS 0100-INPUT-PROCESSING
    OUTPUT PROCEDURE IS 0200-OUTPUT-PROCESSING.
CLOSE INPUT-FILE RESULT-FILE.
STOP RUN.
    .
    .
    .
0200-OUTPUT-PROCESSING SECTION.
0200-OUTPUT-PARA-1.
    OPEN OUTPUT RESULT-FILE.
    RETURN SORT-FILE
        AT END MOVE 1 TO EOF-IND.
    PERFORM 0200-OUTPUT-PARA-2.
        UNTIL EOF-IND = 1.
    GO TO 0200-OUTPUT-PARA-EXIT.
0200-OUTPUT-PARA-2.
    MOVE ITEM-NAME-S TO ITEM-NAME.
    MOVE ITEM-CODE-S TO ITEM-CODE.
    MOVE COUNTER TO SEQ-NBR.
    MOVE PLANT-NAME-S TO PLANT-NAME.
    WRITE RESULT-REC.
    ADD 1 TO COUNTER.
    RETURN SORT-FILE
        AT END MOVE 1 TO EOF-IND.
0200-OUTPUT-PARA-EXIT.
    EXIT.
```

The general rules pertaining to the use of INPUT and OUTPUT PROCEDURE are listed below.

1. INPUT and OUTPUT PROCEDURE must not contain any SORT statements.

2. The INPUT PROCEDURE must consist of one or more sections that are written consecutively and do not form a part of an OUTPUT PROCEDURE. OUTPUT PROCEDURE follows the same pattern and may not form a part of an INPUT PROCEDURE.

3. The INPUT and OUTPUT PROCEDURES must not contain any transfers of control to points outside the procedure.

4. The remainder of the PROCEDURE DIVISION must not contain any transfers of control to points inside the INPUT or OUTPUT PROCEDURES.

5. If an INPUT PROCEDURE is specified, control is passed to the input procedure *before* file-name-1 is sequenced by the SORT statement. Before control passes the last statement in the input procedure, file-name-3 must *not* be opened. The compiler inserts a return mechanism at the end of the last section in the input procedure, and when control passes the last statement in the input procedure, the records that have been released to file-name-1 are sorted.

6. If an output procedure is specified, control passes to it *after* file-name-1 has been sequenced by the SORT statement. File-name-2 must *not* be open at this time. The compiler inserts a return mechanism at the end of the last section in the output procedure, and when control passes the last statement in the output procedure, the return mechanism terminates the sort and passes control to the next executable statement after the SORT statement. Figure 10-10 depicts the SORT INPUT/OUTPUT PROCEDURE operation and Figure 10-11 lists the complete program.

FIGURE 10-10

Schematic: SORT with INPUT/OUTPUT PROCEDURE

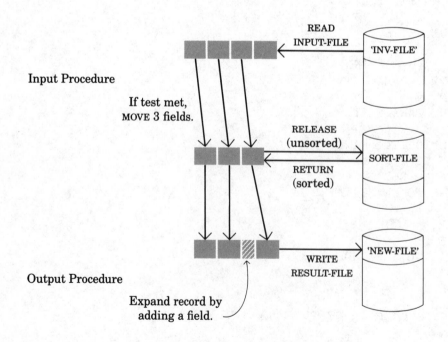

FIGURE 10-11

SORT with INPUT/OUTPUT PROCEDURE

```
000100 IDENTIFICATION DIVISION.
000110 PROGRAM-ID. SORT-IO.
000120*
000130 ENVIRONMENT DIVISION.
000140 CONFIGURATION SECTION.
000150 SOURCE-COMPUTER. - - -.
000160 OBJECT-COMPUTER. - - -.
000170 INPUT-OUTPUT SECTION.
000180 FILE-CONTROL.
000190     SELECT INPUT-FILE ASSIGN TO - - -.
000200     SELECT SORT-FILE ASSIGN TO - - -.
000210     SELECT RESULT-FILE ASSIGN TO - - -.
000220*
000230 DATA DIVISION.
000240 FILE SECTION.
000250 FD  INPUT-FILE
000260     LABEL RECORD IS STANDARD
000270     VALUE OF FILE-ID IS 'INV-FILE'
000280     DATA RECORD IS INV-REC.
000290 01  INV-REC.
000300     03  ITEM-NAME-IN          PIC X(20).
000310     03  ITEM-CODE-IN          PIC 9(05).
000320     03  PLANT-NAME-IN         PIC X(20).
000330     03  PLANT-CODE-IN         PIC X(05).
000340 SD  SORT-FILE
000350     DATA RECORD IS SORT-REC.
000360 01  SORT-REC.
000370     03  ITEM-NAME-S           PIC X(20).
000380     03  ITEM-CODE-S           PIC 9(05).
000390     03  PLANT-NAME-S          PIC X(20).
000400 FD  RESULT-FILE
000410     LABEL RECORD IS STANDARD
000420     VALUE OF FILE-ID IS 'NEW-FILE'
000430     DATA RECORD IS RESULT-REC.
000440 01  RESULT-REC.
000450     03  ITEM-NAME             PIC X(20).
000460     03  ITEM-CODE.
000470         05  CODE-NBR          PIC 9(05).
000480         05  SEQ-NBR           PIC 999.
000490     03  PLANT-NAME            PIC X(20).
000500 WORKING-STORAGE SECTION.
000510 01  MISC-FIELDS.
000520     03  EOF-INDICATOR         PIC 9 VALUE ZERO.
000530     03  EOF-IND               PIC 9 VALUE ZERO.
000540     03  COUNTER               PIC 999 VALUE 001.
000550*
000560 PROCEDURE DIVISION.
000570 MAIN-PROCESSING-CONTROL SECTION.
000580 CONTROL-ROUTINE.
```

continued

FIGURE 10-11

continued

```
000590      SORT SORT-FILE
000600          ON ASCENDING KEY ITEM-CODE-S
000610          INPUT PROCEDURE IS 0100-INPUT-PROCESSING
000620          OUTPUT PROCEDURE IS 0200-OUTPUT-PROCESSING.
000630      CLOSE INPUT-FILE RESULT-FILE.
000640      STOP RUN.
000650*
000660 0100-INPUT-PROCESSING SECTION.
000670 0100-INPUT-PARA-1.
000680      OPEN INPUT INPUT-FILE.
000690      READ INPUT-FILE
000700          AT END MOVE 1 TO EOF-INDICATOR.
000710      PERFORM 0100-INPUT-PARA-2
000720          UNTIL EOF-INDICATOR = 1.
000730      GO TO 0100-INPUT-PARA-EXIT.
000740 0100-INPUT-PARA-2.
000750      IF PLANT-CODE-IN IS EQUAL TO 'WEST '
000760          MOVE ITEM-NAME-IN TO ITEM-NAME-S
000770          MOVE ITEM-CODE-IN TO ITEM-CODE-S
000780          MOVE PLANT-NAME-IN TO PLANT-NAME-S
000790          RELEASE SORT-REC.
000800      READ INPUT-FILE
000810          AT END MOVE 1 TO EOF-INDICATOR.
000820 0100-INPUT-PARA-EXIT.
000830      EXIT.
000840*
000850 0200-OUTPUT-PROCESSING SECTION.
000860 0200-OUTPUT-PARA-1.
000870      OPEN OUTPUT RESULT-FILE.
000880      RETURN SORT-FILE
000890          AT END MOVE 1 TO EOF-IND.
000900      PERFORM 0200-OUTPUT-PARA-2
000910          UNTIL EOF-IND = 1.
000920      GO TO 0200-OUTPUT-PARA-EXIT.
000930 0200-OUTPUT-PARA-2.
000940      MOVE ITEM-NAME-S TO ITEM-NAME.
000950      MOVE ITEM-CODE-S TO ITEM-CODE.
000960      MOVE COUNTER TO SEQ-NBR.
000970      MOVE PLANT-NAME-S TO PLANT-NAME.
000980      WRITE RESULT-REC.
000990      ADD 1 TO COUNTER.
001000      RETURN SORT-FILE
001010          AT END MOVE 1 TO EOF-IND.
001020 0200-OUTPUT-PARA-EXIT.
001030      EXIT.
```

Larger computer systems have access to on-line service facilities.

COMMON ERRORS

Since the basic SORT operation in COBOL is so straightforward, there is little chance of making an error. The one area that may cause some concern is the proper SELECT entry for the sort work file. On many systems there may be a very specific name and entry required for the file on which the sort will take place, so check your machine to be certain. Some systems have to be informed of the size of the file to be sorted and the length of the records used. Also, as mentioned in the chapter, do not include the LABEL RECORD IS entry in the Sort Description.

Remember that when using the first format of the SORT statement (USING/GIVING) the system has the duty of opening and closing the files. This responsibility falls to you only when using the INPUT and/or OUTPUT PROCEDURE options.

With the INPUT and OUTPUT PROCEDURE versions of SORT, you are required to have *all* paragraph names fall within a section name. As shown in the chapter example, this means that the first entry in the PROCEDURE DIVISION must be a section name.

PROGRAMMING TIPS

At various places in the past chapters you were told about some techniques that could be used if your program wouldn't work. Re-evaluation of the design logic and desk checking the program statements are two methods you may have had to use already. Beyond this, however, there are some other problem-solving aids that are available and that depend more on the computer system software than on your abilities to locate errors.

Most computer systems have either specific diagnostic software for a particular language such as COBOL, or generalized software to help locate program errors. In COBOL one such software aid is called READY TRACE, and when this statement is inserted in your program, it will print a listing of the modules that were executed and the sequence of the execution. (Check with your instructor or the operator of your computer system to see exactly how this or a similar routine should be used on your system.)

If you wanted to check the flow of control throughout your entire program, the READY TRACE statement could be inserted in the CONTROL-MODULE paragraph:

```
PROCEDURE DIVISION.
CONTROL-MODULE.
    READY TRACE.
    PERFORM 010-OPENER.
        .
        .
        .
```

If you are concerned about the action of a particular module rather than the entire program, the READY TRACE statement can be inserted wherever you wish. Obviously the execution of READY TRACE takes valuable computer time, so its use should not be abused. In addition, you may not wish to continue the trace action beyond a particular point in the program. If this is so, the RESET TRACE entry will terminate the tracking action. One common practice is to insert READY TRACE just before entering the suspected paragraph and to use RESET TRACE immediately afterward:

```
        .

        .
READY TRACE.
PERFORM CALCULATION-ROUTINE
    UNTIL _____
RESET TRACE.
        .
        .
        .
```

Think in terms of program maintenance!

Program maintenance does apply to you because you are likely to maintain or make changes to your own program during the last debugging stages. At that point, the change of even a single line of code should not be taken lightly. Gerald M. Weinberg, the acknowledged leader in the area of programming psychology, is particularly emphatic on this point. Over the years he has compiled a (confidential) list of the world's most expensive programming errors and all of the top 10 are *maintenance* errors. The top three on his current list are

1. $1,600,000,000
2. $900,000,000
3. $245,000,000

The interesting part is that each of these involved the change of a *single* digit in a program that had been running correctly before! As he puts it, each change was "instituted casually." (Source: *Infosystems*, August 1983, "Kill That Code," p. 49)

SELF-STUDY: QUESTIONS AND ANSWERS

1. The text talks about the constant need for sorting, but I don't understand why it is so important.

   Answer: Data records in a random or unsorted order are difficult and inefficient to work with. You will see an example of this later in the text when the processing of master and detail files is discussed. In general, any type of matching operation where records from one file are compared against records of another file is likely to go much faster if the files have been placed in some type of order. However, realize that sorting is not "free," which means that the cost of the sort has to be balanced against the increased speed of the processing program.

2. How will I know when to do an internal sort as opposed to an external sort?

   Answer: The text gave a rough rule-of-thumb: Files with more than 100 records should be sorted externally. Under 100, it may be worthwhile to sort the records within a table. The most practical answer to the question is that a rule on this—based upon the strengths and weaknesses of your computer system—probably will have been established wherever you work.

   Also, remember that when we say "external" sorting we actually mean that the sorting itself takes place in memory, but that the sorted records are ultimately stored on the sort work file. When sorting in tables, the data remain inside memory.

   Another point you may wish to consider is that the external SORT software, as shown in the chapter, already exists. If you wish to do an internal table sort, you will have to develop your own algorithm for the job.

3. Do I have to use the file names of SORT-FILE, INPUT-FILE, and RESULT-FILE? You seem to have used these names throughout the chapter.

   Answer: Normally, you can use any names you want for the input, sort work, and result files. The only limitation is that your particular computer system may require a specific file name for the sort work file. The most likely situation is that you may choose any names you wish for the files, but may have to have a specific entry for the ASSIGN part of the sort work file entry.

4. In the second version of the SORT statement, can I use OUTPUT PROCEDURE without using INPUT PROCEDURE?

   Answer: Yes, you can. INPUT and OUTPUT PROCEDURE and USING and GIVING may be used in a "mix-and-match" arrangement. The main point to remember is that if you use either INPUT or OUTPUT PROCEDURE, you must reference a section name.

CHAPTER TERMS

ASCENDING	READY TRACE
bubble sort	RESET TRACE
DESCENDING	section name
external sort	selection sort
INPUT PROCEDURE	shell sort
internal sort	SORT
OUTPUT PROCEDURE	sort work file

EXERCISES

1. Explain the difference between internal and external sorting.

2. Under what conditions would you want to sort internally? When would you want to sort externally? Give an example of each use.

3. Assume you have five data records, each containing a single data value (PIC 999). Design the program and draw the flowchart for the steps necessary to put these values in ascending order. You are *not* to use a table, and each value is to be considered and tested as it enters from a file. Use the fields called LARGEST, SECOND-LARGEST, and THIRD-LARGEST, and so on, for the sorted values.

4. Modify the previous exercise so that all the values are read into a table before sorting begins.

5. Modify Exercise 4 so that the values are placed in descending rather than ascending order.

6. If you did both Exercises 4 and 5, you are aware of the slight difference between the plans. Now, modify the plan still further so that the sort sequence (ascending or descending) can be determined just before the process is executed.

7. The text described an internal sorting technique called a bubble sort. Design a program that first reads five values into a table and then sorts these values into descending order by "bubbling" the highest number up to the top.

8. Show the table below after each pass through, using a bubble sort.

   START

9
2
4
5
1

9. What differences exist between a file description for a sort work file and a normal file?

10. When utilizing SORT with USING and GIVING, how are the files opened for the sort process?

11. When utilizing INPUT PROCEDURE, how are the files opened for the sort process?

12. Describe in general terms the action of the computer system during an external sort operation.

13. Data File A (PAY-DATA) contains the following data fields:

Field	Length
ID Number	9 digits
Employee Name	20 characters
Filler	1 character
Rate of Pay	4 digits, dollars and cents
Number of Dependents	2 digits
Filler	19 characters

Write a program to list the contents of the file in ascending order based on the Rate of Pay field. Note that you will have to total the rates of pay and calculate the average pay rate. Output will be as follows:

```
                    EMPLOYEE PAY RATES

    NAME      ID NUMBER      RATE     NUMBER OF DEPENDENTS
    ____      _____        ____     _____

    ____      _____        ____     _____


           TOTAL NUMBER OF EMPLOYEES _____
           AVERAGE HOURLY PAY RATE _____
```

14. Data File B (SALES-DATA) contains the following data fields:

Field	Length
Sales Territory	3 digits
ID Number	5 digits
Name	20 characters
YTD Sales	7 digits, dollars and cents
YTD Sales Returns	6 digits, dollars and cents

Write a program to sort the file into ascending order based on the three-digit sales territory field. After the file has been sorted, provide for printer output of those employees who have net year-to-date sales of over $1000. Output will have the following format:

```
                    EMPLOYEE LISTING

    SALES TERRITORY        NAME ID NUMBER      NET YTD SALES
    _____                _____             _____

    _____                _____             _____


    NUMBER OF RECORDS PROCESSED _____
```

15. Modify Exercise 13 so that the output records are in ascending order by Number of Dependents within the Rate of Pay field. The output format will be the same.

16. Modify Exercise 14 so that the data records are sorted into descending order of YTD Sales within ascending Sales Territory number. The output format will be the same.

17. Modify Exercise 14 so that only those records of employees in Sales Territory 107 with Net YTD Sales greater than $1000 are placed onto the sort work file. The ascending sort is to be done on the employee name field.

Chapter 11
Working with Sequential Files

CHAPTER OUTLINE

Magnetic tape media
    Using tape efficiently
Magnetic disk storage
    Disk characteristics
    Disk addressing
Manipulating sequential files
    Changing or deleting existing records
    On-line updating
    Adding records to a file (merging)
Common errors
Programming tips
Self-study: Questions and answers
Chapter terms
Exercises

LEARNING OBJECTIVES

1. To understand the makeup of magnetic tape and disk storage media.

2. To learn how to use magnetic tape.

3. To understand how the system handles blocked records, label processing, and the end-of-file condition on sequential files.

4. To see how sequential files are updated or maintained by modifying existing records, or by adding records to or deleting records from the file.

5. To see the value of using a diagramming method as a tool in determining program logic.

All the applications discussed so far have dealt with sequential files, and, in general, they all work the same way, although there are differences between card files and tape or sequential disk files.

Magnetic media files offer at least three advantages over cards. First, magnetic media are much faster. Second, records are not limited to 80 characters. Third, special methods exist that allow data to be handled far more efficiently on tape and disk rather than cards. Let's take a look at the specific characteristics of tape and disk.

Magnetic tape media

Magnetic tape is made of plastic that is one half inch wide, and is coated on one side with an easily magnetized material such as iron oxide. Reels containing up to 2400 feet of tape are mounted on *tape drives*, which perform the tasks of reading from or writing onto the tape storage media. The tape transport mechanism (Figure 11-1) physically moves the tape past a read/write head assembly where reading or writing takes place. As with any input file, you *read* from tape *into* memory and *write* from memory *onto* tape. Reading from tape is nondestructive in the sense that the data on tape are still there and can be read repeatedly. Writing onto tape is destructive since the data that originally were on that area of tape are destroyed by the new material being written.

FIGURE 11-1

Tape transport mechanism

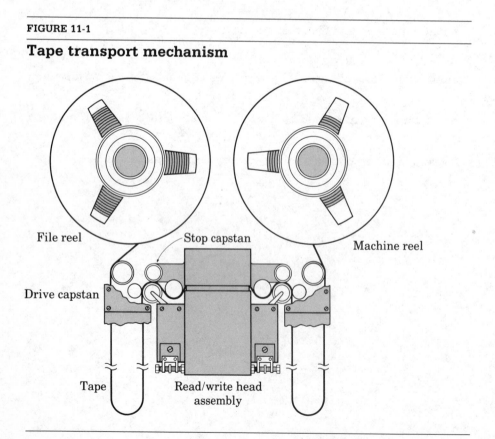

File reel   Stop capstan   Machine reel

Drive capstan

Tape   Read/write head assembly

The data on tape are in the form of a column of tiny magnetic spots, or "bits" (binary digits), written by the electrically activated read/write head. Modern computers use nine-channel tape (an eight-bit byte plus one check bit or parity bit). Older computers often used a seven-channel format consisting of a six-bit code plus one parity bit (Figure 11-2).

Although tape and card records share some similarities, there are several ways in which they differ. At the conclusion of every tape WRITE operation, the computer system automatically skips a small portion of tape (usually about one half inch), which is known as the inter-record gap (IRG). This is something over which the programmer has no control, since the system requires a gap in order to physically handle the tape as it moves through the tape's read-write mechanism. A gap, then, will appear between each tape record.

Record	Gap	Record	Gap	Record	Gap	Record	Gap	Record

When the tape spool is mounted on the tape drive, about 15 feet at the beginning is used as "leader" to thread through the winding system. The actual recording area of tape is recognized by the tape drive because it senses a small, light-reflecting silver patch positioned just after the leader area. The physical end of the tape is marked in a similar way so that reading or writing does not progress beyond the usable area.

Each WRITE instruction advances the tape until we write the last record on the tape file. The system does not "know" that this is the last record; but when the file is CLOSEd, the system writes a special configuration of bits that indicates this is the end of the file (EOF). Later, when a program reads the tape file, the EOF configuration triggers the AT END portion of the sequential file READ statement.

Using tape efficiently

Although the previous diagram is correct in that it does represent the layout of tape records, it is grossly out of perspective, because it does not consider one of the features of magnetic storage media—recording density. The term *recording density* means the closeness with which the columns of magnetic spots are written onto magnetic tape. Some fairly typical recording densities are 800 and 1600 characters per inch (often called bpi for "bytes" per inch in reference to the storage terminology used on most IBM machines). For example, at 800 characters per inch (cpi), an 80-column card record would take up one-tenth of an inch and at 1600 cpi the record would occupy only one-twentieth of an inch. When you think back to the fact that the inter-record gap is approximately one half inch, tape is mostly gaps, as the following illustration indicates:

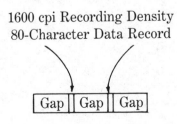

1600 cpi Recording Density
80-Character Data Record

FIGURE 11-2

Tape formats

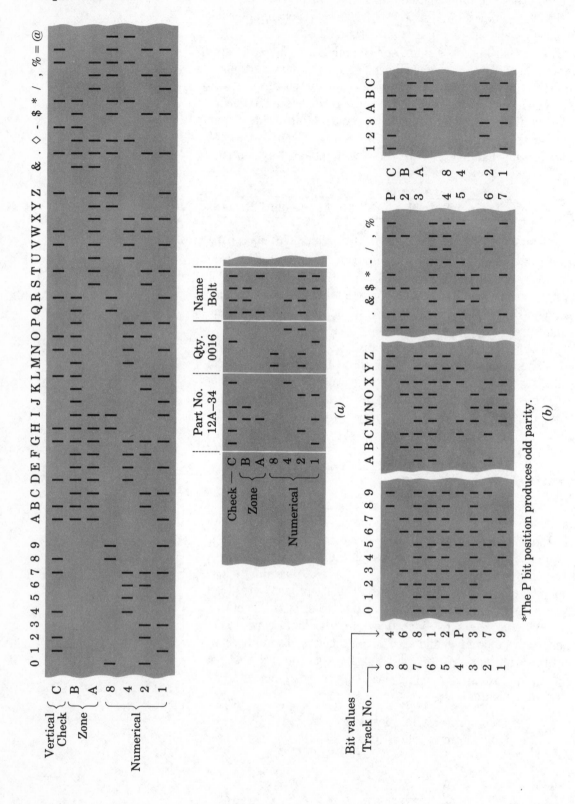

*The P bit position produces odd parity.

Obviously, we are not using tape efficiently, but the problem is easily avoided by "blocking" the tape records. The term *blocking* means we will group a series of records together into a block *before* writing the data onto tape. If we had a *blocking factor* of 3 (that is, three records per block), a *schematic* layout (not actual size) of our tape data would look as follows:

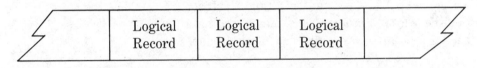

At this point, we need to introduce another term associated with files. A single record—a card record, for example—is known as a *logical* record. It also happens to be comprised of one *physical* record. When records are blocked, as they were in the above diagram, the physical record consists of three logical records followed by an inter-block gap (IBG).

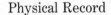

Physical Record

It is possible to block hundreds of records together in a block, with one obvious limiting factor being the amount of memory available in the computer system. On most systems, however, there is an optimum block size that can be determined by use of a formula that takes into consideration the specifics of the hardware being used. Quite often this figure is close to 8000 bytes. Further efficiency in the use of magnetic storage media can be achieved by writing the numeric data in packed format, a topic discussed earlier.

Blocking is extremely simple to do in COBOL. All it requires is a single change in the file description entry:

```
FD  TAPEFILE
    LABEL RECORD IS STANDARD
    VALUE OF FILE-ID IS 'TAPE-DATA'
    BLOCK CONTAINS 3 RECORDS
    DATA RECORD IS TAPE-REC.
01  TAPE-REC.
    ------
    ------  } 80-byte record
    ------
    ------
```

The BLOCK CONTAINS entry triggers the COBOL software system to cause the tape records to be written in blocked format. However, there is *no* change in the PROCEDURE DIVISION statement nor is there any change in the program logic!

Even though the system software does all the work for you, you should understand exactly what is happening. When the system "sees" the BLOCK CONTAINS entry, it sets up a buffer area in memory large enough to hold the block of three records. In our example the buffer is 240 characters long (three times the record size of 80).

Let's assume a file of card records is to be written to magnetic tape, blocked three records per block. The PROCEDURE DIVISION statements are based on the Read-a-record, Write-a-record logic as before. However, the system software overrides this logic to take care of your blocking requirements by doing the following:

1. The first card is read into the CARD-IN area as you would expect.
2. The card data are moved to the tape record area (EMPLOYEE-DATA) (Figure 11-3a).
3. The system encounters the tape WRITE statement, but the record is *not* written onto tape. If the system did so, we would have a tape gap immediately after the record was written onto tape. Instead, the software overrides the WRITE statement and moves the data record to the first record area in the three-record block (Figure 11-3b).
4. The program (using structured logic) reads another card and branches back through the looping process. The second card record is *not* written onto tape, but is moved into the second record area of the three-record block.
5. The buffer area, of course, will be filled after the third card record is moved in. Only then are the contents of the buffer area (block) written onto tape. Again, note that the program logic (as shown in the PROCEDURE DIVISION statements) is done as if the data records were unblocked (Figure 11-3c).
6. The reading of blocked tape files follows the reverse of the pattern illustrated. Again, on either input or output, the *program logic* is based on the manipulation of *unblocked* files.

In Chapter 10 you saw sort programs in which the input and output files were unblocked—that is, no mention was made that any blocking was to be done. Either or both of these files could be in blocked format and still be processed by the SORT software. For example, the INPUT-FILE could have been blocked 3 and RESULT-FILE might have been blocked something other than 3 without any change in the SORT operation. Also, we could have had any combination of magnetic disk and/or magnetic tape files for input, sorting, or output, although a disk would be more appropriate for the sort work file.

Obviously, in order to be able to use a file that has been blocked, the user must know the factor by which the records were blocked when the file was created. Without this information, the file is useless. Sequential disk files follow the same blocking/unblocking pattern with one possible exception. Some disk-oriented systems have special input/output software for disk file activities. On systems of this type the programmer may specify a particular blocking factor by means of the BLOCK CONTAINS entry, but the system software may override this specification in favor of its own more efficient blocking and unblocking activities.

FIGURE 11-3

Buffer action—blocked tape records

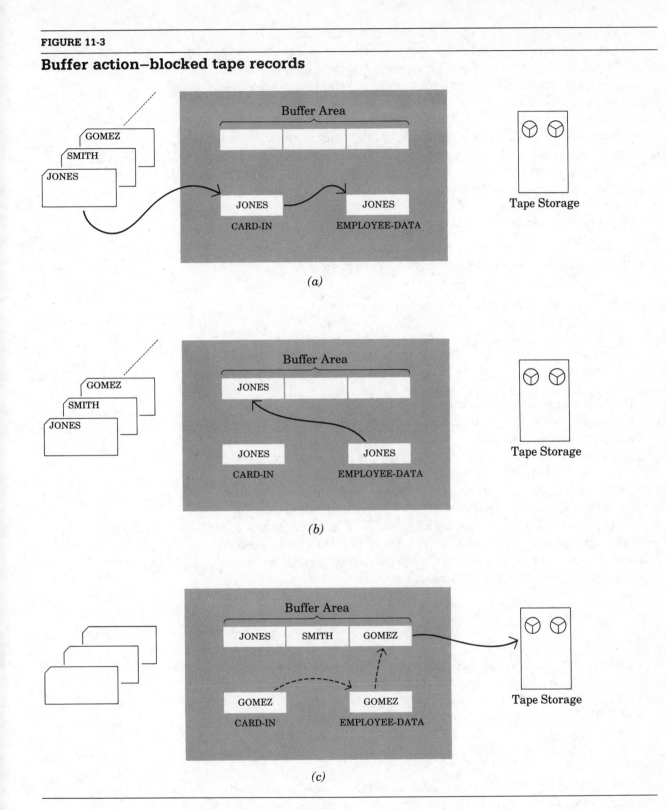

(a)

(b)

(c)

Accidental destruction of a tape file (that is, writing on a tape) can be prevented by means of a plastic file protect ring near the center of the spool. The ring must be on the spool in order for writing to take place. In order to prevent accidental writing over or destruction of a file, the plastic ring is removed. Now the tape cannot be written on and an attempt to do so will again cancel the program. The general rule is "no ring, no write."

From the earlier discussions of tape recording density and the use of blocking, it is obvious that these factors determine how much data can be stored on a single spool of tape. However, a more specific example may put this into better perspective. Suppose we have a file of 10,000 80-character card records that are to be stored on tape. The following table shows how much tape space is required for the *data only*, depending upon the recording density:

10,000 records $\times$ 80 characters = 800,000 characters

Recording density	Data storage
800 cpi	1000 in. or 83.3 ft
1600 cpi	500 in. or 41.67 ft
6250 cpi	128 in. or 10.67 ft

If the data records were written in unblocked form, we would have a gap between each record, or 10,000 gaps. Using the common gap size of six-tenths of an inch, our 10,000 unblocked records would require 6000 inches, or 500 feet, of gaps! Thus there is little advantage to having a high recording density if the data records are unblocked. Even at a medium-high recording density of 1600 characters per inch we would use approximately 541 feet of tape to store only 41 feet of data in unblocked form.

Blocking will change this significantly: We will have far fewer gaps because they will appear only after a *block* is written. If we use a blocking factor of 20—that is, 20 records per block—our 10,000 records will result in 500 blocks with a corresponding number of inter-block gaps:

10,000 records divided by 20 records = 500 blocks
500 blocks $\times$ .6 in. gap = 300 in. of gap
300 in. of gap divided by 12 = 25 ft of gap

Tape blocking also has an important effect upon *transfer rate*, which is the rate at which tape data are read into memory. Common transfer rates range from 60,000 to 100,000 or more characters per second. Our example of 10,000 80-character records (800,000 characters) would take 10 seconds to read using a tape system with a transfer rate of 80,000 characters per second. This 10-second figure, however, is misleading, since this rate pertains to *data* only.

When the system encounters a gap, it stops and then has to start again to read the next portion of data. If we assume a stop-start gap time of eight one-thousandths of a second, we can easily calculate the effect that gaps have upon the time it takes to read tape data into memory. If our 10,000-record file is unblocked, the 10,000 gaps will require 80 seconds:

Sequential File Processing with magnetic tape.

10,000 gaps $\times$ .008 sec per gap = 80 sec

Total read time will then be 90 seconds—10 for the data and 80 for the gaps. If the data are blocked 20, we will now require only four seconds for the passage through the gaps:

500 gaps $\times$ .008 sec per gap = 4 sec

Total read time will now be 14 seconds.

Magnetic disk storage

Most large computer installations are likely to have both magnetic disk and tape drives attached to the computer system because this combination offers operational flexibility. Tape is an excellent backup medium for disk and functions well for certain types of file operations. Disk, on the other hand, offers quick access, which makes it the preferred storage for on-line or quick response applications. In many ways, magnetic disk is similar to magnetic tape, but its major difference is the ability to store data in addressable areas.

Disk characteristics

Many varieties of disk storage units are available today, but they generally share similar characteristics. The disks resemble phonograph records and may be arranged in a stacked order or as single units (Figure 11-4). The disks may be of metal or soft plastic, but both types are extremely smooth

FIGURE 11-4

Disk platter arrangements

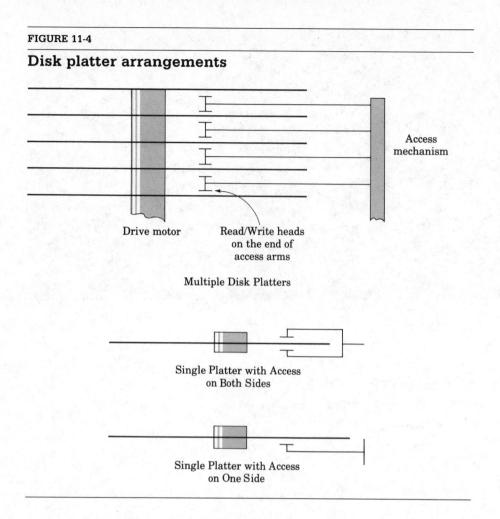

Drive motor

Read/Write heads
on the end of
access arms

Access
mechanism

Multiple Disk Platters

Single Platter with Access
on Both Sides

Single Platter with Access
on One Side

and coated with an easily magnetized substance such as iron oxide. Electrically activated read/write heads on the ends of access arms are used to write information onto or to read information from the surface of the disks. Data are recorded in the form of tiny magnetic spots laid down according to the computer's internal coding format. In the final analysis, however, all the data are stored in a binary format that consists of spots or no spots. As with other magnetic storage media, reading does not harm the data in any way, but writing is destructive since the new data replace (write over) the old data.

The physical disk unit in which the platters are housed is called a *disk drive* and most computer systems have the capability of supporting several drive units. Usually the platter or set of platters that make up disk storage are removable, although some drives (fixed disk drives) contain nonremovable platters. Removable platters are often packaged as a single unit and are known as a *disk pack*.

From the previous figure you can see that the access arms all move in or out across the disk surfaces together. However, only one read/write head is activated at any one moment so that reading or writing takes place on only one part of the disk surface at any time.

On "hard" disks (as opposed to what are known as "soft," or "floppy," disks), the read/write heads do not touch the disk but are extremely close to the surface. A disk drive is a precision instrument—a point particularly evident when you realize that the platter is rotating at a constant speed of close to 3000 revolutions per minute while the access arms are going in and out to read or write information. A dreaded "head crash" occurs when the read/write heads actually make contact with the surface. When this happens not only are the data lost, but part of the disk drive electronics may be destroyed as well.

A relative newcomer to auxiliary storage media are the soft or "floppy" disks brought out in 1972. Called "diskettes" by IBM, the flexible disks are enclosed in a hard plastic cover that has openings for the drive spindle and access mechanism. After their introduction, they began to be used as a cheap auxiliary storage medium for intelligent terminals, office word processing systems, and microcomputers. The original floppies could record data on one side only, but the newer version, called "flippies," can record on both sides. Technical improvements over the years have pushed storage capacity to over one million characters per floppy disk.

Hard disks have two main advantages over soft disks that help to offset their higher cost.

1. Their higher rotational rate permits much faster data retrieval than soft disk.
2. The manufacturing precision of hard disk media and drives allows the storage of far greater amounts of data.

As of this writing, there is no standardization in either size or recording formats on floppy disks. Sizes range from 8 inches down to 2 inches with 5¼ inches being the most popular today. Soft disks differ from the traditional hard disks in one very important aspect. On soft disks the read/write heads actually touch the disk surface. The contact point is lubricated, but after a specific number of revolutions the disk becomes worn and must be discarded (after copying the data onto a new floppy). The disks are relatively cheap (about $3–$4) but not particularly usable for large data files or files that have a great amount of read/write activity.

Disk addressing

So far, a magnetic disk has been very similar to magnetic tape, but we now come to the major point of difference. Tape, as you will recall from an earlier chapter, is a sequential access device in that access to a particular record is accomplished only by serially reading all prior records. Disk, on the other hand, is said to be a direct access device because we can directly access a specific disk record. Access activities of this type will be covered in a later chapter. For now, we are concerned only with disk as a sequential storage device.

Much like the groove in a phonograph record, the surface of a disk consists of a series of smaller and smaller concentric circles called *tracks*. Each of these tracks has an address and can be directly referenced or accessed by the programmer. When reading or writing takes place, the access arms position the read/write heads directly above or below the track that the programmer addressed. Again, the precision of a disk unit may be appreciated when you realize that a track is thinner than the width of a pencil line and each track nearly touches the tracks on either side. The surface of a disk may contain anywhere from 100 to 800 tracks depending upon the size and type of disk. Also, each track normally holds the same amount of data with the data bits on the outer tracks being written slightly farther apart.

Figure 11-5 shows the general addressing structure of a single disk track. The track itself is identified by a series of bits that indicate the home address of that particular track. In a way, it is much like the numbering system used where you live—it indicates your street name and house number. On a disk, the home address is coded to indicate the specific surface and track number, which means that each home address is unique to the disk addressing scheme. The diagram also illustrates the fact that many data records could be (and usually are) stored on one track. If this is done, then each record on the track is identified by means of some identifying bits written prior to the data bits. Just as with magnetic tape, gaps are used to separate the disk material.

When a disk is used in a straight sequential manner, the programming may be identical to that done with magnetic tape. SELECT——ASSIGN TO—— assigns the file to a disk device and, unless told otherwise, the system assumes sequential access. On some systems, you may have to make some minor changes.

```
SELECT ___ ASSIGN TO SYSXX-UT-2314-S.
```

describes a disk device (IBM 2314 disk system) that is being used as a utility (UT) device for sequential (S) access. Other systems may require the additional entry ACCESS IS SEQUENTIAL:

```
SELECT _____
     ASSIGN TO _____
          ACCESS IS SEQUENTIAL.
```

Manipulating sequential files

Up to now, almost all examples have involved reading in and processing of the records from a sequential file. However, one of the major tasks in any data processing installation is that of getting files ready for the type of processing you have been doing. The general term that covers this activity is *file maintenance* or *updating*, and typically involves three specific operations:

1. Making changes to records in a file.
2. Deleting records from a file.
3. Adding records to a file.

FIGURE 11-5

Disk track format

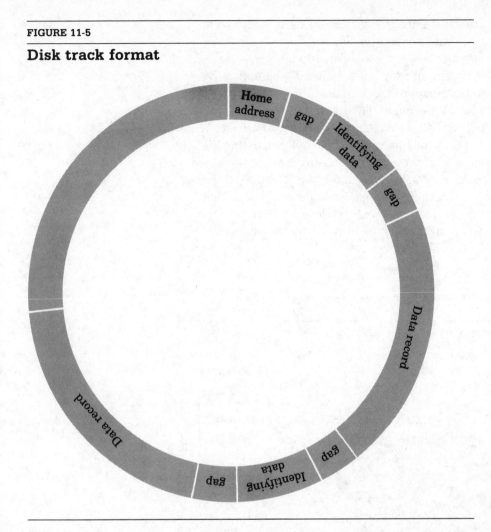

To show you how the updating process works, we will set up a sequential file (disk or tape) 'WORKERS' consisting of a series of employee records having the following format:

Field	Length
Employee SS Number	9 digits
Employee Name	20 characters
Telephone Number	8 characters
	Ex. 555-3817
Status Date (date employed)	6 digits

123456789	JONES, JOHN	555-5555	112672
314803800	LEE, SALLY	566-7777	041580
438316914	SMITH, SUE	556-0140	041580
500305432	ROBERTS, SAM	556-9188	061778
777685948	GONZALES, ED	555-3817	103081
900396542	JOHNSON, ROBERT	566-4444	012478

Note that the records are in ascending order according to social security number—a normal practice with sequential files.

Actually, on straight sequential files you really don't update the existing file; that is, you don't make changes directly on it. Instead, you update by creating a *new* file that contains the appropriate data records.

In a large business operation we might have a great many changes during a specific time period, and these changes would be written to a temporary disk or tape file prior to the updating process. The existing file (WORKERS) is called the "Master File" because it contains master, or relatively unchanging, data. The file containing the changes (CHANGES) would be known as the Detail, or Transaction, File and would contain data that probably will be used only once. The updating program, which we will construct shortly, normally would be run just *prior* to any processing activities that make use of the Master File (Figure 11-6).

FIGURE 11-6

File maintenance process

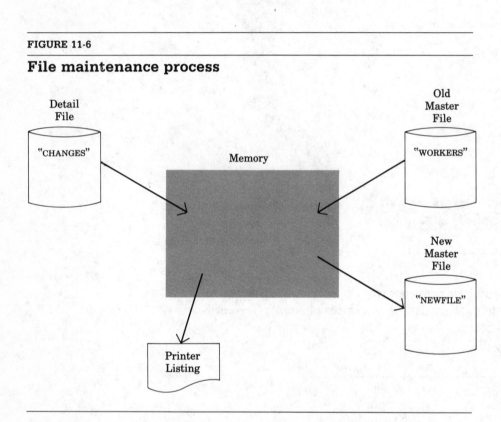

Changing or deleting existing records

The first of our updating activities is that of making changes to existing records in the "WORKERS" file. Let's assume that some of the data records in the file are no longer correct and they must be updated to reflect the following changes:

Employee Sue Smith has married and is now known as SUE BERTOLI. Her new phone number is 496-3462.
Employee Ed Gonzales has changed his telephone number to 583-0014.

Again, note that both files have been put into ascending or sequential order based upon the Social Security Number field. The matter of the sequencing of the files is of extreme importance since it will dictate how the update operation will take place. If either or both of the files were unordered, we would have to use a very inefficient, "brute force" method to find and change specific records. By brute force we mean that you read through the Master File until the matching record is found. Then, the Master File must be closed and reopened in order to find the match for the next Detail record. This approach may be feasible for small files, but the repeated opening and closing of files—particularly tape files—is very time consuming.

The "Brute Force" Method

OPEN the Master and Detail Files.
Read a Detail record.
READ in a Master record.
    IF the SS numbers do not match, continue reading Master records until a match is found or until the end of file is reached.
    IF the SS numbers do match, write the new data record.
CLOSE the Master File.
OPEN the Master File.
Repeat the process for the next Detail record until all changes have been entered.

The alternative—sorting both files and then performing a sophisticated matching operation based on sorted files—is also expensive in that the sort operation does take computer time. However, it is usually far more efficient to work with sorted rather than with unsorted files, and in the "real world" most files are sorted prior to being processed.

In a business situation you would normally run a sequence check of the file records prior to executing the update program. This could be done either in a separate program or as part of the file update process. Instead of taking the brute-force approach, we will make use of the fact that both files are in ascending order in our program logic. Obviously, we will have to read from both files, but we cannot assume that the reading of a record from each file will automatically result in a matching condition. A simple diagram is a handy way to approach the logic of matching file records.

Let's assume that the two files contain the following records as identified by these single-digit key fields:

Detail File: ③   ⑤   EOF Marker

Old Master File: ①   ②   ③   ④   ⑤   ⑥   EOF Marker

We will start by reading a record from each file (two separate READ statements) and then comparing the Social Security Numbers. There are several different approaches that could be used, but let's try this one. If the SS-NBR field from the Old Master File is not equal to the SS-NBR field from the Detail (or Transaction) File, then we can simply write the Old Master record onto the New Master File. A look at our simplified diagram tells you that, in the example above, there could never be an equal (or matching) condition for Old Master record #1.

Since we have not yet found the match for Detail record #3, we will now read another Old Master record *without* reading another Detail record. This process will continue until the Old Master record is equal to the Detail record. Equal SS-NBRs will signal this condition, and now the record *from the Detail File* will be written onto the New Master. Then, the program will read a record from both the Old Master File and the Detail File in order to continue the process again. To help us determine whether this approach will work, we can expand on the previous diagram by using a step-by-step "walk through" of the program. By using this method we have a good chance of spotting logic errors before writing the program.

The priming READS have read one record from each file.

Step 1   *Analysis*

M   D

1   3   Master is not equal to the Detail.

The New Master is written from the Old Master File.
An Old Master record is read.

Step 2   *Analysis*

M   D

2   3   Same as Step 1.

Step 3   *Analysis*

M   D

3   3   Master is equal to the Detail.

The New Master is written from the Detail File.
Both an Old Master and a Detail record are read.

Step 4   *Analysis*

M   D

4   5   Same as Step 1.

Step 5   *Analysis*

M   D

5   5   Same as Step 3.

The program logic is fine to this point, but we have not considered the AT END condition when reading sequential files. When we reach the end of the Detail File, we cannot just stop the program since there may be more records on the Old Master File that have to be written onto the New Master. At first glance it would seem that we can just continue with the 015-UPDATE module because all succeeding Old Master records will be unequal (larger) to the last Detail record. This is true, but we will get into trouble with the IF statement in that paragraph. It will attempt to compare the Master SS-NBR with a nonexisting Detail SS-NBR. In essence, the system will try to compare against garbage, and the program will be terminated.

To get around this problem we will get out of the 015-UPDATE module by means of the end of file indicator (DETAIL-SWITCH) that controls the PER-FORM for the 015-UPDATE module. Upon exiting from that PERFORM, we will enter into another PERFORM that will control another module that duplicates the remaining Old Master records onto the New Master File:

```
PERFORM 015-UPDATE
    UNTIL DETAIL-SWITCH = 1.
PERFORM 030-DUP-OLD-MASTER
    UNTIL OLD-MSTR-SWITCH = 1.
```

Our analysis for the rest of the items will now change.

Step 6		*Analysis*
M	D	
6	EOF	Exit from 030-DUP-OLD-MASTER module.
		Write New Master from Old Master; Read Old Master.

Step 7		*Analysis*
M	D	
EOF	EOF	Exit from 030-DUP-OLD-MASTER module.

Pseudocode specifications for the program are shown in Figure 11-7. The flowchart, the program, and output are shown in Figures 11-8 and 11-9.

FIGURE 11-7

Pseudocode: File update program

```
CONTROL-ROUTINE
    PERFORM 010-OPENER
    PERFORM 015-UPDATE UNTIL detail switch = 1
    PERFORM 030-DUP-OLD-MASTER UNTIL master switch = 1
    PERFORM 035-END-ROUTINE
    STOP RUN


010-OPENER
    Open the files
    Write heading line
    Read a detail record at end move 1 to detail switch
    Read old master record at end move 1 to master switch


015-UPDATE
    IF  social security number old master equals social security
            number detail
        Move detail fields to new master record
        Write new master record
        Move detail fields to print area
        Write a report line on the printer
        Read a detail record at end move 1 to detail switch
        Read old master record at end move 1 to master switch


    ELSE
        PERFORM 030-DUP-OLD-MASTER
    ENDIF


030-DUP-OLD-MASTER
    Move old master fields to new master
    Write new master record
    Move old master fields to print area
    Write a report line on the printer
    Read old master file at end move 1 to master switch


035-END-ROUTINE
    Close files
```

FIGURE 11-8

Flowchart: File update program

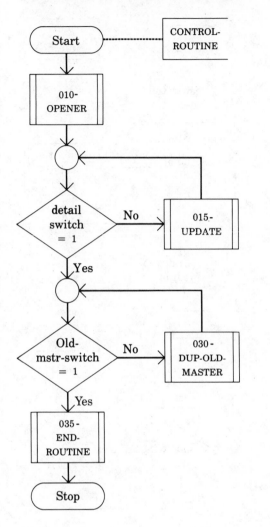

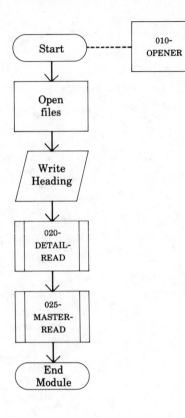

continued

FIGURE 11-8

continued

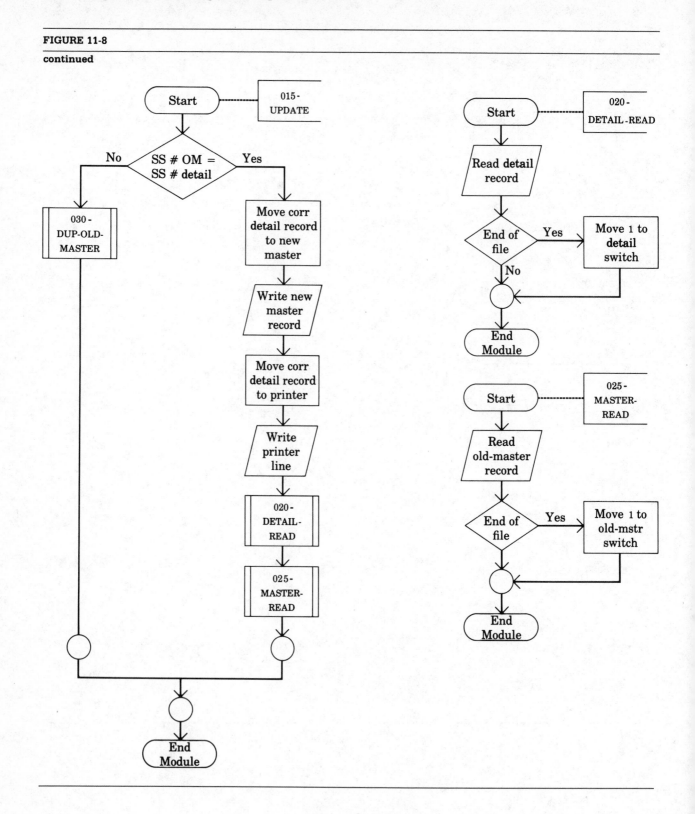

FIGURE 11-8

continued

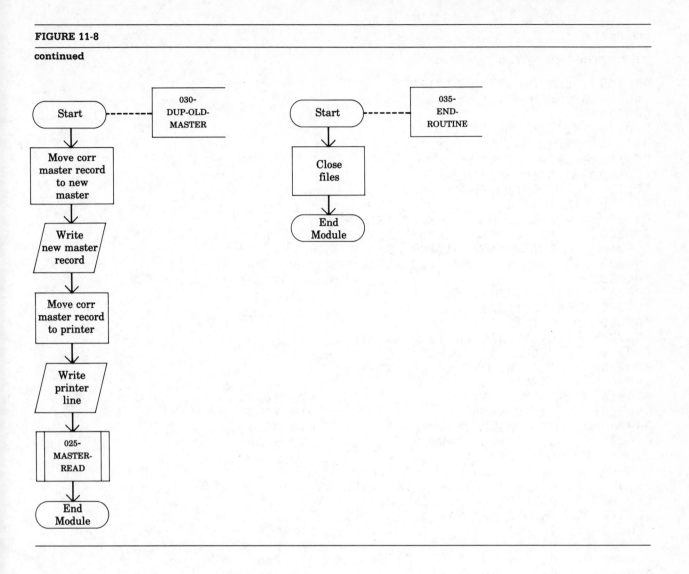

FIGURE 11-9

File update program

```
000100 IDENTIFICATION DIVISION.
000110 PROGRAM-ID. UPDATE1.
000120*
000130 ENVIRONMENT DIVISION.
000140 CONFIGURATION SECTION.
000150 SOURCE-COMPUTER. - - -.
000160 OBJECT-COMPUTER. - - -.
000170 INPUT-OUTPUT SECTION.
000180 FILE-CONTROL.
000190     SELECT DETAIL-FILE ASSIGN TO - - -.
000200     SELECT OLD-MASTER ASSIGN TO - - -.
000210     SELECT NEW-MASTER ASSIGN TO - - -.
000220     SELECT PRINT-FILE ASSIGN TO - - -.
000230*
000240 DATA DIVISION.
000250 FILE SECTION.
000260 FD   DETAIL-FILE
000270      LABEL RECORD IS STANDARD
000280      VALUE OF FILE-ID IS 'CHANGES'
000290      DATA RECORD IS DETAIL-REC.
000300 01   DETAIL-REC.
000310      03   SS-NBR                PIC 9(9).
000320      03   E-NAME                PIC X(20).
000330      03   PHONE                 PIC X(8).
000340      03   STATUS-DATE           PIC 9(06).
000350 FD OLD-MASTER
000360      LABEL RECORD IS STANDARD
000370      VALUE OF FILE-ID IS 'WORKERS'
000380      DATA RECORD IS EMPLOYEE-DATA-OM.
000390 01   EMPLOYEE-DATA-OM.
000400      03   SS-NBR                PIC 9(9).
000410      03   E-NAME                PIC X(20).
000420      03   PHONE                 PIC X(8).
000430      03   STATUS-DATE           PIC 9(06).
000440 FD   NEW-MASTER
000450      LABEL RECORD IS STANDARD
000460      VALUE OF FILE-ID IS 'NEW-FILE'
000470      DATA RECORD IS EMPLOYEE-DATA-NM.
000480 01   EMPLOYEE-DATA-NM.
000490      03   SS-NBR                PIC 9(9).
000500      03   E-NAME                PIC X(20).
000510      03   PHONE                 PIC X(8).
000520      03   STATUS-DATE           PIC 9(06).
000530 FD   PRINT-FILE
000540      LABEL RECORD IS OMITTED
000550      DATA RECORD IS PRINT-LINE.
000560 01   PRINT-LINE                 PIC X(121).
000570*
000580 WORKING-STORAGE SECTION.
000590 01   MISC-FIELDS.
000600      03   DETAIL-SWITCH         PIC 9 VALUE ZERO.
000610      03   OLD-MSTR-SWITCH       PIC 9 VALUE ZERO.
000620 01   PRINT-RECORD.
```

FIGURE 11-9

continued

```
000630        03   FILLER                    PIC X(10) VALUE SPACES.
000640        03   SS-NBR                    PIC 999B99B9999.
000650        03   FILLER                    PIC X(5) VALUE SPACES.
000660        03   E-NAME                    PIC X(30).
000670        03   FILLER                    PIC X(5) VALUE SPACES.
000680        03   PHONE                     PIC X(8).
000690        03   FILLER                    PIC X(5) VALUE SPACES.
000700        03   STATUS-DATE               PIC 99/99/99.
000710        03   FILLER                    PIC X(39) VALUE SPACES.
000720 01  HEAD1.
000730        03   FILLER                    PIC X(15) VALUE SPACES.
000740        03   FILLER                    PIC X(12) VALUE 'REVISED FILE'.
000750        03   FILLER                    PIC X(94) VALUE SPACES.
000760*
000770 PROCEDURE DIVISION.
000780 CONTROL-ROUTINE.
000790      PERFORM 010-OPENER.
000800      PERFORM 015-UPDATE
000810          UNTIL DETAIL-SWITCH = 1.
000820      PERFORM 030-DUP-OLD-MASTER
000830          UNTIL OLD-MSTR-SWITCH = 1.
000840      PERFORM 035-END-ROUTINE.
000850      STOP RUN.
000860 010-OPENER.
000870      OPEN INPUT DETAIL-FILE OLD-MASTER
000880          OUTPUT NEW-MASTER PRINT-FILE.
000890      WRITE PRINT-LINE FROM HEAD1
000900          AFTER ADVANCING 2 LINES.
000910      PERFORM 020-DETAIL-READ.
000920      PERFORM 025-MASTER-READ.
000930 015-UPDATE.
000940      IF SS-NBR OF EMPLOYEE-DATA-OM IS EQUAL TO
000950          SS-NBR OF DETAIL-REC
000960          MOVE CORRESPONDING DETAIL-REC
000970              TO EMPLOYEE-DATA-NM
000980          WRITE EMPLOYEE-DATA-NM
000990          MOVE CORRESPONDING DETAIL-REC
001000                  TO PRINT-RECORD
001010          WRITE PRINT-LINE FROM PRINT-RECORD
001020              AFTER ADVANCING 2 LINES
001030          PERFORM 020-DETAIL-READ
001040          PERFORM 025-MASTER-READ
001050      ELSE
001060          PERFORM 030-DUP-OLD-MASTER.
001070 020-DETAIL-READ.
001080      READ DETAIL-FILE
001090          AT END MOVE 1 TO DETAIL-SWITCH.
001100 025-MASTER-READ.
001110      READ OLD-MASTER
001120          AT END MOVE 1 TO OLD-MSTR-SWITCH.
001130 030-DUP-OLD-MASTER.
001140      MOVE CORRESPONDING EMPLOYEE-DATA-OM
```

continued

FIGURE 11-9

continued

```
001150          TO EMPLOYEE-DATA-NM.
001160     WRITE EMPLOYEE-DATA-NM.
001170     MOVE CORRESPONDING EMPLOYEE-DATA-OM
001180          TO PRINT-RECORD.
001190     WRITE PRINT-LINE FROM PRINT-RECORD
001200          AFTER ADVANCING 2 LINES.
001210     PERFORM 025-MASTER-READ.
001220 035-END-ROUTINE.
001230     CLOSE DETAIL-FILE OLD-MASTER
001240          NEW-MASTER PRINT-FILE.
```

```
     REVISED FILE

123 45 6789     JONES, JOHN              555-5555    11/26/72

314 80 3800     LEE, SALLY               566-7777    04/15/80

438 31 6914     BERTOLI, SUE             496-3462    04/15/80

500 30 5432     ROBERTS, SAM             556-9188    06/17/78

777 68 5948     GONZALES, ED             583-0014    10/30/81

900 39 6542     JOHNSON, ROBERT          566-4444    01/24/78
```

On-line updating

The previous example illustrated the updating process in which a record from a Detail File is matched against a record in the Master File. Obviously, this method works, but it may not be efficient when the number of records to be changed is small. Since COBOL has the capability of ACCEPTing data entry through the keyboard, why not enter the changes "on-line" rather than through the "batch" processing method just shown (Figure 11-10)?

The only extra problem this strategy causes is that we will have to provide for a mechanism to end the terminal input process. This, of course, becomes the equivalent of the AT END part of the sequential file READ statement. You saw this in Chapter 6 in the LOADER1 program that created a sequential file with data entered through the terminal. A similar process is outlined here. We will continue to ACCEPT data until the operator enters a value of all nines for the identification number. This will trigger the system to move a 1 into the DETAIL-SWITCH area:

```
PERFORM 015-UPDATE
    UNTIL DETAIL-SWITCH = 1.
    .
    .
    .

015-UPDATE.
    DISPLAY 'ENTER EMPLOYEE ID NUMBER'
    ACCEPT  id number
    IF  identification number is not equal to all nines
        ACCEPT  remaining fields in the record
    ELSE
        MOVE 1 TO DETAIL-SWITCH.
```

FIGURE 11-10

On—line updating

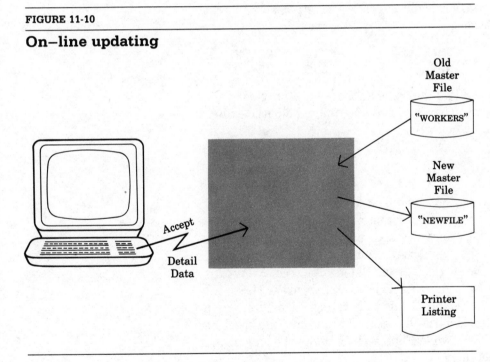

An alternative method is to check directly for all nines in the identification number:

```
PERFORM 015-UPDATE
    UNTIL id number = 999999999.
```

Deleting records from a file follows the same pattern as before. Again, we will match the records to be deleted (contained in the Detail File—CHANGES) with the records in the Master File. This time, when equal social security numbers are found, neither the Master nor the Detail record will be written to the New Master File. Instead, the record will be written to the printer to provide a hard copy record that the deletion was made. This latter point is of considerable importance as you must be able to reconstruct a file in case of accidental destruction. Either a hard copy record or the Old Master and Detail must be kept for this purpose for whatever length of time is appropriate.

Adding records to a file (merging)

The third possibility when updating a file is that of making additions by interspersing the records of one file with the records of another file. In programming terminology this is known as *merging*. Once more we will go back to our original master employee file and create a New Master File that contains the following additions:

```
248399618    ADDISON, CHARLES    551-8890    022582
883111529    MASON, NANCY        556-6346    022482
```

Basically, our program will be the same as those used previously, but with one significant difference. The simplified diagram to help us decide on what logic to use is illustrated below:

Detail File: ② ⑤

Old Master File: ① ③ ④ ⑥

As opposed to the two previous examples, we cannot test for equality because we no longer have a matching situation. The test will be to see whether the SS-NBR of the Old Master is less than that of the Detail File. If it is, an entry is made to the New Master File from the Old Master File and another Old Master record is read. If the Old Master record is *not* less than the Detail record, the New Master File is written from the Detail File and the merged record is entered into the new file listing. As before, a step-by-step analysis will help to visualize the operation. Pseudocode specifications are shown in Figure 11-11 while Figure 11-12 shows the PROCEDURE DIVISION entries and the output.

The priming READS have read one record from each file.

Step 1   *Analysis*

M   D

1   3   Master is less than the Detail.

                       The New Master File is written from the Old Master File.

Step 2		Analysis
M	D	
3	2	Master is *not* less than the Detail.

The New Master is written from the Detail File.
A Detail record is read.

Step 3		Analysis
M	D	
3	5	Same as Step 1.

Step 4		Analysis
M	D	
4	5	Same as Step 1.

Step 5		Analysis
M	D	
6	5	Master is *not* less than the Detail.

The New Master File is written from the Detail File.
The end of file condition is detected in the Detail File
when the Detail File is read.

Step 6		Analysis
M	D	
6	EOF	Exit from 015-UPDATE module.

Write New Master from Old Master.
Read Old Master. End of Master File is detected.

Step 7		Analysis
M	D	
EOF	EOF	Exit from 025-DUP-OLD-MASTER module.

COMMON ERRORS

The chapter examples produced correct output because certain assumptions were met. Note, in the first example we assumed that there would always be a match for an incoming Detail record. The fact that both files are in ascending order does not necessarily guarantee that there will always be a matching situation. The social security number in the Detail record could have been keyed incorrectly. However, our program logic can take care of this problem.

Detail File: ② ④
Master File: ① ② ③ ⑤ EOF

The initial READs will show that the Detail record is higher:

M	D
1	2

FIGURE 11-11

Pseudocode: Merging

```
CONTROL-ROUTINE
    PERFORM 010-OPENER
    PERFORM 015-UPDATE UNTIL detail switch = ON
    PERFORM 030-DUP-OLD-MASTER UNTIL Old Master
        switch = ON
    PERFORM 035-END-ROUTINE
    STOP RUN


010-OPENER
    Open files
    Write heading line
    Read a Detail record at end move ON to Detail switch
    Read Old Master File at end move ON to Old Master switch


015-UPDATE
    IF social security number Master is less than social security
            number Detail
        PERFORM 030-DUP-OLD MASTER
    ELSE
        Move Detail fields to New Master record
        Write New Master record
        Move Detail fields to print area
        Write a report line on the printer
        Read a Detail record at end move ON to detail switch
    ENDIF


030-DUP-OLD-MASTER
    Move Old Master fields to New Master record
    Write New Master record
    Move Old Master fields to print area
    Write a report line on the printer
    Read Old Master File at end move ON to Old Master switch


035-END-ROUTINE
    Close files
```

FIGURE 11-12

Adding records to a file (merging)

```
000770 PROCEDURE DIVISION.
000780 CONTROL-ROUTINE.
000790     PERFORM 010-OPENER.
000800     PERFORM 015-UPDATE
000810         UNTIL DETAIL-SWITCH = 1.
000820     PERFORM 030-DUP-OLD-MASTER
000830         UNTIL OLD-MSTR-SWITCH = 1.
000840     PERFORM 035-END-ROUTINE.
000850     STOP RUN.
000860 010-OPENER.
000870     OPEN INPUT DETAIL-FILE OLD-MASTER
000880         OUTPUT NEW-MASTER PRINT-FILE.
000890     WRITE PRINT-LINE FROM HEAD1
000900         AFTER ADVANCING 2 LINES.
000910     PERFORM 020-DETAIL-READ.
000920     PERFORM 025-MASTER-READ.
000930 015-UPDATE.
000940     IF SS-NBR OF EMPLOYEE-DATA-OM IS LESS THAN
000950         SS-NBR OF DETAIL-REC
000960         PERFORM 030-DUP-OLD MASTER
000970     ELSE
000980         MOVE CORRESPONDING DETAIL-REC
000990             TO EMPLOYEE-DATA-NM
001000         WRITE EMPLOYEE-DATA-NM
001010         MOVE CORRESPONDING DETAIL-REC
001020             TO PRINT-RECORD
001030         WRITE PRINT-LINE FROM PRINT-RECORD
001040             AFTER ADVANCING 2 LINES
001050         PERFORM 020-DETAIL-READ.
001060 020-DETAIL-READ.
001070     READ DETAIL-FILE
001080         AT END MOVE 1 TO DETAIL-SWITCH.
001090 025-MASTER-READ.
001100     READ-OLD-MASTER
001110         AT END MOVE 1 TO OLD-MSTR-SWITCH.
001120 030-DUP-OLD-MASTER.
001130     MOVE CORRESPONDING EMPLOYEE-DATA-OM
001140         TO EMPLOYEE-DATA-NM.
001150     WRITE EMPLOYEE-DATA-NM.
001160     MOVE CORRESPONDING EMPLOYEE-DATA-OM
001170         TO PRINT-RECORD.
001180     WRITE PRINT-LINE FROM PRINT-RECORD
001190         AFTER ADVANCING 2 LINES.
001200     PERFORM 025-MASTER-READ.
001210 035-END-ROUTINE.
001220     CLOSE DETAIL-FILE OLD-MASTER
001230         NEW-MASTER PRINT-FILE.
```

continued

FIGURE 11-12

continued

    REVISED FILE

123 45 6789	JONES, JOHN	555-5555	11/26/72
248 39 9618	ADDISON, CHARLES	551-8890	02/25/82
314 80 3800	LEE, SALLY	566-7777	04/15/80
438 31 6914	SMITH, SUE	556-0140	01/21/79
500 30 5432	ROBERTS, SAM	556-9188	06/17/78
777 68 5948	GONZALES, ED	555-3817	10/30/81
883 11 1529	MASON, NANCY	556-6346	02/24/82
900 39 6542	JOHNSON, ROBERT	566-4444	01/24/78

---

and that another Master can be read in. At that point a matching condition occurs and the New Master record is written from the Detail record:

    M   D
    2   2

Then both the Master and Detail File are read again:

    M   D
    3   4

Since the Detail is higher, another Master record is read in:

    M   D
    5   4

In this case the Master is higher than the Detail, which means that an error condition exists—there can never be a match of the records. The action you take at this point depends upon your individual situation. Most likely you would print an appropriate error message and continue with the remaining Detail records.

Perhaps the single most common error associated with file updating is that of the programmer not considering all the logic alternatives that arise between two or more files. The chapter presented a few conditions, but there is no way a text can cover all the combinations involving multiple files. Experience with students has shown that one common error involves the last record of a file. Frequently students will read the last record but not process it; that is, the record does not get written to either the Master File or to the printer. A similar fault occurs when the last record is recorded or printed twice rather than once.

PROGRAMMING TIPS

Those of you who have been giving some serious thought to the previous examples have probably come up with some "flaws" or conditions under which the programs will not work properly. You would be quite right, of course, because the programs illustrated only one approach to file updating. Let's take a look at some of these additional problem areas.

Perhaps the single most critical point is that both files are supposed to be in ascending order. In our sample program we made this assumption. In a job situation you may be assured by someone that the file is in the proper order, and that it is not necessary to check the sequence of the record in *both* files (or however many files you are using) before writing the New Master File.

Notice what can happen if a file is not in sequential order.

Detail File: ③   ②   ⑦
Master File: ①   ④   ⑤   ⑥   ⑧

The comparison between records ① and ③ proceeds correctly. Record ① is written to the New Master and another Old Master record is read. Now the comparison is between ④ of the Old Master and ③ of the Detail File, and since ④ is not less than ③, record ③ is written (correctly) to the New Master and another record is read from the Detail File. So far, the New Master looks as follows:

①   ③

The next comparison is between ④ and ②, and, since the Old Master is again not less than ②, record ② is written to the New Master File. The end result of not checking the sequence is a New Master File that looks as follows:

①   ③   ②   ④   ⑤   ⑥   ⑦   ⑧

In a way, the addition of records to a file (merging) is almost the reverse of the first example. Originally, you *wanted* matching numbers; in the last case you do *not* want a match of Social Security Numbers since this would indicate an error condition. To confuse things a bit further, it is also possible to have a situation where duplicate numbers are permissible and *both* must be written to the new file. In that case a decision will have to be made as to which duplicate entry has precedence.

Some problems, particularly those using multiple Detail Files, require both matching and merging. For example, a series of Daily Transaction Files are likely to require that data records be matched and then merged into a combined Weekly Transaction File. File manipulation is not limited to any set number of incoming or outgoing files. The only practical limit is the complexity of the problem and the system hardware itself. However, it is your job to provide for all possible error conditions. The easiest way to take care of all these complex situations is to do what we did in the chapter—use a simple diagram to show the file conditions you will encounter. If the conditions seem too complex, diagram each condition separately and then combine them.

SELF-STUDY: QUESTIONS AND ANSWERS

1. How many different kinds of magnetic disks are there?

   Answer: Perhaps the best way to answer the question is to say that disks are either "hard" or "soft" with the soft disk being used mainly on the microcomputer and word processing systems. The so-called "hard" disks can be categorized as of the "moving head" or "fixed head" variety according to how data are accessed. After that, the distinction becomes less clear since we have removable and nonremovable hard disks as well as disks of different diameters. After many years of little change, disk technology is undergoing a revolution in size, storage capacity, and access methods.

2. It hardly seems possible that the BLOCK CONTAINS entry can have such a large effect on my program.

   Answer: From reading the chapter you now have an idea of the power of that very simple entry. The important thing to remember is that it is not "magic" since the software you trigger into it is extremely sophisticated. In general, this software does two things. First, it sets up the memory buffer area for the incoming or outgoing data block. Second, it allows you to write your program in such a way that you do not have to consider where the data are blocked or unblocked.

3. When a tape file is created, what causes the system to write the label onto tape?

   Answer: Earlier in the chapter you saw that executing the CLOSE statement caused the system to write the end of file (EOF) material on the tape. You also read that execution of the OPEN statement caused the system to check the actual tape label against the label requested in the program. When a file is created, the OPEN statement takes the label information from the source (VALUE OF FILE-ID, and so on) and writes this (plus some other information) on the beginning of the tape. The same action is followed for disk files except that the label information is written on the disk index area.

4. The chapter examples showed how a single Detail File was processed against a Master File to produce a new or updated Master. Can multiple Detail Files be used?

Answer: Yes, you certainly can use multiple Detail Files in an updating situation. For example, you might have four Weekly Detail Files that must be merged into a single Monthly Detail File before the main processing program can be run. In effect, you are creating a consolidated Detail File rather than a Master File, but the logic process is still the same.

5. Throughout the chapter you make a great distinction between Master and Detail Files. Is there really that much difference?

Answer: Yes, there is, and it is important that you understand the difference between the two. A note of caution here: Don't treat Master Files lightly. Files of this type contain exactly what the term indicates— master data. As opposed to Detail Files, Master Files are likely to be used by many programs. Detail Files, on the other hand, may only be used once. Master Files are so important that a common practice is to have a duplicate stored nearby (but not in the same place) in case the original gets destroyed.

6. I see the space-saving advantage of blocking tape data, but are there any other advantages?

Answer: Perhaps you forgot about the increased transfer rate of data from tape to memory when data are blocked. Remember that each gap forces the tape drive to come to a complete stop and then start up again. The time (and space) saved by blocking may not seem significant, but when you begin to consider some large files of many *millions* of records, the savings can become tremendously important.

CHAPTER TERMS

BLOCK CONTAINS
buffer area
Detail File (Transaction File)
disk drive
diskette
disk pack
file maintenance
flippy disk
floppy disk
home address (disk)
Inter Block Gap (IBG)
Inter Record Gap (IRG)
logical record

Master File
matching of records
merging of records
nine-channel tape
physical record
recording density
seven-channel tape
soft disk (floppy disk)
tape drive
track (disk storage)
Transaction File (Detail File)
transfer rate
updating

EXERCISES

1. How many channels or tracks do most modern computers use to write onto tape?

2. At what time does the system write an END-OF-FILE (EOF) mark?

3. What are two common tape recording densities?

4. What is meant by the term "head crash"?

5. What is meant by the term *brute force*, in reference to a file search?

6. Define or explain the following terms as they relate to magnetic tape.
   a. end of file
   b. label (internal)
   c. reflective marker
   d. inter-record gap
   e. inter-block gap
   f. blocked records
   g. tape transfer rate
   h. tape protection (from accidental writing)
   i. recording density
   j. transfer rate

7. Define or explain each of the following:
   a. Detail File
   b. Transaction File
   c. Master File
   d. Old Master File
   e. New Master File

8. How does the BLOCK CONTAINS entry affect the logic used by the programmer in the PROCEDURE DIVISION? Explain in detail.

9. Why is the AT END part of the READ statement required when you read from a sequential file?

10. What "triggers" the AT END part of the tape READ statement? Explain in detail.

11. Assume you are working with tape that has a recording density of 1600 characters and a gap size of 0.5 inch. How much tape space will the following files take?
   a. 100,000 80-byte records blocked 5
   b. 65,000 35-byte records blocked 25
   c. 65,000 35-byte records that are unblocked
   d. 50,000 70-byte records blocked 2
   e. 50,000 70-byte records blocked 10

12. Assume a tape transfer rate of 100,000 characters per second and a gap stop/start time of 0.1 second. Use this information to calculate the transfer times for Exercises 11a, 11b, 11d, and 11e.

13. Draw Master-Detail File diagrams to represent the following matching situations in which there are no duplicate key fields:
   a. A file matching situation in which one Detail record is out of sequence. Assume there is one Detail File and one Master File.
   b. A file matching situation in which there are two Detail Files and one Master File. All records are in sequential order.
   c. A file matching situation in which one record from the Master File and one record from the Detail File are out of sequence.
   d. Revise Exercise 13b so that records from one of the Detail Files are out of order.

14. Let's assume that you have decided on the matching logic you wish to use in a program. Explain what will happen when the *first* record in the Detail File is the one that is out of sequence. Then, explain what will happen when the *last* record in the Detail File is out of sequence.

15. Draw Master-Detail File diagrams to represent the following merging situations. Assume that there cannot be any matching key values.
    a. A file merging situation in which both the Master File and single Detail File are in the correct order.
    b. A file merging situation in which the Master File is correct but the Detail File is out of sequence.
    c. A file merging situation involving two Detail Files and a single Master File. All files are in sequential order.

16. A file match-merging situation involves two Detail Files that will be merged into a single combined Detail File. Both files are in sequential order; duplicate Detail keys are permitted; and Detail File A has precedence over Detail File B. Draw the diagram.

17. Modify the PROCEDURE DIVISION logic in the UPDATE1 program in the text to include sequence checking of the Detail File. If an error is found, a message is to be printed on the system console device.

18. In this exercise you will make use of Data Set B (see Appendix D), which contains sales data information blocked 5. The file label name is SALES-DATA. The record format is as follows:

Field	Characters	Type
Sales territory	3	Numeric
ID number	5	Numeric
Salesperson's name	20	Alphabetic
Year to date sales	7	Numeric, packed format, dollars and cents
Year to date sales returns	6	Numeric, packed format, dollars and cents

The sales manager is concerned about sales in territories 103 and 107. This information comprises our Detail File and may be entered via ACCEPT, punched cards, a separate data file, or by means of table values created internally. Write a program that will do the following:
    a. Get the sales territory number as per above.
    b. Read sequentially through the file and print a line of output for each salesperson in the matching sales territory, as shown in the diagram below. Note that the ID number is to be separated into two parts by a dash. Net YTD sales is calculated by subtracting YTD returns from YTD sales.
    c. You are to keep a running total of the net YTD sales and print this at the end of the listing for that particular department. All numeric fields are to be appropriately edited.
    d. In order to go through the tape file a second time to search for the next territory number, you will have to close the tape file and open it again. This program uses "brute force," but should convince you of the inefficiency of the method and of the nature of sequential files.
    e. There is a possibility that a salesperson can have returns that exceed sales in the case of return items that were sold in a previous year. Your program is to account for this situation and print a credit symbol (CR) immediately after the year-to-date net sales figure.

NAME	ID#	YTD SALES	YTD RETURNS	YTD NET SALES
Jones, Fred	20-136	------	------	------
------	------	------	------	------
------	------	------	------	------

TOTAL NET YTD SALES-TERRITORY 103

Smith, Sam	50-904	------	------	------
------	------	------	------	------
------	------	------	------	------

TOTAL NET YTD SALES-TERRITORY 107

PROGRAMMED BY

19. Modify the problem presented in Exercise 18 by first sorting the file into ascending order based on the sales territory field. Then, program for efficient data access and retrieval.

20. The data for this problem will be a master payroll disk (Data Set A) with the external file name "PAYDATA."

Field	Length	Example
Social Security number	9	Numeric, DISPLAY
Employee name	20	Alphabetic
Filler	1	—
Rate of pay	4	Numeric, dollar and cents, packed format
Number of dependents	2	Numeric, DISPLAY
Insurance deduction	4	Numeric, packed format, dollars and cents
Credit Union deduction	5	Numeric, packed format, dollars and cents
Other deductions	5	Numeric, packed format, dollars and cents

In order to calculate payroll information, you will need to know the actual number of hours each employee has worked this week. This information will be on a disk file with the external file name "HOURS" and has the following format:

Field	Length	Example
Employee SS number	9	431265972
Hours worked	2	41

Data

```
05012539540
06044391638
19045630140
23096577742
24686461508
30416529840
35021410141
55543861940
```

Both files are in ascending order by Social Security Number, but not all employees work each week. Therefore, before processing any data, make sure the Detail record and Master record match. Write a program to do the following:

a. First, use a loader program to create the "HOURS" file with the data being entered via DISPLAY and ACCEPT statements.

b. Using the data from both files, calculate Gross Pay, Total Deductions, and Net Pay for each employee.

c. The deductions for Group Insurance, United Crusade, and the Credit Union are given in the Master Payroll record. The deduction amount for Income Tax, however, will have to be calculated. Our company uses the following rule:

   1. If the employee has three or fewer dependents, a flat 20% of the Gross Pay figure is deducted.

   2. If the employee has more than three dependents, 18% is used as the deduction rate.

d. All employees working in excess of 40 hours per week are paid on a time-and-a-half basis.

e. Output fields are to be appropriately spaced on a print line and edited according to the following format:

Name	SS Nbr	Gross Pay	Inc Tax	Insurance	Credit Union	Other	Total Ded	Total Pay
		Total					Total	Total

Note: The deductions for each employee are totaled and made part of the output line. In addition, the Grand Totals of the Gross Pay, Total Deductions, and Net Pay amounts are to be printed at the end of the program to provide accounting controls.

f. There may be no match for a detail record. This possibility will be detected by your program logic and should be planned for. Have an appropriate error message printed whenever this occurs.

Chapter 12
Working with Indexed Files

CHAPTER OUTLINE

LEARNING OBJECTIVES

1. To learn how to create indexed-sequential files and to see how data records can be accessed (a) sequentially from the beginning of the file, (b) sequentially from a different starting point within the file, and (c) randomly, based on a key field.

2. To learn some of the variations or options that may be used with indexed-sequential files, including: (a) multiple keys, (b) permitting alternate keys with duplicates, and (c) combined sequential and random access.

3. To see how the FILE STATUS entry can be used to determine more accurately the result of any disk I/O operation.

4. To see how indexed-sequential files can be updated using the REWRITE and DELETE statements.

$\mathbf{U}$sing a disk storage device as an ordinary sequential file is often necessary, but one of the most important advantages of disk over other media is its ability to store data in addressable disk areas. The fact that the data areas can be accessed directly opens up a whole range of possibilities that were not available with card and tape files. Some of these possibilities are listed below and will be explored in the chapter.

1. The most obvious possibility is that of being able to access a record "directly," rather than using the sequential read method discussed in previous chapters. A more accurate term describing this capability is *random access*, since we can get any specific record without having to read all prior records in the file. The "secret" to this and all the other direct access variations is that an *index* containing the location of the data records is created when the file is first established.

2. Indexed-sequential files, as the name implies, may be accessed either randomly or sequentially.

3. In general, modifications to an indexed file do not require that a new file be created. With straight sequential files, any change, addition, or deletion dictated that a new file be created. With indexed files, individual records may be modified, inserted, or deleted without creating a new file.

4. File modifications are much easier for the programmer since the normal record matching/merging logic is not required.

5. The marvelous benefits of indexed-sequential files are not without cost, however. The cost is in terms of increased processing time to create the file and in the use of larger amounts of disk storage as opposed to straight sequential files.

Disk storage for direct access to large files.

Basic operations on indexed files

The heart of all indexed file operations is the index, which may be used even when the file is being accessed sequentially. Fortunately, the programmer does not have to be concerned with the details of creating the index as this feature is activated by a single entry in the SELECT statement. As a matter of fact, it is the entries within SELECT that provide the system with the necessary information that permits the various indexed file operations described earlier. One word of caution: Although indexed file operations tend to be *generally* the same in COBOL, each system is likely to have a few small differences. Unfortunately, even one "small" difference is enough to abort your program. *Check your manual!*

Creating an indexed-sequential file

One entry in the SELECT alerts the system that an indexed file is being created (or used), but, unfortunately, this entry may vary slightly from system to system. On some, the following entry does the job:

```
SELECT _____
       ASSIGN TO SYSXXX-DA-2314-I
```

The letters DA establish it as a Direct Access file while I indicates that the file will have an index. On most systems, the ORGANIZATION IS INDEXED entry is used:

```
SELECT _____
       ASSIGN TO _____
       ORGANIZATION IS INDEXED
```

The index that will be created is based upon a key field within the data record. This field normally is something like Part Number, Customer Number, Social Security Number, and so on, and is chosen by the programmer. The programmer names and establishes the field within the DATA DIVISION and communicates this name to the software through the RECORD KEY entry in the SELECT statement:

```
SELECT _____
       ASSIGN TO _____
       ORGANIZATION IS INDEXED
       ACCESS IS SEQUENTIAL
       RECORD KEY IS key field.
```

Figure 12-1 is a variation of the LOADER1 program that was used to create a straight sequential file in Chapter 6. You will recall that we created an inventory file based upon data values entered by means of DISPLAY and ACCEPT statements. This time we will create an indexed-sequential file based upon the key field PART-NBR.

FIGURE 12-1

Creating an indexed-sequential file

```
000100 IDENTIFICATION DIVISION.
000110 PROGRAM-ID. LD-NDEX.
000120*
000130 ENVIRONMENT DIVISION.
000140 CONFIGURATION SECTION.
000150 SOURCE-COMPUTER. - - -.
000160 OBJECT-COMPUTER. - - -.
000170 INPUT-OUTPUT SECTION.
000180 FILE-CONTROL.
000190     SELECT DISK-FILE
000200         ASSIGN TO - - -
000210         ORGANIZATION IS INDEXED
000220         ACCESS IS SEQUENTIAL
000230         RECORD KEY IS PART-NBR.
000240*
000250 DATA DIVISION.
000260 FILE SECTION.
000270 FD  DISK-FILE
000280     LABEL RECORD IS STANDARD
000290     VALUE OF FILE-ID IS 'INDSEQ'
000300     DATA RECORD IS RECORD-OUT.
000310 01  RECORD-OUT.
000320     03   PART-NBR                 PIC X(05).
000330     03   PART-NAME                PIC X(10).
000340     03   BIN-NBR                  PIC 999.
000350 WORKING-STORAGE SECTION.
000360 01  MISC-FIELDS.
000370     03   EOF-SWITCH               PIC 9 VALUE ZERO.
000380*
000390 PROCEDURE DIVISION.
000400 CONTROL-MODULE.
000410     OPEN OUTPUT DISK-FILE.
000420     PERFORM 010-ENTER-DATA
000430         UNTIL EOF-SWITCH = 1.
000440     CLOSE DISK-FILE.
000450     DISPLAY 'END OF PROGRAM'.
000460     STOP RUN.
000470 010-ENTER-DATA.
000480     DISPLAY 'ENTER 5 DIGIT PART NUMBER'.
000490     ACCEPT PART-NBR.
000500     DISPLAY 'ENTER PART NAME'.
000510     ACCEPT PART-NAME.
000520     DISPLAY 'ENTER BIN NUMBER'.
000530     ACCEPT BIN-NBR.
000540     DISPLAY 'IF LAST RECORD, ENTER 1; ELSE ENTER ZERO'.
000550     ACCEPT EOF-SWITCH.
000560     WRITE RECORD-OUT
000570         INVALID KEY
000580             DISPLAY 'LOADER ERROR'
000590             MOVE 1 TO EOF-SWITCH.
```

continued

FIGURE 12-1

continued

PART NBR	PART NAME	BIN NUMBER
16612	BOLTS	550
21976	HAMMER	013
30433	CLAMP	642
32559	PLIERS	189
38662	NAILS	444
41357	WRENCH	893

Several new entries or lines worth noting appear in the program.

1. The ASSIGN TO ------ entry may require a special name, such as DISK or DIRECT-ACCESS on your system.

2. ORGANIZATION IS INDEXED is the entry that tells the software to generate an index to the data during execution of the LD-NDEX program. The index itself is created in memory and then stored on disk, as shown below.

3. The ACCESS IS SEQUENTIAL entry is optional (but is assumed by the system if omitted) and tells the system that the data records are in sequential order in terms of a designated key field. Since DISK-FILE was opened OUTPUT, the system will write records to the disk file sequentially from the starting disk file location.

4. The RECORD KEY IS PART-NBR entry designates the key field on which the data records are indexed. Note that PART-NBR is a field *within the disk* record. The value stored in that field is the key by which that data record will be stored, indexed, and retrieved. The COBOL software that creates the index to the disk data will go to the PART-NBR field and use the value it contains to build the index. In general, the index contains the record key data and the disk area on which the record is stored. Schematically, the index will look as follows:

INDEX

Record key (part number)	Disk location
16612	------
21976	------
30433	------
32559	------
38662	------
41357	------

5. Note that the key field, PART-NBR, was designated as PIC X(5). On some systems, the key field *must* be PIC X, while on others it *cannot* be PIC X. In addition, most systems require that the RECORD KEY field be the *first* field in the record. Thus, PART-NAME could not serve as the primary record key. Later in the chapter you will see that alternate keys are permitted, but the main key must still be the first field in the record.

6. The OPEN OUTPUT DISK-FILE statement causes the system to activate the software that will create the index. Values are entered via ACCEPT and written onto the disk, and it is at this time that the system actually creates the index. Note that the program used a slightly different form of the WRITE statement:

```
WRITE RECORD-OUT
    INVALID KEY
    ------
```

The INVALID KEY portion of the WRITE statement is required and is activated if the RECORD KEY value is not higher than the previous key value.

The DISPLAY and MOVE statements will be executed on the INVALID KEY condition and will terminate the program. However, you are not obligated to terminate. Instead, you may wish to print or display an appropriate error message and continue processing.

Sequential retrieval

Programming for *sequential* retrieval of data records in an indexed-sequential file is essentially the same as programming to create the file. The SELECT contains the same entries as before and, since the DISK-FILE is OPENED AS INPUT, the ORGANIZATION IS INDEXED entry tells the system that an index to the "INDSEQ" file already exists. Execution of the OPEN statement makes the disk index information available to the system for retrieval purposes. Since the file is being accessed sequentially, the disk READ statement must contain the AT END entry and READing of the disk file records begins with the first record in the file. When the disk file is OPENed, the software consults the index to find the disk location of the *beginning* record on the file. During the READ loop operation, the pointer automatically goes to the next data record each time the READ statement is executed. Figure 12-2 illustrates the process.

Because the index contains the location of each disk record, the programmer has an additional option at his or her disposal when sequentially accessing an indexed-sequential file. The system software assumes sequential retrieval to start at the beginning of the file, only if not told otherwise. Several different methods might be used to enter a different starting value, but the ACCEPT statement would be the most likely candidate. As shown in Figure 12-3, the starting value is entered into the PART-NBR field by ACCEPT. Then, the START statement is used to initialize the system to begin retrieval at the record in the disk file that matches the value just entered. (*Note:* START

FIGURE 12-2

Sequential retrieval

```
000100 IDENTIFICATION DIVISION.
000110 PROGRAM-ID. DISKSEQ1.
000120******************************************
000130*                                        *
000140*          SEQUENTIAL RETRIEVAL          *
000150*                                        *
000160*          INDEXED SEQUENTIAL FILE       *
000170*                                        *
000180******************************************
000190 ENVIRONMENT DIVISION.
000200 CONFIGURATION SECTION.
000210 SOURCE-COMPUTER. - - -.
000220 OBJECT-COMPUTER. - - -.
000230 INPUT-OUTPUT SECTION.
000240 FILE-CONTROL.
000250     SELECT DISK-FILE
000260         ASSIGN TO - - -
000270         ORGANIZATION IS INDEXED
000280         ACCESS IS SEQUENTIAL
000290         RECORD KEY IS PART-NBR.
000300     SELECT PRINT-FILE ASSIGN TO - - -.
000310*
000320 DATA DIVISION.
000330 FILE SECTION.
000340 FD  DISK-FILE
000350     LABEL RECORD IS STANDARD
000360     VALUE OF FILE-ID IS 'INDSEQ'
000370     DATA RECORD IS DISK-RECORD.
000380 01  DISK-RECORD.
000390     03  PART-NBR          PIC X(5).
000400     03  PART-NAME         PIC X(10).
000410     03  BIN-NBR           PIC 9(3).
000420 FD  PRINT-FILE
000430     LABEL RECORD IS OMITTED
000440     DATA RECORD IS OUTPUT-RECORD.
000450 01  OUTPUT-RECORD         PIC X(121).
000460 WORKING-STORAGE SECTION.
000470 01  MISC-FIELDS.
000480     03  DISK-EOF-SWITCH   PIC X(3) VALUE 'OFF'.
000490 01  HEAD-LINE.
000500     03  FILLER            PIC X(14) VALUE SPACES.
```

FIGURE 12-2

continued

```
000510        03   FILLER              PIC X(6) VALUE 'NUMBER'.
000520        03   FILLER              PIC X(13) VALUE SPACES.
000530        03   FILLER              PIC X(4) VALUE 'NAME'.
000540        03   FILLER              PIC X(13) VALUE SPACES.
000550        03   FILLER              PIC X(3) VALUE 'BIN'.
000560        03   FILLER              PIC X(68) VALUE SPACES.
000570 01  MAIN-LINE.
000580        03   FILLER              PIC X(15) VALUE SPACES.
000590        03   PART-NBR-PR         PIC X(5).
000600        03   FILLER              PIC X(10) VALUE SPACES.
000610        03   PART-NAME-PR        PIC X(10).
000620        03   FILLER              PIC X(10) VALUE SPACES.
000630        03   BIN-NBR-PR          PIC 9(3).
000640        03   FILLER              PIC X(68) VALUE SPACES.
000650*
000660 PROCEDURE DIVISION.
000670 CONTROL-MODULE.
000680        PERFORM 010-OPENER.
000690        PERFORM 020-PROCESS-DISK-DATA
000700            UNTIL DISK-EOF-SWITCH IS EQUAL TO ' ON'.
000710        PERFORM 030-CLOSER.
000720        STOP RUN.
000730 010-OPENER.
000740        OPEN INPUT DISK-FILE OUTPUT PRINT-FILE.
000750        WRITE OUTPUT-RECORD FROM HEAD-LINE
000760            AFTER ADVANCING PAGE.
000770        MOVE SPACES TO OUTPUT-RECORD.
000780        WRITE OUTPUT-RECORD AFTER ADVANCING 2 LINES.
000790        READ DISK-FILE
000800            AT END MOVE ' ON' TO DISK-EOF-SWITCH.
000810 020-PROCESS-DISK-DATA.
000820        MOVE PART-NBR TO PART-NBR-PR.
000830        MOVE PART-NAME TO PART-NAME-PR.
000840        MOVE BIN-NBR TO BIN-NBR-PR.
000850        WRITE OUTPUT-RECORD FROM MAIN-LINE
000860            AFTER ADVANCING 1 LINE.
000870        READ DISK-FILE
000880            AT END MOVE ' ON' TO DISK-EOF-SWITCH.
000890 030-CLOSER.
000900        CLOSE DISK-FILE, PRINT-FILE.
```

only positions the file for retrieval—it does not read in the data.) The INVALID KEY entry is executed if the system cannot find the start key in the index to the disk file.

$$\text{START file-name } \underline{\text{KEY}} \text{ IS } \left[\left\{ \begin{array}{l} \underline{\text{EQUAL}} \ \underline{\text{TO}} \\ \underline{=} \\ \underline{\text{GREATER}} \ \ \underline{\text{THAN}} \\ \underline{>} \\ \underline{\text{NOT}} \ \underline{\text{LESS}} \ \underline{\text{THAN}} \end{array} \right\} \text{data-name} \right]$$

INVALID KEY imperative statement

Figure 12-3 shows, in skeletal form, a modification of our DISKSEQ1 program to allow for the use of the START statement.

FIGURE 12-3

Using START with sequential retrieval

```
01  DISK-RECORD.
    03  PART-NBR _____
    03  PART-NAME _____
    03  BIN-NBR _____
        .
        .
        .

PROCEDURE DIVISION.
CONTROL-MODULE.
    PERFORM 010-OPENER.
    IF DISK-EOF-SWITCH = 'OFF'
        PERFORM 030-SEQ-READ.
    PERFORM 020-PROCESS-DISK-DATA
        UNTIL DISK-EOF-SWITCH = ' ON'.
        .
        .
        .

010-OPENER.
    OPEN INPUT DISK-FILE _____
    DISPLAY 'ENTER STARTING PART NUMBER'.
    ACCEPT PART-NBR.
    START DISK-FILE
        KEY IS EQUAL TO PART-NBR
        INVALID-KEY
            PERFORM 040-ERROR-ROUTINE.
020-PROCESS-DISK-DATA.
        .
        .
        .

030-SEQ-READ.
    READ DISK-FILE
        AT END MOVE ' ON' TO DISK-EOF-SWITCH.
040-ERROR-ROUTINE.
    MOVE ' ON' TO DISK-EOF-SWITCH.
```

Random retrieval

As mentioned earlier in the chapter, the beauty of an indexed-sequential file is that the file records can be accessed both sequentially and randomly. So far we have retrieved records sequentially from the beginning of the file and, by using START, from a specified starting point within the file. The next example (Figure 12-4) illustrates the random retrieval process. Several points are worth noting.

1. The SELECT entry specifies that ACCESS IS RANDOM rather than SEQUENTIAL that was used before. PART-NBR is still our KEY field.

2. The program ACCEPTS a PART-NBR value until the number of 99999 is entered. This "dummy" number is used on the assumption that it could never be a valid part number.

3. In keeping with the logic of the retrieval method, the READ statement used with random retrieval uses INVALID KEY rather than AT END.

4. In the example, the programmer entered the values 32559, 16612, 41857, and 99999 in response to the prompt 'ENTER PART NUMBER OF RECORD DESIRED'. When a valid part NUMBER is entered, the system compares that to the key values in the index. When a match is found, the system takes the corresponding disk location from the index and retrieves the data record. Note that it is not necessary to test (with an IF statement) to see if the correct record was brought in. The test is built into the INVALID KEY part of the statement. If a matching record is not found, the statement following INVALID KEY is executed.

Figure 12-5 shows the logic in Warnier/Orr format while Figure 12-6 depicts the flowchart format.

FIGURE 12-4

Random retrieval

```
000100 IDENTIFICATION DIVISION.
000110 PROGRAM-ID. RAND1.
000120***************************************
000130*                                     *
000140*           RANDOM RETRIEVAL          *
000150*                                     *
000160*          INDEXED SEQUENTIAL FILE    *
000170*                                     *
000180***************************************
000190 ENVIRONMENT DIVISION.
000200 CONFIGURATION SECTION.
000210 SOURCE-COMPUTER. - - -.
000220 OBJECT-COMPUTER. - - -.
000230 INPUT-OUTPUT SECTION.
000240 FILE-CONTROL.
000250     SELECT DISK-FILE
000260         ASSIGN TO - - -
000270         ORGANIZATION IS INDEXED
000280         ACCESS IS RANDOM
000290         RECORD KEY IS PART-NBR.
000300     SELECT PRINT-FILE ASSIGN TO - - -.
000310*
000320 DATA DIVISION.
000330 FILE SECTION.
000340 FD  DISK-FILE
000350     LABEL RECORD IS STANDARD
000360     VALUE OF FILE-ID IS 'INDSEQ'
000370     DATA RECORD IS DISK-RECORD.
000380 01  DISK-RECORD.
000390     03  PART-NBR          PIC X(5).
000400     03  PART-NAME         PIC X(10).
000410     03  BIN-NBR           PIC 9(3).
000420 FD  PRINT-FILE
000430     LABEL RECORD IS OMITTED
000440     DATA RECORD IS OUTPUT-RECORD.
000450 01  OUTPUT-RECORD         PIC X(121).
000460 WORKING-STORAGE SECTION.
000470 01  HEAD-LINE.
000480     03  FILLER            PIC X(14) VALUE SPACES.
000490     03  FILLER            PIC X(6) VALUE 'NUMBER'.
000500     03  FILLER            PIC X(13) VALUE SPACES.
000510     03  FILLER            PIC X(4) VALUE 'NAME'.
000520     03  FILLER            PIC X(13) VALUE SPACES.
000530     03  FILLER            PIC X(3) VALUE 'BIN'.
000540     03  FILLER            PIC X(68) VALUE SPACES.
```

FIGURE 12-4

continued

```
000550 01  MAIN-LINE.
000560      03   FILLER                PIC X(15) VALUE SPACES.
000570      03   PART-NBR-PR           PIC X(5).
000580      03   FILLER                PIC X(10) VALUE SPACES.
000590      03   PART-NAME-PR          PIC X(10).
000600      03   FILLER                PIC X(10) VALUE SPACES.
000610      03   BIN-NBR-PR            PIC 9(3).
000620      03   FILLER                PIC X(68) VALUE SPACES.
000630*
000640 PROCEDURE DIVISION.
000650 CONTROL-MODULE.
000660      PERFORM 010-OPENER.
000670      PERFORM 020-PROCESS-DISK-DATA
000680          UNTIL PART-NBR IS EQUAL TO '99999'.
000690      DISPLAY 'END OF RETRIEVAL'.
000700      CLOSE DISK-FILE, PRINT-FILE.
000710      STOP RUN.
000720 010-OPENER.
000730      OPEN INPUT DISK-FILE OUTPUT PRINT-FILE.
000740      WRITE OUTPUT-RECORD FROM HEAD-LINE
000750          AFTER ADVANCING 2 LINES.
000760      MOVE SPACES TO OUTPUT-RECORD.
000770      WRITE OUTPUT-RECORD AFTER ADVANCING 2 LINES.
000780      DISPLAY 'ENTER PART NUMBER OF RECORD DESIRED'.
000790      ACCEPT PART-NBR.
000800      IF PART-NBR IS NOT EQUAL TO '99999'
000810          PERFORM 030-DISK-READ.
000820 020-PROCESS-DISK-DATA.
000830      MOVE PART-NBR TO PART-NBR-PR.
000840      MOVE PART-NAME TO PART-NAME-PR.
000850      MOVE BIN-NBR TO BIN-NBR-PR.
000860      WRITE OUTPUT-RECORD FROM MAIN-LINE
000870          AFTER ADVANCING 1 LINE.
000880      DISPLAY 'ENTER PART NUMBER OF RECORD DESIRED'.
000890      ACCEPT PART-NBR.
000900      IF PART-NBR IS NOT EQUAL TO '99999'
000910          PERFORM 030-DISK-READ.
000920 030-DISK-READ.
000930      READ DISK-FILE
000940          KEY IS PART-NBR
000950          INVALID KEY
000960              PERFORM 040-ERROR-ROUTINE.
000970 040-ERROR-ROUTINE.
000980      DISPLAY 'PART NUMBER ' PART-NBR ' IS INCORRECT'.
000990      MOVE '99999' TO PART-NBR.
```

FIGURE 12-5

Random retrieval: Warnier/Orr diagram

FIGURE 12-6

Random retrieval: Flowchart

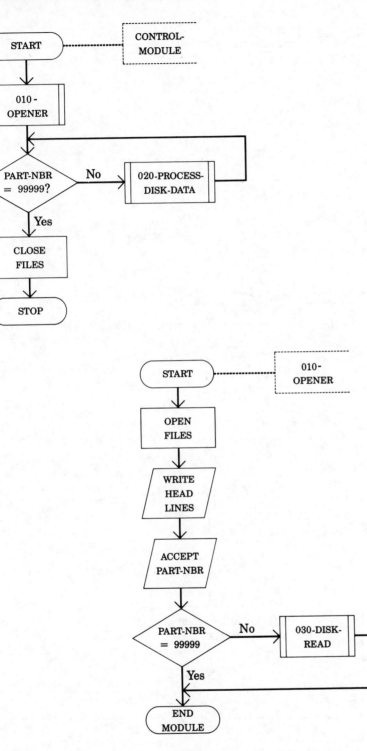

continued

FIGURE 12-6

continued

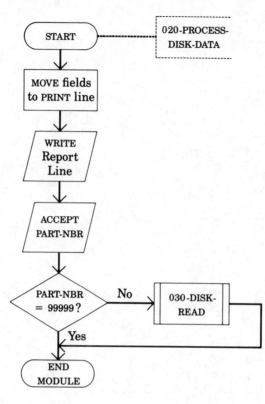

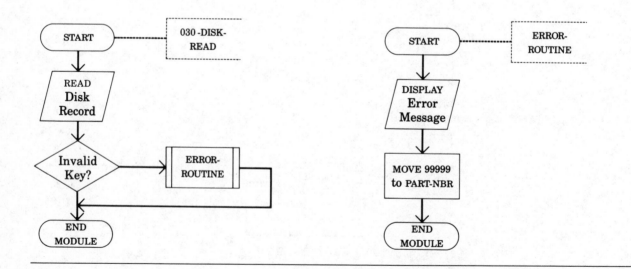

Using alternate keys

Earlier in the chapter, it was mentioned that indexed files could be set up such that the system would create an index based on more than a single key field. The operation is easy to do and provides a great amount of flexibility in randomly accessing data records. In the examples used so far, the only access has been through the primary key as identified by the RECORD KEY IS phrase in the SELECT entry. A far better arrangement would be to have access based on the part name as well. All that is required is the entry

```
ALTERNATE RECORD KEY IS PART-NAME
```

in the SELECT for the program that *creates* the file. Then, the *same* entry is used in the program that *accesses* the file. The next example (Figure 12-7) shows in skeletal form how this is done from a file called 'TWOKEYS'. Note that the prompt message asks the user to enter one of two types of fields that is ACCEPTed from the keyboard. The READ DISK-FILE statement *must* indicate the name of the alternate key to be used since a file can be created with *multiple* alternate keys. In previous examples we always indicated the *prime* access key by the entry

```
READ DISK-FILE
    KEY IS PART-NBR
    ------ .
```

Technically, the KEY IS entry is not required if you are using the primary key (RECORD KEY IS PART-NBR). However, it is good programming practice to do so anyway.

FIGURE 12-7

Using alternate keys

```
      SELECT DISK-FILE
          ASSIGN TO _____
          ORGANIZATION IS INDEXED
          ACCESS IS RANDOM
          RECORD KEY IS PART-NBR
          ALTERNATE RECORD KEY IS PART-NAME.
          .
          .
          .

  010-OPENER.
      OPEN INPUT DISK-FILE _____
      DISPLAY 'IF YOU WISH TO RETRIEVE RECORDS BASED'.
      DISPLAY 'ON THE PART NUMBER, ENTER A 1. IF YOU '.
      DISPLAY 'WISH TO USE PART NAME, ENTER A 2'.
      ACCEPT CHOICE-SWITCH.
      IF CHOICE-SWITCH = 1
          PERFORM READ-PART-NBR
      ELSE
          PERFORM READ-PART-NAME.
          .
          .
          .

  READ-PART-NAME.
      DISPLAY 'ENTER 5 DIGIT PART NUMBER'.
      ACCEPT PART-NBR.
      READ DISK-FILE
          KEY IS PART-NBR
          INVALID KEY
              PERFORM ERROR-ROUTINE-1.
          .
          .
          .

  READ-PART-NBR.
      DISPLAY 'ENTER 10 CHARACTER PART NAME'.
      ACCEPT PART-NAME.
      READ-DISK-FILE
          KEY IS PART-NAME
          INVALID KEY
              PERFORM ERROR-ROUTINE-2.
          .
          .
          .
```

A further extension of the alternate key capability is that the system can be made to look for duplicate key values. You will recall that the normal procedure is that the *record key* must be unique; that is, a record with a duplicate key is not permitted. However, duplicate *alternate* keys are permitted. In the following example, our basic loader program was used to create a file with duplicate bin numbers as an alternate key:

```
SELECT DISK-FILE
    ASSIGN TO _____
    ORGANIZATION IS INDEXED
    ACCESS MODE IS SEQUENTIAL
    RECORD KEY IS PART-NBR
    ALTERNATE RECORD KEY IS BIN-NBR
        WITH DUPLICATES.
```

The data records loaded to the 'DUPS' file are shown below:

12345	CLAMP	102	00631
16612	SHEARS	046	01895
18903	VISE	102	07586
19946	PULLEY	189	02450
25991	HANDLE	462	00845
27803	MALLET	102	01267

A program that retrieves *all* records with a particular bin number is shown in Figure 12-8.

The program differs from the previous random retrieval program in several ways.

1. Since the file was created with an ALTERNATE RECORD KEY WITH DUPLICATES, this entry is included in the SELECT.

2. In the 010-OPENER paragraph the bin number of the bin records desired (bin 102 in this case) is ACCEPTed from the terminal. The bin number is checked to see if it equals the dummy value of 999. If it does, the end-of-file action is triggered.

3. Entry of a valid bin number (not 999) causes the system to perform the 030-GET-FIRST-RECORD routine, which is a *random read* based on the BIN-NBR key. This statement has the net effect of acting as a priming read for the rest of the READS that will take place in the program. An error routine is triggered on the INVALID KEY condition. The BIN-NBR is moved to WORK-ING-STORAGE where it will be used for comparison. At this point, both BIN-NBR and BIN-NBR-WS contain a value of 102.

4. The 020-PRINT-AND-GET-DUPLICATES paragraph moves and prints the data from the records, which were just brought in with random read statement. The next read is a *sequential* read that will now continue the usual move-write-read process that has always been used for sequential retrieval. Normally, two different types of READS (random and sequential) cannot be used with a file. However, it is permitted with indexed files if the SELECT specifies the ACCESS IS DYNAMIC entry as we have done (line 300).

FIGURE 12-8

Alternate keys with duplicates

```
000100 IDENTIFICATION DIVISION.
000110 PROGRAM-ID. DUPBIN1.
000120*****************************************
000130*                                         *
000140*              INDEXED SEQUENTIAL FILE     *
000150*                                         *
000160*              USING ALTERNATE KEY         *
000170*                                         *
000180*              WITH DUPLICATE ENTRIES      *
000190*                                         *
000200*****************************************
000210 ENVIRONMENT DIVISION.
000220 CONFIGURATION SECTION.
000230 SOURCE-COMPUTER. - - -.
000240 OBJECT-COMPUTER. - - -.
000250 INPUT-OUTPUT SECTION.
000260 FILE-CONTROL.
000270     SELECT DISK-FILE
000280         ASSIGN TO - - -
000290         ORGANIZATION IS INDEXED
000300         ACCESS IS DYNAMIC
000310         RECORD KEY IS PART-NBR
000320         ALTERNATE RECORD KEY IS BIN-NBR
000330             WITH DUPLICATES.
000340     SELECT PRINT-FILE ASSIGN TO - - -.
000350*
000360 DATA DIVISION.
000370 FILE SECTION.
000380 FD   DISK-FILE
000390     LABEL RECORD IS STANDARD
000400     DATA RECORD IS DISK-RECORD.
000410 01   DISK-RECORD.
000420     03   PART-NBR          PIC X(5).
000430     03   PART-NAME         PIC X(10).
000440     03   BIN-NBR           PIC X(3).
000450     03   PRICE             PIC 999V99.
000460 FD   PRINT-FILE
000470     LABEL RECORD IS OMITTED
000480     DATA RECORD IS OUTPUT-RECORD.
000490 01   OUTPUT-RECORD         PIC X(121).
000500 WORKING-STORAGE SECTION.
000510 01   MISC-FIELDS.
000520     03   EOF-INDICATOR     PIC 9 VALUE ZERO.
000530     03   BIN-NBR-WS        PIC XXX.
000540 01   HEAD-LINE.
000550     03   FILLER            PIC X(14) VALUE SPACES.
000560     03   FILLER            PIC X(6) VALUE 'NUMBER'.
000570     03   FILLER            PIC X(13) VALUE SPACES.
000580     03   FILLER            PIC X(4) VALUE 'NAME'.
000590     03   FILLER            PIC X(13) VALUE SPACES.
000600     03   FILLER            PIC X(3) VALUE 'BIN'.
000610     03   FILLER            PIC X(11) VALUE SPACES.
000620     03   FILLER            PIC X(5) VALUE 'PRICE'.
000630     03   FILLER            PIC X(52) VALUE SPACES.
000640 01   MAIN-LINE.
000650     03   FILLER            PIC X(15) VALUE SPACES.
000660     03   PART-NBR-PR       PIC X(5).
000670     03   FILLER            PIC X(10) VALUE SPACES.
000680     03   PART-NAME-PR      PIC X(10).
```

FIGURE 12-8

continued

```
000690      03   FILLER             PIC X(10) VALUE SPACES.
000700      03   BIN-NBR-PR         PIC 9(3).
000710      03   FILLER             PIC X(10) VALUE SPACES.
000720      03   PRICE-PR           PIC $ZZZ.99.
000730      03   FILLER             PIC X(51) VALUE SPACES.
000740*
000750 PROCEDURE DIVISION.
000760 CONTROL-MODULE.
000770      PERFORM 010-OPENER.
000780      PERFORM 020-PRINT-AND-GET-DUPLICATES
000790           UNTIL EOF-INDICATOR IS EQUAL TO 1.
000800      DISPLAY 'END OF RETRIEVAL FOR BIN # ', BIN-NBR-WS.
000810      CLOSE DISK-FILE, PRINT-FILE.
000820      STOP RUN.
000830 010-OPENER.
000840      OPEN INPUT DISK-FILE OUTPUT PRINT-FILE.
000850      WRITE OUTPUT-RECORD FROM HEAD-LINE
000860           AFTER ADVANCING 2 LINES.
000870      MOVE SPACES TO OUTPUT-RECORD.
000880      WRITE OUTPUT-RECORD AFTER ADVANCING 2 LINES.
000890      DISPLAY 'ENTER BIN NUMBER OF RECORD DESIRED'.
000900      ACCEPT BIN-NBR.
000910      IF BIN-NBR IS NOT EQUAL TO '999'
000920           PERFORM 030-GET-FIRST-RECORD
000930      ELSE
000940           MOVE 1 TO EOF-INDICATOR.
000950      IF EOF-INDICATOR = ZERO
000960           MOVE BIN-NBR TO BIN-NBR-WS.
000970 020-PRINT-AND-GET-DUPLICATES.
000980      IF BIN-NBR NOT = BIN-NBR-WS
000990           MOVE 1 TO EOF-INDICATOR
001000      ELSE
001010           MOVE PART-NBR TO PART-NBR-PR
001020           MOVE PART-NAME TO PART-NAME-PR
001030           MOVE BIN-NBR TO BIN-NBR-PR
001040           MOVE PRICE TO PRICE-PR
001050           WRITE OUTPUT-RECORD FROM MAIN-LINE
001060               AFTER ADVANCING 2 LINES
001070           PERFORM 050-SEQUENTIAL-READ.
001080 030-GET-FIRST-RECORD.
001090      READ DISK-FILE
001100           KEY IS BIN-NBR
001110           INVALID KEY
001120               PERFORM 040-ERROR-ROUTINE.
001130 040-ERROR-ROUTINE.
001140      DISPLAY 'BIN # ', BIN-NBR, ' IN ERROR'.
001150      MOVE 1 TO EOF-INDICATOR.
001160 050-SEQUENTIAL-READ.
001170      READ DISK-FILE NEXT RECORD
001180           AT END MOVE 1 TO EOF-INDICATOR.
```

NUMBER	NAME	BIN	PRICE
12345	CLAMP	102	$ 6.31
18903	VISE	102	$ 75.86
27803	MALLET	102	$ 12.67

5. The 020-PRINT-AND-GET-DUPLICATES paragraph will continue executing to the end of the file if we let it. However, we are interested only in retrieving those records with a bin number of 102. The IF statement at the end of the paragraph keeps checking each sequentially retrieved record. As soon as a bin number that does not match the WORKING-STORAGE value is encountered, the looping action is terminated.

The FILE STATUS entry

The entries within a file SELECT phrase have grown in relation to the complexity of operations we wish to perform on the data records. In most cases, if the operation is unsuccessful, the system provides for a method of "escape" by means of the INVALID KEY routine. The programs shown so far have included a general message devised by the programmer that might give a very rough idea of the problem encountered:

```
READ DISK-FILE
    INVALID KEY
    DISPLAY 'PART NUMBER ' PART-NBR ' INCORRECT'.
```

Fortunately, COBOL offers the programmer access to a series of internal codes generated by the execution of any input/output statement that references an indexed file. To gain access to this information the programmer may insert another line into the SELECT entry as shown below:

FILE STATUS IS data-name

FILE and STATUS are reserved words and data-name is the name of a two-character alphanumeric field that is described in the WORKING-STORAGE SECTION. (The field cannot be described in the FILE SECTION.)

```
SELECT DISK-FILE
    ASSIGN TO _____
    ORGANIZATION IS INDEXED
    ACCESS IS RANDOM
    RECORD KEY IS PART-NBR
    FILE STATUS IS CONDITION-CODE.
    .
    .
    .
WORKING-STORAGE SECTION.
01  MISC-FIELDS.
    03  CONDITION-CODE.
        05  FIRST-DIGIT     PIC X.
        05  SECOND-DIGIT    PIC X.
```

Immediately after the execution of an I/O statement that references a file, the system moves a two-character code to the named field—CONDITION-CODE in our example. The two characters are known as *status key 1* (FIRST-

DIGIT) and *status key 2* (SECOND-DIGIT) and contain information concerning the status of the system as a result of the input or output operation. The programmer may then use this information if it is appropriate to the program:

```
READ DISK-FILE
     KEY IS PART-NBR
     INVALID KEY
          PERFORM ERROR-ROUTINE.
     .
     .
     .
ERROR-ROUTINE.
          (IF statements to see whether the job should be
          aborted or continued based on the information
          supplied by the FILE STATUS field)
```

Listed below are some of the status codes used on *one manufacturer's system*. These codes are not necessarily valid on your system and are included only to show you how the FILE STATUS works. Consult your manual.

Status Key 1

0   Successful completion of the input/output operation.

1   AT END—attempted to read sequentially and the EOF marker was encountered.

2   Invalid key.

3   Permanent error due to some type of input/output problem.

9   General error that will be indicated by the value in right-most character of the status code field.

Status Key 2

0   No further information is available. A successful operation will generate a 00 condition in the keys.

If status key 1 contains a '2', which indicates an INVALID KEY, status key 2 may contain the following:

1   Sequence error in a sequentially accessed file.

2   Duplicate key value.

3   No record found.

4   An attempt has been made to write beyond the file boundary.

If status key 1 contains a '9', which indicates a general error, status key 2 may contain the following:

0   Invalid operation.

1   File not opened prior to execution of a statement that uses the file.

2   File not closed prior to an OPEN attempt.

3   File not available.

4   Invalid OPEN.

5   Invalid device.

6   Undefined current record pointer status while working in sequential access mode.

7   Invalid record length.

8   Invalid indexed file—the file contains inconsistent data and no recovery is possible.

Updating indexed files

When we were working with *straight* sequential files, the only way a file could be updated was by creating a new file that contained the desired records. The tasks of modifying (or changing) a record and deleting a record required that a matching operation take place. This operation required that both the Detail and Master File be in the same order and that appropriate matching logic be present in the update programs. The use of an indexed-sequential file relieves the programmer of much of this work since the file can be updated directly (without creating a new file). In addition, the program matching logic is not needed since the software performs this task by consulting the index to find the desired record.

Modifying with the REWRITE statement

To show you how updating works, we will use a file called 'MODIFY' that has the following format:

PART NUMBER	PART NAME	BIN NUMBER	PRICE
16612	BOLTS	559	00012
21976	HAMMER	013	01136
30433	CLAMP	457	00642
32559	PLIERS	189	00763
38662	NAILS	444	00195
41857	WRENCH	684	01496

Because there is a significant difference in the way updating takes place, we will need to use a slightly different version of the OPEN statement. When we were working with straight sequential files, both the Detail File and the Old Master File were opened as INPUT, while the New Master File was opened as OUTPUT. However, in the case of an indexed file update, the system will first have to READ the record and then REWRITE the revised record on top of the old data. The net effect of this operation is that the file will be treated as both an INPUT and an OUTPUT file. The OPEN version that allows this to happen follows:

OPEN I-O file-name.

As mentioned earlier, a special version of the WRITE statement—called REWRITE—is used to modify a record in an indexed-sequential file. The REWRITE statement follows the same format as the regular WRITE statement we have used so far, but it can only be used with a file that has been opened I-O. The general format is

REWRITE record-name [FROM identifier]
    INVALID KEY imperative statement

where record-name refers to a logical record in the FILE SECTION of the DATA DIVISION. Certain rules must be followed when using REWRITE.

1. The file must be opened I-O.
2. The number of characters being written must be equal to the number of characters in the record that is replaced.
3. The record written by the REWRITE statement is no longer available in the FILE SECTION.
4. If the record key on the disk does not match the record key that was entered, the INVALID KEY condition is invoked and updating does not take place.

Figure 12-9 shows how the modifying and REWRITEing of a record take place. Several points are worth noting.

1. Access is RANDOM and the record key is PART-NBR.
2. The DISK-FILE is OPENed I-O in order to be able to use the REWRITE statement later in the program.
3. The program prompts for the entry of the identifying key PART-NBR and the two fields that could possibly be changed—BIN-NBR and PRICE. The PART-NBR value is ACCEPTed into the DISK-RECORD record area, while the bin number and price are ACCEPTed into a WORKING-STORAGE area. If the bin number and price had been entered into the DISK-RECORD area, the values would be destroyed by the following disk READ operation.
4. The DISK-FILE record is read based on the PART-NBR key field. The fields are moved to an output line and printed to provide a listing of the original values in the record.
5. Then, the changed BIN-NBR and/or PRICE values are moved into the DISK-RECORD area and the REWRITE operation takes place. The record is also written on the printer to provide a comparison with the original data.
6. The ACCEPT-change process terminates when PART-NBR is entered as all nines.

FIGURE 12-9

Updating with REWRITE

```
000100 IDENTIFICATION DIVISION.
000110 PROGRAM-ID.   UP1.
000120*************************************************
000130*                                               *
000140*               UPDATING AN                      *
000150*                                               *
000160*           INDEXED SEQUENTIAL FILE              *
000170*                                               *
000180*************************************************
000190 ENVIRONMENT DIVISION.
000200 CONFIGURATION SECTION.
000210 SOURCE-COMPUTER. - - -.
000220 OBJECT-COMPUTER. - - -.
000230 INPUT-OUTPUT SECTION.
000240 FILE-CONTROL.
000250      SELECT DISK-FILE
000260          ASSIGN TO - - -
000270          ORGANIZATION IS INDEXED
000280          ACCESS IS RANDOM
000290          RECORD KEY IS PART-NBR.
000300      SELECT PRINT-FILE
000310*
000320 DATA DIVISION.
000330 FILE SECTION.
000340 FD   DISK-FILE
000350      LABEL RECORD IS STANDARD
000360      VALUE OF FILE-ID IS 'MODIFY'
000370      DATA RECORD IS DISK-RECORD.
000380 01   DISK-RECORD.
000390      03   PART-NBR              PIC X(5).
000400      03   PART-NAME             PIC X(10).
000410      03   BIN-NBR               PIC 9(3).
000420      03   PRICE                 PIC 999V99.
000430 FD   PRINT-FILE
000440      LABEL RECORD IS OMITTED
000450      DATA RECORD IS OUTPUT-RECORD.
000460 01   OUTPUT-RECORD             PIC X(121).
000470 WORKING-STORAGE SECTION.
000480 01   MISC-FIELDS.
000490      03   BIN-NBR-WS            PIC 999.
000500      03   PRICE-WS              PIC 999V99.
000510 01   HEAD-LINE.
000520      03   FILLER                PIC X(14) VALUE SPACES.
000530      03   FILLER                PIC X(6) VALUE 'NUMBER'.
000540      03   FILLER                PIC X(13) VALUE SPACES.
000550      03   FILLER                PIC X(4) VALUE 'NAME'.
000560      03   FILLER                PIC X(13) VALUE SPACES.
000570      03   FILLER                PIC X(3) VALUE 'BIN'.
000580      03   FILLER                PIC X(11) VALUE SPACES.
000590      03   FILLER                PIC X(5) VALUE 'PRICE'.
000600      03   FILLER                PIC X(52) VALUE SPACES.
```

FIGURE 12-9

continued

```
000610 01   MAIN-LINE.
000620      03   FILLER             PIC X(15) VALUE SPACES.
000630      03   PART-NBR-PR        PIC X(5).
000640      03   FILLER             PIC X(10) VALUE SPACES.
000650      03   PART-NAME-PR       PIC X(10).
000660      03   FILLER             PIC X(10) VALUE SPACES.
000670      03   BIN-NBR-PR         PIC 9(3).
000680      03   FILLER             PIC X(10) VALUE SPACES.
000690      03   PRICE-PR           PIC $ZZZ.99.
000700      03   FILLER             PIC X(51) VALUE SPACES.
000710*
000720 PROCEDURE DIVISION.
000730 CONTROL-MODULE.
000740      PERFORM 010-OPENER.
000750      PERFORM 020-PROCESS-DISK-DATA
000760          UNTIL PART-NBR IS EQUAL TO '99999'.
000770      DISPLAY 'END OF RETRIEVAL'.
000780      CLOSE DISK-FILE, PRINT-FILE.
000790      STOP RUN.
000800 010-OPENER.
000810      OPEN I-O DISK-FILE OUTPUT PRINT-FILE.
000820      WRITE OUTPUT-RECORD FROM HEAD-LINE
000830          AFTER ADVANCING 2 LINES.
000840      MOVE SPACES TO OUTPUT-RECORD.
000850      WRITE OUTPUT-RECORD AFTER ADVANCING 2 LINES.
000860      DISPLAY 'ENTER PART NUMBER OF RECORD TO BE CHANGED'.
000870      ACCEPT PART-NBR.
000880      DISPLAY 'ENTER OLD OR NEW BIN NUMBER'.
000890      ACCEPT BIN-NBR-WS.
000900      DISPLAY 'ENTER OLD OR NEW PRICE'.
000910      ACCEPT PRICE-WS.
000920      IF PART-NBR IS NOT EQUAL TO '99999'
000930          PERFORM 030-DISK-READ.
000940 020-PROCESS-DISK-DATA.
000950      MOVE BIN-NBR-WS TO BIN-NBR, BIN-NBR-PR.
000960      MOVE PRICE-WS TO PRICE, PRICE-PR.
000970      REWRITE DISK-RECORD
000980          INVALID KEY
000990              DISPLAY 'PART NUMBER ', PART-NBR, ' IS INCORRECT'
001000              STOP RUN.
001010      MOVE PART-NBR TO PART-NBR-PR.
001020      MOVE PART-NAME TO PART-NAME-PR.
001030      WRITE OUTPUT-RECORD FROM MAIN-LINE
001040          AFTER ADVANCING 2 LINES.
001050      DISPLAY 'ENTER PART NUMBER OF RECORD TO BE CHANGED'.
001060      ACCEPT PART-NBR.
001070      DISPLAY 'ENTER OLD OR NEW BIN NUMBER'.
001080      ACCEPT BIN-NBR-WS.
001090      DISPLAY 'ENTER OLD OR NEW PRICE'.
001100      ACCEPT PRICE-WS.
```

continued

FIGURE 12-9

continued

```
001110        IF PART-NBR IS NOT EQUAL TO '99999'
001120             PERFORM 030-DISK-READ.
001130  030-DISK-READ.
001140        READ DISK-FILE
001150             KEY IS PART-NBR
001160             INVALID KEY
001170                DISPLAY 'PART NUMBER ', PART-NBR, ' IS INCORRECT'
001180                STOP RUN.
001190        MOVE PART-NBR TO PART-NBR-PR.
001200        MOVE PART-NAME TO PART-NAME-PR.
001210        MOVE BIN-NBR TO BIN-NBR-PR.
001220        MOVE PRICE TO PRICE-PR.
001230        WRITE OUTPUT-RECORD FROM MAIN-LINE
001240             AFTER ADVANCING 2 LINES.
```

Shown below is the output from the update program. The operator keyed in 30433 as the PART-NBR, 402 as the revised BIN-NBR-WS, and 00642 as the PRICE-WS entry. The system then printed the values in the original record and then the updated version of the same record. The second pair of lines reflects a change in the item price from $14.96 to $13.78.

NUMBER	NAME	BIN	PRICE
30433	CLAMP	457	$ 6.42
30433	CLAMP	402	$ 6.42
41857	WRENCH	684	$ 14.96
41857	WRENCH	684	$ 13.78

Removing records—the DELETE statement

The DELETE statement logically removes a record from the disk file and has the following format:

DELETE file-name RECORD

    INVALID KEY imperative statement

Note that the record is "logically" removed from the file rather than physically deleted. This is accomplished by flagging the index entry to that record, not by actually deleting it from the disk data area. The DELETE statement may be used with indexed files that are accessed in either SEQUENTIAL or RANDOM mode; but, with SEQUENTIAL ACCESS, the INVALID KEY phrase is omitted. When used with a sequential access operation, the DELETE statement is used in conjunction with the last successfully executed sequential READ statement. Execution of the DELETE statement then logically removes the last record read in. When the file is accessed in either the RANDOM or DYNAMIC mode, the INVALID KEY phrase must be included. As with the REWRITE statement, the file must be OPENed I-O in order to use DELETE.

Our example will make use of the

```
ACCESS IS DYNAMIC
```

entry because the program will access the file both randomly and sequentially. The file is the same as the previous updating example, and, in response to the prompt 'ENTER PART NUMBER OF RECORD TO BE DELETED', the operator will first enter 21976 and then 38662 when asked the second time. After these two records have been removed by the DELETE statement, the operator enters 99999 to trigger the end of the file deletion process.

Then, since DISK-FILE is being accessed in the DYNAMIC mode, the file is CLOSEd and then OPENed as INPUT and accessed sequentially to print a listing of the records that remain on the file. Figure 12-10 shows the pertinent parts of the program.

FIGURE 12-10

Example of DELETE statement usage

```
      SELECT DISK-FILE
          ASSIGN TO _____
          ORGANIZATION IS INDEXED
          ACCESS IS DYNAMIC
          RECORD KEY IS PART-NBR.
               .
               .
               .


PROCEDURE DIVISION.
CONTROL-MODULE.
    PERFORM 010-OPENER.
    PERFORM 020-PROCESS-DISK-DATA
        UNTIL PART-NBR IS EQUAL TO '99999'.
    DISPLAY 'END OF FILE DELETION PROCESS'.
    PERFORM 030-OPENER.
    PERFORM 040-READ-AND-PRINT
        UNTIL EOF-INDICATOR = 1.
    CLOSE DISK-FILE, PRINT-FILE.
    STOP RUN.
010-OPENER.
    OPEN I-O DISK-FILE OUTPUT PRINT-FILE.
    WRITE OUTPUT-RECORD FROM HEAD-LINE
        AFTER ADVANCING 2 LINES.
    MOVE SPACES TO OUTPUT-RECORD.
    WRITE OUTPUT-RECORD AFTER ADVANCING 2 LINES.
020-PROCESS-DISK-DATA.
    DISPLAY 'ENTER PART NUMBER OF RECORD TO BE DELETED'.
    ACCEPT PART-NBR.
    IF PART-NBR IS NOT EQUAL TO '99999'
        DELETE DISK-FILE RECORD
            INVALID KEY
                DISPLAY 'PART NUMBER IS INCORRECT'
                STOP RUN.
```

---

continued

FIGURE 12-10

continued

```
030-OPENER.
    CLOSE DISK-FILE.
    OPEN INPUT DISK-FILE.
    READ DISK-FILE NEXT RECORD
        AT END MOVE 1 TO EOF-INDICATOR.
040-READ-AND-PRINT.
    MOVE PART-NBR TO PART-NBR-PR.
    MOVE PART-NAME TO PART-NAME-PR.
    MOVE BIN-NBR TO BIN-NBR-PR.
    MOVE PRICE TO PRICE-PR.
    WRITE OUTPUT-RECORD FROM MAIN-LINE
        AFTER ADVANCING 2 LINES.
    READ DISK-FILE NEXT RECORD
        AT END MOVE 1 TO EOF-INDICATOR.
```

NUMBER	NAME	BIN	PRICE
16612	BOLTS	550	$ .12
30433	CLAMP	457	$ 6.42
32559	PLIERS	189	$ 7.63
41857	WRENCH	893	$ 14.96

Adding records to an indexed file

Adding records to an indexed-sequential file follows the same pattern that was used in creating the file originally. The difference is that the system has to be alerted to the fact that the records being entered are to be added to an *existing* file. If this information is not transmitted to the software, the system will simply create a new file with the same name as the old file, which will result in the destruction of the old data file. The SELECT entries are shown below:

```
SELECT DISK-FILE
    ASSIGN TO _____
    ORGANIZATION IS INDEXED
    ACCESS IS RANDOM
    RECORD KEY IS PART-NBR.
    .
    .
    .

FD  DISK-FILE
    LABEL RECORD IS STANDARD
    VALUE OF FILE-ID IS 'MODIFY'
    .
    .
    .
```

In this example the 'MODIFY' file contains the same records we started with at the beginning of this section.

PART NUMBER	PART NAME	BIN NUMBER	PRICE
16612	BOLTS	550	00012
21976	HAMMER	013	01136
30433	CLAMP	457	00642
32559	PLIERS	189	00763
38662	NAILS	444	00195
41857	WRENCH	684	01496

Figure 12-11 shows the PROCEDURE DIVISION entries for the program. Note that the DISK-FILE is opened I-O, which indicates to the system that the 'MODIFY' file already exists. Therefore, data records will be added to the file *and* the index. The PART-NBRs of the added records do not have to be in sequential order, although this would be the normal practice. Whether the keys are in ascending order or not, the PART-NBR keys will be inserted into their proper place in the index so that execution of a sequential retrieval program will result in a listing that is in ascending key order. Figure 12-12 shows the output from the disk-add program and the output from the execution of a sequential listing of the 'MODIFY' file.

COMMON ERRORS

Beginning programmers seem to make relatively few errors when working with disk files. Those errors that are made can be summarized as follows:

1. Not differentiating between a straight sequential disk file and an indexed-sequential file that is handled sequentially. The difference, of course, is that a straight sequential disk file will *not* include the ORGANIZATION IS INDEXED entry.
2. Not recognizing that an indexed-sequential file can be treated in either a sequential or random manner. In either case, the file access mode determines whether ACCESS IS SEQUENTIAL or ACCESS IS RANDOM will be used.
3. Forgetting to set up the key field in either the right place in the record or in the correct format (PIC X or PIC 9).
4. Another type of error is that of using an IF statement to test whether or not the disk system retrieved the correct record during random retrieval. As mentioned earlier, there is no need for the programmer to do this checking since it is done automatically by the system software. An incorrect match will be detected and invoke the INVALID KEY part of the statement. At that point you may wish to execute an error routine to see what caused the error or to either abort or continue processing.
5. Make sure that, when using the REWRITE statement, the new record is exactly the same size as the old record.
6. Finally, a reminder that the file must be opened as I-O when records are added to the file. Opening it just as OUTPUT will result in destruction of the old file.

FIGURE 12-11

File addition program

```
000720 PROCEDURE DIVISION.
000730 CONTROL-MODULE.
000740     PERFORM 010-OPENER.
000750     PERFORM 020-PROCESS-DISK-DATA
000760         UNTIL PART-NBR IS EQUAL TO '99999'.
000770     DISPLAY 'END OF FILE ADDITION PROCESS'.
000780     CLOSE DISK-FILE, PRINT-FILE.
000790     STOP RUN.
000800 010-OPENER.
000810     OPEN I-O DISK-FILE OUTPUT PRINT-FILE.
000820     WRITE OUTPUT-RECORD FROM HEAD-LINE
000830         AFTER ADVANCING 2 LINES.
000840     MOVE SPACES TO OUTPUT-RECORD.
000850     WRITE OUTPUT-RECORD AFTER ADVANCING 2 LINES.
000860     DISPLAY 'ENTER PART NUMBER OF RECORD TO BE ADDED'.
000870     ACCEPT PART-NBR.
000880 020-PROCESS-DISK-DATA.
000890     MOVE PART-NBR TO PART-NBR-PR.
000900     DISPLAY 'ENTER PART NAME'.
000910     ACCEPT PART-NAME.
000920     MOVE PART-NAME TO PART-NAME-PR.
000930     DISPLAY 'ENTER BIN NUMBER'.
000940     ACCEPT BIN-NBR.
000950     MOVE BIN-NBR TO BIN-NBR-PR.
000960     DISPLAY 'ENTER PRICE'.
000970     ACCEPT PRICE.
000980     MOVE PRICE TO PRICE-PR.
000990     WRITE DISK-RECORD
001000         INVALID KEY
001010             PERFORM ERROR-ROUTINE.
001020     IF PART-NBR NOT = TO '99999'
001030         WRITE OUTPUT-RECORD FROM MAIN-LINE
001040             AFTER ADVANCING 2 LINES.
001050         PERFORM ACCEPT-ROUTINE.
001060 ERROR-ROUTINE.
001070     DISPLAY 'ERROR IN PART NUMBER ', PART-NBR.
001080     MOVE '99999' TO PART-NBR.
001090 ACCEPT-ROUTINE.
001100     DISPLAY 'ENTER PART NUMBER OF RECORD TO BE ADDED'.
001110     ACCEPT PART-NBR.
```

FIGURE 12-12

Results of file addition operation

NUMBER	NAME	BIN	PRICE
19403	CUTTER	075	$ 8.56
36997	VISE	391	$ 73.91

Added Records

NUMBER	NAME	BIN	PRICE
16612	BOLTS	550	$ .12
19403	CUTTER	075	$ 8.56
21976	HAMMER	013	$ 11.36
30433	CLAMP	457	$ 6.42
32559	PLIERS	198	$ 7.63
36997	VISE	391	$ 73.91
38662	NAILS	444	$ 1.95
41857	WRENCH	684	$ 14.96

Listing of revised file

PROGRAMMING TIPS

Perhaps the single most important programming tip concerning indexed file operations is that a disk is "touchy" in that what appear to be minor infractions of the rules may result in a program abend. The following admonitions emphasize how critical some of the entries are: (1) Be careful that the RECORD KEY field is in the proper place within the record. (It *must* be the first field or it *cannot* be the first field.) (2) Be sure that the field is of the proper type (x or 9).

Considerable differences may exist in the range between microcomputers and mainframes so the caveat "consult your manual" should be heeded. Some systems permit the creation of indexed files by means of a program as shown in the chapter, but only after extensive information has been provided to special disk software designed for this purpose.

The next point was discussed earlier in the text, but needs to be mentioned again. For greater clarity and future ease of maintenance, place READ and WRITE statements in separate paragraphs that are PERFORMed when needed. Later, if the input/output file has to be changed, only a single correction in the program need be made; as opposed to making a change in each and every place where the READ or WRITE is used. In theory, each file would have only one READ or WRITE statement associated with it in the entire program. Note the following examples:

```
020-BEGINNING-MODULE.
    OPEN _____
    READ CUSTOMER-DISK-FILE
        AT END _____.
030-PROCESSING-LOOP.
    _____

    _____

    WRITE CUSTOMER-PRINTER-FILE
        AFTER ADVANCING _____.
    READ CUSTOMER-DISK-FILE
        AT END _____.
```

A better arrangement is as follows:

```
020-BEGINNING-MODULE.
    OPEN _____.
    PERFORM READ-ROUTINE.
030-PROCESSING-LOOP.
    _____.

    _____.

    PERFORM PRINTER-OUTPUT.
    PERFORM READ-ROUTINE.
        .

        .

        .

READ-ROUTINE.
    READ CUSTOMER-DISK-FILE
        AT END _____.
PRINTER-OUTPUT.
    WRITE CUSTOMER-PRINT-FILE
        AFTER ADVANCING _____.
```

If you think your program is complex, consider that "it took 400 IBM programmers more than 4,000,000 hours to write approximately 500,000 lines of computer code for the five on-board computers that guided the first space-shuttle mission."* (Author's note: That works out to approximately one line of code per day per programmer over a five-year period!)

*Source: *Psychology Today*, January 1984, p. 77.

SELF-STUDY: QUESTIONS AND ANSWERS

1. None of the examples used blocked data on disk. Why not?

   Answer: The reason you never saw BLOCK CONTAINS with any of the disk examples was that the entry is usually optional. With tape files the input/output software does the blocking and unblocking described in an earlier chapter. On some disk systems a BLOCK CONTAINS entry in the file description follows the same process. On the more sophisticated systems, however, the disk I/O software may ignore your blocking instructions and pick its own optimum blocking factor.

2. You discussed straight-sequential disk access and sequential access of an indexed-sequential disk file. Why would you ever use straight-sequential disk access if you have the possibility of using indexed-sequential access?

   Answer: If you had a lot of disk files you were going to access sequentially *from the first record*, it would be better to set up those files on a straight-sequential basis. The reason for this is that doing the same operation on an indexed-sequential file is not quite as efficient since the system is obligated to check the index to determine the location of the first record. Also, you save disk space that would have been needed for the index.

3. Why shouldn't I set up every indexed file with *every* field as a key field? That would give me the most flexibility in being able to access the records I want.

   Answer: In theory you could set up an indexed file with the index based on every field. However, there are three good reasons why you wouldn't or shouldn't. First, the index itself can get very large. Conceivably, the index could exceed the size of the data file. Second, some systems have limits (such as five) on the number of keys permitted. Third, a file with a great many indexes takes longer to create, longer to update, and longer to access.

CHAPTER TERMS

ACCESS IS DYNAMIC	key (RECORD KEY)
ACCESS IS RANDOM	ORGANIZATION IS INDEXED
ACCESS IS SEQUENTIAL	random access
ALTERNATE RECORD KEY	READ – NEXT RECORD
DELETE	RECORD KEY IS
DUPLICATES	REWRITE
FILE STATUS	sequential access
indexed-sequential file	START
INVALID KEY	status key

EXERCISES

1. The field on which an indexed file is based is known as the _____ .

2. What is the function of the ORGANIZATION IS INDEXED entry? Explain in detail.

3. What is the purpose of the RECORD KEY entry? Give an example of it in use.

4. Explain why AT END is *not* used with a random-access disk READ.

5. To begin using a sequential index file at a point other than the beginning, a _____ statement must be used.

6. What must you add to a READ statement, if you are using an *alternate* key for retrieval?

7. To read records with duplicate keys from an indexed file you will need to first access _____ , then access the rest of the file _____ .

8. In order to do two different types of accesses within a program, the file must be defined as _____ .

9. To get a system generated code which tells the status of the file being used, what must be added to the SELECT statement?

10. When doing an update operation on a random access file, the WRITE statement is replaced by _____ .

11. A deleted record from an indexed file is _____ , and not actually removed from the file.

12. What does INVALID KEY do in the following?
   a. Sequential access of an indexed-sequential file using START.
   b. Random access of an indexed-sequential file.

13. Write a program to create a straight sequential disk file called 'SEQSALES' using Data Set B (see Appendix D). The record format is as follows, and data values will be entered by means of the ACCEPT statement.

Field	Characters	Type
Sales Territory	3	Numeric
ID Number	5	Numeric
Salesperson's Name	20	Alphabetic
Year to Date Sales	7	Numeric
Year to Date Sales Returns	6	Numeric

14. Modify Exercise 13 to create an indexed-sequential file called IS-FILE.

15. Use the file created in Exercise 13 and program for the following.
   a. Sequential retrieval and printout of the data records starting with the beginning of the file.
   b. Sequential retrieval and printout of the data records starting with some record number other than the beginning record.

16. Use the file created in Exercise 14 to provide for random retrieval. Consult Appendix D and pick out six identification numbers. Write a program to randomly retrieve the matching disk records and print appropriate lines of output.

Chapter 13
Writing Reports

CHAPTER OUTLINE

Carriage control

Using the LINAGE **clause**

The Report Writer feature

What can Report Writer do?

Some DATA DIVISION entries

Some PROCEDURE DIVISION entries

More DATA DIVISION entries

Common errors

Programming tips

Self-study: Questions and answers

Chapter terms

Exercises

LEARNING OBJECTIVES

1. To let you become acquainted with one of the optional features of COBOL—Report Writer—that is usually implemented only on the larger computer systems.

2. To have you get some feeling for the power of Report Writer in its ability to handle various report features such as: page headings, page footings, control breaks, group indication, and summing.

In previous chapters you saw several ways in which the programmer could control the action of the printer in order to turn out nice-looking reports. One technique involved starting the print action at the top of a new page by means of the SPECIAL-NAMES section and the reserved word C01. If you recall, C01 (Cee zero one) is a word that allows the programmer to assign a name to the first printing line on the top of a new page:

```
CONFIGURATION SECTION.
SPECIAL-NAMES.
    C01 IS PAGE-TOP.
        .
        .
        .
010-OPENER
        .
        .
        .
    WRITE PRINT-LINE
        FROM HEAD-LINE-1
        AFTER ADVANCING PAGE-TOP.
```

A second method involved the use of a reserved word PAGE that caused automatic skipping to the first printing position on a new page:

```
WRITE PRINT-LINE
    FROM HEAD-LINE-1.
    AFTER ADVANCING PAGE.
```

Carriage control

Now we are ready to take a deeper look at the ways in which the programmer can exercise better control over print operations. How is this done? Many printers, particularly the older ones, are equipped with a special carriage control tape that is used to control printer spacing. The tape (usually made of paper, although plastic "paper tape" is also available) is laid alongside the printer form, cut to the proper length and the two ends glued together to form a loop (Figure 13-1). The tape loop is then placed onto the carriage control mechanism so that one complete revolution of the tape loop moves one complete page through the printer.

The numbers at the top of the tape refer to tape *channels* 01 through 12, which are used to trigger paper advancing and skipping. A punch in channel *01* (C01) always designates the first printing position or line on the tape. Punches made in any of the channels 02 through 11 designate places on the form to which the programmer can skip. On most printers, skipping to a specific channel punch is faster and more efficient than normal ADVANCING down the page:

```
SPECIAL-NAMES.
    CO1 IS PAGE-TOP.
    CO7 IS FIRST-BODY-LINE.
           .
           .
           .
    WRITE PRINT-LINE
        FROM MAIN-DATA-LINE
        AFTER ADVANCING FIRST-BODY-LINE.
```

Many of the newer printers do not have the traditional carriage control mechanism. Instead, this function may be performed by a cassette tape, floppy disk, or by a programmable microcomputer that is a physical part of the printer. Note that each production program that uses the printer is likely to require its own tape to conform to the required advancing and skipping points on the page. COBOL still allows carriage tape operations on modern printers because of the tens of thousands of old COBOL programs that are still being run using traditional carriage control entries.

FIGURE 13-1

Carriage control tape and printed form

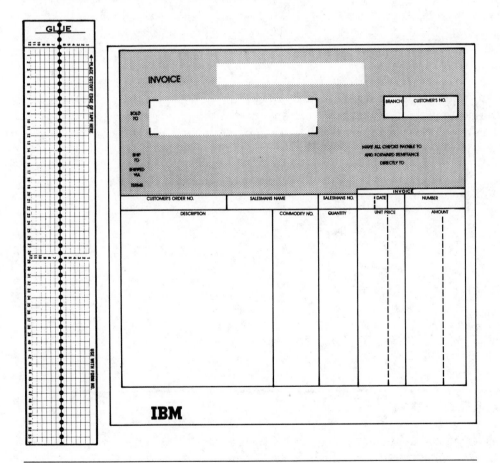

By the way, the entry

    AFTER ADVANCING 0 LINES

is permissible and usually means that normal advancing of one line down the page is suppressed. (On some systems, however, ADVANCING 0 LINES is used to take the programmer to the top of the next page.) Be careful when using zero LINES—overstriking may occur.

A punch in channel 12 designates the last printing line on a page and, when detected by the system, causes (on most printers) the control unit to skip over the page perforations and go to the top of the next page.

In addition, 74 ANS COBOL provides for a check for the end-of-page condition by means of the reserved word END-OF-PAGE, or EOP. (Unfortunately, this option is not often implemented on most versions of COBOL.) The format provides for the END-OF-PAGE test as part of the WRITE statement and is usually implemented through the LINAGE option, which is discussed in the next section.

WRITE record-name [FROM identifier-1]

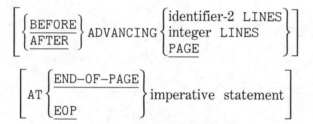

As you can see, end-of-page processing can be a little awkward, particularly since it limits the portability of a program from one machine to another. Most programmers avoid the problem by setting up a line counter and adding to it every time a line is printed. When the counter reaches or exceeds a specific value (usually about 56), the programmer clears the counter, performs the required end-of-page activities and then goes to the top of the next page:

    77 LINE-COUNTER-WS   PIC 99 VALUE ZERO.
         .
         .
         .

    WRITE PRINT-LINE
        AFTER ADVANCING 1 LINE.
    ADD 1 TO LINE-COUNTER-WS.
    IF LINE-COUNTER-WS IS GREATER THAN 56
        PERFORM EOP-ROUTINE.

Using the LINAGE clause

Line counting may appear to be a simple matter, but the method is successful only if the programmer remembers to add the appropriate amount to the line counter *every* time the WRITE statement is used. ANS 1974 COBOL provided an optional way of taking care of the problem by means of the LINAGE clause.

The LINAGE clause is written in the File Description (FD) of the printer file, and its sole purpose is to automatically initialize and increment the line counter.

When LINAGE is used, the system assumes that the printed page is divided into three sections—a top margin, the body of the report (including a *footing* area within the body), and a bottom margin.

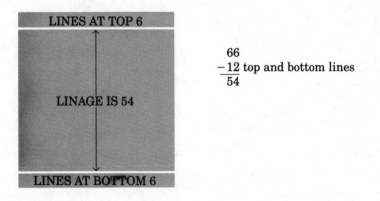

LINAGE entry is the only required entry: the others are optional. Suppose we have a 66-line page and wish to print a multi-page report that does not require any headings. If we wanted one-inch margins (6 lines) at both the top and bottom, our entry would be as follows:

```
FD  PRINT-FILE
    LABEL RECORDS ARE OMITTED
    DATA RECORD IS PRINT-LINE
    LINAGE IS 54
        LINES AT TOP 6
        LINES AT BOTTOM 6.
```

LINES AT TOP 6

LINAGE IS 54

LINES AT BOTTOM 6

$$\begin{array}{r} 66 \\ -12 \text{ top and bottom lines} \\ \hline 54 \end{array}$$

In this illustration, the LINAGE entry tells the system to do the following things.

1. Set up a special line counter called LINAGE-COUNTER (a reserved word) with an initial value of 1. Note that the programmer *cannot* set up this area as it is done automatically by the COBOL software.

2. Automatically add to LINAGE-COUNTER by the appropriate amount each time the WRITE statement is used.

3. If a WRITE statement will cause printing to occur *beyond* the 54 lines of the main body of the report, the system will automatically advance to the top of a new page *before* printing.

Now, let's consider a second example where we want to print headings at the top of each new page. Assume that we need a 1½ inch blank area at the top (9 lines) and 1 inch at the bottom (6 lines). In addition, we will create a 6-line FOOTING area at the end of the body of the report that will be used to trigger the END-OF-PAGE option discussed earlier:

```
FD  PRINT-FILE
    LABEL RECORDS ARE OMITTED
    DATA RECORD IS PRINT-LINE
    LINAGE IS 51 LINES
        WITH FOOTING AT 45
        LINES AT TOP 9
        LINES AT BOTTOM 6.
01  PRINT-LINE      PIC X(121).
```

FIGURE 13-2

LINAGE example

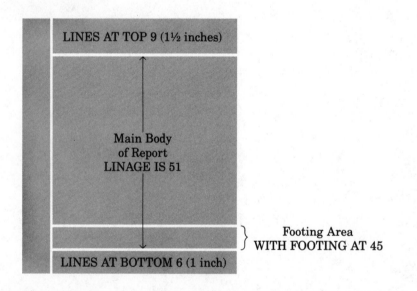

The entry, LINAGE IS 51 LINES, is calculated as follows:

66 lines per page
15 less the blank lines at top and bottom (9 + 6 = 15)
――
51

The WITH FOOTING AT 45 allows us a 6-line area *within* the 51 lines designated above. This area acts as a sort of trigger or warning mechanism. Whenever a WRITE statement causes the LINAGE-COUNTER value to exceed the value stated in the WITH FOOTING entry (45 in our example), the system will generate an END-OF-PAGE condition. Note that this is considerably different from the first example in which the system *automatically* advanced to the top of a new page. With this FOOTING feature, the programmer can utilize the AT END-OF-PAGE option to perform end-of-page activities (such as printing page totals) and to print headings at the top of the new page:

```
          .
          .
          .
      WRITE PRINT-LINE
          FROM MAIN-DATA-LINE
          AFTER ADVANCING 2 LINES
          AT END-OF-PAGE
              PERFORM END-PAGE-ROUTINE.
          .
          .
          .
  END-PAGE-ROUTINE.
      WRITE PRINT-LINE
          FROM PAGE-TOTAL-LINE
              AFTER ADVANCING 2 LINES.
      WRITE PRINT-LINE
          FROM HEADING-LINE
              AFTER ADVANCING PAGE.
```

The Report Writer feature

ANS COBOL contains Report Writer, a module that allows the programmer to produce reports by use of a number of special DATA DIVISION entries and PROCEDURE DIVISION statements. In essence, we are talking about a trade-off of effort. The Report Writer feature requires more coding in the DATA DIVISION but much less in the PROCEDURE DIVISION. Rather than writing the program statements to move or manipulate the data, the programmer describes the physical appearance of the report and lets the system generate the statements (internally) to accomplish the task. Unfortunately, relatively few COBOL compilers support the Report Writer feature for at least three reasons. First, because it imposes an overhead burden on the system. Second, because most programmers are not aware of the power of Report Writer. And third, because a separate language—RPG or Report Program Generator—is often available for just this purpose. In this chapter we will not attempt to cover all the features of Report Writer, but we will examine its highlights.

What can Report Writer do?

Some of the output formats that can be specified are listed below.

1. *Report Headings.* A report heading is a single page of output that is printed once and typically lists the report name, date, for whom prepared, and so on.

2. *Page Headings*. A page heading option causes a page heading to be printed at the top of each page of the report except for the report heading page. In addition, the system will automatically generate and increment a page counter, thus freeing the programmer from this task.

3. *Control Headings*. Control headings are printed at the start of a specified control group. All control headings with the exception of the final control break may appear multiple times on a page.

4. *Body Lines or Detail Lines*. Of all the lines formatted and printed by Report Writer, the body or detail lines of the report are the only lines under control of the programmer. Among the options that can be chosen is GROUP INDICATE, an entry that takes care of the group indication activities discussed in Chapter 7.

5. *Control Footings*. A control footing entry typically summarizes or prints the total of a group of detail lines. You saw this type of output in the section on control breaks. There, you printed minor and/or intermediate control footing totals whenever a break occurred. Final totals are considered to be a special form of control footings.

6. *Page Footings*. So far, you have not seen any page footings in the text, mainly because they are used mainly with long reports. When a report is likely to exceed perhaps 10 pages, the reader may desire that cumulative running totals be printed at the bottom of each page. This helps to give the reader a general sense of perspective as the report progresses.

7. *Report Footing*. A report footing is roughly equivalent to final totals printed at the end of the report. With Report Writer, it is preceded by a page heading and is the last page of the report.

Figure 13-3 identifies these entries in a typical printed report.

Some DATA DIVISION entries

As mentioned earlier, the heart of the Report Writer lies in the DATA DIVISION. The first change occurs in the file description for the print line when the DATA RECORD IS—— entry is replaced by REPORT IS——. Unlike DATA RECORD IS——, which is followed by an 01 entry, REPORT IS *cannot* be followed by any sort of breakdown. Instead, the system, upon seeing REPORT IS, will expect to find a complete description of report lines in a special area within the WORKING-STORAGE SECTION called the REPORT SECTION:

```
FD  PRINTER-FILE
    LABEL RECORDS OMITTED
    REPORT IS SALES-REPORT.
WORKING-STORAGE SECTION.
    .
    .
    .

REPORT SECTION.
RD  SALES-REPORT
    .
    .
    .
```

FIGURE 13-3

General output formats: Report Writer

```
              SUBSCRIPTION REPORT      )    Report
                WESTERN REGION         }    Heading
                  APRIL 19__           )
```

```
              SUBSCRIPTION REPORT
                  APRIL 19__


                                        Page 2      )   Page
                                                    }   Heading
        NAME            ADDRESS         BALANCE   END DATE    )

   JONES, EDWIN    456 19TH ST LODI, CA   $ 43.76   12 31 85  )
   SMITH, SHIRLEY  PO BOX 48 SACTO, CA    $ 19.59   06 15 85  }  Detail
   NEWTON, JOHN    RT 15 RENO, NEV        $107.16   08 30 84  }  Lines
   CARDOZA, RAUL   1004 ELM ST S F, CA    $ 00.00   05 30 83  )
   FONG, ROBERT    274 FIR DR BRYTE, CA   $ 51.91   11 28 83  )


   TOTAL - WESTERN REGION                $222.42    )  Control
                                                    }  Footing
```

```
              SUBSCRIPTION REPORT
                WESTERN REGION
                  APRIL 19__


   TOTAL NUMBER OF SUBSCRIPTIONS          2,835     )   Report
   BALANCE OWED                       $51,316.28    }   Footing
```

The entries within the Report Description area (RD) depend upon the physical layout or format that you want the report to take. The entries that are usually included are listed below.

1. The PAGE LIMIT entry, which specifies the maximum number of lines that will be printed on a page. This entry is required if the report is to have page headings.

   Example:

   ```
   PAGE LIMIT 56 LINES
   ```

2. The line on which the heading is to be printed is specified by the HEADING entry. If we want the heading to start on line 3, we would use the following entry.

   ```
   HEADING 3
   ```

3. The first and last lines on which the detail or body lines of the report will appear are indicated by the FIRST DETAIL and LAST DETAIL entries.

   Example:

   ```
   FIRST DETAIL  8
   LAST DETAIL 42
   ```

Our expanded Report Description is shown below. Note that the period goes at the end of all the entries:

```
RD   SALES-REPORT
     PAGE LIMIT       56 LINES
     HEADING          3
     FIRST DETAIL     8
     LAST DETAIL      42.
```

The entries described so far are relatively simple and straightforward. However, they do not take advantage of the power of Report Writer. The one entry that, perhaps, more than any other, triggers into the more powerful features of the language is one called CONTROL. This entry is made immediately after the RD line and specifies the different levels of controls that can be used in the report. You are already familiar with these from the chapter on control breaks. There you saw that reports frequently make use of minor, intermediate, and major breaks that are initiated by a change of values in control fields. The programmer can name any number of fields on which control breaks are to be based and, in addition, may use the reserved word FINAL to initiate all the appropriate breaks at the end of the report. Control break fields are listed in a hierarchical order from highest to lowest with FINAL being the highest control level possible. In the following example, we are specifying a FINAL total, an intermediate control based on the field called REGION, and a minor control on the field called DEPARTMENT:

```
RD   SALES-REPORT
     CONTROL IS FINAL REGION DEPARTMENT
     .
     .
     .
```

If we wanted just a final total, the entry would simply be:

```
CONTROL IS FINAL
     .
     .
     .
```

There remains, however, one additional item to consider. If we are planning for a final total, then we also have to allow for a place—a FOOTING area—in which it can be printed. The FOOTING entry indicates the first line on which the footing (or totals) will be printed. Our expanded Report Description is shown below:

```
RD   SALES-REPORT
     CONTROL IS FINAL
     PAGE LIMIT       56 LINES
     HEADING          3
     FIRST DETAIL     8
     LAST DETAIL      42
     FOOTING          44.
```

At this point our sample RD entry is complete and we can proceed to describe to Report Writer the exact layout of the lines that will be generated. Each type of line is identified and described in sequence. We will assume that our report does *not* require a separate page for a report heading, so the first item to be described is the PAGE HEADING (which may be abbreviated PH). The reserved word TYPE alerts the system to the nature of the line being described:

```
01  TYPE IS PAGE HEADING.
```

The rest of the description is done much the same as it was in the past but with the additional help of the reserved words LINE and COLUMN:

```
01   TYPE IS PAGE HEADING.
     03   LINE 3.
          05   COLUMN 21     PIC X(12) VALUE 'ABC COMPANY'.
     03   LINE 5.
          05   COLUMN 11     PIC X(10) VALUE 'DEPARTMENT'.
          05   COLUMN 31     PIC X(12) VALUE 'SALES AMOUNT'.
```

The entries above describe a heading line that will be printed on line 3 of the page and that will begin in column 21. The second heading line will be printed on line 5 and each column heading will appear where designated by the COLUMN entry. Although we did not show it, a Report Heading line (REPORT HEADING or RH) would be described in the same way.

The DETAIL lines (may be abbreviated DE) are described much as you have done before when setting up the body line of a report:

```
01  BODY-LINE TYPE DETAIL.
```

At this point we again want to use the LINE entry to specify the lines on which we want the body of the report to be printed. The problem is that, unlike headings that are designated to be printed on a specific line, detail lines will be printed at various places within the body of the report. In addition, we will want to tell the system the type of line spacing that is needed, much like the ADVANCING clause used with the WRITE statement. With Report Writer, this information is conveyed by using LINE PLUS. LINE PLUS 1 indicates single spacing while LINE PLUS 2 indicates double spacing.

Following that, the programmer identifies the columns on which specific data fields are to be printed. The entry must also include PIC (PICTURE) and the reserved word SOURCE, which indicates the origin or source of the data that will be printed. The net effect of these entries is that they replace the series of MOVE statements with which you are so familiar. The two methods are contrasted in Figure 13-4.

We will assume that our incoming data records are from the SALES-DATA file (Chapter 7; BREAK1 program) and have the following format:

```
01   SALES-REC.
     03   FILLER       PIC X(05).
     03   DEPARTMENT   PIC 9(02).
     03   FILLER       PIC X(02).
     03   SALES-AMT    PIC 999V99.
```

FIGURE 13-4

Handling detail lines

Traditional Method

```
01   INPUT-RECORD.
     03   NAME-IN     PIC A(20).
     03   ADDRESS-IN  PIC X(20).
     03   SS-NBR-IN   PIC 9(09).
     .
     .
     .

01   MAIN-BODY-LINE.
     03   FILLER      PIC X.
     03   FILLER      PIC X(5) VALUE SPACES.
     03   NAME-OUT    PIC A(20).
     03   FILLER      PIC X(5) VALUE SPACES.
     03   ADDRESS-OUT PIC X(20).
     03   FILLER      PIC X(5) VALUE SPACES.
     03   SS-NBR-OUT  PIC 9(09).
     .
     .
     .

PROCEDURE DIVISION.
     .
     .
     .

     MOVE NAME-IN    TO  NAME-OUT.
     MOVE ADDRESS-IN TO  ADDRESS-OUT.
     MOVE SS-NBR-IN  TO  SS-NBR-OUT.
     .
     .
     .
```

With Report Writer

```
01   BODY-LINE TYPE DETAIL.
     03   LINE PLUS 2.
          05   COLUMN 6      PIC A(20) SOURCE NAME-IN.
          05   COLUMN 31     PIC X(20) SOURCE ADDRESS-IN.
          05   COLUMN 56     PIC 9(09) SOURCE SS-NBR-IN.
```

The DEPARTMENT and SALES-AMT fields will become the SOURCE fields for the data elements in our detail BODY-LINE:

```
01   BODY-LINE TYPE DETAIL.
     03   LINE PLUS 1.
          05   COLUMN 15   PIC 99 SOURCE DEPARTMENT.
          05   COLUMN 34   PIC $$$$.99 SOURCE SALES-AMT.
```

After describing the detail line(s), the next step is to lay out the control footings and their associated control heading lines. In this case we are not concerned with control breaks, and need only a final total or CONTROL FOOTING (CF) of the SALES-AMT values. Our description follows much the same pattern as before with one exception, which illustrates the nature and power of Report Writer:

```
01   TYPE IS CONTROL FOOTING FINAL.
     03   LINE PLUS 2.
          05   COLUMN 10 PIC X(11) VALUE 'FINAL TOTAL'.
          05   COLUMN 32 PIC $$$$$$.99 SUM SALES-AMT.
          05   COLUMN 43 PIC X(3) VALUE '***'.
```

Note the use of the word SUM. This single entry causes Report Writer to sum the values of the SALES-AMT field as the records are being processed. Not only does Report Writer relieve you of this task that would normally be done in the PROCEDURE DIVISION, it also automatically sets up the work area for the summing process. The complete REPORT SECTION is shown in Figure 13-5.

FIGURE 13-5

Sample Report Writer entries

```
FD   PRINTER-FILE
     LABEL RECORDS ARE OMITTED
     REPORT IS SALES-REPORT.

          .
          .
          .

REPORT SECTION.
RD SALES-REPORT
     CONTROL IS FINAL
     PAGE LIMIT        56 LINES
     HEADING            3
     FIRST DETAIL       8
     LAST DETAIL       42
     FOOTING           44.
01   TYPE IS PAGE HEADING.
     03   LINE 3.
          05   COLUMN 21      PIC X(12) VALUE 'ABC COMPANY'.
     03   LINE 5.
          05   COLUMN 11      PIC X(10) VALUE 'DEPARTMENT'.
          05   COLUMN 32      PIC X(12) VALUE 'SALES AMOUNT'.
01   BODY-LINE TYPE DETAIL.
     03   LINE PLUS 1.
          05   COLUMN 15      PIC 99 SOURCE DEPARTMENT.
          05   COLUMN 34      PIC $$$$.99 SOURCE SALES-AMT.
01   TYPE IS CONTROL FOOTING FINAL.
     03   LINE PLUS 2.
          05   COLUMN 10      PIC (11) VALUE 'FINAL TOTAL'.
          05   COLUMN 32      PIC $$$$$$.99 SUM SALES-AMT.
          05   COLUMN 43      PIC X(3) VALUE '***'.
```

Some PROCEDURE DIVISION entries

In contrast to the DATA DIVISION entries you just experienced, the PROCE-DURE DIVISION entries are quite simple. Three statements are used to activate the Report Writer: INITIATE, GENERATE, and TERMINATE. The formats are:

```
INITIATE report-name
GENERATE data-name
TERMINATE report-name
```

As before, the programmer still must open the appropriate files and perform the priming read operation prior to activating the Report Writer features:

```
PROCEDURE DIVISION.
CONTROL-MODULE.
    PERFORM 010-INITIALIZATION.
       .
       .
       .
010-INITIALIZATION.
    OPEN INPUT SALES-FILE
        OUTPUT PRINTER-FILE.
    INITIATE SALES-REPORT.
    READ SALES-FILE
        AT END MOVE 1 TO EOF-INDICATOR.
```

The INITIATE statement starts the report process and automatically prints a report heading (if specified in the program), the first page heading, and control headings when appropriate. It also resets all page and line counters prior to starting the report.

The GENERATE statement is used within the program loop to process detail lines. If control breaks are specified in the DATA DIVISION entries, Report Writer will automatically generate the specified control footing prior to processing the next detail line:

```
CONTROL-MODULE.
    PERFORM 010-INITIALIZATION.
    PERFORM 020-READ-AND-PRINT
        UNTIL EOF-INDICATOR = 1.
       .
       .
       .
020-READ-AND-PRINT.
    GENERATE BODY-LINE.
    READ SALES-FILE
        AT END MOVE 1 TO EOF-INDICATOR.
```

Note that "hidden" within the GENERATE statement is the summing or totaling process as indicated by the word SUM in the DATA DIVISION entry for the CONTROL FOOTING line.

The TERMINATE statement ends the execution of the Report Writer features by producing the necessary control breaks (if specified in the DATA DIVISION) at this point, along with FINAL control footings. However, the TERMINATE statement does not CLOSE the files—this must be done by the programmer in a separate statement. Figure 13-6 shows our complete program.

FIGURE 13-6

Report Writer program

```
000100 IDENTIFICATION DIVISION.
000110 PROGRAM-ID.  RW1.
000120**********************************
000130*                              *
000140*     SAMPLE REPORT WRITER      *
000150*                              *
000160**********************************
000170*
000180 ENVIRONMENT DIVISION.
000190 CONFIGURATION SECTION.
000200 SOURCE-COMPUTER. - - - -.
000210 OBJECT-COMPUTER. - - - -.
000220 INPUT-OUTPUT SECTION.
000230 FILE-CONTROL.
000240     SELECT SALES-FILE ASSIGN TO - - - -.
000250     SELECT PRINTER-FILE ASSIGN TO - - - -.
000260*
000270 DATA DIVISION.
000280 FILE SECTION.
000290 FD  SALES-FILE
000300     LABEL RECORD IS STANDARD
000310     VALUE OF FILE-ID IS 'SALES-DATA'
000320     DATA RECORD IS SALES-REC.
000330 01  SALES-REC.
000340     03  FILLER              PIC X(05).
000350     03  DEPARTMENT          PIC 9(02).
000360     03  FILLER              PIC X(02).
000370     03  SALES-AMT           PIC 999V99.
000380 FD  PRINTER-FILE
000390     LABEL RECORD IS OMITTED
000400     REPORT IS SALES-REPORT.
000410 WORKING-STORAGE SECTION.
000420 01  MISC-FIELDS.
000430     03  EOF-INDICATOR       PIC 9 VALUE ZERO.
000440 REPORT SECTION.
000450 RD  SALES-REPORT
000460     CONTROL IS FINAL
000470     PAGE LIMIT          56 LINES
000480     HEADING              3
000490     FIRST DETAIL         8
000500     LAST DETAIL         42
000510     FOOTING             44.
000520 01  TYPE IS PAGE HEADING.
000530     03  LINE 3.
000540         05  COLUMN 21       PIC X(12) VALUE 'ABC COMPANY'.
000550     03  LINE 5.
000560         05  COLUMN 11       PIC X(10) VALUE 'DEPARTMENT'.
000570         05  COLUMN 31       PIC X(12) VALUE 'SALES AMOUNT'.
```

---

continued

FIGURE 13-6

continued

```
000580 01   BODY-LINE TYPE DETAIL.
000590      03   LINE PLUS 1.
000600           05   COLUMN 15       PIC 99 SOURCE DEPARTMENT.
000610           05   COLUMN 34       PIC $$$$.99 SOURCE SALES-AMT.
000620 01   TYPE IS CONTROL FOOTING FINAL.
000630      03   LINE PLUS 2.
000640           05   COLUMN 10       PIC X(11) VALUE 'FINAL TOTAL'.
000650           05   COLUMN 32       PIC $$$$$$.99 SUM SALES-AMT.
000660           05   COLUMN 43       PIC X(03) VALUE '***'.
000670*
000680 PROCEDURE DIVISION.
000690 CONTROL-MODULE.
000700      PERFORM 010-INITIALIZATION.
000710      PERFORM 020-READ-AND-PRINT
000720           UNTIL EOF-INDICATOR = 1.
000730      PERFORM 030-END-ROUTINE.
000740      STOP RUN.
000750 010-INITIALIZATION.
000760      OPEN INPUT SALES-FILE
000770           OUTPUT PRINTER-FILE.
000780      INITIATE SALES-REPORT.
000790      READ SALES-FILE
000800           AT END MOVE 1 TO EOF-INDICATOR.
000810 020-READ-AND-PRINT.
000820      GENERATE BODY-LINE.
000830      READ SALES-FILE
000840           AT END MOVE 1 TO EOF-INDICATOR.
000850 030-END-ROUTINE.
000860      TERMINATE SALES-REPORT.
000870      CLOSE SALES-FILE PRINTER-FILE.
```

```
                ABC   COMPANY
DEPARTMENT             SALES AMOUNT

     01                    $594.60
     01                    $483.25
     02                    $916.64
     02                    $742.81
     03                    $533.86
     05                    $759.95
     05                    $261.04
     09                    $360.00
     12                    $926.17
     12                    $593.01
     12                    $600.00

FINAL TOTAL               $6771.33
```

More DATA DIVISION entries

As mentioned earlier, Report Writer has a great many features, and only the BASIC ones were covered in the previous section. However, there are a few more options that are quite powerful and that you should know about.

If you recall, we mentioned that the software provides for various levels of control breaks and all the activities that are associated with control totals. In the previous example you saw how the system can be made to accumulate a grand total and print this at the end of the report. Now, let's see how Report Writer would handle minor and intermediate totals in addition to a final total.

Figure 13-7 is a duplicate of the output from the intermediate totals program that appeared in Chapter 7 (Figure 7-12).

Let's set up Report Writer to produce similar output. The first change would occur in the CONTROL entry of the Report Description where we will list (from highest to lowest) the fields on which the breaks are to be based:

```
RD   SALES-REPORT
     CONTROL IS FINAL TERRITORY DEPARTMENT
```

The entry above "says" that there will be a final total plus an intermediate break based on the TERRITORY field and a minor break based on the DEPARTMENT field. (We will assume both of these fields are in the incoming data record.) Right after the description of the DETAIL line we will set up a CONTROL FOOTING (CF) for each of the two levels of breaks:

```
01   BODY-LINE TYPE DETAIL.
     03   LINE PLUS 1.
          05   COLUMN 8    PIC 999 SOURCE IS TERRITORY.
          05   COLUMN 25   PIC 99 SOURCE IS DEPARTMENT.
          05   COLUMN 40   PIC $$$$.99 SOURCE IS SALES-AMT.
01   INT-LINE TYPE CONTROL FOOTING TERRITORY.
     03   LINE PLUS 2.
          05   COLUMN 15   PIC X(15) VALUE
                                'TERRITORY TOTAL'.
          05   COLUMN 38   PIC $(6).99 SUM SALES-AMT
                                RESET ON TERRITORY.
          05   COLUMN 49   PIC XX VALUE '**'.
01   MINOR-LINE TYPE CONTROL FOOTING DEPARTMENT.
     03   LINE PLUS 2.
          05   COLUMN 15   PIC X(16) VALUE 'DEPARTMENT TOTAL'.
          05   COLUMN 39   PIC $(5).99 SUM SALES-AMT
                                RESET ON DEPARTMENT.
          05   COLUMN 49   PIC X VALUE '*'.
01   TYPE IS CONTROL FOOTING FINAL.
     03   LINE PLUS 2.
          05   COLUMN 15   PIC X(11) VALUE 'FINAL TOTAL'.
          05   COLUMN 37   PIC $(7).99 SUM SALES-AMT.
          05   COLUMN 49   PIC XXX VALUE '***'.
```

FIGURE 13-7

Output: Intermediate break program

TERRITORY	DEPARTMENT	SALES AMOUNT
415	01	$594.60
415	01	$483.25
	MINOR TOTAL	$1077.85 *
415	02	$916.64
415	02	$742.81
	MINOR TOTAL	$1659.45 *
	INTERMEDIATE TOTAL	$2737.30 **
621	03	$533.86
	MINOR TOTAL	$533.86 *
621	05	$759.95
621	05	$261.04
	MINOR TOTAL	$1020.99 *
	INTERMEDIATE TOTAL	$1554.85 **
643	09	$360.00
	MINOR TOTAL	$360.00 *
	INTERMEDIATE TOTAL	$360.00 **
789	12	$926.17
789	12	$593.01
789	12	$600.00
	MINOR TOTAL	$2119.18 *
	INTERMEDIATE TOTAL	$2119.18 **
	FINAL TOTAL	$6771.33

The key entries that trigger Report Writer's control break software are the reserved words CONTROL FOOTING and RESET. CONTROL FOOTING "tells" the system to prepare for a control break based on a specified field (TERRITORY). As discussed earlier, the SUM entry causes the system to sum the SALES-AMT values for each record that is processed. The difficulty is that we want the summing process to stop whenever a control break is encountered. Just as we did in Chapter 7, we want the system to roll the sum into the next highest accumulator and then reset the lower-level accumulator back to zero, prior to processing the next detail record. Of course, that is exactly what the CONTROL FOOTING, SUM, and RESET entries accomplish.

Group indication is specified by the GROUP INDICATE entry in the description of the detail line. It may be used on any field to suppress the printing of duplicate control field values. In our previous example we could have group indicated either or both the TERRITORY and DEPARTMENT fields:

```
01   BODY-LINE TYPE DETAIL.
     03   LINE PLUS 1.
          05   COLUMN 8     PIC 999 SOURCE IS TERRITORY
                                GROUP INDICATE.
          05   COLUMN 25    PIC 99 SOURCE IS DEPARTMENT
                                GROUP INDICATE.
          05   COLUMN 40    PIC $$$$.99 SOURCE IS SALES-AMT.
```

COMMON ERRORS

One potential source of error has already been mentioned, but bears repeating. The LINAGE-COUNTER field is set up by the COBOL system software when the LINAGE IS entry is detected in the file description. Therefore, it is *incorrect* for you to do the following:

```
77   LINAGE-COUNTER     PIC 99 VALUE ZERO.
```

Your program *cannot* in any way modify this field through the use of ADD, SUBTRACT, MOVE, and so on. However, you can *access* the value that is contained in LINAGE-COUNTER. For example, under certain circumstances you may wish to initiate a middle-of-the-page routine when the LINAGE-COUNTER reaches a specific value or range:

```
IF LINAGE-COUNTER IS EQUAL TO 30
     PERFORM CENTER-OF-PAGE-PROCESSING.
```

or

```
IF LINAGE-COUNTER IS GREATER THAN 25
     AND LINAGE-COUNTER IS LESS THAN 30
          PERFORM CENTER-OF-PAGE-PROCESSING.
```

An additional item to be considered is that, if a FOOTING area is designated, it must be of a size such that regular spacing cannot go completely through it into the LINES AT BOTTOM area. Depending upon how you have your program set up, this could trigger an advance to the top of the next page before you are ready.

As to Report Writer, relatively few execution errors are likely to be made since the bulk of the effort occurs in the DATA DIVISION. In theory, any errors would be caught during compilation. One point to be aware of is that even though Report Writer is functional on your computer, all the features may not be included. For example, the GROUP INDICATE feature is sometimes omitted, which means that you will have to program around the problem.

PROGRAMMING TIPS

As you know, this chapter deals with special mechanisms available in some versions of COBOL that relieve the programmer of a few of the chores associated with turning out nice-looking reports. As reports get more and more complicated—with formats that include page headings, group and detail printing, group indication, page footings or totals, and so on—it becomes imperative that you prepare very accurate, complete, and neat documentation. Don't be hesitant about using preprinted printer spacing charts. Be extremely neat; print and count the lines and spaces very carefully. If you are using your own line counter, be sure to account for every line, including blank lines and special lines that are generated only under error conditions. The extra time spent on these details at the beginning really pays off in the end when time may be less plentiful.

SELF-STUDY: QUESTIONS AND ANSWERS

1. I am not sure I understand what the FOOTING entry does when you are using LINAGE IS.

   Answer: It is a little confusing at first, but perhaps another look at the FOOTING entry will help. The FOOTING entry is not required. If it is omitted, the system will automatically generate an advance to the first printing line on the next page, whenever a WRITE statement starts to print in the LINES AT BOTTOM area. This, of course, is exactly what you want the system to do—*not* print in that area. Note that the system checks the LINAGE-COUNTER before printing, to see if it will go into that area.

Leaving out the FOOTING entry is fine, as long as you do not need to print totals or any other ending material on that page *before* being sent to the top of the new page. By specifying WITH FOOTING AT, you designate an area at the end of the main body area that, upon being entered by the LINAGE-COUNTER value, triggers the internal END-OF-PAGE indicator used by the system. This works to your advantage, because it gives you a mechanism that allows you to perform an end-of-page and/or a new-page heading routine gracefully.

2. I understand the general nature of the DATA DIVISION entries for Report Writer, but one thing puzzles me. When you specify more than one control footing, how does the system know which is the minor or intermediate or major control?

Answer: Fortunately, the answer to that is fairly easy. Remember that the format for the control entry specifies that the items be entered according to a *hierarchical* structure with the highest named first. Thus, if we said

```
CONTROL IS FINAL DEPARTMENT
```

DEPARTMENT would be considered to be the minor control field. If we had said

```
CONTROL IS FINAL TERRITORY DEPARTMENT
```

then TERRITORY is the intermediate control field and DEPARTMENT is the minor control.

3. Can Report Writer be used along with regular COBOL programming?

Answer: Yes, it can, but it may not always be practical to do so. As the name indicates, Report Writer is particularly useful when you are required to prepare reports that require relatively little file and/or data manipulation. Therefore, the use of Report Writer is often limited to a general class of problems that involve control breaks and totals. Beyond that, you must also realize that many, if not most, COBOL programmers are not familiar with Report Writer. To further complicate the problem, relatively few systems have the Report Writer software. This means that, as advantageous as Report Writer is, it is not as portable (from one system to another) as is straight COBOL code.

CHAPTER TERMS

CARRIAGE CONTROL
carriage control tape
channels 01 through 12 (carriage control)
COLUMN
CONTROL
Control Breaks
Control Footings (CF)
Control Headings (CH)
counting lines
DETAIL (DE)
Detail Lines
END-OF-PAGE
EOP (END-OF-PAGE)
FINAL
FIRST DETAIL
Footings
GENERATE
GROUP INDICATE
HEADING

INITIATE
LAST DETAIL
LINAGE
LINAGE-COUNTER
LINE; LINE PLUS
PAGE
Page Footings (PF)
Page Headings (PH)
PAGE LIMIT
Report Footing (RF)
Report Headings (RH)
REPORT IS
REPORT SECTION
Report Writer
RESET
SOURCE
SPECIAL-NAMES
SUM
WITH FOOTING

EXERCISES

1. What entries in the file description are used to split a report page into three sections?

2. With Report Writer, the statement LINE PLUS _____ gives double line spacing.

3. What reserved word does the same as MOVE when using Report Writer?

4. What three statements activate Report Writer?

5. Write the *complete* FD entry for the following situations that use LINAGE.
   a. PRINTER-FILE; PRINT-REC; 66-line page; 3 lines at the top; 6 lines at the bottom; no footing.
   b. PRINTER-FILE; PRINT-REC; 66-line page; 3 lines at the top; 6 lines at the bottom; with a footing area of 3 lines.
   c. OUTPUT-FILE; PRINTER-REC; 88-line page; 8 lines at the top; 8 lines at the bottom; no footing.
   d. OUTPUT-FILE; PRINTER-REC; 88-line page; 16 lines at the top; 8 lines at the bottom; with an 8-line footing area.

6. Write the Report Description entries based on the following information:
   a. RD DATA-REPORT
      One control field (FIELD-A); no FINAL total; 56 printing lines; a heading will appear on line 5; the first and last detail lines are 7 and 43; no footing.
   b. RD SALES-REPORT
      Three control fields (COUNTRY, REGION, STATE) plus a FINAL total; 60 print lines; heading will start on line 6; the first and last detail lines will be on lines 12 and 50; footing at line 55.

7. Make up page heading entries (centered) for a 120-character line based on the following information:
   (line 4)   GISMO COMPANY
   (line 6)   INVENTORY REPORT FOR (current month)
   (line 8)   PART NAME/STOCK NUMBER/BIN NUMBER/QUANTITY

8. Make up detail line entries based on the following information:
   a. Line name is STUB; double spacing;
      column 16 source is PART-NAME—20 characters;
      column 42 source is STOCK-NUMBER—8 digits;
      column 60 source is BIN-NUMBER—4 digits;
      column 75 source is QUANTITY-ON-HAND—6 digits.
   b. Line name is PAY-LINE; single spacing;
      column 15 source is SS-NBR—9 digits;
      column 30 source is EMP-NAME—20 alphabetic characters;
      column 60 source is GROSS-PAY—7 digits, dollars and cents, edited;
      column 70 source is DEDUCTIONS—6 digits, dollars and cents, edited;
      column 80 source is NET-PAY—7 digits, dollars and cents, edited.
   c. Line name is SALES; single spacing;
      column 12 source is REGION—3 digits;
      column 20 source is AREA-CODE—4 digits;
      column 32 source is SALES-FIGURES—6 digits, dollars and cents.

9. Write the control footing entry based on the information provided by Exercise 8c. Assume that REGION is the minor control field and sum the SALES-FIGURES on this basis. Use double spacing.

10. Modify Exercise 9 above to provide for an intermediate control footing based on REGION, and a minor control footing based on AREA-CODE. Use double spacing for the minor break and triple spacing for the intermediate break.

    Also, include a FINAL control footing that prints the total of the SALES-FIGURES values. Double space. Use the caption "REPORT TOTALS" and print two asterisks before the total sales figure.

11. Make up a FINAL control footing line based on the information from Exercise 8b. Provide for the print of totals from the GROSS-PAY, DEDUCTIONS, and NET-PAY fields after double spacing.

Appendixes

Appendix A.   COBOL **reserved words**

ACCEPT
ACCESS
ADD
ADVANCING
AFTER
ALL
ALPHABETIC
ALSO
ALTER
ALTERNATE
AND
ARE
AREA
AREAS
ASCENDING
ASSIGN
AT
AUTHOR

BEFORE
BLANK
BLOCK
BOTTOM
BY

CALL
CANCEL
CD
CF
CH
CHARACTER
CHARACTERS
CLOCK-UNITS
CLOSE
COBOL
CODE
CODE-SET
COLLATING
COLUMN
COMMA
COMMUNICATION
COMP
COMPUTATIONAL
COMPUTE
CONFIGURATION
CONTAINS
CONTROL
CONTROLS
COPY
CORR
CORRESPONDING
COUNT
CURRENCY

DATA
DATE
DATE-COMPILED
DATE-WRITTEN
DAY
DE
DEBUG-CONTENTS
DEBUG-ITEM
DEBUG-LINE
DEBUG-NAME
DEBUG-SUB-1
DEBUG-SUB-2
DEBUG-SUB-3
DEBUGGING
DECIMAL-POINT
DECLARATIVES
DELETE
DELIMITED
DELIMITER
DEPENDING
DESCENDING
DESTINATION
DETAIL
DISABLE
DISPLAY
DIVIDE
DIVISION
DOWN
DUPLICATES
DYNAMIC

EGI
ELSE
EMI
ENABLE
END
END-OF-PAGE
ENTER
ENVIRONMENT
EOP
EQUAL
ERROR
ESI
EVERY
EXCEPTION
EXIT
EXTEND

FD
FILE
FILE-CONTROL
FILLER
FINAL

FIRST
FOOTING
FOR
FROM

GENERATE
GIVING
GO
GREATER
GROUP

HEADING
HIGH-VALUE
HIGH-VALUES

I-O
I-O-CONTROL
IDENTIFICATION
IF
IN
INDEX
INDEXED
INDICATE
INITIAL
INITIATE
INPUT
INPUT-OUTPUT
INSPECT
INSTALLATION
INTO
INVALID
IS

JUST
JUSTIFIED

KEY

LABEL
LAST
LEADING
LEFT
LENGTH
LESS
LIMIT
LIMITS
LINAGE
LINAGE-COUNTER
LINE
LINE-COUNTER
LINES
LINKAGE
LOCK

LOW-VALUE
LOW-VALUES

MEMORY
MERGE
MESSAGE
MODE
MODULES
MOVE
MULTIPLE
MULTIPLY

NATIVE
NEGATIVE
NEXT
NOT
NUMBER
NUMERIC

OBJECT-COMPUTER
OCCURS
OMITTED
OPEN
OPTIONAL
ORGANIZATION
OVERFLOW

PAGE
PAGE-COUNTER
PERFORM
PIC
PICTURE
PLUS
POINTER
POSITION
POSITIVE
PRINTING
PROCEDURE
PROCEDURES
PROCEED
PROGRAM
PROGRAM-ID

QUEUE
QUOTE
QUOTES

RANDOM
READ
RECEIVE
RECORD
RECORDS
REDEFINES
REEL
REFERENCES
RELATIVE
RELEASE
REMAINDER
REMOVAL
RENAMES
REPLACING
REPORT
REPORTING
REPORTS
RERUN
RESERVE
RESET
RETURN
REVERSED
REWIND
REWRITE
RIGHT
ROUNDED
RUN

SAME
SEARCH
SECTION
SECURITY
SELECT
SEND
SENTENCE
SEPARATE
SEQUENCE
SEQUENTIAL
SET
SIGN
SIZE
SORT
SORT-MERGE
SOURCE
SOURCE-COMPUTER
SPACE
SPACES
SPECIAL-NAMES

STANDARD
STANDARD-1
START
STATUS
STRING
SUB-QUEUE-1
SUB-QUEUE-2
SUB-QUEUE-3
SUBTRACT
SUM
SUPPRESS
SYMBOLIC
SYNC
SYNCHRONIZED

TABLE
TALLYING
TAPE
TERMINAL
TERMINATE
TEXT
THAN
THROUGH
THRU
TIME
TIMES
TOP
TRAILING
TYPE

UNIT
UNSTRING
UNTIL
UPON
USAGE
USE
USING

VALUE
VALUES
VARYING

WHEN
WITH
WORDS
WORKING-STORAGE

ZERO
ZEROES
ZEROS

Appendix B. COBOL **format notation**

This appendix contains a general format summary of the valid statements in COBOL. It is not intended to be a complete list of all COBOL entries, but it does include the most commonly used features of the language. For a complete list of the valid entries on a particular machine you should check the appropriate COBOL specification manual.

The notation for the reference formats is as follows:

1. Words printed in capital letters are reserved words.
2. Underlined reserved words are required unless that portion of the entry is optional.
3. Lowercase words are terms supplied by the programmer.
4. Brackets [ ] indicate optional entries.
5. Braces { } indicate alternative features, one of which may be chosen.
6. Ellipses (. . .) indicate repetition of part of the entry.

Formats for the IDENTIFICATION DIVISION

```
IDENTIFICATION DIVISION.
PROGRAM-ID. program-name.
[AUTHOR. [comment-entry] . . . ]
[INSTALLATION. [comment-entry] . . . ]
[DATE-WRITTEN. [comment-entry] . . . ]
[DATE-COMPILED. [comment-entry] . . . ]
[SECURITY. [comment-entry] . . . ]
```

Formats for the ENVIRONMENT DIVISION

```
ENVIRONMENT DIVISION.
CONFIGURATION SECTION.
SOURCE-COMPUTER. computer-name [WITH DEBUGGING MODE] .
OBJECT-COMPUTER. computer-name
SPECIAL-NAMES. implementor-name is mnemonic-name
INPUT-OUTPUT SECTION.
FILE-CONTROL.
```

Format 1:

```
SELECT [OPTIONAL] file-name
    ASSIGN TO implementor-name-1 [, implementor-name-2] . . .

    [; RESERVE integer-1 [ AREA  ] ]
                        [ AREAS ]

    [; ORGANIZATION is SEQUENTIAL]

    [; ACCESS MODE IS SEQUENTIAL].
```

Format 2:

```
SELECT file-name
    ASSIGN TO implementor-name-1 [, implementor-name-2] . . .
```

$$\left[; \underline{\text{RESERVE}}\,\text{integer-1}\begin{bmatrix}\text{AREA}\\\text{AREAS}\end{bmatrix}\right]$$

```
    ; ORGANIZATION IS RELATIVE
```

$$\left[; \underline{\text{ACCESS}}\ \text{MODE IS}\left\{\begin{array}{ll}\underline{\text{SEQUENTIAL}}&[, \underline{\text{RELATIVE}}\ \text{KEY IS data-name-1}]\\\left\{\begin{array}{l}\underline{\text{RANDOM}}\\\underline{\text{DYNAMIC}}\end{array}\right\}&, \underline{\text{RELATIVE}}\ \text{KEY IS data-name-1}\end{array}\right\}\right].$$

Format 3:

```
SELECT file-name
    ASSIGN TO implementor-name-1 [, implementor-name-2] . . .
```

$$\left[; \underline{\text{RESERVE}}\,\text{integer-1}\begin{bmatrix}\text{AREA}\\\text{AREAS}\end{bmatrix}\right]$$

```
    ; ORGANIZATION IS INDEXED
```

$$\left[; \underline{\text{ACCESS}}\ \text{MODE IS}\left\{\begin{array}{l}\underline{\text{SEQUENTIAL}}\\\underline{\text{RANDOM}}\\\underline{\text{DYNAMIC}}\end{array}\right\}\right]$$

```
    ; RECORD KEY IS data-name-1
[; ALTERNATE RECORD KEY IS data-name-2 [WITH DUPLICATES]] . . .
```

Formats for the DATA DIVISION

```
DATA DIVISION.
FILE SECTION.
FD  file-name
```

$$\left[; \underline{\text{BLOCK}}\ \text{CONTAINS}\,[\text{integer-1}\ \underline{\text{TO}}]\,\text{integer-2}\left\{\begin{array}{l}\underline{\text{RECORDS}}\\\underline{\text{CHARACTERS}}\end{array}\right\}\right]$$

```
[; RECORD CONTAINS [integer-3 TO] integer-4 CHARACTERS]
```

$$; \underline{\text{LABEL}}\left\{\begin{array}{l}\underline{\text{RECORD}}\ \text{IS}\\\underline{\text{RECORDS}}\ \text{ARE}\end{array}\right\}\left\{\begin{array}{l}\underline{\text{STANDARD}}\\\underline{\text{OMITTED}}\end{array}\right\}$$

$$\left[; \underline{\text{VALUE}}\ \underline{\text{OF}}\ \text{implementor-name-1 IS}\left\{\begin{array}{l}\text{data-name-1}\\\text{literal-1}\end{array}\right\}\right.$$

$$\left.\left[, \text{implementor-name-2 IS}\left\{\begin{array}{l}\text{data-name-2}\\\text{literal-2}\end{array}\right\}\right]\ .\ .\ .\ \right]$$

$$\left[; \underline{\text{DATA}}\left\{\begin{array}{l}\underline{\text{RECORD}}\ \text{IS}\\\underline{\text{RECORDS}}\ \text{ARE}\end{array}\right\}\text{data-name-3}\,[, \text{data-name-4}]\ .\ .\ .\ \right]$$

```
            record description entry
SD  file-name

    [; RECORD CONTAINS [integer-1 TO] integer-2 CHARACTERS]

    ⎡      ⎧RECORD IS   ⎫                                ⎤
    ⎢; DATA⎨            ⎬ data-name-1 [, data-name-2] . . .⎥ .
    ⎣      ⎩RECORDS ARE ⎭                                ⎦

            record description entry

⎡01  record-name
⎢02-49 record description entry
⎣ WORKING-STORAGE SECTION.

⎡77-level-description-entry⎤
⎢record-description-entry  ⎥ . . .
⎣                         ⎦
```

Formats for data description entries

Format 1:

```
                ⎧data-name-1⎫
level-number    ⎨           ⎬
                ⎩FILLER     ⎭

    [; REDEFINES data-name-2]

    ⎡  ⎧PICTURE⎫                      ⎤
    ⎢; ⎨       ⎬ IS character-string  ⎥
    ⎣  ⎩PIC    ⎭                      ⎦

    ⎡               ⎧COMPUTATIONAL⎫ ⎤
    ⎢               ⎪COMP         ⎪ ⎥
    ⎢; [USAGE IS]   ⎨DISPLAY      ⎬ ⎥
    ⎣               ⎩INDEX        ⎭ ⎦

    ⎡             ⎧LEADING ⎫                      ⎤
    ⎢; [SIGN IS]  ⎨        ⎬ [SEPARATE CHARACTER] ⎥
    ⎣             ⎩TRAILING⎭                      ⎦

    ⎡         ⎧integer-1 TO integer-2 TIMES DEPENDING ON data-name-3⎫
    ⎢; OCCURS ⎨                                                     ⎬
    ⎣         ⎩integer-2 TIMES                                      ⎭

            ⎡⎧ASCENDING ⎫                                  ⎤
            ⎢⎨          ⎬ KEY IS data-name-4 [, data-name-5] . . . ⎥ . . .
            ⎣⎩DESCENDING⎭                                  ⎦

            [INDEXED BY index-name-1 [, index-name-2] . . .]⎤
```

$$\left[; \left\{\begin{array}{l}\underline{\text{SYNCHRONIZED}}\\\underline{\text{SYNC}}\end{array}\right\} \left[\begin{array}{l}\underline{\text{LEFT}}\\\underline{\text{RIGHT}}\end{array}\right]\right]$$

$$\left[; \left\{\begin{array}{l}\underline{\text{JUSTIFIED}}\\\underline{\text{JUST}}\end{array}\right\} \text{RIGHT}\right]$$

[; <u>BLANK</u> WHEN <u>ZERO</u>]

[; <u>VALUE</u> IS literal].

Format 2:

$$66 \quad \text{data-name-1;} \ \underline{\text{RENAMES}} \ \text{data-name-2} \left[\left\{\begin{array}{l}\underline{\text{THROUGH}}\\\underline{\text{THRU}}\end{array}\right\} \text{data-name-3}\right].$$

Format 3:

$$88 \quad \text{condition-name;} \left\{\begin{array}{l}\underline{\text{VALUE}} \text{ IS}\\\underline{\text{VALUES}} \text{ ARE}\end{array}\right\} \text{literal-1} \left[\left\{\begin{array}{l}\underline{\text{THROUGH}}\\\underline{\text{THRU}}\end{array}\right\} \text{literal-2}\right]$$

$$\left[, \text{literal-3} \left[\left\{\begin{array}{l}\underline{\text{THROUGH}}\\\underline{\text{THRU}}\end{array}\right\} \text{literal-4}\right]\right] \ . \ . \ . \ .$$

Formats for the PROCEDURE DIVISION

<u>ACCEPT</u> identifier [<u>FROM</u> mnemonic-name]

$$\underline{\text{ACCEPT}} \ \text{identifier} \ \underline{\text{FROM}} \left\{\begin{array}{l}\underline{\text{DATE}}\\\underline{\text{DAY}}\\\underline{\text{TIME}}\end{array}\right\}$$

$$\underline{\text{ADD}} \left\{\begin{array}{l}\text{identifier-1}\\\text{literal-1}\end{array}\right\} \left[\begin{array}{l}, \text{identifier-2}\\, \text{literal-2}\end{array}\right] \ . \ . \ . \ \underline{\text{TO}} \ \text{identifier-m} \ [\underline{\text{ROUNDED}}]$$

[, identifier-n [<u>ROUNDED</u>]] . . . [; ON <u>SIZE</u> <u>ERROR</u> imperative-statement]

$$\underline{\text{ADD}} \left\{\begin{array}{l}\text{identifier-1}\\\text{literal-1}\end{array}\right\}, \left\{\begin{array}{l}\text{identifier-2}\\\text{literal-2}\end{array}\right\} \left[\begin{array}{l}, \text{identifier-3}\\, \text{literal-3}\end{array}\right] \ . \ . \ .$$

<u>GIVING</u> identifier-m [<u>ROUNDED</u>] [, identifier-n [<u>ROUNDED</u>]] . . .

[; ON <u>SIZE</u> <u>ERROR</u> imperative-statement]

$$\underline{\text{ADD}} \left\{\begin{array}{l}\underline{\text{CORRESPONDING}}\\\underline{\text{CORR}}\end{array}\right\} \text{identifier-1} \ \underline{\text{TO}} \ \text{identifier-2} \ [\underline{\text{ROUNDED}}]$$

[; ON <u>SIZE</u> <u>ERROR</u> imperative-statement]

$$\underline{\text{CLOSE}} \ \text{file-name-1} \left\{\begin{array}{l}\underline{\text{REEL}}\\\underline{\text{UNIT}}\end{array}\right\} \left[\text{WITH} \left\{\begin{array}{l}\underline{\text{NO REWIND}}\\\underline{\text{LOCK}}\end{array}\right\}\right] \ . \ . \ .$$

<u>COMPUTE</u> identifier-1 [<u>ROUNDED</u>] [, identifier-2 [<u>ROUNDED</u>]] . . .

= arithmetic-expression [; ON <u>SIZE</u> <u>ERROR</u> imperative-statement]

<u>DISPLAY</u> $\begin{Bmatrix} \text{identifier-1} \\ \text{literal-1} \end{Bmatrix}$ $\begin{bmatrix} \text{, identifier-2} \\ \text{, literal-2} \end{bmatrix}$ . . . [<u>UPON</u> mnemonic-name]

<u>DIVIDE</u> $\begin{Bmatrix} \text{identifier-1} \\ \text{literal-1} \end{Bmatrix}$ <u>INTO</u> identifier-2 [<u>ROUNDED</u>]

[, identifier-3 [<u>ROUNDED</u>]] . . . [; ON <u>SIZE</u> <u>ERROR</u> imperative-statement]

<u>DIVIDE</u> $\begin{Bmatrix} \text{identifier-1} \\ \text{literal-1} \end{Bmatrix}$ <u>INTO</u> $\begin{Bmatrix} \text{identifier-2} \\ \text{literal-2} \end{Bmatrix}$ <u>GIVING</u> identifier-3 [<u>ROUNDED</u>]

[, identifier-4 [<u>ROUNDED</u>]] . . . [; ON <u>SIZE</u> <u>ERROR</u> imperative-statement]

<u>DIVIDE</u> $\begin{Bmatrix} \text{identifier-1} \\ \text{literal-1} \end{Bmatrix}$ <u>BY</u> $\begin{Bmatrix} \text{identifier-2} \\ \text{literal-2} \end{Bmatrix}$ <u>GIVING</u> identifier-3 [<u>ROUNDED</u>]

[, identifier-4 [<u>ROUNDED</u>]] . . . [; on <u>SIZE</u> <u>ERROR</u> imperative-statement]

<u>DIVIDE</u> $\begin{Bmatrix} \text{identifier-1} \\ \text{literal-1} \end{Bmatrix}$ <u>INTO</u> $\begin{Bmatrix} \text{identifier-2} \\ \text{literal-2} \end{Bmatrix}$ <u>GIVING</u> identifier-3 [<u>ROUNDED</u>]

<u>REMAINDER</u> identifier-4 [; ON <u>SIZE</u> <u>ERROR</u> imperative-statement]

<u>DIVIDE</u> $\begin{Bmatrix} \text{identifier-1} \\ \text{literal-1} \end{Bmatrix}$ <u>BY</u> $\begin{Bmatrix} \text{identifier-2} \\ \text{literal-2} \end{Bmatrix}$ <u>GIVING</u> identifier-3 [<u>ROUNDED</u>]

<u>REMAINDER</u> identifier-4 [; ON <u>SIZE</u> <u>ERROR</u> imperative-statement]

<u>EXIT</u> [<u>PROGRAM</u>].

<u>GO</u> <u>TO</u> [procedure-name-1]

<u>GO</u> <u>TO</u> procedure-name-1 [, procedure-name-2] . . . , procedure-name-n

<u>DEPENDING</u> ON identifier

<u>IF</u> condition; $\begin{Bmatrix} \text{statement-1} \\ \underline{\text{NEXT}}\ \underline{\text{SENTENCE}} \end{Bmatrix}$ $\begin{Bmatrix} \text{; }\underline{\text{ELSE}}\text{ statement-2} \\ \text{; }\underline{\text{ELSE}}\ \underline{\text{NEXT}}\ \underline{\text{SENTENCE}} \end{Bmatrix}$

<u>INSPECT</u> identifier-1 <u>TALLYING</u>

$\left\{ \text{, identifier-2 }\underline{\text{FOR}} \left\{ , \begin{Bmatrix} \underline{\text{ALL}} \\ \underline{\text{LEADING}} \\ \underline{\text{CHARACTERS}} \end{Bmatrix} \begin{Bmatrix} \text{identifier-3} \\ \text{literal-1} \end{Bmatrix} \right\} \left[\begin{Bmatrix} \underline{\text{BEFORE}} \\ \underline{\text{AFTER}} \end{Bmatrix} \text{INITIAL} \begin{Bmatrix} \text{identifier-4} \\ \text{literal-2} \end{Bmatrix} \right] \right\} \ldots \right\} \ldots$

<u>INSPECT</u> identifier-1 <u>REPLACING</u>

$\left\{ \begin{matrix} \underline{\text{CHARACTERS}} \ \underline{\text{BY}} \begin{Bmatrix} \text{identifier-6} \\ \text{literal-4} \end{Bmatrix} \left[\begin{Bmatrix} \underline{\text{BEFORE}} \\ \underline{\text{AFTER}} \end{Bmatrix} \text{INITIAL} \begin{Bmatrix} \text{identifier-7} \\ \text{literal-5} \end{Bmatrix} \right] \\ \left\{ , \begin{Bmatrix} \underline{\text{ALL}} \\ \underline{\text{LEADING}} \\ \underline{\text{FIRST}} \end{Bmatrix} \right\} \left\{ , \begin{Bmatrix} \text{identifier-5} \\ \text{literal-3} \end{Bmatrix} \underline{\text{BY}} \begin{Bmatrix} \text{identifier-6} \\ \text{literal-4} \end{Bmatrix} \left[\begin{Bmatrix} \underline{\text{BEFORE}} \\ \underline{\text{AFTER}} \end{Bmatrix} \text{INITIAL} \begin{Bmatrix} \text{identifier-7} \\ \text{literal-5} \end{Bmatrix} \right] \right\} \ldots \end{matrix} \right\} \ldots$

$$\underline{\text{MOVE}} \begin{Bmatrix} \text{identifier-1} \\ \text{literal} \end{Bmatrix} \underline{\text{TO}} \text{ identifier-2} \,[\,, \text{identifier-3}\,] \, \ldots$$

$$\underline{\text{MOVE}} \begin{Bmatrix} \underline{\text{CORRESPONDING}} \\ \underline{\text{CORR}} \end{Bmatrix} \text{identifier-1} \ \underline{\text{TO}} \ \text{identifier-2}$$

$$\underline{\text{MULTIPLY}} \begin{Bmatrix} \text{identifier-1} \\ \text{literal-1} \end{Bmatrix} \underline{\text{BY}} \text{ identifier-2}\,[\underline{\text{ROUNDED}}]$$

$$\left[\,, \text{identifier-3}\,[\underline{\text{ROUNDED}}]\,\right] \ \ldots \ [\,; \text{ON}\,\underline{\text{SIZE}}\,\underline{\text{ERROR}}\,\text{imperative-statement}\,]$$

$$\underline{\text{MULTIPLY}} \begin{Bmatrix} \text{identifier-1} \\ \text{literal-1} \end{Bmatrix} \underline{\text{BY}} \begin{Bmatrix} \text{identifier-2} \\ \text{literal-2} \end{Bmatrix} \underline{\text{GIVING}}\,\text{identifier-3}\,[\underline{\text{ROUNDED}}]$$

$$\left[\,, \text{identifier-4}\,[\underline{\text{ROUNDED}}]\,\right] \ \ldots \ [\,; \text{ON}\,\underline{\text{SIZE}}\,\underline{\text{ERROR}}\,\text{imperative-statement}\,]$$

$$\underline{\text{OPEN}} \begin{Bmatrix} \underline{\text{INPUT}}\,\text{file-name-1}\begin{bmatrix}\underline{\text{REVERSED}}\\ \text{WITH}\,\underline{\text{NO}}\,\underline{\text{REWIND}}\end{bmatrix} \quad \left[\,, \text{file-name-2}\begin{bmatrix}\underline{\text{REVERSED}}\\ \text{WITH}\,\underline{\text{NO}}\,\underline{\text{REWIND}}\end{bmatrix}\right]\,\ldots \\ \underline{\text{OUTPUT}}\,\text{file-name-3}\,[\text{WITH}\,\underline{\text{NO}}\,\underline{\text{REWIND}}]\,[\,, \text{file-name-4}\,[\text{WITH}\,\underline{\text{NO}}\,\underline{\text{REWIND}}]]\,\ldots \\ \underline{\text{I-O}}\,\text{file-name-5}\,[\,, \text{file-name-6}]\,\ldots \\ \underline{\text{EXTEND}}\,\text{file-name-7}\,[\,, \text{file-name-8}]\,\ldots \end{Bmatrix} \ldots$$

$$\underline{\text{OPEN}} \begin{Bmatrix} \underline{\text{INPUT}}\ \text{file-name-1}\,[\,, \text{file-name-2}]\,\ldots \\ \underline{\text{OUTPUT}}\ \text{file-name-3}\,[\,, \text{file-name-4}]\,\ldots \\ \underline{\text{I-O}}\ \text{file-name-5}\,[\,, \text{file-name-6}]\,\ldots \end{Bmatrix} \ldots$$

$$\underline{\text{PERFORM}}\,\text{procedure-name-1}\left[\begin{Bmatrix}\underline{\text{THROUGH}}\\ \underline{\text{THRU}}\end{Bmatrix}\text{procedure-name-2}\right]$$

$$\underline{\text{PERFORM}}\,\text{procedure-name-1}\left[\begin{Bmatrix}\underline{\text{THROUGH}}\\ \underline{\text{THRU}}\end{Bmatrix}\text{procedure-name-2}\right]\begin{Bmatrix}\text{identifier-1}\\ \text{integer-1}\end{Bmatrix}\underline{\text{TIMES}}$$

$$\underline{\text{PERFORM}}\,\text{procedure-name-1}\left[\begin{Bmatrix}\underline{\text{THROUGH}}\\ \underline{\text{THRU}}\end{Bmatrix}\text{procedure-name-2}\right]\underline{\text{UNTIL}}\,\text{condition-1}$$

$$\underline{\text{PERFORM}}\,\text{procedure-name-1}\left[\begin{Bmatrix}\underline{\text{THROUGH}}\\ \underline{\text{THRU}}\end{Bmatrix}\text{procedure-name-2}\right]$$

$$\text{VARYING} \begin{Bmatrix} \text{identifier-2} \\ \text{index-name-1} \end{Bmatrix} \underline{\text{FROM}} \begin{Bmatrix} \text{identifier-3} \\ \text{index-name-2} \\ \text{literal-1} \end{Bmatrix}$$

$$\underline{\text{BY}} \begin{Bmatrix} \text{identifier-4} \\ \text{literal-3} \end{Bmatrix} \underline{\text{UNTIL}} \text{ condition-1}$$

$$\left[\underline{\text{AFTER}} \begin{Bmatrix} \text{identifier-5} \\ \text{index-name-3} \end{Bmatrix} \underline{\text{FROM}} \begin{Bmatrix} \text{identifier-6} \\ \text{index-name-4} \\ \text{literal-3} \end{Bmatrix} \right.$$

$$\underline{\text{BY}} \begin{Bmatrix} \text{identifier-7} \\ \text{literal-4} \end{Bmatrix} \underline{\text{UNTIL}} \text{ condition-2}$$

$$\left[\underline{\text{AFTER}} \begin{Bmatrix} \text{identifier-8} \\ \text{index-name-5} \end{Bmatrix} \underline{\text{FROM}} \begin{Bmatrix} \text{identifier-9} \\ \text{index-name-6} \\ \text{literal-5} \end{Bmatrix} \right.$$

$$\left. \left. \underline{\text{BY}} \begin{Bmatrix} \text{identifier-10} \\ \text{literal-6} \end{Bmatrix} \underline{\text{UNTIL}} \text{ condition-3} \right] \right]$$

$\underline{\text{READ}}$ file-name RECORD [$\underline{\text{INTO}}$ identifier] [; AT $\underline{\text{END}}$ imperative-statement]

$\underline{\text{READ}}$ file-name [$\underline{\text{NEXT}}$] RECORD [$\underline{\text{INTO}}$ identifier]

   [; AT $\underline{\text{END}}$ imperative-statement]

$\underline{\text{READ}}$ file-name RECORD [$\underline{\text{INTO}}$ identifier] [; $\underline{\text{INVALID}}$ KEY imperative-statement]

$\underline{\text{READ}}$ file-name RECORD [$\underline{\text{INTO}}$ identifier]

   [; $\underline{\text{KEY}}$ IS data-name]

   [; $\underline{\text{INVALID}}$ KEY imperative-statement]

$\underline{\text{RELEASE}}$ record-name [$\underline{\text{FROM}}$ identifier]

$\underline{\text{RETURN}}$ file-name [$\underline{\text{INTO}}$ identifier-1] AT $\underline{\text{END}}$ imperative-statement

$$\underline{\text{SEARCH}} \text{ identifier-1} \left[\underline{\text{VARYING}} \begin{Bmatrix} \text{identifier-2} \\ \text{index-name-1} \end{Bmatrix} \right] [\text{; AT } \underline{\text{END}} \text{ imperative-statement-1}]$$

$$; \underline{\text{WHEN}} \text{ condition-1} \begin{Bmatrix} \text{imperative-statement-2} \\ \underline{\text{NEXT}}\,\underline{\text{SENTENCE}} \end{Bmatrix}$$

$$\left[; \underline{\text{WHEN}} \text{ condition-2} \begin{Bmatrix} \text{imperative-statement-3} \\ \underline{\text{NEXT}}\,\underline{\text{SENTENCE}} \end{Bmatrix} \right] . . .$$

SEARCH ALL identifier-1 [; AT END imperative-statement-1]

$$; \underline{WHEN} \left\{ \begin{array}{l} \text{data-name-1} \\ \text{condition-name-1} \end{array} \right\} \left\{ \begin{array}{l} \text{IS } \underline{EQUAL} \text{ TO} \\ \text{IS} = \end{array} \right\} \left\{ \begin{array}{l} \text{identifier-3} \\ \text{literal-1} \\ \text{arithmetic-expression-1} \end{array} \right\} \right\}$$

$$\left[\underline{AND} \left\{ \begin{array}{l} \text{data-name-2} \\ \text{condition-name-2} \end{array} \right\} \left\{ \begin{array}{l} \text{IS } \underline{EQUAL} \text{ TO} \\ \text{IS} = \end{array} \right\} \left\{ \begin{array}{l} \text{identifier-4} \\ \text{literal-2} \\ \text{arithmetic-expression-2} \end{array} \right\} \right\} \right] \dots$$

$$\left\{ \begin{array}{l} \text{imperative-statement-2} \\ \underline{NEXT}\ \underline{SENTENCE} \end{array} \right\}$$

$$\underline{SET} \left\{ \begin{array}{l} \text{identifier-1 [, identifier-2]} \dots \\ \text{index-name-1 [, index-name-2]} \dots \end{array} \right\} \underline{TO} \left\{ \begin{array}{l} \text{identifier-3} \\ \text{index-name-3} \\ \text{integer-1} \end{array} \right\}$$

$$\underline{SET} \text{ index-name-4 [, index-name-5]} \dots \left\{ \begin{array}{l} \underline{UP}\ \underline{BY} \\ \underline{DOWN}\ \underline{BY} \end{array} \right\} \left\{ \begin{array}{l} \text{identifier-4} \\ \text{integer-2} \end{array} \right\}$$

$$\underline{SORT} \text{ file-name-1 ON} \left\{ \begin{array}{l} \underline{ASCENDING} \\ \underline{DESCENDING} \end{array} \right\} \text{KEY data-name-1 [, data-name-2]} \dots$$

$$\left\{ \begin{array}{l} \underline{INPUT}\ \underline{PROCEDURE} \text{ IS section-name-1} \left[\left\{ \begin{array}{l} \underline{THROUGH} \\ \underline{THRU} \end{array} \right\} \text{section-name-2} \right] \\ \underline{USING} \text{ file-name-2 [, file-name-3]} \dots \end{array} \right\}$$

$$\left\{ \begin{array}{l} \underline{OUTPUT}\ \underline{PROCEDURE} \text{ IS section-name-3} \left[\left\{ \begin{array}{l} \underline{THROUGH} \\ \underline{THRU} \end{array} \right\} \text{section-name-4} \right] \\ \underline{GIVING} \text{ file-name-4} \end{array} \right\}$$

$$\underline{START} \text{ file-name} \left[\underline{KEY} \left\{ \begin{array}{l} \text{IS } \underline{EQUAL}\ \text{TO} \\ \text{IS} = \\ \text{IS } \underline{GREATER}\ \text{THAN} \\ \text{IS} > \\ \text{IS } \underline{NOT}\ \underline{LESS}\ \text{THAN} \\ \text{IS } \underline{NOT} < \end{array} \right\} \text{data-name} \right]$$

[; INVALID KEY imperative-statement]

$$\underline{STOP} \left\{ \begin{array}{l} \underline{RUN} \\ \text{literal} \end{array} \right\}$$

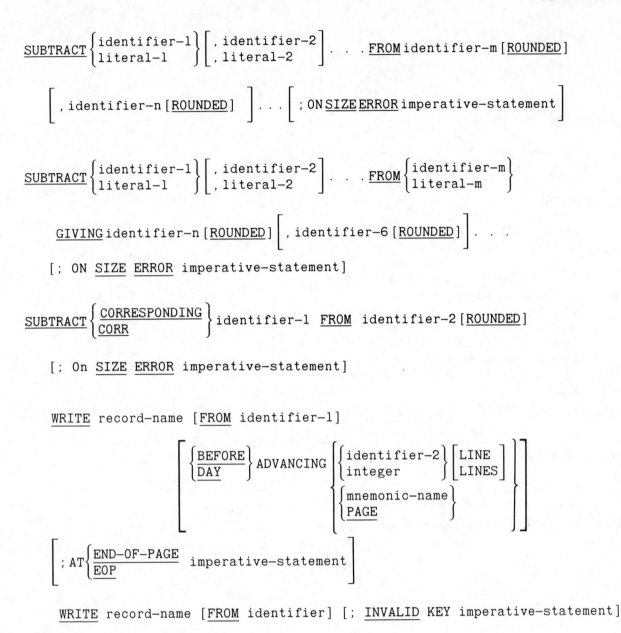

SUBTRACT $\begin{Bmatrix} \text{identifier-1} \\ \text{literal-1} \end{Bmatrix} \begin{bmatrix} \text{, identifier-2} \\ \text{, literal-2} \end{bmatrix} \ldots$ FROM identifier-m [ROUNDED]

$\begin{bmatrix} \text{, identifier-n} [\underline{ROUNDED}] \end{bmatrix} \ldots \begin{bmatrix} \text{; ON} \underline{SIZE} \underline{ERROR} \text{ imperative-statement} \end{bmatrix}$

SUBTRACT $\begin{Bmatrix} \text{identifier-1} \\ \text{literal-1} \end{Bmatrix} \begin{bmatrix} \text{, identifier-2} \\ \text{, literal-2} \end{bmatrix} \ldots$ FROM $\begin{Bmatrix} \text{identifier-m} \\ \text{literal-m} \end{Bmatrix}$

GIVING identifier-n [ROUNDED] $\begin{bmatrix} \text{, identifier-6} [\underline{ROUNDED}] \end{bmatrix} \ldots$

[; ON SIZE ERROR imperative-statement]

SUBTRACT $\begin{Bmatrix} \underline{CORRESPONDING} \\ \underline{CORR} \end{Bmatrix}$ identifier-1 FROM identifier-2 [ROUNDED]

[; On SIZE ERROR imperative-statement]

WRITE record-name [FROM identifier-1]

$\begin{bmatrix} \begin{Bmatrix} \underline{BEFORE} \\ \underline{DAY} \end{Bmatrix} \text{ADVANCING} \begin{Bmatrix} \begin{Bmatrix} \text{identifier-2} \\ \text{integer} \end{Bmatrix} \begin{bmatrix} \text{LINE} \\ \text{LINES} \end{bmatrix} \\ \begin{Bmatrix} \text{mnemonic-name} \\ \underline{PAGE} \end{Bmatrix} \end{Bmatrix} \end{bmatrix}$

$\begin{bmatrix} \text{; AT} \begin{Bmatrix} \underline{END-OF-PAGE} \\ \underline{EOP} \end{Bmatrix} \text{ imperative-statement} \end{bmatrix}$

WRITE record-name [FROM identifier] [; INVALID KEY imperative-statement]

Miscellaneous formats

RELATION CONDITION:

$\begin{Bmatrix} \text{identifier-1} \\ \text{literal-1} \\ \text{arithmetic-expression-1} \\ \text{index-name-1} \end{Bmatrix} \begin{Bmatrix} \text{IS [NOT]} \underline{\text{GREATER THAN}} \\ \text{IS [NOT]} \underline{\text{LESS THAN}} \\ \text{IS [NOT]} \underline{\text{EQUAL}} \text{ TO} \\ \text{IS [NOT]} > \\ \text{IS [NOT]} < \\ \text{IS [NOT]} = \end{Bmatrix} \begin{Bmatrix} \text{identifier-2} \\ \text{literal-2} \\ \text{arithmetic-expression-2} \\ \text{index-name-2} \end{Bmatrix}$

CLASS CONDITION:

identifier IS [NOT] $\begin{Bmatrix} \underline{NUMERIC} \\ \underline{ALPHABETIC} \end{Bmatrix}$

SIGN CONDITION:

arithmetic-expression is [NOT] $\left\{ \begin{array}{l} \underline{POSITIVE} \\ \underline{NEGATIVE} \\ \underline{ZERO} \end{array} \right\}$

PICTURE CLAUSE CHARACTERS

A	Alphabetic character
B	Blank space
P	Decimal scaling position
S	Sign
V	Assumed decimal point
Z	Zero suppression
9	Numeric character
0	Zero insertion character
.	Decimal point edit character
,	Comma edit character
+	Plus sign edit character
−	Minus sign edit character
CR	Credit symbol edit character
DB	Debit symbol edit character
*	Asterisk symbol edit character
$	Dollar sign

Report Writer and linage formats

DATA DIVISION entries

LINAGE and REPORT clause in FILE SECTION

$$\left[; \underline{LINAGE} \text{ IS } \left\{ \begin{array}{l} data-name-5 \\ integer-5 \end{array} \right\} LINES \left[, \text{ with } \underline{FOOTING} \text{ AT } \left\{ \begin{array}{l} data-name-6 \\ integer-6 \end{array} \right\} \right] \right.$$

$$\left[, LINES \text{ AT } \underline{TOP} \left\{ \begin{array}{l} data-name-7 \\ integer-7 \end{array} \right\} \right] \left[, LINES \text{ AT } \underline{BOTTOM} \left\{ \begin{array}{l} data-name-8 \\ integer-8 \end{array} \right\} \right] \right]$$

$$\left[; \left\{ \begin{array}{l} \underline{REPORT} \text{ IS} \\ \underline{REPORTS} \text{ ARE} \end{array} \right\} report-name-1 [, report-name-2] \ldots \right]$$

REPORT SECTION entries

<u>REPORT SECTION</u>
<u>RD</u> *report-name*
   WITH <u>CODE</u> *mnemonic-name*

$$\left\{\begin{matrix} \underline{\text{CONTROL}}\text{ IS} \\ \underline{\text{CONTROLS}}\text{ ARE} \end{matrix}\right\} \left\{\begin{matrix} \underline{\text{FINAL}} \\ \textit{identifier-1}\,[\textit{identifier-2}]\ldots \\ \underline{\text{FINAL}}\;\textit{identifier-1}\,[\textit{identifier-2}]\ldots \end{matrix}\right\}$$

$$\underline{\text{PAGE}} \left[\begin{matrix} \underline{\text{LIMIT}}\text{ IS} \\ \underline{\text{LIMITS}}\text{ ARE} \end{matrix}\right] \textit{integer-1} \left\{\begin{matrix} \underline{\text{LINE}} \\ \underline{\text{LINES}} \end{matrix}\right\}$$

[<u>HEADING</u> *integer-2*]
[<u>FIRST</u> <u>DETAIL</u> *integer-3*]
[<u>LAST</u> <u>DETAIL</u> *integer-4*]
[<u>FOOTING</u> *integer-5*].

REPORT GROUP DESCRIPTION ENTRY

Format 1:

01 [*data-name-1*]

$$\underline{\text{LINE}}\text{ NUMBER IS} \left\{\begin{matrix} \textit{integer-1} \\ \underline{\text{PLUS}}\;\textit{integer-2} \\ \underline{\text{NEXT}}\;\underline{\text{PAGE}} \end{matrix}\right\}$$

$$\underline{\text{NEXT}}\text{ GROUP IS} \left\{\begin{matrix} \textit{integer-1} \\ \underline{\text{PLUS}}\;\textit{integer-2} \\ \underline{\text{NEXT}}\;\underline{\text{PAGE}} \end{matrix}\right\}$$

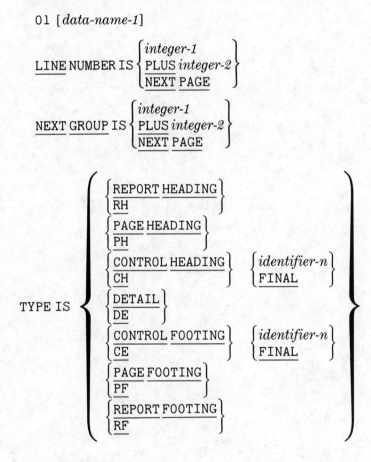

USAGE Clause.

Format 2:

nn [*data-name-1*]
  LINE Clause—See Format 1
  USAGE Clause.

Format 3:

nn [*data-name-1*]
<u>COLUMN</u> NUMBER IS *integer-1*
<u>GROUP</u> INDICATE
<u>JUSTIFIED</u> Clause
<u>LINE</u> Clause—See Format 1
<u>PICTURE</u> Clause

$$\underline{\text{RESET}} \text{ ON} \begin{Bmatrix} \textit{identifier-1} \\ \underline{\text{FINAL}} \end{Bmatrix}$$

<u>BLANK</u> <u>WHEN</u> <u>ZERO</u> Clause

$$\underline{\text{SOURCE}} \text{ IS} \begin{Bmatrix} \underline{\text{TALLY}} \\ \textit{identifier-2} \end{Bmatrix}$$

$$\underline{\text{SUM}} \begin{Bmatrix} \underline{\text{TALLY}} \\ \textit{identifier-3} \end{Bmatrix} \begin{bmatrix} \underline{\text{TALLY}} \\ \textit{identifier-4} \end{bmatrix} \dots [\underline{\text{UPON}} \textit{ data-name}]$$

<u>VALUE</u> IS *literal-1*
<u>USAGE</u> Clause.

COBOL Verbs for Indexed Files

<u>DELETE</u> file—name <u>RECORD</u>
 <u>INVALID</u> KEY imperative statement
<u>REWRITE</u> record—name [<u>FROM</u> identifier]
 <u>INVALID</u> KEY imperative statement

PROCEDURE DIVISION entries

GENERATE Statement
 <u>GENERATE</u> *identifier*

INITIATE Statement
 <u>INITIATE</u> *report-name-1* [*report-name-2*] . . .

TERMINATE Statement
 <u>TERMINATE</u> *report-name-1* [*report-name-2*] . . .

USE Sentence
 <u>USE</u> <u>BEFORE</u> <u>REPORTING</u> *data-name*.

Appendix C.   Answers to selected chapter exercises

Chapter 1   Computers and problem solving

1. Report; edit; and file manipulation
4. Easier to correct errors; easier to maintain
6. Linear sequence; selection structure (IFTHENELSE); controlled loop or iteration (DOWHILE)
13. IDENTIFICATION DIVISION   identifies or names the program
    ENVIRONMENT DIVISION tells the system about the environment in which the program will operate
    DATA DIVISION   describes the data records and fields that will be used in the program
    PROCEDURE DIVISION   directs the computer to execute specific instructions in a specified sequence
14. a. STUDENT-FILE
    b. LIST-RECORD
    c. CONTROL-ROUTINE
       010-OPENER
       020-READER
       030-CLOSER
    d. To act as the main processing loop in the program
    e. Gets files ready for processing
    f. When the value in the EOF-INDICATOR field is changed from 0 to 1, it tells the system to stop executing the program loop.

Chapter 2   Getting started in COBOL

1. Non-numeric literal
3. Operating system
5. Run time
8. Figurative
11. One character or one byte
15. a. Incorrect; NUMBER is a reserved word
    b. Incorrect; no period
    c. Correct; but a poor choice of field names
    d. Correct; but the commas are not required
    e. Incorrect; the statement is not complete
    f. Incorrect; OVERFLOW is a reserved word
    g. Correct
    h. Incorrect; used MORE instead of MOVE
    i. Incorrect; there is a blank in the SS-NUMBER field instead of a hyphen
16. a. Correct
    b. Correct
    c. Incorrect; no ending quote
    d. Incorrect; you cannot work numerically with non-numeric literals
    e. Incorrect; no ending period
    f. Incorrect; you don't have to tell it how many SPACES
    g. Incorrect; you can't do arithmetic on non-numeric literals
    h. Correct
    i. Incorrect; you can't manipulate figurative constants
19. a. Numeric constant
    b. Non-numeric literals
    c. Non-numeric literal
    d. Illegal numeric constant
    e. Non-numeric literal
    f. Numeric constant

    g. Figurative constant
    h. Numeric constant
    i. Non-numeric literal
    j. Non-numeric literal

20. PROGRAM-ID

22. The purpose of the SELECT entry is to give an internal name to a file and to indicate what input/output device that file will use. (Note: On some systems, particularly microcomputers, the SELECT entry may also designate the external file name as well.)

25. Yes, a one record file is possible.

Yes, a record can consist of a single field.

The maximum size of a field is determined by what type of field it is. Numeric fields are limited to 18 digits; alphabetic and alphanumeric fields are limited to 120 characters.

Chapter 3   Setting up the program

3. Magnetic recording media such as tape and disk require the LABEL RECORD IS STANDARD entry

4. The period after OMITTED is incorrect and should be deleted

8. FILLER

11. If its level number is larger than the one before it

13. Elementary

15. '98.65' is not a numeric value

17. The programmer did not allow one position for carriage control

19. **a.** Incorrect; period missing
    b. Incorrect; space in program name
    c. Incorrect; dash missing in PROGRAM-ID
    d. Correct
    e. Incorrect; period missing
    f. Incorrect; FD entry should begin in column eight
    g. Incorrect; dash should not be there; however, this is a properly formed (although poorly chosen) COBOL name and could be used to name a file, a record, a field, or a COBOL paragraph

22.
```
01   EMPLOYEE-RECORD.
     03   FILLER        PIC X(20).
     03   SS-NBR        PIC 9(9).
     03   EMP-NAME      PIC X(21).     or A(21).
     03   ADDRESS-IN    PIC X(20).
     03   CODE-FIELD    PIC 99.
```

25.

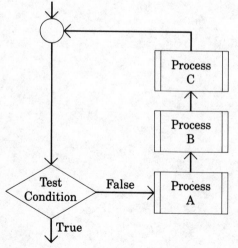

26. a. PIC 9(4).
　b. PIC 9(4).
　c. PIC 999V99.
　d. PIC 9(4)V99.
　e. PIC 99V99.
　f. PIC V999.
　g. PIC V99999.

29.

a. 567	(left-most digit is truncated)	**a.** ABCbb	
b. 45·50		**b.** ABC	
c. 3·000	(left-most two digits are truncated)	**c.** ABbCDb	
d. 0000·	(left-most four digits are truncated)	**d.** bbbbb	
e. 00000			
f. bbbbb			

Chapter 4   Handling data—Part I

2. TOP-OF-PAGE is *not* a reserved word
4. $bb1,234.56
6. ADD FIELD-A FIELD-B TO TOTAL.
8. TO and GIVING cannot be used together within an ADD statement
10. Field name is missing
12. FIELD-B is not numeric. It is an edit field and cannot be worked upon arithmetically.
15. Since we were not going to refer to these fields within the program, we could use the reserved word FILLER designed just for this purpose
18. Yes, alphabetic or alphanumeric fields would have worked just as well
19. a. 01　HEAD-1.

```
        03  FILLER      PIC X.
        03  FILLER      PIC X(52) VALUE SPACES.
        03  FILLER      PIC X(16) VALUE 'INCOME STATEMENT'.
        03  FILLER      PIC X(52) VALUE SPACES.
```

　b. 01　HEAD-2.

```
        03  FILLER      PIC X.
        03  FILLER      PIC X(30) VALUE SPACES.
        03  FILLER      PIC X(23) VALUE
                                  'FOR THE YEAR ENDED 1985'.
        03  FILLER      PIC X(79) VALUE SPACES.
```

　c. 01　HEAD-3.

```
        03  FILLER      PIC X.
        03  FILLER      PIC X(79) VALUE SPACES.
        03  FILLER      PIC X(23) VALUE
                                  'FOR THE YEAR ENDED 1985'.
        03  FILLER      PIC X(30) VALUE SPACES.
```

20. a. EDIT-FIELD PIC ZZZ.99.
　b. EDIT-FIELD PIC $$$$.99.
　c. EDIT-FIELD PIC Z,ZZZ.99.
　d. EDIT-FIELD PIC $$,$$$.99.
　e. EDIT-FIELD PIC ZZZ.99CR.
　f. EDIT-FIELD PIC ZZZ.99+.
　g. EDIT-FIELD PIC $99,999.99DB.
　h. EDIT-FIELD PIC 999B99B9999.

22. a. Correct
　b. Incorrect; you cannot add to a literal
　c. Incorrect; you cannot have TO and GIVING in the same ADD statement
　d. Correct
　e. Correct
　f. Incorrect; AND is not permitted
　g. Correct
　h. Incorrect; improper use of ROUNDED

    i. Correct

    j. Incorrect; you cannot use any symbols in arithmetic operations

    k. Correct

23. **a.** Correct

    b. Correct

    c. Incorrect; you cannot subtract from a literal

    d. Correct

    e. Incorrect; format requires FROM

    f. Correct

    g. Incorrect use of ROUNDED

    h. Incorrect placement of period

    i. Incorrect; LINES is a reserved word

    j. Incorrect use of ROUNDED

25. **a.** `COMPUTE X = (A + B) / C.`

    b. `COMPUTE X = A / C + B.`

    c. `COMPUTE X = A ** 2 + B ** 3.`

    d. `COMPUTE X = 6 * A * B + 4 * R * Q * G.`

    e. `COMPUTE X = (6 * A * B) / (4 * Q * G).`

    f. `COMPUTE X ROUNDED = (6 * A * B) / (4 * Q * G).`

    g. `COMPUTE X - (A + A ** 2 + (A ** 3 - 15)) / T.`

    h. `COMPUTE X ROUNDED = (A + B) / C ON SIZE ERROR`
        `PERFORM MESSAGE-ROUTINE.`

    i. `COMPUTE R = R + 1.`

Chapter 5   Conditional operations in COBOL

1. A relational test is done to see if one field is greater than, less than, or equal to another field.

   A sign test is done to see if a field is positive or negative.

   A class test is done to see if a field contains all alphabetic or all numeric characters.

4. Programs are easier to read and easier to maintain if level 88 entries are used.

6. **a.** `IF A-FIELD IS NOT EQUAL TO ZERO PERFORM ROUTINE-1.`

    b. `IF A-FIELD IS GREATER THAN LIMIT`
        `ADD 1 TO COUNTER-A`
    `ELSE`
        `SUBTRACT CONSTANT FROM COUNTER-B.`

    c. `IF NAME-FIELD IS NOT ALPHABETIC`
        `DISPLAY 'NAME FIELD NOT ALPHABETIC'`
           `UPON CONSOLE`
        `ADD 1 TO COUNT-B.`
    `ADD 1 TO COUNT-C.`

    d. `IF AMT-OF-PAY IS NOT NUMERIC`
        `DISPLAY 'DATA OF WRONG TYPE'`
           `UPON CONSOLE`
    `ELSE`
        `MOVE BODY-LINE TO OUTPUT-LINE`
        `WRITE OUTPUT-LINE`
           `AFTER ADVANCING 3 LINES.`
    `MULTIPLY SUB-TOTAL BY RATE`
        `GIVING ANSWER-1.`

8. **a.** `IF A > B`
        `COMPUTE X = A - B`
        `MOVE ZEROS TO`
           `TOTAL-3`
    `ELSE`
        `COMPUTE X = B - A`
        `COMPUTE Q = (R + Z) ** 2.`

```
        MOVE MSG-2 TO
            OUTPUT-LINE.
        WRITE OUTPUT-LINE
            AFTER ADVANCING
                3 LINES.
     b. IF A > B
            COMPUTE X = A - B
            MOVE ZEROS TO
                TOTAL-3
        ELSE
            COMPUTE X = B - A
            COMPUTE Q = (R + Z) ** 2
            MOVE MSG-2 TO OUTPUT-LINE
            WRITE OUTPUT-LINE
                AFTER ADVANCING 3 LINES.
     c. IF A = B
            COMPUTE X = A + B
            ADD 1 TO TOTAL-X
            IF COUNT IS EQUAL TO 5
                NEXT SENTENCE
            ELSE
                PERFORM 080-INT-PROCESSING
                PERFORM 100-CALCULATOR
                    UNTIL SW-1 = 1
        ELSE
            IF A IS GREATER THAN B
                SUBTRACT 1 FROM TOTAL-A
            ELSE
                ADD 1 TO TOTAL-A
                IF Q IS NOT EQUAL TO R
                    PERFORM 060-TESTER
                    PERFORM 090-FINISHER
                ELSE
                    NEXT SENTENCE.
        MOVE SPACES TO AREA-A.
```

 9. **a.** Valid; true
    b. Valid; false
    c. Valid; true
    d. Valid; true
    e. Invalid
    f. Invalid
    g. Valid; true
    h. Valid; false
10. **a.** A = B; C = D
    b. A = B; C = D; Q < R
    c. A < B; Q = R; C = D
    d. C = D; Q = R; A < B
    e. C NOT = Q; A = B
    f. C NOT = Q; F < T; A = B

Chapter 6   Handling data—Part II

1. MOVE FIELD-A OF DATA2 TO FIELD-A OF DATA1.
   or MOVE FIELD-A IN DATA2 TO FIELD-A IN DATA1.
3. For ease of program maintenance
5. COMP-3
8. DATE

11. **a.** NO-OF-SALES PIC 999 VALUE ZEROS.
    b. COUNTER-1 PIC 9(5) VALUE ZEROS.
    c. AREA-1 PIC 9(5)V99 COMP-3 VALUE ZEROS.
    d. AREA-1 PIC 9(4)V99 COMP VALUE ZEROS.
    e. AREA-1 PIC 9(6)V99 VALUE ZEROS.
    f. DATA-AREA PIC 9(4)V99 COMP-3.
12. **a.** KONSTANT PIC 999V999 VALUE 763.714.
    b. FUDGE-AMT PIC 99V99 VALUE 21.65 COMP.
    c. ONE-AMT PIC 9 VALUE 9 COMP-3.
    d. THREE-FIELD PIC 999 VALUE 006 COMP.
    e. MESSAGE PIC X(14) VALUE 'BAD INPUT DATA'.
    f. DATA-AREA PIC 9(4) COMP.
13. **a.** 4 bytes
    b. 4 bytes
    c. 2 bytes
    d. 2 bytes
    e. 4 bytes
    f. 2 bytes

Chapter 7   Control breaks and programmed switches

1. Minor break or minor total; intermediate break or intermediate total
2. You should check for the higher level break first, since a higher level break normally triggers a lower level break.
4. "Flag" or "sentinel"
5. The second example is not permitted since VALUE is not permitted with REDEFINES.
6. A control break occurs when the value in a designated field of the first input record has a value different from that of the next or second input record. Rolling a total is the act of adding a total into a higher-level total. For example, a minor total will be rolled into an intermediate-level total, and so on.
7. The "first record" problem is that there is no valid number against which to compare it. Even if we assume that the computer system accepts the comparing process, the first record will always trigger a minor break. The chapter showed two ways around the problem. One was by moving the control break value from the first record into a compare area; the second method was to use a switch to bypass the comparing operation on the first record.
9. A detail printed report prints one line per record plus the appropriate total lines. A group or summary printed report prints one line for each control group.
10. Group indication occurs when the printing of the identifying material for a group occurs only for the first record of that group. One exception to this is if the group-indicated report were to go onto a new page, the first line on the new page would print the complete line of identifying material.

Chapter 8   Working with tables of data

1. A table consists of adjacent or contiguous memory locations set aside for the storage of data.

4. OCCURS cannot be at the 01 level.

5. Subscript

6. PERFORM 010-ADDER VARYING COUNT
          FROM 1 BY 2 UNTIL COUNT IS GREATER THAN 99.

8. PERFORM 010-ADDER VARYING COUNT
          FROM 5 BY 5 UNTIL DATA-FIELD (COUNT)
                IS LESS THAN ZERO

(Although the PERFORM will work as indicated, the logic is that it would be possible to go outside the range of the table before a zero value is encountered. Exercise 9 asks you to plan for this possibility.)

10. Nine times

13. Negative subscripts are not permitted.

15. a. 03   RETURNS PIC 9(4) OCCURS 50 TIMES.

  b. 03   SALES-AMT PIC 9(4)V99 OCCURS 50 TIMES COMP-3.

  c. 03   EMPLOYEE-NAMES PIC A(20) OCCURS 70 TIMES.

  d. 03   TABLE-INFO OCCURS 60 TIMES.
          05   AMOUNT-IN   PIC 9(4).
          05   ITEM-DESCRIPTION   PIC X(30).

  e. 03   TABLE-INFO OCCURS 60 TIMES.
          05   AMOUNT-IN   PIC 9(4) COMP-3.
          05   ITEM-DESCRIPTION   PIC X(30).

  f. 03   TABLE-DATA OCCURS 10 TIMES.
          05   SS-NBR   PIC 9(9) COMP-3.
          05   E-NAME   PIC X(30).
          05   RATE   PIC S99V999 COMP-3.
          05   HOURS   PIC S99.

17. a. COMPUTE ANS (5) = A * A + B * B

  b. COMPUTE ANS (J) = A * A + B * B

  c. COMPUTE TOTAL = SALES(1) + SALES(2) + SALES(3).

  d. ADD 6 TO ANS(7).

  e. COMPUTE AMOUNT(X) = AMOUNT(X) + 1.3.

18. 01 DATA-VALUES.
      03   FILLER   PIC 9V99 VALUE 6.75.
      03   FILLER   PIC 9V99 VALUE 9.42.
      03   FILLER   PIC 9V99 VALUE 8.56.
      03   FILLER   PIC 9V99 VALUE 1.49.
    01 TABLE-DATA REDEFINES DATA-VALUES.
      03   TABLE-L PIC 9V99 OCCURS 4 TIMES.

22. 03 TABLE-DATA OCCURS 4 TIMES.
      05   NAME   PIC X(20).
      05   SS-NBR   PIC 9(9).
      05   SCHOOL-CLASS   PIC X(9).

```
          .
          .
          .

    PERFORM ENTER-DATA VARYING KOUNT
          FROM 1 BY 1 UNTIL KOUNT IS GREATER THAN 4.
          .
          .
          .

ENTER-DATA.
    DISPLAY 'PLEASE ENTER STUDENT NAME'.
    ACCEPT NAME (KOUNT).
    DISPLAY 'PLEASE ENTER SOCIAL SECURITY NUMBER'.
    ACCEPT SS-NBR (KOUNT).
    DISPLAY 'PLEASE ENTER CLASS: FRESHMAN; SOPHOMORE;'.
    DISPLAY 'JUNIOR; SENIOR'.
    ACCEPT SCHOOL-CLASS (KOUNT).
```

Chapter 9   More about tables

2. Pointer or index values
3. INDEXED BY; SET
5. The index field *must not* be defined in the WORKING-STORAGE SECTION.
7. The binary search cannot use the GREATER THAN test.
8. Ten slots or 20 bytes of memory
9.
```
01   TEMP-TABLE.
      03   DAY-TEMP   OCCURS 365 TIMES.
            05   YR   PIC 999V9 OCCURS 10 TIMES.
```
.
.
a. DISPLAY YR (312, 7).
b. DISPLAY YR (X, R).
c.
```
01   TEMP-TABLE.
      03   YR-TEMP   OCCURS 10 TIMES.
            05   DAY-TEMP   PIC 999V9
                  OCCURS 365 TIMES.
```

Chapter 10   Sorting

1. Internal sorting is done in memory in tables and usually is limited to few values—perhaps fewer than 100.
   External sorting involves large volumes of data and requires the use of external storage such as disk or tape.
3. One possible plan and flowchart is shown below.

```
Read in value A and place in storage area called
   LARGEST
Read in value B into HOLD-1 and compare against
   value stored in LARGEST
   If HOLD-1 is greater than the value in LARGEST,
      move LARGEST to SECOND-LARGEST and move HOLD-1
      to SECOND-LARGEST
   Else move HOLD-1 to SECOND LARGEST
Read value C into HOLD-1 and compare against
   value stored in LARGEST
   If HOLD-1 is greater than the value in LARGEST,
      move the value in LARGEST to HOLD-2
      move SECOND-LARGEST to THIRD-LARGEST
      move HOLD-1 to LARGEST
      move HOLD-2 to SECOND-LARGEST
   Else compare HOLD-1 against the value stored in
      SECOND-LARGEST
      If HOLD-1 is greater than SECOND-LARGEST, move
         SECOND-LARGEST to THIRD-LARGEST and move
         HOLD-1 to SECOND-LARGEST
      If HOLD-1 is not greater than SECOND-LARGEST,
         move HOLD-1 to THIRD-LARGEST
```

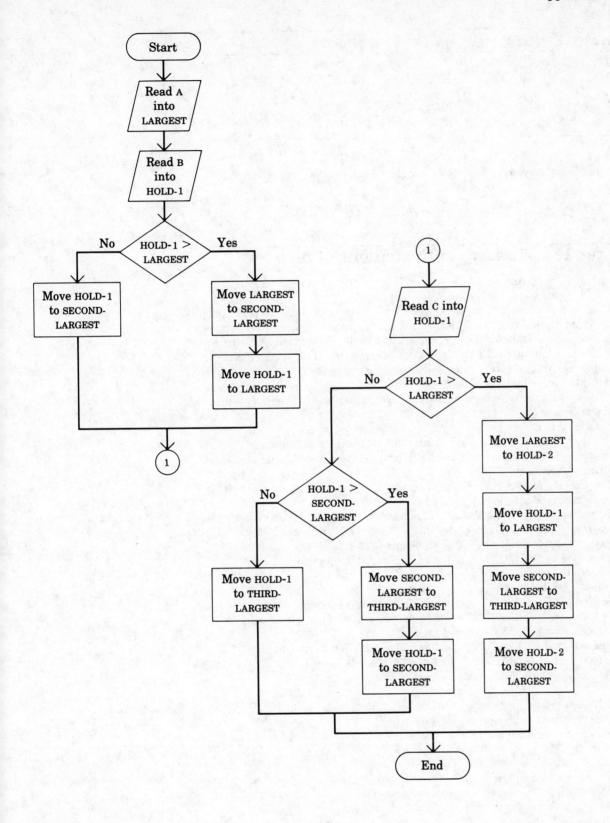

8. Start	Pass 1	Pass 2	Pass 3	Pass 4(end)
9	1	1	1	1
2	9	2	2	2
6	2	9	5	5
5	6	5	9	6
1	5	6	6	9

9. For sort files the FD is replaced by SD and the LABEL RECORDS clause is omitted.

Chapter 11   Working with sequential files

2. When the file is CLOSEd

3. 800 and 1600 bpi

5. The "brute force" approach to working with files involves reading through a file until the appropriate record is found, closing the file, reopening it, and performing the same process again for the next record that needs to be found. A far better approach is to first put both files into order. Then, you can program so that the matching records can be found on one pass, or reading, of the data file.

7. **a.** A file that contains data of temporary value or is likely to be used only once. Typical examples include *daily* charge transactions, *weekly* inventory adjustments, and so on.

   b. See Detail File.

   c. As opposed to a Detail, or Transaction file, a Master File contains data that change relatively infrequently and which are likely to be used by many different application programs.

   d. The existing Master File that is going through, or has just gone through, an updating process is the Old Master File.

   e. The latest version of the Master that is being developed from the processing of the Detail File and the old Master File is called the New Master File.

11. **a.** 8,000,000 bytes divided by 1600 = 5000 inches of data
    100,000 records divided by 5 (blocking factor) = 20,000 gaps
    1/2 inch per gap = 10,000 inches of gaps
    equals a total of 15,000 inches = 1250 ft for the file

   b. 65,000 × 35 = 2,275,000 bytes divided by 1600 = 1422 inches of data
    65,000 records divided by 25 (blocking factor) = 2600 gaps
    1/2 inch per gap = 1300 inches of gaps
    equals a total of 1422 + 1300 = 2722 inches = 226.8 ft for the file

12. **a.** 800,000 characters divided by 100,000 = 80 seconds for data
    2000 gaps × .1 = 200 seconds for gaps
    　　　　　　　　Total 280 seconds

   b. 2,275,000 characters divided by 100,000 = 22.75 seconds for data
    2600 gaps × .1 = 260 seconds for gaps
    　　　　　　　　Total 282.75 seconds

13. **a.** M:　1　2　3　4　5　6
    　　D:　2　5　1

   b. M:　1　2　3　4　5　6　7
    　　D1:　2　5　7
    　　D2:　1　3　4

   c. M:　1　2　3　4　5　6
    　　D:　2　5　1　6

   d. M:　1　2　3　4　5　6　7
    　　D1:　2　7　5
    　　D2:　1　3　4

Chapter 12   Working with indexed files

1. Key field
3. The purpose of the RECORD KEY entry is to identify to the system the name of the field that contains the key by which that record is indexed.
6. RECORD KEY IS name
8. ACCESS IS DYNAMIC
9. FILE STATUS IS
10. The REWRITE statement
11. Flagged or logically removed from the index

Chapter 13   Writing reports

1. LINAGE
   LINES AT TOP
   LINES AT BOTTOM
3. SOURCE
4. INITIATE
   GENERATE
   TERMINATE
5. a. FD   PRINTER-FILE
         LABEL RECORD IS OMITTED
         DATA RECORD IS PRINT-REC
         LINAGE IS 66
             LINES AT TOP 3
             LINES AT BOTTOM 6.
   b. FD   PRINTER-FILE
         LABEL RECORD IS OMITTED
         DATA RECORD IS PRINT-REC
         LINAGE IS 57
             WITH FOOTING AT 54
             LINES AT TOP 3
             LINES AT BOTTOM 6.
   c. FD   OUTPUT-FILE
         LABEL RECORD IS OMITTED
         DATA RECORD IS PRINTER-REC
         LINAGE IS 75
             LINES AT TOP 8
             LINES AT BOTTOM 8.
   d. FD   OUTPUT-FILE
         LABEL RECORD IS OMITTED
         DATA RECORD IS PRINTER-REC
             WITH FOOTING AT 56
             LINES AT TOP 16
             LINES AT BOTTOM 8.
8. a. 01   STUB TYPE DETAIL.
         03   LINE PLUS 2.
             05   COLUMN 16   PIC X(20) SOURCE PART-NAME.
             05   COLUMN 42   PIC 9(8)
                             SOURCE STOCK-NUMBER.
             05   COLUMN 60   PIC 9(4) SOURCE BIN-NUMBER.
             05   COLUMN 75   PIC 9(6)
                             SOURCE QUANTITY-ON-HAND.

b. 01　PAY-LINE TYPE DETAIL.
　　　03 LINE PLUS 1.
　　　　　05　COLUMN 15　PIC 9(9) SOURCE SS-NBR.
　　　　　05　COLUMN 30　PIC A(20) SOURCE EMP-NAME.
　　　　　05　COLUMN 60　PIC $99,999.99 SOURCE
　　　　　　　　　　　　　　　　　　GROSS-PAY.
　　　　　05　COLUMN 70　PIC $9,999.99 SOURCE
　　　　　　　　　　　　　　　　　　DEDUCTIONS.
　　　　　05　COLUMN 80　PIC $99,999.99 SOURCE
　　　　　　　　　　　　　　　　　　NET-PAY.

c. 01　SALES TYPE DETAIL.
　　　03　LINE PLUS 1.
　　　　　05　COLUMN 12　PIC 999 SOURCE REGION.
　　　　　05　COLUMN 20　PIC 9(4) SOURCE AREA-CODE.
　　　　　05　COLUMN 32　PIC $9,999.99 SOURCE
　　　　　　　　　　　　　　　　　　SALES-FIGURES.

Appendix D.   Data for use in problems

Data set A

```
            1         2         3         4         5
   1234567890123456789012345678901234567890123456789012345

 1  010114101SMITH ELBERT      M075003120005000010004036A
 2  010116104BARNHART STANLEY  S112501065010000000004019R
 3  050124101WALSH JUDITH      M065502120005000000004016A
 4  050125395PEARSON SAMUEL    M077505120000000025004036A
 5  060443916LEE KIMBERLY      S045001065002500000038A76
 6  140133010CHICANE HERB      M047501120000000015004036C
 7  190456301HARKELRODE CLARA  M052504120000000150040189
 8  220133512KOCHINIS ANGELO   S096501065000000200040194
 9  230965777RUSE WAYNE        M085002120005000000004236A
10  270134109MOORE SAMUEL      M077503120002500000004036A
11  304165298BILBERRY DALTON   M077501120000000005004036A
12  320135004MARTIN SUSAN      M055008120002500000003919R
13  346945678FUJIMOTO KEN      S113001065015000000004019R
14  350214101STOLL GEORGE      S095502120005000000004119C
15  365593864EVANS ROBERT      M065508120000000000004036C
16  410954321GARCIA FRAN       M054505120000000015004236A
17  555438619DEE ELLIS         S045001065000000000004027R
18  666666666BRONSON PATTY     M075003120002500000003819R
19  684836197ROSSI JACK        M065004120000000100040100
20  745678432JOHNSON PAM       S085001065005000000004027R
```

Data set B

```
              1         2         3         4
    12345678901234567890123456789012345678901234567890
```

```
 1  10700415MARTIN PEARSON      0105080012027
 2  10300532JOE SMITH           0139055013615
 3  10400617MIKE GONZALES       0137017000000
 4  10701009GEORGE STOLL        0145626002584
 5  10701362SUSAN HASHIMOTO     0139581011559
 6  10401589ABBY JOHNSON        0131519000000
 7  10301666PATRICK JACKSON     0565265042617
 8  10501743JOHN BOSCH          0125554002125
 9  10701824OTTO EHRLIN         0468923001063
10  10302340SHARON HELM         0155581000000
11  10302785JORDAN HOTCHKISS    1032665468555
12  10402965ALVIN WALL          0146277195360
13  10603524PATRICK WONG        0190088000000
14  10703955WAYNE MOORE         0138000000961
15  10404876VERNA APPLEWHITE    0195091000000
16  10705291ANGELA CHANG        1176804001875
17  10505900LISA MOULTON        0132586132586
18  10506893DANIEL PARKER       0968427336597
19  10307444CURTIS HAHN         0660061271783
20  10608321RAYMOND BUTLER      0539609143268
21  10508965DIXIE RHINEHART     0773647051556
22  10709401SARA THOMAS         0131033000000
23  10609653LINDA HAYES         0139998086317
24  10610468FRED WILSON         1047752186537
25  10311639DICK HENNING        0865419256856
```

Appendix E.   Some bits and pieces

The origin of COBOL: Captain Grace M. Hopper

The origins of COBOL go back to the earliest days of computing, when the Harvard Mark series of the mid-1940s and the UNIVAC I were programmed in their own peculiar machine code. At that time, the languages we now know—FORTRAN, BASIC, COBOL, PASCAL—simply did not exist. Library routines such as those to sort or take square roots were also unknown. Instead, programmers had to copy long strings of code from one program to another in order to do these operations.

One of the pioneers in the development of high-level languages was Captain Grace M. Hopper of the U.S. Navy, who is still very active in data processing today. She is considered the grand matriarch of computing and was one of the driving forces behind the creation of user groups that shared their ideas about the solutions to these common problems. Captain Hopper presented a paper on compiler construction and has, since then, contributed more than fifty additional publications on software and programming languages. Her work led to her appointment on the Defense Department-sponsored Committee on Data System Languages (Codasyl) in 1959.

Her work on the committee was instrumental in developing COBOL, the first language not identified with any specific manufacturer and compatible with a wide variety of machines. Since that time she has been a leader in language standardization and has continued to shepherd COBOL through its many revisions. A Ph.D. in mathematics, Grace Hopper is today, at age 75 and with 40 years of data-processing experience, a highly sought-after lecturer. In her words, "We haven't even begun to exploit its [the computer's] potential."*

Program "bugs"

Captain Grace Hopper has participated in many notable "firsts" during her long career in the data-processing industry. Perhaps one of the most interesting of these had to do with the origin of the term "program bug," or "debugging." As she recalls it, "In 1945, while working in a World-War-I-vintage, non-air-conditioned building on a hot, humid, summer day, the computer stopped. We searched for the problem and found a failing relay—one of the big signal relays."

"Inside, we found a moth that had been beaten to death. We pulled it out with tweezers and taped it to the log book. From then on, when the officer came in to ask if we were accomplishing anything, we told him we were 'debugging' the computer."*

Program loops: Lady Lovelace

History buffs are aware that in the 1830s Charles Babbage, an English mathematical genius, envisioned a new kind of calculating machine, which he called The Analytical Engine. His machine differed from previous calculators in that it would perform all types of mathematical calculations that could be combined to solve any type of problem. The Analytical Engine, of course, contained the essential components of the modern computer. Specifically, he planned to have:

1. a "mill" (CPU) where the data would be processed;
2. a "store" (memory) to house the data being worked on and to hold the results of computations;

*Source: Computerworld, November 16, 1981

3. punched cards that specified the operations to be performed and the address of that instruction;
4. perhaps most importantly, the ability to make conditional branches within the program.

Many of his writings were interpreted and expanded by his friend Lady Ada Augusta Lovelace, daughter of the poet Lord Byron. A mathematical genius in her own right (in a time when women were not expected to excel in such areas), she mastered his plans and was able to correct some errors in his work.

One of her most important contributions was recognizing that the same sequence of instructions might have to be repeated many times within the program and that it would be possible to plan for this within the program. Thus, she not only originated the idea of program loops but is considered to have been the world's first programmer. Her name lives on today in the new Department-of-Defense-sponsored programming language called Ada.*

*Source: Computerworld, July 27, 1981

Documentation is an important part of both programming and operations.

Appendix F. COBOL programming and documentation standards

COBOL programming standards

I Design Considerations

  A. Overall design

    1. All programs are to be designed using a top-down or stepwise refinement which involves the subdividing of a program into smaller and smaller functional modules or paragraphs. It starts with the design of the main control module which PERFORMS other modules. Some of these other modules may, in turn, PERFORM submodules. This relationship is expressed in a top-down hierarchy chart.

    2. All programs are to be designed to use the three basic program structures: Sequence; Ifthenelse; and, Dowhile.

Structure	COBOL *Statements*
Sequence	Any statement that does not transfer control
Ifthenelse	IF or IF/ELSE statement
Dowhile	PERFORM UNTIL

    3. Programs are to be designed to be read from top to bottom and to be largely self-documenting and understandable. Choosing meaningful field, record and internal file names is imperative. Names should be descriptive of the data they represent. Paragraph names should be representative of the function they perform.

    4. A main control module (paragraph) is to be used to provide over-all program control. It will consist mainly of PERFORM statements that execute program submodules. The STOP RUN statement should appear here and not in a PERFORMed paragraph.

    5. Generally, PROCEDURE DIVISION paragraphs are to be placed in the sequence of their first reference. All paragraph names are to be numbered and named in a manner that permits the insertion of other paragraphs during program modification. Place a blank line between the DIVISIONS and before each paragraph.

    6. Program run-time efficiency is not to be achieved at the cost of clear, maintainable code. If you have any doubt about this rule, check with your instructor.

    7. Avoid "tricky" logic in favor of simple processes that would be common and understandable to most programmers.

  B. Subprogram design

    1. Generally, modules are to perform a single function or task. It is possible that the function may be accomplished by a single statement or it may require a series of statements (examples: reading a record; printing headings; end-of-page processing; filling a table; input data validation). You should aim for paragraphs in which the individual statements are closely related to each other. Sometimes the term *cohesion* is used to refer to the strength of the relationship of the statements. PERFORMING single statement modules may appear to be inefficient but is desirable in terms of program structure, clarity, and ease of maintenance. If possible, limit paragraphs to fifty or fewer lines so that they can be printed on a single page. If your routine is larger, you should be able to logically break it into smaller sections.

    2. For all paragraphs, control enters at the top and exits at the bottom ("one entrance; one exit").

3. There should be only one READ or WRITE statement for each file. Special spacing requirements may make this rule difficult to comply with, but certainly the main READ and WRITE operations should be resident in PERFORMed paragraphs.

4. Common routines (such as those used to READ and WRITE) are to be placed at the end of the program.

II. Program Documentation

A. A neatly-drawn, top-down hierarchy chart is to be included with every program as part of the final documentation. Starting at the second level, each box is to be numbered and/or lettered in a consistent, logical manner that will allow insertion of other modules if the program is modified.

B. You may be required to document the program logic by means of flowcharts, pseudocode or a specific documentation method such as Warnier/Orr diagrams. If any of these methods are used, the programmer must take care to see that the final version of the program logic is accurately shown in the documentation.

C. Any narrative material is to be written in a manner that reflects proper use of the English language.

D. A chart or diagram is to be used to show data input and output formats.

E. Printer spacing charts are to be used to layout the various line formats. All printed output will be from one standard output line, as designated in the FILE SECTION of the DATA DIVISION.

F. Documentation within the program is outlined below.

1. IDENTIFICATION DIVISION
   a. The AUTHOR entry in the IDENTIFICATION DIVISION is to be used to indicate the programmer's name, class section, assignment number and due date.
   b. The DATE-COMPILED entry is to be used to show the compilation date of the source program listing.
   c. A brief description of the purpose of the program is to be enclosed within a box of asterisks.

   Example:

   ```
   PROGRAM-ID.  SUBSCR.
   AUTHOR.   SUSAN JONES
             SECTION 2  MWF  10 AM
             ASSIGNMENT #3
             DUE _____.
   DATE-COMPILED.    (on most systems, leave blank for compiler to
                      insert current date)


   ****************************************
   *    THIS PROGRAM IS DESIGNED TO       *
   *    READ AND PRINT A LISTING          *
   *    OF SUBSCRIBERS.                   *
   ****************************************
   ```

2. ENVIRONMENT DIVISION
   a. Use meaningful file names in SELECT entries.
   b. List the most frequently used files first or list the files in the order in which they are used.

3. DATA DIVISION—FILE SECTION
   a. Use optional entries in the FD area rather than using system defaults.

   Example:

   ```
   LABEL RECORD IS _____
   ```

b. Use meaningful file, record, and field names. Develop a consistent naming pattern so that fields can be readily identified as to their source, destination, or type. Follow the old rule: "When in doubt; spell it out!"

Example:

```
01  INPUT-PAY-RECORD.
    03  NAME-IN
    03  PAY-CODE-IN
        etc.
```

c. Each successive level number should be indented four spaces and equal level numbers are to be aligned on the same column. Leave at least a one-number gap between level numbers.

```
01  INPUT-PAY-RECORD.
    03  EMPLOYEE-NAME.
        05  EMP-FIRST-NAME
        05  EMP-INITIAL
        05  EMP-LAST-NAME
    03  EMP-SS-NUMBER
```

d. Provide a brief, variable dictionary or description of the input and/or output fields if this is appropriate.

Example:

```
 01  SUBSCRIPTION-RECORD.
 **************************************************
 * THE INPUT RECORD CONTAINS                      *
 * SUBSCRIBER NAME           NAME-IN              *
 * SUBSCRIBER ADDRESS        ADDRESS-IN           *
 * PRIOR BALANCE OWED        ORIG-BALANCE         *
 * MONTHLY BILL              MO-BILL              *
 * SUBSCRIPTION END DATE     ENDING-DATE          *
 * SUBSCRIPTION CODE         CODE-1   3 DIGITS    *
 *                           CODE-2   2 DIGITS    *
 **************************************************
        03 NAME-IN
        03 ADDRESS-IN
```

4. DATA DIVISION—WORKING-STORAGE SECTION
   a. Organize the section to make it as easy as possible to locate the data.
   b. Your instructor may require you to include a variable dictionary at some point in the DATA DIVISION. If so, it is to be boxed within asterisks and is to list each *major* variable used within the program and its purpose.
   c. WORKING-STORAGE entries (level 01) should be grouped according to data types.

   > Switches or Indicators
   > Counters
   >> Item Counters; Line Counters, and so on.
   >> Dollar Amount Counters
   > Error Messages
   > Output Lines
   >> Page Headings
   >> Column Headings
   >> Report Lines
   >> Total Lines
   > Tables

d. Switches should be identified by an appropriate prefix or suffix attached to a descriptive field name.

Example:

```
    03  END-OF-FILE-SW
```

or

```
    03  SW-EOF
```

Establish a consistent pattern for indicating the "off" or "on" condition of a switch. Also, it is better programming practice to use something other than zero '0' or one '1' to indicate the switch condition. Level 88 entries can be used to clarify the settings.

Example:

```
03  EOF-SW      PIC X VALUE 'N'.
    88  OUT-OF-RECORDS VALUE 'Y'.
```

e. Switch and/or counter uses should be documented at this point.

Example:

```
WORKING-STORAGE SECTION.
01  SWITCHES-AND-COUNTERS
    03  EOF-SW       PIC X VALUE 'N'.
        88  OUT-OF-RECORDS VALUE 'Y'.
    03  RECORD-COUNTER PIC 999 VALUE ZERO.
    03  SALES-COUNTER  PIC S9(5)V99 VALUE ZERO.
********************************************************
* THE EOF-SW FIELD CHANGES FROM                        *
*   'N' TO 'Y' AFTER THE LAST RECORD                   *
*   HAS BEEN PROCESSED.                                 *
* THE RECORD-COUNTER IS USED TO                         *
*   ACCUMULATE THE NUMBER OF INPUT                      *
*   RECORDS PROCESSED.                                  *
* THE SALES-COUNTER ACCUMULATES                         *
*   INDIVIDUAL DAILY SALES FROM                         *
*   SEVERAL DEPARTMENTS.                                *
********************************************************
```

f. Define all numeric and non-numeric literals in WORKING-STORAGE. Do not define them in the PROCEDURE DIVISION. An exception to this rule would be the use of the common literal 1.

```
Avoid:  MOVE ' INVALID KEY DATA VALUE'
                 TO PRINTER-RECORD.
Poor:   MOVE MESSAGE-1 TO PRINTER-RECORD.
Good:   MOVE MSSG-1-INVALID-KEY TO PRINTER-RECORD
```

g. Use level 88's, conditional names, wherever appropriate. Their use aids both in program maintenance and documentation.

h. Avoid level 77 entries in favor of fields grouped under an 01 entry.

i. Line up PIC entries for easy visual reference. Make all PIC entries at least two digits in length.

Example:

```
    PIC X(02) rather than PIC X(2).
```

j. Printer output lines should clearly indicate the carriage control position if this is required by your system.

k. Output fields that contain edit characters should be identified in some manner so as to lessen the chance of attempting to work on these fields arithmetically.

Example:

```
03  DEPT-SALES-ED   PIC $Z,ZZ9.99.
```

5. PROCEDURE DIVISION

a. The PROCEDURE DIVISION is to start with a PROCEDURE DICTIONARY that lists the *major* paragraphs and a *brief* explanation of their functions.

Example:

```
PROCEDURE DIVISION.
******************************************************
*              PROCEDURE DICTIONARY              *
* 010-OPENER: OPENS THE FILES; PRINTS            *
*             THE HEADING; AND DOES A            *
*             PRIMING READ.                      *
* 020-READER: MOVES FIELDS TO THE                *
*             REPORT LINE FOR EDITING;           *
*             ACCUMULATES A SALES TOTAL;         *
*             WRITES A LINE;                     *
*             READS ANOTHER RECORD.              *
* 030-CLOSER: MOVES FIELDS AND WRITES            *
*             A TOTAL LINE;                      *
*             CLOSES THE FILES.                  *
******************************************************
        PERFORM 010-OPENER.
           etc.
```

b. Each module or paragraph within the PROCEDURE DIVISION is to start with a *brief* description of its function set off by a box of asterisks. Any unusual programming constructs or activities are to be *thoroughly* documented.

Example:

```
010-OPENER.
******************************************************
*                                               *
* THIS MODULE OPENS THE FILES;                   *
*   WRITES TWO HEADING LINES                     *
*   AT THE TOP OF A NEW PAGE;                    *
*   AND DOES A PRIMING READ.                     *
*                                               *
******************************************************
        OPEN INPUT _____
           etc.
```

c. As far as possible, paragraphs are to be included in the order in which they are performed. The exceptions are those common routines (such as READ and WRITE) that are to be placed at the end of the program.

d. If PERFORM THRU is used with an EXIT paragraph, the EXIT paragraph name is to be the same as the original paragraph followed by the word 'EXIT.'

Example:

```
PERFORM 020-READER THRU 020-READER-EXIT.
```

III. COBOL Coding Conventions
   A. Code only one verb per line. This includes placing ELSE, NEXT SENTENCE on a line with no other code.
   B. ELSE must be aligned with its associated IF. Imperative statements within the IF are to be indented. Nested IF statements are to comply with these rules of indention.

Example:

```
Column     12      16      20
           IF   condition-1
                    statement
                    statement
                IF   condition-2
                         statement
                         statement
                ELSE
                         statement
                         statement
           ELSE
                statement
                statement
```

   C. Spell out "greater than" and "less than" rather than using the ">" and "<" symbols.
   D. Do not nest IF statements beyond three deep.
   E. In general, avoid complex IF statements, particularly those involving the use of negative testing. Some compilers do not generate the same code when NOT's are combined with AND's and OR's.
   F. A series of MOVE's should be coded in the order in which the fields are found within the file. In addition, some shops/instructors require that common code elements be aligned.

Example:

```
MOVE     NAME-IN     TO   NAME-OUT.
MOVE     ADDRESS-IN  TO   ADDRESS-OUT.
```

   G. Indent with READ and WRITE statements.

Example:

```
READ PAYROLL-INPUT-FILE
     AT END _____.
WRITE PRINT-RECORD
     AFTER ADVANCING _____.
```

   H. The use of COMPUTE versus the individual arithmetic statements ADD, SUB-TRACT, MULTIPLY, and DIVIDE may be regulated by the instructor.
   I. Prohibited.
      1. The use of GO TO statements, except in limited circumstances as approved by the instructor. Usually this means using a *downward* GO TO in

conjunction with PERFORM THRU and the EXIT statement. An additional valid use is in conjunction with the INPUT/OUTPUT PROCEDURE option of the SORT statement.

2. If PERFORM THRU is permitted, intervening paragraphs between the entry and exit paragraphs are prohibited.

3. Literals are not to be defined in the PROCEDURE DIVISION.

4. Some shops/instructors may prohibit certain uses of the DISPLAY statement.

5. Many shops prohibit the use of MOVE CORRESPONDING for two reasons: (a) it can make program maintenance more difficult; (b) the MOVE CORRESPONDING may be implemented in different ways by different compilers.

```
000100 IDENTIFICATION DIVISION.
000110 PROGRAM-ID.  SAMPDOC1.
000120 AUTHOR. SUSAN JONES
000130          SECTION 2  MWF 10 AM
000140          ASSIGNMENT 3
000150          DUE _____.
000160 DATE-COMPILED.
000170*
000180************************************************
000190*      THIS PROGRAM IS DESIGNED TO       *
000200*   READ AND PRINT A LISTING OF          *
000210*   STUDENT RECORDS ON THE               *
000220*   'STUREC' FILE.                       *
000230************************************************
000240*
000250 ENVIRONMENT DIVISION.
000260 CONFIGURATION SECTION.
000270 SOURCE-COMPUTER.  _____.
000280 OBJECT-COMPUTER.  _____.
000290 INPUT-OUTPUT SECTION.
000300 FILE-CONTROL.
000310     SELECT STUDENT-FILE ASSIGN TO _____.
000320     SELECT PRINT-FILE ASSIGN TO _____.
000330*
000340 DATA DIVISION.
000350 FILE SECTION.
000360 FD  STUDENT-FILE
000370     LABEL RECORD IS STANDARD
000380     VALUE OF FILE-ID IS 'STUREC'
000390     DATA RECORD IS STUDENT-RECORD.
000400 01  STUDENT-RECORD.
000410*
000420*********************************************
000430*   THE INPUT RECORD CONTAINS          *
000440*   STUDENT NAME        NAME-IN        *
000450*   ADDRESS             ADDRESS-IN     *
000460*   SOCIAL SECURITY #   SS-NUMBER-IN   *
000470*********************************************
000480*
000490     03  NAME-IN          PIC A(20).
```

```
000500       03  ADDRESS-IN        PIC X(20).
000510       03  SS-NUMBER-IN      PIC 9(09).
000520 FD  PRINT-FILE
000530     LABEL RECORD IS OMITTED
000540     DATA RECORD IS PRINTER-RECORD.
000550 01  PRINTER-RECORD        PIC X(121).
000560 WORKING-STORAGE SECTION.
000570*
000580***********************************************
000590*   THE EOF-INDICATOR FIELD IS USED       *
000600*   AS A SWITCH THAT WILL CHANGE          *
000610*   FROM 'OFF' TO 'ON ' AFTER THE         *
000620*   LAST RECORD HAS BEEN PROCESSED.       *
000630*                                         *
000640*   THE INPUT FIELDS ARE MOVED TO         *
000650*   APPROPRIATE FIELDS IN THE             *
000660*   REPORT-LINE RECORD.                   *
000670***********************************************
000680*
000690 01  MISC-FIELDS.
000700       03  EOF-INDICATOR     PIC XXX VALUE 'OFF'.
000710       03  END-MESSAGE       PIC X(14) VALUE ' END OF REPORT'.
000720 01  HEAD-LINE.
000730       03  FILLER            PIC X.
000740       03  FILLER            PIC X(54) VALUE SPACES.
000750       03  FILLER            PIC X(12) VALUE 'STUDENT LIST'.
000760       03  FILLER            PIC X(54) VALUE SPACES.
000770 01  REPORT-LINE.
000780       03  FILLER            PIC X.
000790       03  FILLER            PIC X(10) VALUE SPACES.
000800       03  NAME-PR           PIC A(20).
000810       03  FILLER            PIC X(10) VALUE SPACES.
000820       03  ADDRESS-PR        PIC X(20).
000830       03  FILLER            PIC X(10) VALUE SPACES.
000840       03  SS-NUMBER-PR      PIC 9(09).
000850       03  FILLER            PIC X(41) VALUE SPACES.
000860*
000870 PROCEDURE DIVISION.
000880*
000890***********************************************
000900*            PROCEDURE DICTIONARY         *
000910*   010-OPENER: OPENS THE FILES; PRINTS   *
000920*               THE HEADING; AND DOES     *
000930*               A PRIMING READ            *
000940*   020-READER: MOVES FIELDS AND WRITES   *
000950*               LINE; READS A RECORD      *
000960*   030-CLOSER: CLOSING ACTIVITIES        *
000970***********************************************
000980*
000990 CONTROL-MODULE.
001000     PERFORM 010-OPENER.
001010     PERFORM 020-READER
001020         UNTIL EOF-INDICATOR = 'ON '.
001030     PERFORM 030-CLOSER.
001040     STOP RUN.
001050 010-OPENER.
001060*
```

```
001070*******************************************
001080*  THIS MODULE OPENS THE FILES;         *
001090*    WRITES THE HEADING LINE            *
001100*    AT THE TOP OF A NEW PAGE           *
001110*    AND DOES A PRIMING READ.           *
001120*******************************************
001130*
001140      OPEN INPUT STUDENT-FILE OUTPUT PRINT-FILE.
001150      MOVE HEAD-LINE TO PRINTER-RECORD.
001160      WRITE PRINTER-RECORD
001170          AFTER ADVANCING PAGE.
001180      READ STUDENT-FILE
001190          AT END MOVE 'ON ' TO EOF-INDICATOR.
001200 020-READER.
001210*
001220*******************************************
001230*  THE 020-READER MODULE MOVES THE      *
001240*  INPUT FIELDS TO THE REPORT LINE,     *
001250*  WRITES A LINE, AND READS             *
001260*  ANOTHER RECORD.                      *
001270*******************************************
001280*
001290      MOVE NAME-IN TO NAME-PR.
001300      MOVE ADDRESS-IN TO ADDRESS-PR.
001310      MOVE SS-NUMBER-IN TO SS-NUMBER-PR.
001320      WRITE PRINTER-RECORD
001330          AFTER ADVANCING 2 LINES.
001340      READ STUDENT-FILE
001350          AT END MOVE 'ON ' TO EOF-INDICATOR.
001360 030-CLOSER.
001370*
001380*******************************************
001390*  THIS MODULE PRINTS AN END            *
001400*  MESSAGE AND CLOSES THE FILES.        *
001410*******************************************
001420*
001430      MOVE END-MESSAGE TO PRINTER-RECORD.
001440      WRITE PRINTER-RECORD
001450          AFTER ADVANCING 2 LINES.
001460      CLOSE STUDENT-FILE PRINT-FILE.
```

Index